OXFORD WORLD'S CLASSICS

THE OXFORD SHAKESPEARE

General Editor · Stanley Wells

The Oxford Shakespeare offers new and authoritative editions of Shakespeare's plays in which the early printings have been scrupulously re-examined and interpreted. An introductory essay provides all relevant background information together with an appraisal of critical views and of the play's effects in performance. The detailed commentaries pay particular attention to language and staging. Reprints of sources, music for songs, genealogical tables, maps, etc. are included where necessary; many of the volumes are illustrated, and all contain an index.

ANTHONY B. DAWSON is Professor Emeritus at the University of British Columbia. He is an editor, theatre historian, and literary critic who has published widely on Shakespeare and the early modern theatre.

PAUL YACHNIN, co-editor with Anthony B. Dawson of *Richard II* in the Oxford Shakespeare, is Tomlinson Professor of Shakespeare Studies at McGill University. His publications include *Stage-Wrights* and *The Culture of Playgoing in Early Modern England* (with Anthony B. Dawson).

D0190665

THE OXFORD SHAKESPEARE

OXFORD WORLD'S CLASSICS

WILLIAM SHAKESPEARE

Richard II

Edited by
ANTHONY B. DAWSON
and
PAUL YACHNIN

OXFORD
UNIVERSITY PRESS

OXFORD
UNIVERSITY PRESS

Great Clarendon Street, Oxford OX2 6DP

Oxford University Press is a department of the University of Oxford.
It furthers the University's objective of excellence in research, scholarship,
and education by publishing worldwide in

Oxford   New York

Auckland   Cape Town   Dar es Salaam   Hong Kong   Karachi
Kuala Lumpur   Madrid   Melbourne   Mexico City   Nairobi
New Delhi   Shanghai   Taipei   Toronto

With offices in

Argentina   Austria   Brazil   Chile   Czech Republic   France   Greece
Guatemala   Hungary   Italy   Japan   Poland   Portugal   Singapore
South Korea   Switzerland   Thailand   Turkey   Ukraine   Vietnam

Oxford is a registered trade mark of Oxford University Press
in the UK and in certain other countries

Published in the United States
by Oxford University Press Inc., New York

First published 2011
First published as an Oxford World's Classics paperback 2011

British Library Cataloguing in Publication Data

Data available

Library of Congress Cataloging-in-Publication Data

Data available

Typeset by RefineCatch Limited, Bungay, Suffolk
Printed in Great Britain
on acid-free paper by
Clays Ltd, St Ives plc

ISBN 978-0-19-818642-7 (hbk.)
ISBN 978-0-19-960228-5 (pbk.)

2

ACKNOWLEDGEMENTS

Our edition, the last of the Oxford series, has been a long while gestating and during that time we have incurred a number of debts. To previous editors of the play, especially Peter Ure (Arden 2), Stanley Wells (Penguin), Andrew Gurr (Cambridge), John Jowett et al. (Complete Oxford), and Charles Forker (Arden 3), we owe dozens of insights both textual and semantic. Several graduate student research assistants have contributed significantly and cheerfully to the shaping of this edition. Amy Scott provided assistance with bibliography early in the project and excellent service on a number of matters, especially the images, toward the end. Karen Oberer worked through the text with Paul Yachnin before he and Anthony Dawson analysed and shaped it again; the earlier process is vestigial but foundational. David Anderson provided assistance with the commentary, again at an early stage, while Andrew Brown and Katie Davison helped with indexing and proofs near the end. Colleagues have also graciously lent their help. Of these we would like to thank especially Patsy Badir, Bradin Cormack, David George, Gordon McMullan, Michael Neill, Patricia Parker, Steve Partridge, and Carol Rutter. We thank Kate Rumbold and Christie Carson for timely advice about sourcing of images. The staff of the Folger Shakespeare Library, especially Georgianna Ziegler, have been hugely supportive; the Folger collection has been an indispensable resource. The Shakespeare Association of America sponsored a research seminar on *Richard II*, led by Paul Yachnin, whose members helped deepen our understanding of the play. Steven Mullaney was a member of that seminar; his thinking about the theatre and the play has been of considerable value. We are pleased to acknowledge the careful and creative contributions of our copy-editor, Christine Buckley, whose judicious attention to detail rescued us from error on many occasions. More than anything, it is a pleasure to thank the General Editor. Many Oxford editors have said it before us; it is true: Stanley Wells is a model of patience, deep learning, and great intellectual generosity. He has no part in any of the faults of this edition, but a substantial share in anything in it that is sound and insightful. Finally, we would like to thank each other—this is not the first time that we have worked together collaboratively, and we are pleased that the spirit of cooperation and friendly debate established in our earlier work together has remained as vital as in the past.

CONTENTS

LIST OF ILLUSTRATIONS

1. Map of England showing the key locations mentioned in the play.

INTRODUCTION

Richard II occupies an important place in the Shakespeare canon. Written in 1595, at a point when Shakespeare was finding his full stride as a poet and dramatist, the play marks a transition from the earlier history plays (the 'first tetralogy' comprising the three parts of *Henry VI* and *Richard III*) in which the terrible mechanisms of civil war and naked power dominate the scene. Here a new note is audible, a more nuanced representation of the political conflicts of the English past in which character and politics are so deeply intertwined as to be inextricable. The language too is suppler and more richly elaborated. Overall, there is a sense of emerging mastery, as there is too in the other plays he completed in that very productive year, *A Midsummer Night's Dream* and *Romeo and Juliet*. In *Dream* he takes the comic genre in which he had worked in several earlier plays to new heights of complexity while *Romeo*, with its subtle blend of chance and inevitability, does something similar for tragedy (his only previous tragedy had been the bloody and savage revenge play, *Titus Andronicus*). *Richard II* dextrously combines history play and tragedy, giving to its narrative of bad government and usurpation a tragic shape that Shakespeare would, in a richer vein, take up again a decade later in *King Lear*. Indeed, the title-page of the earliest edition, in 1597, calls it 'The Tragedie of King Richard the second', though in the Folio of 1623 it appears with the other history plays and is entitled 'The life and death of King Richard the Second'. However it is designated, it clearly traces a kind of tragic fall from kingly authority and pomp to lonely, painful imprisonment and violent death.

Within that frame, Shakespeare develops an historical theme that had great political immediacy for its first audiences, due largely to its concern with royal succession at a time when the question of who would inherit the throne occupied by the ageing and childless Queen Elizabeth was on everyone's mind. The play confronts head-on an important contemporary debate about political, indeed monarchical, legitimacy. But it is also a drama, so that the ideological issues are fleshed out in terms of the conflict between two main characters whose struggle defines the action.

Who, the play asks, is right—the anointed king who insists on his divinely sanctioned claim to the throne but who at the same time abuses his power and flouts the traditional legal principles that underlie his legitimacy, or the victim of the king's abuse who promises to be a more effective monarch but is, nevertheless, a usurper? This question is central to the play and hovers in the background of the three that follow it, the two parts of *Henry IV* and *Henry V*, which together form the 'second' tetralogy (though the historical events they dramatize come before those depicted in the 'first' tetralogy—and are indeed at the root of the civil bloodshed so prevalent in those earlier plays). Whether Shakespeare, when he sat down to write *Richard II*, planned to compose a series of plays is not known, but it seems likely that he entertained the idea of putting together a sequence that would in some ways parallel that earlier one. At the least, he was acutely aware of the political resonances of the historical events he extracted from the chronicles he raided as sources and alert to the kinds of debate current in his immediate context. In what follows we take up these questions of topicality and political meaning, and examine how Shakespeare embeds them in character and language; and we trace as well how they have been embodied in performance both in Shakespeare's own time and over the centuries since.

The Play in Its Time

The Earl and the Queen   On 7 February 1601, a special performance of *Richard II* was mounted by Shakespeare's company, the Lord Chamberlain's Men, at the Globe theatre on the south bank of the Thames. It was special because it had been commissioned by some followers of the Earl of Essex, the disgruntled former favourite of the ageing Queen Elizabeth. As one of the players later stated, the company reluctantly agreed to present what they considered an 'old' play since they had been offered forty shillings in addition to their regular take to do so.[1] On the day following the performance, Essex and his men, reacting to what rightly

---

[1] The player in question was Augustine Phillips, the only one examined in connection with the incident. He testified that the players were offered 'forty shillings more than their ordinary' for 'the play of the deposing and killing of King Richard the second' (Chambers, ii. 325–6). The play was 'old' since it had been written and performed six years before, in 1595.

2. The courtly and flamboyant Earl of Essex shown in all his finery in a portrait by Marcus Gheeraerts the Younger from *c*.1597.

seemed to them as the laying of a trap to capture and convict the Earl of treason, staged a kind of spontaneous uprising, hoping to engage the citizens of London in their own behalf. They intended not to dethrone Elizabeth and put Essex in her place (as has frequently been claimed), but to restore the Earl's favour with the Queen, convince her to dismiss some of her closest counsellors (men who were the Earl's enemies), and to pave the way for James VI of Scotland to become Elizabeth's official heir.[1] The

---

[1] Paul Hammer presents an exhaustive and persuasive account of these events, carefully weighing the conflicting claims made by various participants. We are much indebted to his interpretation of the documentary evidence. See

disorganized uprising was quickly put down and the Earl and several of his followers were later executed for treason.

Not long after these events, in August 1601, William Lambard, an antiquary and archivist at Elizabeth's court, presented the Queen with a list of manuscripts held in the Tower and, as she was examining his report, her eye 'fell upon the reign of King Richard II [presumably a subheading of the list] saying "I am Richard II know ye not that?"'.[1] Lambard carefully allowed that 'such a wicked imagination was determined and attempted by a most unkind Gent. the most adorned creature that ever your Majesty made', i.e., Essex. And the Queen responded, rather cryptically, 'He that will forget God, will also forget his benefactors; this tragedy was played forty times in open streets and houses.'[2] These facts, if facts they are (the Essex 'rebellion' narrative is complex and depends to some degree on how one reads the evidence, and the Lambard story is from a household manuscript and may be embellished or even entirely fictional), have given rise to a great deal of speculative commentary on the place of this play, and indeed of the theatre more generally, in late Elizabethan culture and politics.

What can we learn from these tantalizing bits of documentary data? What do they mean? We'd best admit immediately that they are surrounded by uncertainty. For one thing, the commissioned play may not have been Shakespeare's, though most scholars now believe it was.[3] Assuming that, what were the conspirators thinking? The play portrays its two central characters, Richard and Henry Bolingbroke (presumably identified with Elizabeth and Essex respectively), in an even-handed, even ambiguous way; it hardly reads like propaganda for the overthrow

---

also Jonathan Bate's lively account of this complex series of incidents, which independently reaches similar conclusions (Bate, pp. 233–67).

[1] All quotations from early modern texts have been modernized, unless otherwise noted.

[2] Chambers, ii. 326–7.

[3] Other candidates have been suggested, especially the manuscript play now known as *Woodstock*, which presents a much less sympathetic portrait of Richard than Shakespeare does. But the court depositions make this unlikely: one of the conspirators stated that the 'play was of King Harry the 4th, and of the killing of King Richard the second' (Gelly Meyrick, in Chambers, ii. 324) and Augustine Phillips, a member of the acting company, corroborated that it dramatized the 'deposing and killing' of Richard. Since *Woodstock* covers only the earlier part of Richard's reign, before the deposition and the rise of Henry, it is not a likely candidate.

of an arbitrary and tyrannical monarch. It nevertheless looks as if the men who commissioned the performance, possibly without Essex's knowledge, were seeking some kind of historical parallel with the politics of their immediate situation, one that might offer either a positive or a negative exemplum or both. Perhaps they were also seeking to effect a kind of solidarity among themselves as they sought to advance the Earl's cause. At this point, importantly, they had no idea that any sort of intervention would take place the following day; Essex, however, and some of his closest associates, including some of those who had commissioned the play, had earlier met secretly at Drury House to plan an intervention.[1] They clearly interpreted the play as supporting their position, but how? Some may have had specifically dynastic motives: two of the men who commissioned the performance were Sir Charles and Sir Jocelyn Percy, brothers of the ninth Earl of Northumberland and descendants of the Northumberland who, in the play, is a key ally helping Henry gain the throne; another was Lord Monteagle who had a family connection with Thomas Mowbray, Duke of Norfolk. Others in Essex's circle also had connections with characters in the play, not least the Earl himself, who recognized Henry Bolingbroke as an ancestor.[2] Such dynastic considerations underpinned another, related interest: Essex, along with other members of the aristocracy, was personally and ideologically troubled by what he saw as the loss, under Elizabeth, of traditional aristocratic privilege and independence from the monarchy. Indeed Essex himself had, over the previous decade, sought to vindicate ideas of aristocratic honour and thus to restrict royal power.[3] He was therefore disdainful of some of Elizabeth's closest advisors, several of whom had risen from lower social ranks. Essex saw them as upstarts, 'caterpillars of the commonwealth', to use Bolingbroke's derisive epithet (2.3.165); a

[1] Essex apparently later admitted that he and other nobles and gentlemen had at that time resolved to repair to her Majesty to 'humbly' seek redress for 'the injuries and indignities our enemies had daily offered us' (quoted in Hammer, p. 12). They planned this for some indeterminate future time (maybe around mid-February), but the events of the evening of 7 Feb. (including Essex's refusal to obey a Privy Council order to appear at court because he had been warned of a trap) precipitated the chaotic action that took place the next day—see Hammer, pp. 12–15, and Bate, pp. 234–6.

[2] Hammer, pp. 28–9.

[3] See Richard McCoy, *The Rites of Knighthood: the Literature and Politics of Elizabethan Chivalry* (Berkeley, Calif., 1989), Ch. 4, and Norbrook, 'Liberal'.

major goal of Essex's intended intervention was to loosen their hold on Elizabeth and install himself and others of like mind and blood, in their place. Thus, what David Norbrook calls 'aristo-cratic constitutionalism' was to some extent at stake, and this position can be easily read into Shakespeare's play.

While the Privy Council was able, in the examinations that followed, to construct a version of events that implicated Essex in a coup, this was, as Hammer shows, far from his original intention—which was merely to displace the 'caterpillars' and regain the Queen's trust. Nevertheless, any attempt to sequester the Queen and compel her to do things she did not want to do could be seen as tantamount to treason. Indeed both factions in this conflict hoped to pin treason on the other. As for the role of the commissioned Globe performance, which has loomed large in interpretations of the play for decades, it now looks rather like a local and not terribly important side event. Indeed, Leeds Barroll made this point many years ago, pointing out that there were no repercussions for the players, who were never regarded by the authorities as somehow in cahoots with the conspirators. The Council only examined one member of the Chamberlain's Men, Augustine Phillips, who adroitly claimed a merely commercial interest in the company taking on the commission (it was he who spoke of the players' reluctance to mount an 'old' play). The Council apparently accepted this, since only a couple of weeks later, on 24 February, the Lord Chamberlain's Men appeared at court to present 'interludes and plays', and were paid accord-ingly.[1] That very day Elizabeth had signed the death warrant for her former favourite, and he was executed the following morning.

As can be seen from this narrative, the commissioning of the performance turns out to be a complex and ambiguous event, in need of careful interpretation. To understand it properly we need to imagine a group of lively young aristocrats, the sort of men who enjoyed going to the theatre and discussing the implications of what they witnessed, seizing on a play that they remembered, and bringing it to bear on their hopes for a better commonwealth. A performance of *Richard II* gave them something to think and talk about, a dramatic event with restricted though still real relevance to their hopes and expectations. Moreover, the play they

---

[1] Barroll, p. 447.

chose was no doubt linked in their minds to Shakespeare's later plays in the same series, the two parts of *Henry IV* and *Henry V* (performed between 1597 and 1599), since the whole tetralogy seems to have been a favourite of their leader.[1] As Hammer points out, they likely thought of the early parts of *Richard II*, the initiating play of the tetralogy, as portraying the kinds of injustices that Essex felt he was the victim of, wrongs perpetrated by an arbitrary monarch. But they must also have been aware that they could not be seen as advocating usurpation and regicide like that represented by the second half of the play. Indeed that was never their intention—their aims were much less radical, if also naïve and rash. For them the portrayal of Henry in Acts 4 and 5 might well have served as a 'negative example'—the kind of thing to avoid.[2] It is very doubtful that they saw the performance as a call to arms.

Thus the claims often made for the relevance of *Richard II* to the politics of the time need some adjustment. There is good evidence to suggest that readers and playgoers did regard the play as pertinent, but this does not mean that it played a decisive role in public life, and it certainly does not prove anything about the politics of the play itself or its author. Different interpreters then as now read it according to their own interests and desires (early modern interpretive dilemmas thereby mirroring those of recent criticism).

One of those interpreters was, of course, the Queen herself. And here we face the problem of how to construe her telling remark about Richard II and her apparent linkage of playing and conspiracy. What did she mean by claiming that the 'tragedy' of Richard II was 'played forty times in open streets and houses'? Could this possibly refer to Shakespeare's company doing a kind of

---

[1] Hammer suggests this as a way of understanding part of an accusation of treason that was being developed by the authorities before the supposed *coup*. This is contained in a document from *c*.1600 (the dating is uncertain), part of which reads: 'the earl himself [was] so often present at the playing thereof, and with great applause giving countenance and liking to the same' (Chambers, ii. 323). Key here is what 'thereof' refers to; Hammer very plausibly argues, given that the context is a 'treasonous book' about Henry's usurpation and the death of Richard (John Hayward's *First Part of the Life and Raigne of King Henrie the IIII*, published in 1599), that 'thereof' refers not, as has been suggested, to some unknown play based on the 'treasonous book', but to the subject matter, indeed Bolingbroke himself, as presented in the first three plays of the Lancastrian tetralogy (pp. 21–2).

[2] Hammer, p. 34.

Elizabethan street theatre, presumably with the design to finger the Queen as an untrustworthy monarch? Such an eventuality is simply unimaginable. All the theatre companies presented their plays inside playhouses, and occasionally, if they were lucky, they received commissions to play at court or in aristocratic houses. The Queen is clearly speaking metaphorically. But granting that, she still seems to be referring to performances, though not necessarily the one on 7 February. Let's parse what she actually says—that '*this* tragedy was played out . . .' (emphasis added). She is in the middle of a sentence about how Essex, formerly her majesty's 'most adorned creature', betrayed the faith required of him to both God and herself—this betrayal is what she calls a 'tragedy'; she seems, that is, to be thinking of 'tragedy' in the traditional, medieval *de casibus* sense—a depiction of the fall of a great man from the heights to the depths. And hence it seems most likely that the 'playing' she is referring to is that of the Earl himself, a man much given to extravagant displays, and has little to do with performances on the part of Shakespeare's, or any other, company. He, that is, busied himself playing out his own tragedy.[1]

That the Queen identifies with her distant predecessor Richard is of course evident from her remark. But there is nothing in what she says that links that self-identification with plays about Richard. Indeed, as Barroll shows, the 'Richard II model was an old one', much mentioned in poetry and personal correspondence.[2] Still, Elizabeth's remark clearly alludes to her sense of her own vulnerability. She was, after all, getting old (just shy of her sixty-eighth birthday), she had no heir, and was a lone woman (albeit a supremely talented one) in a nest of scheming male vipers. She had no illusions about her position, and she knew her history. Since naming an heir would subject her to the influence of those that supported her choice and the wrath of those who did not, she held back, aware as she had been throughout her career of the political value of maintaining a finely tuned

[1] It is also possible that in speaking of such a tragedy being frequently played out, she might have meant simply that failures such as those of Essex to heed God's word and honour one's benefactors are all too prevalent among human beings generally. See as well Barroll (pp. 447–8) and Hammer (p. 25), who cast similarly sceptical light on the relevance of Elizabeth's much-quoted comment.

[2] Barroll quotes two public servants from many years earlier both of whom say they will not give falsely flattering advice to Elizabeth, and would refuse playing the part of 'King Richard the Second's men' (p. 448).

balance. So her forebear, Richard, also without an heir though lacking her political skills, provided an image of extreme susceptibility, of what could happen to her if she lost control of her government. How she might have reacted to Shakespeare's play is unknown, but we can easily imagine that she would recognize her predecessor's folly in not seeking to keep the various factions under control by balancing their competing claims. If the play exemplified to some of Essex's men the kind of behaviour that they thought she indulged in, to her it might well have represented a path deliberately not taken, a failure, on her predecessor's part, of intelligence and courage. Her self-representation as Richard II, while appearing as a sign of weakness, might, on the contrary, be seen not as an actual identification but as one more manoeuvre in the repertory of strategies she deployed to maintain the balance she had so expertly managed for most of her reign.

A Question of Censorship Because of the sensitivity of the play's subject matter, claims have often been made that it was censored by the watchful officials who oversaw both theatrical performance and book publication during the period. But was it? The short (and unsatisfactory) answer is, we cannot be sure. Here is what we do know: the first three quarto editions of *Richard II*, published in 1597 (Q1) and 1598 (Q2 and Q3), lack a crucial scene, depicting the deposition of King Richard (4.1.155–318), which does appear in Q4 (1608), Q5 (1615), and the Folio edition of Shakespeare's plays published in 1623 (F). The question that immediately arises is whether that scene was part of the original play and was cut, or whether it was composed not long before the publication of Q4 and inserted. If the former, was it omitted in the print versions published during Elizabeth's lifetime but played on the stage, or was it barred from both media?

While allowing for uncertainty, we think it likely that the full text as we have it was written all at the same time (late 1595[1])— i.e. that it was not extensively revised some ten years after it was

---

[1] Forker (pp. 111–19) provides a full account of the evidence for this date. While it could have been written a year or so earlier, or some time in 1596, both its style and what external evidence there is (including its relation to certain source texts such as Daniel's *Civil Wars* and the anonymous *Woodstock*) support the 1595 dating. If the 9 Dec. 1595 performance alluded to by Sir Edward Hoby (see below, pp. 78–9) does indeed refer to Shakespeare's play, then that would strongly suggest a 1595 date.

Peace shall go sleepe with turkes and infidels,
And in this seate of peace, tumultuous warres,
Shall kin with kin, and kinde with kinde confound:
Disorder, horror, feare, and mutiny,
Shall heere inhabit, and this land be cald,
The field of Golgotha and dead mens sculs,
Oh if you raise this house against this house,
It will the wofullest diuision proue,
that euer fell vpon this cursed earth,
Left child, childs children crie against you heere:
North. Well haue you argued sir, and for your paines,
Of Capitall treason, we arrest you heere:
My Lord of Westminster, be it your charge,
to keepe him safely till his day of triall.
Bull. Let it be so, and loe on wednesday next,
We solemnly proclaime our Coronation,
Lords be ready all.   *Exeunt.*
                    Manent West. Carlil, Aumerle.
Abbot. A wofull Pageant haue we heere beheld.
Car. The woe's to come, the children yet vnborne,
Shall feele this day as sharpe to them as thorne.
Aum. You holy Clergy men is there no plot,
To ridde the realme of this pernitious blot?
Abbot. My Lo. before I freely speake my mind herein,
You shall not onely take the Sacrament,
To burie mine intents, but also to effect,
What euer I shall happen to deuise:
I see your browes are full of discontent,
Your harts of sorrow, and your eies of teares,
Come home with me to supper, Ile lay a plot,
Shall shew vs all a merrie daie.   *Exeunt.*
                    Enter the Queene with her attendants.
Quee. This way the King will come, this is the way,
To Iulius Caesars ill erected Tower,
To whose flint bosome, my condemned Lord,
I doo onde a prisoner by proud Bullingbrooke,
                                        H 2   Heere

Oh if you raise this house against his house,
It will the wofullest diuision proue,
That euer fell vpon this cursed earth:
Prevent it, resist it, and let it not be so,
Least child, childs children crie against you woe.
North. Well haue you argued sir, and for your paynes,
Of Capitall treason, we arrest you here:
My Lord of Westminster, be it your charge,
To keepe him safely till his day of triall.
May it please you Lords, to graunt the common suite,
Fetch hither *Richard,* that in common view
He may surrender, so we shall proceed without suspition.
Yorke. I will be his conduct.
Bull. Lords, you that here, are vnder our arest,
Procure your Sureties for your dayes of answeres,
Litle are we beholding to your loue,
And litle looke for at your helping hands.
                    Enter king Richard.
Rich. Alacke why am I sent for to a King,
Before I haue shooke off the regall thoughts
Wherewith I raignd, I hardly yet haue learnt
To insinuate, flatter, bow, and bend my limbes?
Giue Sorrow leaue a while to tutor me to this submission:
Yet I well remember the fauours of these men,
Were they not mine? did they not sometimes cry all hayle
To me? so *Iudas* did to *Christ*: but he in twelue,
Found trueth in all but one; I in twelue thousand none:
God saue the King, will no man say Amen?
Am I both Priest and Clarke? well then, Amen,
God saue the King, although I be not hee,
And yet Amen, if heauen do thinke him mee:
To doe what seruice am I sent for hither?
Yorke. To doe that office of thine owne good will,
Which tired maiestie did make thee offer,
The resignation of thy State and Crowne
To *Harry Bullingbrooke.*
Rich. Seaze the Crowne.
                                        Heere

3 & 4. Pages from the first quarto of 1597 (left) and the fourth quarto of 1608. In the former, the text moves directly from the arrest of Carlisle to the Aumerle conspiracy at the end of 4.1, hence omitting the 'deposition' scene, while the latter shows the inclusion of that scene.

originally written—and that it was performed more or less intact throughout its history, though in the print version the deposition scene was excised. Let us take these two issues one at a time. First, why do we regard the scene as part of the original play? An important factor is the style of the sequence, which is entirely consonant with the rest of the play, and with the style of other plays written in the mid-1590s, and very different from the mode of *Macbeth*, *Antony and Cleopatra*, or other plays written after 1605. The verse is more regular and less supple than in the later plays, there is more rhyme, more self-conscious wordplay, more parallelism and antithesis. Here is a passage from the scene that illustrates all these features:

> BOLINGBROKE
> I thought you had been willing to resign.
> RICHARD
> My crown I am, but still my griefs are mine.
> You may my glories and my state depose
> But not my griefs; still am I king of those.
> BOLINGBROKE
> Part of your cares you give me with your crown.
> RICHARD
> Your cares set up do not pluck my cares down.
> My care is loss of care, by old care done,
> Your care is gain of care, by new care won.
> The cares I give I have, though given away,
> They tend the crown yet still with me they stay.
>
> (4.1.190–9)

There is nothing like this in any of the later plays but plenty of it in plays like *Romeo and Juliet* (1595), as well as in other parts of *Richard II*.

One piece of evidence that has been adduced to argue that the deposition scene as we have it was added later (1606–7) is the title-page of one copy of Q4, which reads in part 'The Tragedy of King Richard the Second: With new additions of the Parliament Scene, and the deposing of King Richard, As it hath been lately acted by the King's Majesty's servants, at the Globe.'[1] From this it

---

[1] There are ten extant copies, three of which have no title-page; the title-page of the other six reproduces that of the earlier quartos, naming the players as 'the Lord Chamberlain his servants', even though Shakespeare's company had become the King's servants shortly after the accession of James I in 1603. If the survival

has been claimed that the 'additions' had been recently composed and that the performance referred to as 'lately acted' was the first to present the deposition[1]—though we should remember that publishers' blurbs are not always to be trusted, and that 'new additions' could easily refer to passages new to print. Another issue is the question of motivation. Why would this passage have been added at that point? Barroll suggests that an increased interest in character development, as exemplified in the mature tragedies, might have led Shakespeare to add the scene,[2] but Shakespeare had always been interested in character, and indeed the whole play is an extended study of the complex personality of Richard, especially as he turns more introspective in the latter half. Moreover, there is little evidence of any other revisions. It seems unlikely that a new scene would have been added without any other significant changes being made (beyond a few verbal substitutions).

Another way to determine whether the scene was added or cut is to compare the sequencing in the earliest printed versions to that in the fuller text of 1608. In Q1–Q3, the transition is relatively crude: Henry announces the date of his coronation but the various appellants, whose mutual accusations of treason in the first segment of the scene resonate with the deposition of Richard, are seemingly forgotten; we then move directly to the plot

rate of this text parallels the printing rate, this suggests that the printing of the Q4 text was well advanced before the new title-page was devised.

[1] Most prominent among those who propose a later date of composition for the scene are David Bergeron ('The Deposition Scene in *Richard II*', *Renaissance Papers 1974* (1975), 31–7) and Leeds Barroll. Barroll questions the assumption that because the deposition is missing from the first three quartos it must have been cut; it could have been added. But his argument focuses mainly on print, not performance—he even says that 'the Elizabethan authorities perceived in connection with the Essex plot a threat much more serious than acted plays: i.e., the printed book' (p. 452). This could be seen to support the contention that the printed book of *Richard II* was censored while the live performances were not. Bergeron (in a follow-up article, '*Richard II* and Carnival Politics', *SQ* 42 (1991), 33–43) regards the play as a whole as destabilizing itself in a carnivalesque way and hence not really susceptible to political censorship, but censors are hardly such sensitive readers. Janet Clare ('The censorship of the deposition scene in *Richard II*', *RES* NS 41.161 (1990), 89–94) believes that the scene was written when the rest of the play was, but disallowed by Edmund Tilney, the Master of the Revels, and hence was neither performed nor printed till well into James's reign. Richard Dutton casts doubt on her argument and shows that 'it is quite probable' (though still uncertain) that the censorship derived from 'those who licensed the play for printing' rather than from Tilney's office (pp. 24–5).

[2] Barroll, p. 449.

developed by Westminster, Carlisle, and Aumerle. In the full text, Northumberland insists on granting the 'commons' suit' by having Richard appear to acknowledge his crimes, Bolingbroke reminds the appellant lords of their 'days of answer' (thus solidifying the possible parallels with the conflict between Henry and Richard), and only after Richard has appeared and adroitly avoided having to proclaim his misdeeds does Bolingbroke announce his coronation. As the principals exit, in all the texts, Westminster remarks 'A woeful pageant have we here beheld' (4.1.321) and the conspiracy is announced. Proponents of the view that the deposition was added later regard Westminster's line as a reference to the arrest of Carlisle, but the latter's response ('the woe's to come . . . ') hardly seems consistent with that interpretation. Moreover, the word 'pageant' is much more suitable to the elaborate show that Richard and Bolingbroke have just been enacting than to the rough but not especially theatrical arrest of Carlisle. If the text as we have it in Q1 is what Shakespeare originally wrote, then we have to wonder why he did not provide a fuller transition to the moment of conspiracy that marks the end of the scene. Certainly the rhythm of events seems truncated. While of course the scene could have been played in its diminished state, the skipping from one plot element to another (gage-throwing, the arrest of Carlisle, the announcement of the coronation, and the conspiracy) lacks dramatic punch. Our conclusion therefore is that the play as originally written was subject to censorship and that the printed text of Q4/F[1] represents a return to something like Shakespeare's original.

The next question is whether the censorship extended to performance or was confined to the printed text. If the scene had been barred from the stage, could we not expect some fuller and subtler stitching to prepare it for performance than what we get in Q1? Moreover, as Gurr remarks,[2] if the scene had been disallowed from the outset, the fact that it wasn't printed till 1607 means that the players would have had to keep a copy of it handy for over a decade in hopes to secure permission for it at some future time, something they would not likely have done. We might also

---

[1] F is superior to Q4 and no doubt derives from a more reliable manuscript—see *Textual Analysis*, pp. 109–10.

[2] Gurr, p. 9.

wonder whether the young gentlemen who commissioned the performance in 1601 would have done so if they had not seen it in its full form at some earlier point.

A question raised by some of those who challenge the notion that the play was censored is why, if it was, the deposition sequence might have been excised while the apparently more objectionable murder of the deposed king was allowed to stand. A possible answer, as Cyndia Clegg has shown, is that the deposition scene gives prominence to an issue that was contentious in the 1590s, namely the competing roles of Parliament and the monarchy.[1] It is noteworthy in this context that the 1608 title-page refers to the 'addition' as 'the Parliament Scene'. Furthermore Northumberland, in a number of speeches, insists on the import-ance of granting the 'commons' suit' as expressed by Parliament. Having just arrested Carlisle for 'capital treason', he proceeds to say, 'May it please you, lords, to grant the commons' suit' (4.1.155) and he follows that up (in Q4 and 5, but not in F) with the demand 'Fetch hither Richard, that in common view | He may surrender—so we shall proceed | Without suspicion' (156–8; in F these lines are assigned to Bolingbroke). Later, Northumberland becomes more and more insistent that Richard should 'read | These accusations and these grievous crimes | Committed by your person and your followers . . . | That by con-fessing them, the souls of men | May deem that you are worthily deposed' (4.1.222–7); when Richard puts him off, he refuses to yield, repeating the request several times, till Bolingbroke finally intervenes (271). Clegg very plausibly observes that this repeated demand implies 'that Parliament can and does act without the king, and indeed that Parliament takes precedence over the king' (p. 445). Since this is consistent with ideas that had occasioned actual press censorship in the 1590s (such as the move to curtail Robert Parsons's *A conference about the next succession* . . . (1595), a text Clegg discusses at some length), it could easily have pro-vided a rationale for censoring the scene. She points out that Shakespeare probably wrote the play before this issue arose con-troversially in relation to Parsons's book and that 'performing the

---

[1] Cyndia Susan Clegg, '"By the choise and inuitation of al the realme": *Richard II* and Elizabethan Press Censorship', *SQ* 48 (1997), 432–48. She offers a careful analysis showing that the weight of circumstantial evidence, while not definitive, suggests the likelihood of press censorship.

play with the . . . scene present may not have been a problem' (p. 446). Indeed there is evidence to suggest that the ecclesiastical authorities who censored the press were stricter and more draconian than the Master of the Revels, who looked after the theatre.[1] Clegg's comparison of the practices of the two offices leads her to conclude that the wholesale excision of a long scene, only parts of which could have been found offensive, is more typical of the ecclesiastical court than the Revels office.

Overall, our view of the public standing of the play in its own time may be summarized as follows. Although it is doubtful that the play itself had any significant relation to the 'rebellion' of the Earl of Essex or his followers, it did speak obliquely to the Earl's public persona, in particular his courtship of the common people.[2] It also touched on issues that were controversial and potentially dangerous in the final years of Elizabeth's reign, most especially the matter of aristocratic independence from the monarchy and the conflict between Parliament and the crown over the authority of each. Possible analogies with the role played by Essex, especially in the period between the latter's ignominious return from Ireland in September 1599 and his arrest in February 1601, may also have played a part in rendering the play temporarily suspect, but any such whisperings did not lead to censorship—the play had already appeared in three different editions before Essex fell into disgrace. What did lead to censorship, in print but not in performance, was most likely the spectacle of a monarch's deposition as well as the prominence of Parliament's role in the play as originally composed. Whether Shakespeare sympathized with the goals of Parliament is not clear—he seems most interested in presenting an ideological struggle, theatrically embodied in the persons of his protagonists. But in framing the struggle as he did, he would have been well aware that he was fashioning a position that had a political component, even though

---

[1] See Gurr, pp. 9–10. Dutton suggests that the mechanism of control may not have been the ecclesiastical authorities but the Stationers' Company itself: 'the preservation of their cartel was always a strong argument for not allowing anything to be published that might cause offence' (p. 24). And perhaps the possible connection with Essex was one of the factors in their thinking. We might note in this regard that Parsons's book was dedicated to Essex and that it had to be printed in Antwerp.

[2] On this point, see Hammer, p. 23, and Jeffrey S. Doty, 'Shakespeare's *Richard II*, "Popularity", and the Early Modern Public Sphere', *SQ* 61 (2010), 183–205.

his immediate goals were theatrical. The play, in fact, may be seen as posing a question about the relation between art and politics, especially an art such as theatre, where the public dimension is inescapably in the foreground.

Performing Politics

In 2.1, the Duke of York counsels the King not to seize the property of the dead John of Gaunt and not to deprive Gaunt's son Henry Bolingbroke, the Duke of Hereford, of the 'rights and royalties' (2.3.119) of his inheritance:

> If you do wrongfully seize Hereford's rights,
> Call in the letters patents that he hath
> By his attorneys-general to sue
> His livery, and deny his offered homage,
> You pluck a thousand dangers on your head,
> You lose a thousand well-disposèd hearts
> And prick my tender patience to those thoughts
> Which honour and allegiance cannot think.
>
> (2.1.201–8)

What thoughts can honour and allegiance *not* think? York has already said that Richard is in danger of dismantling the very system of legitimate inheritance that undergirds his kingship: 'for how art thou a king | But by fair sequence and succession?' (198–9). Could he now have in mind the possibility of thinking about the rights of subjects themselves to stand up against their ruler when they think he is doing wrong? Views of what York— and Shakespeare—might have had in mind have differed widely since at least the eighteenth century.[1] Indeed those differences might go all the way back to Shakespeare's time. The Essex party's commissioned performance of the play, discussed above, suggests that at least some people thought the play countenanced resistance to autocratic rule. On the other side, Thomas Heywood remarked that history plays 'instructed such as cannot read in the discovery of all our English Chronicles . . . [which] are writ with this aim . . . to teach the subjects obedience to their king, to show the people the untimely ends of such as have moved tumults,

---

[1] For an overview of differing opinions about the play, see Black, pp. 524–33, and Forker, *Critical*, pp. 65–89.

commotions and insurrections, to present them with the flourishing estate of such as live in obedience, exhorting them to allegiance, dehorting them from all traitorous and felonious stratagems.'[1]

Richard II has been seen as a 'divine right' play where the monarch is God's deputy on earth with his right to rule under-written by divinity and not by the people. That reading finds much support in the text. In the second scene, to take one instance, Gaunt tells the Duchess of Gloucester that he cannot avenge her husband's murder because the king can be judged only by God:

> God's is the quarrel, for God's substitute,
> His deputy anointed in his sight,
> Hath caused his death, the which if wrongfully
> Let heaven revenge, for I may never lift
> An angry arm against his minister.

(1.2.37–41)

One of the most influential versions of the 'divine right' inter-pretation, that of Ernst Kantorowicz, focuses on the early modern legal doctrine of 'the king's two bodies', which held that the monarch had both a mortal 'body natural' as a private person and also a 'body politic' that was sacred and immortal—a mystical, everlasting embodiment of the state.[2] On this account, the play endorses an idea of sacral kingship by telling the tragic story of the sundering of Richard's unified duplex body, which culminates when Richard does what no other person can do—depose the king. 'It is a scene of sacramental solemnity,' Kantorowicz says, 'since the ecclesiastical ritual of undoing the effects of consecra-tion is no less solemn or of less weight than the ritual which has built up the sacramental dignity.'[3]

In contrast, *Richard II* has been read as an oppositional play where the ruler is supposed to be the servant of the common-wealth and where his rule is assured by common law and the consent of the people.[4] York's admonition to Richard, which

---

[1] Thomas Heywood, *An Apology for Actors* (London, 1612), sigs. F3^{r-v}.

[2] Kantorowicz's thinking, and especially its application to *Richard II*, has been usefully historicized and soundly critiqued by Norbrook, 'Body'.

[3] Kantorowicz, p. 35.

[4] Two of the best arguments along these lines are Hamilton, and Rebecca Lemon, *Treason by Words: Literature, Law, and Rebellion in Shakespeare's England* (Ithaca, NY, 2006), pp. 52–78.

states that the kingship depends upon the legal principle of inheritance, lends strong support to this view. So does the dying Gaunt's remark, 'Landlord of England art thou now, not king, | Thy state of law is bondslave to the law' (2.1.113–14), which David Norbrook glosses insightfully by pointing to its evocation of the classical distinction between the political realm of free speech and action and the domestic sphere of mastery and subservience.[1]

There is as well the straightforward fact that Richard is a bad king in as much as he has overtaxed his subjects and failed to serve the national interest, which for many makes his removal necessary even if not strictly legitimate:

> ROSS
>> The commons hath he pilled with grievous taxes
>> And quite lost their hearts. The nobles hath he fined
>> For ancient quarrels and quite lost their hearts. . . .
> WILLOUGHBY
>> But what in God's name doth become of this?
> NORTHUMBERLAND
>> Wars hath not wasted it, for warred he hath not,
>> But basely yielded upon compromise
>> That which his noble ancestors achieved with blows.
>> More hath he spent in peace than they in wars.
>
> (2.1.246–55)

Where a 'divine right' reading of the play would see a 'sacramental solemnity' in the deposition scene, then, other readings might be more attuned to how the operations of raw power and political necessity must be dressed up as ritual performances, or observe how prominent is the secular authority of Parliament in the process of removing the king from office. We can note in this regard how the design of the scene in which the removal takes place would have positioned the several thousand playgoers who attended the first performances as both witnesses and judges of the king's deposition.[2]

---

[1] Norbrook, 'Liberal', p. 43.

[2] For a valuable account about how the play situates the playgoers as judges, witnesses, and participants in the political action, see Phyllis Rackin, *Stages of History: Shakespeare's English Chronicles* (Ithaca, NY, 1990), pp. 119–35.

In light of these very different opinions about the play's political meaning, it will be useful to consider the play against the background of the political thinking of Shakespeare's time and also to analyse just what the playwright did with the story of the ill-fated King, versions of which he read in Edward Hall, Samuel Daniel, *The Mirror for Magistrates*, and, most of all, Raphael Holinshed.[1] In Holinshed, the history of the fall of Richard and the accession to power of Bolingbroke come at the end of an account of years of violent struggle between the nobles and the King, in which appeals to and threats against the common people, frame-ups of enemies, ambushes, and murder are more or less common features. The boy-king, Holinshed tells us, was led astray by bad companions to follow 'the steps of lewd demeanour' (p. 418). In 1388, the lords deployed the authority of what came to be called the 'Merciless Parliament' in order to launch a bloody purge of the King's courtiers. As the King grew into manhood, he consolidated his power and struck back, arranging the murder of the Duke of Gloucester at Calais in 1397 and then convening Parliament in order to legitimize further acts of revenge.

Holinshed is forthright about Richard's failings as a ruler. He reports that the King's actions against the nobility, the extravagance of his court, and his exactions of money from the common people threatened 'the great destruction of the realm in general, but also of every singular person in particular' (p. 496). But Holinshed is also clear about the violence and abuses on the other side. From the beginning of the reign, people feared that John of Gaunt would attempt to wrest the crown from his nephew; and Gaunt's brother Gloucester, portrayed as a plain-speaking, honest, patriotic Englishman in the play *Woodstock*, which Shakespeare also knew, is summed up by Holinshed as 'that noble man, fierce of nature, hasty, willful, and given more to war than to peace; and in this greatly to be discommended, that he was ever repining against the King in all things' (p. 489). Holinshed is also interested in the relationship between the citizens of London on one side and the king and nobles on the other, and he provides numerous accounts of the organization and operation of the civic community of London. He is a

---

[1] The relationship between *Richard II* and its sources will be dealt with more fully below, pp. 44–56.

conscientious and savvy student of politics who is well aware that people are the primary makers of history. Although he does remark that God punished Richard for his 'foul enormities' (p. 508), he is not much interested in theoretical questions about worldly history versus divine providence or about the sources of political legitimacy.

Shakespeare cuts the history of cyclical violence from his tragic retelling in order to shape the play's action as a fall, a story of Richard's trespasses and punishment. He does not emulate Holinshed's even-handed judgement of all the characters in the story; indeed, if we listen to Gaunt and his son, it seems that violent death and high taxes originate with Richard rather than being simply the ever-present condition of doing monarchical politics. Shakespeare truncates Holinshed's history and amplifies the goodness and badness of the competitors in order to be able to frame an effective and emotionally gratifying dramatic arc. He also changes Holinshed in order to highlight the key relationship between power and legitimacy. In the play, an indubitably legitimate but incompetent and unpopular king is deposed by an able and admired rival who does not have a manifestly legitimate claim to the throne. That particular focus necessarily brings into prominence the questions about authority, power, and legitimacy that had been variously debated over at least the previous hundred years.

The history plays are first of all works of political art. That does not mean that they contain political messages dressed up in period costume and iambic pentameter but that their political meanings are integral to the formal organization of plot, character, and language. And because they are works of theatrical art, their political meanings are also, to a high degree, a matter of collective, active response—something that is produced by the text, the actors, and the playgoers working in concert. Steven Mullaney's description of the Elizabethan theatre as 'a new forum within which . . . collective thinking could take place' makes the point explicit:

The open air amphitheaters of early modern London . . . introduced new dimensions, in a quite literal sense, to an already extensive early modern performative sphere, producing a complex cognitive space for playwrights, players, and audiences to occupy and experience—an inhabited affective technology . . . designed to resonate with an audience newly uncertain of its individual or collective identities, and thus to sound out the gaps that had opened up in the heart of the Elizabethan social body.[1]

Mullaney's description of Shakespeare's playhouse as a 'technology' that enabled collective thinking and feeling about political questions can help us move away from a traditional approach to the play, which holds that *Richard II* embodies one or another Shakespearian argument about kingship and power. Mullaney allows us to see the play more accurately and more fully as a complex, unfolding action intended to entertain, arouse strong feelings and make possible disciplined political thinking among a group of several thousand playgoers.

Of course, Shakespeare's own interest in political matters is clear enough from the play itself as well as from what we can gather about his reading. He studied English history, reading more than would have been necessary to construct the plot of *Richard II*. In the play, he goes far beyond merely recounting the story, adapting multiple versions of the history of a formative struggle in early fourteenth-century England in order to frame questions of great resonance for people in his own time. Given that, it is entirely appropriate to see the play as an invitation to readers and playgoers to think about precisely what York did not want to allow himself to consider: what is the nature and source of political authority and under what circumstances is it legitimate to resist or even to overthrow that authority?

These questions had considerable currency in the sixteenth century. Their vogue arose from both religious and secular conflicts (and often from thoroughly mixed kinds of conflict). From 1530 to 1560, the national religion took five distinct forms. The state religion shifted from Roman Catholicism (a supranational religious organization) to a hybrid of the 'Old Faith' and the reformed religion under Henry VIII, to full-fledged Protestantism under his son Edward, to Mary's Catholicism, and finally back to Protestantism under Elizabeth. The Reformation unsettled religious and political unity across Europe and sparked people's thinking about the claims of individual conscience against the

---

[1] Steven Mullaney, 'Affective Technologies: Toward an Emotional Logic of the Elizabethan Stage', in *Environment and Embodiment in Early Modern England*, ed. Mary Floyd-Wilson and Garrett Sullivan (London, 2006), pp. 73–4.

demands of political obedience and about the legitimacy of resistance to political authority in the service of the higher goals of divine truth and salvation. On the Continent, Martin Luther, whose own conscience was a powerful force for political change, declared the lawfulness of active resistance against militant Catholic magistrates.[1] During the reign of Henry's Catholic daughter Mary, English Protestant reformers fled to Europe, from where they wrote in support of the claims of conscience against political obedience, which for them meant acting in allegiance to divine and natural law rather than in conformity to the commands of the prince. They also countenanced the common person's duty to disobey evil magistrates. John Ponet, who advocated tyrannicide against Mary, cited the story of the Roman emperor Nero to make his point: 'Who were to be blamed for these cruel acts? He for doing them, or others for flattering him, or the Senate and people of Rome in suffering him? Surely there is none to be excused, but all to be blamed. . . . he is a good citizen that doth none evil . . . he is a better that letteth [prevents] others, that they shall not do hurt or injustice.'[2] On the other side, when Elizabeth restored Protestantism after the death of her sister Mary, there were those, including the Pope, who encouraged her subjects to feel free in their souls to kill her and so restore England to the Catholic Church. It was a Christian duty, the Catholic polemicists argued, to commit regicide.[3]

The Elizabethan authorities responded to the campaign by Catholic controversialists and to the Marian tradition of 'resistance theory'. In *An Homilie against Disobedience and Wylfull Rebellion*, which was designed to be read aloud in churches on a regular basis, English men and women were told that obedience to the monarch was the chief Christian virtue (note the language of the *Homilie*, which makes the first man and woman into 'subjects', the Fall into a 'rebellion', and Lucifer into the original rebel):

[1] Quentin Skinner, *The Foundations of Modern Political Thought*, 2 vols. (Cambridge, 1978), ii. 200–1.

[2] Quoted in Richard Strier, 'Faithful Servants: Shakespeare's Praise of Disobedience', *The Historical Renaissance: New Essays on Tudor and Stuart Literature and Culture*, ed. Heather Dubrow and Richard Strier (Chicago, 1988), p. 109.

[3] See Richard L. Greaves, 'Concepts of Political Obedience in Late Tudor England: Conflicting Perspectives', *Journal of British Studies*, 22 (Autumn 1982), 23–34 (p. 33).

For as long as in this first kingdom [Paradise] the subjects continued in due obedience to God their king, so long did God embrace all his subjects with his love, favour and grace, which to enjoy is perfect felicity. Whereby it is evident that obedience is the principal virtue of all virtues and indeed the very root of all other virtues and the cause of all felicity. But as all felicity and blessedness should have continued with the continuance of obedience, so with the breach of obedience and breaking in of rebellion, all vices and miseries did withal break in and overwhelm the world. The first author of which rebellion, the root of all vices and mother of all mischiefs, was Lucifer, first God's most excellent creature and most bounden subject, who by rebelling against the majesty of God, of the brightest and most glorious angel is become the blackest and most foulest fiend and devil, and from the height of heaven is fallen into the pit and bottom of hell.[1]

Questions about the limits and nature of rule went on in secular as well as in religious terms. Ponet's mention of the Emperor Nero points to the importance of classical republicanism in early modern arguments against political absolutism.[2] The anti-imperialist thinking of Roman historians such as Tacitus and Polybius emphasized a (usually elite and male) community of responsibility and authority for matters of public concern (the Latin word *respublica* means 'the public thing'). These ideas were taken up by sixteenth-century humanists such as George Buchanan in Scotland and Thomas Smith in England. They are heard often in Shakespeare, as when, in *Antony and Cleopatra*, Pompey reminds the triumvirs about the anti-imperialist motive behind the assassination of Julius Caesar:

> What was't
> That moved pale Cassius to conspire? And what
> Made the all-honoured, honest Roman Brutus,
> With the armed rest, courtiers of beauteous freedom,
> To drench the Capitol but that they would
> Have one man but a man?
>
> (2.6.14–19)

Linked to republicanism in early modern thinking were traditional common-law ideas that emphasized the place of monarchy under

---

[1] *An Homilie against Disobedience and Wylfull Rebellion. The First Part* (London, 1570), A1ᵛ.

[2] For an excellent survey of the topic, see Hadfield, pp. 17–53.

the law and the limitations upon the monarch set by the law-making capacity of Parliament. Henry of Bracton wrote in the thirteenth century, 'law makes the king. Let him therefore bestow upon the law what the law bestows upon him, namely rule and power. For there is no *rex* where will rules rather than *lex*.'[1] Also important was the time-honoured idea of the commonwealth, a word that parallels 'republic' by articulating the value of a commonality of interests cutting across the competing interests of individual estates or ranks of people. In *De Republica Anglorum* (1583), Thomas Smith defined the term as 'a society of common doing of a multitude of free men collected together and united by common accord and covenants among themselves, for the conservation of themselves as well in peace as in war'.[2] That the commonwealth is about taking free, collective action as well as about having shared interests means that the court's preying upon the commonwealth (2.3.164–6; 3.4.33–5) can be seen as an act against the freedom as well as against the material well-being of the people.

In order to get a sense of where *Richard II* stands in all this controversy, consider one of the most salient differences between Holinshed and Shakespeare. Holinshed pays a great deal of attention to the relationship between the warring nobles on the one side and the citizens and officials of London on the other, whereas Shakespeare tends to reduce London and the commons inside and outside London to an undifferentiated mass. We can get a good sense of this by comparing their respective versions of Bolingbroke and Richard's entry into London in the wake of the deposition. In Holinshed, the entries happen on different days, with Bolingbroke's described in more detail and including descriptions of his welcome on his way toward London:

As for the duke . . . It was a wonder to see what great concourse of people and what number of horses came to him on the way as he thus passed the countries till his coming to London where . . . the mayor rode forth to receive him and a great number of other citizens. . . . in every town and village where he passed, children rejoiced, women clapped their hands, and men cried out for joy. But to speak of the great numbers of people

---

[1] Quoted in Hamilton, p. 11.

[2] Sir Thomas Smith, *De Republica Anglorum: A Discourse on the Commonwealth of England* (1583), ed. L. Alston (repr. Shannon, 1972), p. 20.

that flocked together in the fields and streets of London at his coming I here omit; neither will I speak of the presents, welcomings, lauds, and gratifications made to him by the citizens and commonality.

But now to the purpose. The next day after his coming to London, the king from Westminster was had to the Tower and there committed to safe custody. Many evil-disposed persons assembling themselves together in great numbers intended to have met with him and to have taken him from such as had the conveying of him that they might have slain him. But the mayor and aldermen gathered to them the worshipful commoners and grave citizens, by whose policy and not without much ado, the other[s] were revoked from their evil purpose. (p. 501)

In Shakespeare, the scene is recounted by York to his wife. We can note the addition of an extended theatrical simile and also how Shakespeare picks up Holinshed's focusing sentence, 'But now to the purpose', by having the Duchess suggest that while the people's attention might have been on Bolingbroke, hers is on Richard:

> . . . all tongues cried 'God save thee Bolingbroke!'
> You would have thought the very windows spake,
> So many greedy looks of young and old
> Through casements darted their desiring eyes
> Upon his visage . . .
>
> DUCHESS
> Alack poor Richard, where rode he the whilst?
> YORK
> As in a theatre the eyes of men
> After a well-graced actor leaves the stage
> Are idly bent on him that enters next,
> Thinking his prattle to be tedious,
> Even so, or with much more contempt, men's eyes
> Did scowl on gentle Richard. No man cried God save him,
> No joyful tongue gave him his welcome home,
> But dust was thrown upon his sacred head,
> Which with such gentle sorrow he shook off, . . .
> That had not God for some strong purpose steeled
> The hearts of men, they must perforce have melted
> And barbarism itself have pitied him.
> But heaven hath a hand in these events
> To whose high will we bound our calm contents.
>
> (5.2.11–38)

Holinshed's carefully differentiated and active members of London civic society are transformed by Shakespeare into a rabble of gaping, ill-judging playgoers. If we compare the play's and the chronicle's representations of the English polity, it is clear that Shakespeare tends to minimize the active role of the commons and to diminish almost altogether the place of the citizenry in the constitution of the state. His whole picture of Ricardian England seems tilted toward the nobles and the king, with high-ranking clergy taking part and speaking well, but with the commons on the sidelines and, with one or two exceptions, without voice. It is important also that while Holinshed uses the word 'citizen' regularly (as above, 'the worshipful commoners and grave citizens'), Shakespeare does not use the word once. Holinshed's 'citizens' are Shakespeare's 'subjects'; the latter word and its cognates appear eighteen times in the play. These facts about the play's vocabulary, especially the omission of the word 'citizen', might seem to indicate its overall support of a movement within state-sponsored writing in the 1590s, a dominant reframing of the people as subjects of the crown rather than as citizens with traditional rights and responsibilities under civic as well as royal authority.[1]

That Shakespeare's exclusive use of the word 'subject' is deliberate in this play, and therefore part of its particular design, is clear from the numerous appearances of the word 'citizen' in the first tetralogy, especially *Richard III*, and in Roman plays such as *Julius Caesar* and *Coriolanus*, where he is evidently more interested in the representation of more variegated state structures than the high-centred polity of Henrician England. The near evacuation of the citizenry from the constitution of the state in this play is of a piece with John of Gaunt's paean to England as 'this teeming womb of royal kings' (2.1.51), where the value of the nation is keyed to the glory of its Christian warrior-kings. About Gaunt's speech, the philosopher David Hume remarked, 'in the elaborate panegyric of England . . . and the detail of its advantages, [there is] not a word of its civil constitution as anywise different from or superior to that of other European kingdoms: An omission which cannot be supposed in any English

---

[1] See Patrick Collinson, '*De Republica Anglorum*: Or, History with the Politics put back in', in *Elizabethan Essays* (London, 1994), pp. 1–29; and Hadfield, p. 17.

author that wrote since the Restoration, at least since the Revolution.'[1]

But as is clear from what we have already described, the play's evident 'royalism' is far from uncritical. The numerous descriptions of the way kingship is embedded in the law and dependent at least to a degree on the will of Parliament, not to mention the representation of the King's own incompetence and insouciance, make it difficult to see Richard as God's deputy on earth, a bearer of Gaunt's recollected royal, Christian standard. That Richard's story cannot amount to a convincing case for divine right is most evident when the King himself is defending the view vociferously, as if he knew it to be a fiction in which he would dearly like to believe:

> Not all the water in the rough rude sea
> Can wash the balm off from an anointed king.
> The breath of worldly men cannot depose
> The deputy elected by the Lord;
> For every man that Bolingbroke hath pressed
> To lift shrewd steel against our golden crown,
> God for his Richard hath in heavenly pay
> A glorious angel. Then if angels fight,
> Weak men must fall, for heaven still guards the right.
>
> (3.2.54–62)

Despite such claims, Richard's portrayal of himself as sacred is everywhere in question. But, while he might not be a credible representative of divine right rule, he is nevertheless a compelling figure of sacrificial kingship. As we will discuss below (pp. 60–1), the play weaves together images of the fertile earth and the shedding of human blood. Yet Richard's is the only blood that we see spilled on the stage; and once it is shed, the new King reinforces its apparently magical, sacrificial power by expressing 'woe | That blood should sprinkle me to make me grow' (5.6.45–6).[2] Richard's

---

[1] Quoted in Brian Vickers, *Shakespeare: The Critical Heritage, 1623–1800*, 6 vols. (London, 1974–81), iv. 48.

[2] The difference between a sacred and a sacrificial king is subtle but important. A sacrificial figure takes part in a ritual that is set apart from ordinary life as sacred but the figure is not in itself sacred; divine right rulers are sacred in themselves. Earlier murdered kings and princes were regarded as saints: see D. W. Rollason, 'The cults of murdered royal saints in Anglo-Saxon England', *Anglo-Saxon England*, 11 (Cambridge, 1983), 1–22.

5. The Wilton Diptych, a hinged wooden panel dating from c.1395, showing King Richard kneeling (left) before the enthroned Virgin and her child, who are surrounded by angels. The young King is being presented by three saints who stand behind, Edmund (an Anglo-Saxon martyred king), Edward the Confessor, and John the Baptist.

sacrificial role highlights a severe limitation in the view of the play as oppositional. How powerful can the play's oppositional argument be when it seems to bend so much of its dramatic energy and formal properties of action, characterization, and imagery toward making its audience weep for the death of the King?

If we recall Mullaney's characterization of the playhouse as 'a cognitive space' and 'an . . . affective technology', we will be able to see how the King's sacrificial death, which might make us shed tears, was intended not to constitute a political argument but rather to open an opportunity for an audience to think feelingly through questions about the nature and limits of rule and especially the question of legitimacy and power. The playgoers' shared, affective cognition would no doubt be advanced by the play's critical treatment of the idea of divine right. But the point is that—when we think about the performance of the play before thousands of English men and women, the great majority of them commoners—the play's royalist dimension emerges as entirely of a piece with its populism and its operative democratizing tendencies. The play fashioned its playgoers in 1595 as witnesses to and judges of an historical event that bore on enduring political questions that were, if anything, more rather than less prominent as the ageing Queen grew more autocratic. As the *Homilie against Disobedience* makes clear, the monarchy claimed that its power derived from and was interwoven with the divine, and as such was essentially beyond question; but Shakespeare's play raised the 'religio-providentialist view of the state' precisely as a question.[1] On this account, the play is radical, but not primarily because of its ideological content, much of which is in any case deeply conservative. It is radical because of its cultivation of the public practices of discussing, debating, and judging among ordinary people.

Finally, it is worth noting how the play presents its popular audience with two images of their own activity as feeling judges of the fate of kings. One, which we have looked at already, is negative. By representing playgoing in critical terms, the royal entry recounted by York to his wife invites its audience to feel pity for the deposed King and to probe the question of the legitimacy of his deposition. The London crowds who cheer Bolingbroke and who throw dust on Richard's 'sacred head' (5.2.30) are certainly full of emotion, but their thoughtless excitement and rage make York and the Duchess recoil. The Londoners' bad example seems designed to make any audience recoil. York's pity for the very man whom he helped depose and his distaste for the commoners' enthusiasm lead directly to the question about power and legitimacy. York's answer to that question is moreover so jejune and self-serving that the question remains only more pressingly in need of an answer. Since 'barbarism itself' would have taken Richard's part out of pity, York reasons, it must be the case that 'God for some strong purpose steeled | The hearts of men' (34–6). He is content, ironically enough, to take the Londoners' brutal mistreatment of Richard as evidence for the providential justice of his own shift of allegiance from one king to another.

---

[1] The phrase is from Mervyn James, *Society, Politics and Culture* (Cambridge, 1986), p. 417.

The second image of the audience's political thinking and feeling is positive. The garden scene (3.4) is first of all an emblematic elaboration of the theme of the 'garden-state', which receives memorable treatment in Gaunt's panegyric and is reiterated throughout the play. The scene is critical of Gaunt in as much as the gardeners emphasize the necessity of violence in the commonwealth where the Duke imagines the state as pacific by nature, its Christian, kingly violence being directed outward. Where Gaunt's England is 'This other Eden, demi-paradise' (2.1.42), the garden-state imagined by the gardeners is awash in metaphorical blood:

> Go thou and like an executioner
> Cut off the heads of too-fast-growing sprays
> That look too lofty in our commonwealth—
> All must be even in our government.
>
> (3.4.33–6)

The gardeners are thus more in tune with Gaunt's son Boling-broke, whose vow 'to weed and pluck away' the 'caterpillars of the commonwealth' (2.3.165–6) leads to the summary execution of Richard's followers.

In addition to being a critical emblem of the state, the scene is also an allegorization of playgoing in the most positive light possible. Or, more precisely, it allegorizes performance itself as a politically well-informed and meaningful practice. The Queen and her ladies are the playgoers here and the gardeners the players. She opens the scene with a request for some form of recreation, 'To drive away the heavy thought of care' (3.4.2). Her companions suggest bowling, then dancing, then storytelling, and then singing; but all to no avail. Finally the gardeners enter— from the Queen's point of view, as if at last to provide some entertainment and diversion. They will 'talk of state', she says as she steps back to watch and listen, 'for every one doth so | Against a change' (3.4.27–8). In the event, she gets something rather different from what she might have anticipated. The gardeners not only talk about politics, they self-consciously play at government, as if trimming and weeding were the same as taking counsel and controlling potential rivals. The playgoers at *Richard II* in 1595, with the Queen ageing, the succession unsettled, and a number of rival candidates vying for pre-eminence, would have been

6. Gardeners, like those in 3.4, going about their business of pruning, binding, and rooting away, from William Lawson, *A New Orchard and Garden* (1648).

similarly keen for 'talk of state'. What is presented to the playgoers is, however, far from a scene of people gossiping in ignorance or darting their 'desiring eyes' to catch a glimpse of their social superiors.

The Gardener and his two men are capable of articulate, well-informed and thoughtful discussion and judgement about matters of public concern.[1] Responsible for the upkeep of the orchards and gardens at one of the Duke of York's estates, possibly his home at Langley, the Gardener is a worker and also the supervisor and teacher of other workers. Their talk of political violence is moderated by their emphasis on the nation as a commonwealth, by the good order of the garden (they cut off bushy, green excrescences rather than the heads of men named Bushy and Green), and by their hierarchical yet collaborative working relationship—what Smith calls a 'society of common doing'. The

---

[1] The best discussion of the garden scene, and one to which we are indebted, is in James Siemon, *Word Against Word* (Amherst and Boston, 2002), pp. 181–92.

scene shows how ordinary people make reasoned judgements. When he is confronted by the angry Queen, who, intruding into the theatrical performance to which she is a witness, mistakenly characterizes his speech as 'harsh' and 'rude' (74), the Gardener explains what she calls 'a second fall of cursèd man' in the secular terms of factionalist court politics:

> King Richard, he is in the mighty hold
> Of Bolingbroke. Their fortunes both are weighed:
> In your lord's scale is nothing but himself
> And some few vanities that make him light,
> But in the balance of great Bolingbroke,
> Besides himself, are all the English peers,
> And with that odds he weighs King Richard down.
>
> (83–9)

By showing the Queen picking up the latest political information from such a surprising source, the scene suggests playfully how the playhouse itself was part of an emerging news business, and the scene also shows specifically how ordinary people gathered and disseminated knowledge about public affairs, without which of course they could not form reliable political judgements.[1] First, they learn the news by talk:

> GARDENER   Hold thy peace.
> He that hath suffered this disordered spring
> Hath now himself met with the fall of leaf.
> The weeds which his broad-spreading leaves did shelter
> That seemed in eating him to hold him up
> Are plucked up root and all by Bolingbroke—
> I mean the Earl of Wiltshire, Bushy, Green.
> SERVANT
> What, are they dead?
> GARDENER   They are, and Bolingbroke
> Hath seized the wasteful King.
>
> (47–55)

News spreads by means of conversation but also through an epistolary network to which many people have access by dint of household relations:

---

[1] For more on theatre and news, see Dawson and Yachnin, pp. 182–207.

SERVANT

What, think you the King shall be deposed?

GARDENER

Depressed he is already and deposed
'Tis doubt he will be. Letters came last night
To a dear friend of the good Duke of York's
That tell black tidings.

(67–71)

The effect of this popular informational network is that Richard's fall is known to everyone in the kingdom except, it seems, to the Queen and her ladies. With what must be a mix of kindness toward the Queen and an assertion of his own and his fellows' veracity and dignity, the Gardener counsels the Queen to enquire on her own behalf: 'Post you to London and you will find it so, | I speak no more than everyone doth know' (90–1).

In light of the foregoing discussion, we might say that the politics of the play is a rich orchestration of at least one hundred years of historical and political thinking and debate, a body of writing that was produced during a period of remarkable innovation and controversy in English and European history. To say that and to leave it at that, however, would be to mistake the play that Shakespeare wrote for a chronicle like Holinshed or a polemical work such as John Ponet's *Shorte Treatise of Politike Power* (1556). An account of *Richard II*'s politics, we suggest, must include also the emotional force of its carefully wrought plot and characters, the complexity of its dramatic presentation of various views of kingship and government, and the power of the performance itself to cultivate a 'society of common doing' among the playgoing public.

The Character of History

Shakespeare was not a historiographer, so we should not expect to find in his works either a programmatic theory of history or a curriculum of historical education. However, he was an historical dramatist, which means that his history plays are not only literary works and theatrical scripts but also works that engage with questions about the shape and motive force of history and about the nature and value of historical knowledge. What, we want to ask, are Shakespeare's practices as a writer of historical drama? What emerges from those practices as the principle of Shakespearian history? And why was he so interested in history in the first place, interested enough to devote at least ten of the thirty-eight plays he wrote to the subject of English history?[1] And since, finally, he was an artist before he was an historian, we want to ask how Shakespearian history was shaped by his techniques as a dramatist—a maker of plot, poetic language, and character.

This period in England saw an extraordinary efflorescence of historical writing and publication, including works on classical and modern history, global histories such as Walter Ralegh's *History of the World* (1614), translations of the historical writings of Antiquity and modern Italy and France, local histories, and studies of historical method.[2] History served a range of uses. It played a central role in the polemical struggles of the English Reformation, with a work such as John Foxe's 'martyrology', *Acts and Monuments of the English Church* (1563), arguing for the apostolic primacy of the English Church. The many histories of England, like those by Raphael Holinshed, Edward Hall, and Samuel Daniel, inculcated national pride and aroused a sense of political belonging in their readers. History was good for its own sake, good because it told the truth, and particularly valuable for its capacity to educate. It made its readers better rulers or subjects and it encouraged Christian virtue. John Stow praised 'chronicles and histories' for their civic and moral instructiveness:

Amongst other books ... there are few to be preferred before the chronicles and histories. What examples of men deserving immortality, of exploits worthy great renown, of virtuous living of the posterity to be embraced, of wise handling of weighty affairs ... what encouragement of nobility to noble feats, what discouragement of unnatural subjects

---

[1] We're counting only the ten plays identified in the Folio as 'Histories', and not including *King Lear*, *Macbeth*, and *Cymbeline*, nor are we counting historical plays which he may have had a hand in, such as *Sir Thomas More* and *Edward III*.

[2] Two excellent studies of early modern English history are F. J. Levy, *Tudor Historical Thought* (San Marino, Calif., 1967; repr. Toronto, 2004); and Daniel Woolf, *The Social Circulation of the Past: English Historical Culture, 1500–1730* (Oxford, 2003); for local history, see Richard Helgerson, *Forms of Nationhood: The Elizabethan Writing of England* (Chicago, 1992), pp. 105–47.

from wicked treasons ... to conclude, what persuasions to honesty, godliness, and virtue of all sort, what dissuasions from the contrary.[1]

Richard II achieved a number of the standard purposes of historical writing. It educated playgoers, both literate and illiterate, about the history of the nation and the exemplary actions and fates of the nation's past leaders. In our view, however, Shakespeare made several special contributions to the growth of history as a form of knowledge. These included his cultivation among the playgoers of a sense of belonging to a nation consecrated by the shedding of royal blood, his education of the audience in critical history, and his development of dramatic character as the agent of historical change and principal interpreter of what those changes might mean. Shakespeare's emphasis on character is of a piece with his insight that history is as much a matter of human imagining as it is an effect of forces, events, and contingencies.

Richard II and Shakespeare's history plays as a group are remarkable because they had the capacity to involve the playgoers in a formative experience of their own Englishness by providing moving spectacles of the English past. Thomas Nashe lauded the theatrical power of the death of Talbot in *I Henry VI*, one of Shakespeare's earliest plays, in terms that bear on the particular character and social value of the history play genre. 'How would it have joyed brave Talbot', Nashe asked, '. . . to think that after he had lain two hundred years in his tomb, he should triumph again on the stage and have his bones new embalmed with the tears of ten thousand spectators'.[2] *Richard II* was able to tune to an even higher pitch than *Henry VI* the history play's ability to create an English community by focusing on the shedding of royal blood and by linking the king's blood with that of Christ.

The imagery of blood begins with Bolingbroke's reference to Abel's blood, which cries out to him for justice (1.1.104–6), and with Richard's allusion to the medical procedure of bleeding (1.1.157); this then leads to many images of blood as soiling

---

[1] John Stow, 'Epistle Dedicatorie', in *A Summarie of the Chronicles of England* (London, 1579), n.p.

[2] Thomas Nashe, *Pierce Penilesse his Supplication to the Divell* (1592), sig. F3; edited version in *Works*, ed. R. B. McKerrow; rev. F. P. Wilson, 5 vols. (Oxford, 1958), i. 212.

and also vitalizing, culminating in the moment near the end, which gives us, at last, the spectacle of violence and sight of blood promised from the start of the play, when Richard's life-blood is spilled onto the stage: 'Exton, thy fierce hand | Hath with the King's blood stained the King's own land' (5.5.109–10). Consider, against the background of this pattern of imagery, how the Bishop of Carlisle's dire prophecy of civil war might have affected a crowd of people in 1595, some of them Londoners, many from the villages and towns of the English countryside, many acquiring their first powerful sense of what it might mean to be English. Did they perhaps feel the blood of their ancestors and their ancestors' rulers under their feet in the very soil of the yard of the Theatre?

> My lord of Hereford here, whom you call king,
> Is a foul traitor to proud Hereford's king
> And if you crown him, let me prophesy
> The blood of English shall manure the ground
> And future ages groan for this foul act.
> Peace shall go sleep with Turks and infidels
> And in this seat of peace tumultuous wars
> Shall kin with kin and kind with kind confound.
> Disorder, horror, fear and mutiny
> Shall here inhabit and this land be called
> The field of Golgotha and dead men's skulls.
>
> (4.1.135–45)

Carlisle's prophecy can stir up the playgoers to take to heart the dire future effects of the deposition scene they are watching. Indeed many of those present in the Theatre would already have seen the 'tumultuous wars', here foretold by the Bishop, in Shakespeare's first tetralogy, the sequence that dramatizes the violent struggles up to the conquest of Richard III by the future Henry VII and that adumbrates the movement from the deposition of Richard II to the start of the playgoers' own epoch, under the reign of Henry VII's granddaughter, Elizabeth. On this account, the centre of gravity of the play has to do with an historical action in which the onlookers in the playhouse are implicated. They are inheritors of a troubled legacy because the play places them as the beneficiaries of the violent transactions of their national history and because the arc of the action, which twice offers and then rescinds the pleasurable spectacle of violence (in the joust scene in 1.3 and before Flint Castle in 3.3), tends to make the audience wish for the assault that results in Richard's murder. The form of the play thus makes the audience a party to the regicide. By these means, Shakespeare cultivates in his audience members an awareness of themselves as a sacramental political community bound together by their shared, guilty indebtedness for the spiritual nourishment and theatrical pleasure afforded them by their ancestor king's blood.

At the same time, and with a quite different valence, the play also educated the playgoers in critical history—in sharp-eyed ways of understanding the very history plays that were able to draw from them their collective tears of national sorrow and pride. The first scene demonstrates well Shakespeare's craft as a maker of provocative dramatic action. If we did not already know the history (and many of Shakespeare's playgoers would have been learning their English history at the playhouse), we would not understand just what is unfolding before us. No one tells us that Bolingbroke's appeal against Mowbray for the murder of Gloucester is a proxy attack on the King. We are not told exactly what lies behind the controversy and we are not sure just who did what. When faced with a direct accusation of murder, Mowbray's reply is ambiguous: 'For Gloucester's death, | I slew him not, but to my own disgrace | Neglected my sworn duty in that case' (1.1.132–4). The interpretive problems aroused by the first scene are addressed but not entirely resolved by the second, where we do learn that the King was responsible, but not that the killing was wrongful (or, on the other hand, that it was justified).

By not telling us what we need to know, Shakespeare tells us just what we do need to know in order to arouse our spirit of critical historical enquiry. A similar detail of dramatic construction is discernible in the exchanges among Northumberland, Ross, and Willoughby that begin without a pause after Gaunt's death and Richard's appropriation of Bolingbroke's inheritance (2.1.224–end). The conspirators, left together on stage, lament the state of the nation and the unjust treatment of Gaunt's son. Northumberland informs the others that Bolingbroke has already gathered a small army and a fleet of warships and is waiting for the King to depart for Ireland before initiating the invasion of England (2.1.277–98). Northumberland insists that the return of the Duke will restore England to its former glory. After this scene of conspiracy, every statement about Bolingbroke's 'coming . . . |

But for his own' (2.3.147–8) is liable to awaken a spirit of enquiry among the audience. Shakespeare's ordering of events serves well to put in question the Duke's claim that he is seeking only to right the wrong of his disinheritance.

This educative work also goes on in the play's language. Many exchanges enact the destabilization of language, putting the characters' self-understandings and descriptions of their world in question—from the accusations of treason in the first scene to the more vexed situation after Richard's overthrow, when words such as 'treason', 'honour', 'troth', and 'villain' retain their denotative stability but are unable to find a steady perch in the world. York's outrage against his son Aumerle (who, from another point of view, might be one of the few true men left in England) represents a high point in the play's encouragement of the critical scrutiny of language. 'Treason, foul treason!' York shouts after he discovers his son's part in the conspiracy to kill the new King at Oxford, 'Villain, traitor, slave!' (5.2.72). His words can claim no determinate meaning within the topsy-turvy political world of the play, and it is not surprising that the scene shifts into domestic farce as York calls out for his boots and the Duchess tries to stop him from leaving: 'Saddle my horse. | God for his mercy, what treachery is here! . . . Give me my boots, I say, saddle my horse. | Now by mine honour, by my life, by my troth, | I will appeach the villain' (5.2.74–9). It is up to the spectators in the theatre to attempt to normalize this cluster of value-laden words, all of them having been made indeterminate by our inability to discern the hand of God in the struggle for royal power.

These two functions—arousing a sense of what we could call 'sacramental nationhood' and simultaneously inculcating a disciplined scepticism about the truth of history—might seem to be at cross-purposes since critical history fosters doubt about providentialism, the idea that God's hand is above all, directing human affairs, bringing moral intelligibility to historical events, and keeping a sharp eye on the fortunes of the 'Chosen Nation' of England.[1] But critical history and Christian nationhood were

---

[1] For Shakespeare's histories' critical view of providentialism, see H. A. Kelly, *Divine Providence in the England of Shakespeare's Histories* (Cambridge, Mass., 1970).

able to coexist as aims of Shakespeare's histories because their Christianity was not doctrinal but rather a way of thinking and feeling about the world. We might even say that, in this play and others, Shakespeare transmuted the Christianity of his age so that the world he represents is both secular and consecrated. We can get a sense of how this works when, at the end of the play, the new King picks up the image of blood and draws out its Christological resonance:

> Lords, I protest my soul is full of woe
> That blood should sprinkle me to make me grow. . . .
> I'll make a voyage to the Holy Land
> To wash this blood off from my guilty hand.
>
> (5.6.45–6, 49–50)

Richard's royal blood is something that marks out a sinful act and something that provides life-giving nourishment to the sinner. Of course, Richard is not Christ, even though he associates his fall from power with the betrayal and killing of the Christian saviour. We can understand Richard's deposition readily enough in straightforward political terms, and we can easily explain his assumption of a Christlike role as an attempt to make himself feel better about his loss of worldly power. We can also understand Bolingbroke's profession of remorse as an act of political expediency rather than as a convincing statement about the sacredness of Richard's blood. All that said, the Christological quality of the King's death is no mere fantasy either, but a pervasive, formative way by which the characters make sense of their history as well as a way by which they present their history to the audience to be judged.

The third important feature of Shakespeare's history, then, is dramatic character itself. Shakespeare is interested in how particular personalities help to make history. The character of his Richard is more complex in itself and more determinative of the history the play recounts than is the Richard that appears in the sources Shakespeare drew on. Richard's character also is able to arouse a complex response from us—one that is capable of both judgement and sympathy. This Richard differs from the mostly one-dimensional figures of the King we encounter in the source texts. Lastly, Shakespeare brings character forward since it is the characters rather than the world that determine the meaning of history. That does not mean that Shakespeare rules Fortune or Providence out of his account of historical change, but rather that the operation of these forces is not presented as a given about the world itself. Since Shakespeare refrains from bringing on stage any indubitable sign of supernatural agency, the role of Providence especially must always remain open to interpretation.[1] Historical analysis has to do with deciding about what God wants, what his plans are for the world. York justifies his change of allegiance by reasoning that the bad treatment of Richard is itself proof that his overthrow has divine sanction. But analysis also has to do with this-worldly questions about the legality or morality of, for example, seizing property for what are arguably justifiable state uses (such as quashing a rebellion in Ireland) or removing a legitimate but tyrannical king. The task of interpretation is carried out by the characters as they act and speak in the world of the play, but the work of evaluation does not end with them since the audience too is invited to make sense of history and judge the rightness or wrongness of the actions of the historical actors. In Shakespeare, our efforts to understand and judge the action and the world in which the action unfolds must always go through our analytic and emotional engagement with the characters.

Inventing Genre In the time of national celebration that followed the defeat of the Spanish Armada in 1588, the novice writer Shakespeare invested most of his time and effort in the composition of a series of plays about King Henry VI, an undertaking that required him to dig into the massive English chronicles by Edward Hall, Raphael Holinshed, and others for material about the English past.[2] From about 1589 to 1593, he completed what emerged as a grand arc of four plays, culminating with the villainous rule of Richard III and the start of the Tudor royal

---

[1] Plausible exceptions include the witchcraft of Joan la Pucelle in *1 Henry VI* and the 'wonderful' English victory at Agincourt in *Henry V* (4.8.112).

[2] It is likely that the multi-play sequences themselves were an important part of how Shakespeare developed historiographical competence in his audience. The first *Henry IV* play, for example, looks back on the action of *Richard II* in ways that an audience can evaluate against their playhouse-based knowledge of Ricardian history.

line.[1] The success of his historical drama is indicated by the strong notice it attracted from other, older writers. Robert Greene claimed Shakespeare was a plagiarist and self-promoter, and he even turned a line from *3 Henry VI* into a barb against the author: 'there is an upstart crow, beautified with our feathers, that with his *tiger's heart wrapped in a player's hide*, supposes he is as well able to bombast out a blank verse as the best of you; and being an absolute *Johannes fac totum*, is in his own conceit the only Shake-scene in a country'.[2]

English history helped to make Shakespeare's career in the 1590s. But Shakespeare was also hard at work during these years making the genre of the history play itself. The traditional division of dramatic 'kinds'—either comedy or tragedy—afforded Shakespeare little space for a kind of drama that would be seen as an altogether new genre. That is reflected on the title-pages of our play. The first quarto (1597) is titled *The Tragedie of King Richard the second,* as are all the quarto editions up to 1615. In fact, the designation makes good sense since there was no dramatic genre called 'history' when Shakespeare wrote *Richard II*, since the word 'history' was more or less interchangeable with the word 'story' and therefore meaningless as the name of a particular genre, and since the play itself is well described as a tragedy, which for the Elizabethans designated a serious story of a disastrous fall from high place. Seriousness and high place were important matters for the genre, especially since the tragic drama of the time tended toward what Philip Sidney condemned as 'mongrel tragi-comedy' on account of its formal, tonal, and social heterogeneity.[3] Shakespeare, always a brilliant experimenter with form, evidently did not feel constrained by such classical strictures. *Titus Andronicus*, to take one example, mingles farce and tragedy in ways that would unsettle the expectations of any audience, even an Elizabethan

---

[1] The persuasive argument that *1 Henry VI* was written after the second and third *Henry VI* plays suggests that Shakespeare might well have developed the idea of writing his first tetralogy while he was writing what became the middle plays in it. See 'Introduction', *King Henry VI, Part 1*, ed. Edward Burns, Arden 3 (London, 2000), pp. 69–73.

[2] Robert Greene, *Greenes Groats-worth of Wit* (1592), sig. F1. The line he is parodying, and which he expects his reader to recall, is 'O tiger's heart wrapped in a woman's hide!' (1.4.138).

[3] Philip Sidney, *An Apology for Poetry*, in *Selected Poetry and Prose*, ed. David Kalstone (New York, 1970), p. 262.

one. But with *Richard II*, Shakespeare seems to have undertaken to write a play that might have pleased even as stringent a critic as Sidney. It is a drama about the fall and murder of a king, a play where there is no clowning, few commoners, and where even the gardeners speak in verse.

On its own account, then, *Richard II* is Shakespeare's most austere achievement in the genre of tragedy, where the subject matter just happens to be English history. We can only guess whether he intended the play, when he was writing it, to be the first in a second tetralogy.[1] He had already written one four-play sequence, so the possibility of writing another could not have been far from his mind. Once we see the play in that larger context, it becomes clear that Shakespeare was doing something far more radical than either developing a 'mongrel' form or realizing a classical model. The subject matter of English history, which was the focus of about half his dramatic writing through the 1590s, deformed the traditional genres from within, especially that of tragedy, creating a new super-genre able to hold within it elements of tragedy and comedy. It is able indeed to absorb whole tragedies because the form of the history super-genre must include, at least as a possibility, more than one play in any given work. That the action need not come to a full stop at the end of any given play means that the acts of the characters are not conditioned by a bent toward a definitive comic or tragic ending. Time surges forward beyond the end of any individual history play, bringing new beginnings that usher in the future and also transform the past. When dramatic temporality is unbound from the shaping force of tragedy or comedy, it becomes available to particular, competing constructions and revisions on the part of the characters. History grounded in such an idea of unbound time is neither linear nor recursive, but revolutionary in the full sense of the word, since each new substantial advance is at the same time a revision of everything that preceded it.

---

[1] Gurr argues (pp. 4–6) that Shakespeare must have planned the sequence from the moment he started writing *Richard II* because it anticipates many elements in the later plays. This is persuasive but not definitive since, as a matter of principle, elements in any text become anticipatory only when they are picked up and developed in later texts; as any storyteller knows, narratives are written by looking backward as well as forward.

To get a clearer idea of the differences between tragedy and history as those genres were being shaped by Shakespeare, let us consider two young men who live through the fatal happenings in their respective play-worlds. Edgar in *King Lear*, about whom we care a great deal, survives the catastrophe that ends his play, but we give little thought to what his life might be like in the future. Aumerle (who, as a matter of fact, disappears from the sequence after *Richard II*) gains a powerful forward-moving momentum by virtue of the two comic scenes in which he and his mother race against his father to get to King Henry and then beg the King to pardon Aumerle's treason (while Aumerle's father argues with equal vehemence that his son should be killed).[1] Henry himself draws attention to the indecorum of the action—'Our scene is altered from a serious thing | And now changed to "The Beggar and the King"' (5.3.78–9). There is rough and tonally complex comedy in *King Lear* also, but the affecting family comedy in *Richard II* with its evocation of the pathos of ordinary life helps to change the temporal orientation of this tragedy from within. For all we care, there is no world after the deaths of Lear and Cordelia. We can note how Shakespeare uses apocalyptic imagery to enhance the sense that this is the final ending.[2] After Richard's death, in contrast, the world is changed but intact; the characters still have their lives ahead of them. Aumerle disappears, but other sons, Northumberland's Hotspur and Bolingbroke's Hal, not to mention Northumberland and the new King himself, have vital stories in the plays that follow. They have their history, including the history that preceded them, to create and re-create.

Of course, Shakespeare did not invent plays about English history. John Bale's mid-century polemical play, *King Johan*, the anonymous *Famous Victories of Henry V* (*c*.1583–8), and Christopher Marlowe's *Edward II* (*c*.1591–2), which influenced Shakespeare directly, are among many instances of the dramatic adaptation of chronicle history in the period.[3] But the sheer number of Shakespeare's histories, the scale of his achievement as

---

[1] In the most illuminating reading of the scenes, Sheldon P. Zitner emphasizes how ordinary life and language can provide a critical view of aristocratic politics. See 'Aumerle's Conspiracy', *Studies in English Literature*, 14 (1974), 239–57.

[2] See *King Lear*, ed. Stanley Wells (Oxford, 2000), 24.259 and note.

[3] See Irving Ribner, *The English History Play in the Age of Shakespeare* (rev. edn., London, 1965), pp. 30–91.

the leading Elizabethan theatrical historian, and the formative changes he made within historical tragedy all influenced contemporary thinking about dramatic genre and contributed to the growth of interest in history as a distinct kind of knowledge about the world. By gathering the ten English histories (out of thirty-six plays in all) into a separate section, the editors of the First Folio in effect added a new genre to the two classical ones.[1] The first page after the dedications presents 'A Catalogue of the several Comedies, Histories, and Tragedies contained in this Volume'. To some extent, this was a matter of mere convenience and reflects the simple fact that all the 'Histories' share the same subject matter. But the tripartite organization of the volume also suggests some level of recognition on the part of Heminge and Condell of Shakespeare's fashioning of a new kind of dramatic literature. That recognition of generic innovation is borne out by the title that the editors gave the play—'The Life and Death of King Richard the Second'. We might say that biography, as an element of historical writing about a larger world, here takes the place of tragedy (the word used on the quarto title-pages), where time and the world are summed up in the arc of a single person's fall from greatness.

Dramatizing the Histories of Richard II   Shakespeare took pains with *Richard II*, researching the King's reign and fall from power with great care in a number of sources and shaping a large amount of material, much of it contradictory, into a compressed, coherent and moving dramatic narrative. That 'history' is designed to heighten both the emotional and critical engagement of the audience and to bring forward dramatic characters, including women characters, as foundational to the play's appeal to the audience in the first place, as prime movers of historical change and as the key interpreters of the meaning of history.[2]

---

[1] The editors and/or the printer did not make use of the category of tragicomedy, which had been made fashionable by writers like John Fletcher and Shakespeare himself, and which might have served for plays such as *Cymbeline* or *The Tempest*, which are classified respectively as a tragedy and a comedy.

[2] The most judicious and lucid discussion of the sources of *Richard II*, and the one to which we are most indebted, is Bullough, pp. 353–82. Forker's discussion of the sources (pp. 123–65) is remarkably and helpfully detailed.

Among the works Shakespeare read were Marlowe's *Edward II* and Samuel Daniel's poetic history, *The First Four Books of the Civil Wars* (1595), both of which are important for their own interest in character. He likely also saw Marlowe's play in performance, and he must have seen a performance of the anonymous play, *Thomas of Woodstock* (*c*.1591–5), since he drew on it though it was not published in his time. Certainly he knew *The Mirror for Magistrates* (1559), although its moralizing representations of crime and punishment do not seem to have greatly influenced his more worldly understanding of political life and death. He is also likely to have read Lord Berners's translation of Jean Froissart's *Chronicle* (1525; 1545); it was an available and lively eyewitness account of the King's last years by a French visitor to the English court. From his work on the first tetralogy, he would already have been familiar with Edward Hall's *The Union of the Two Noble and Illustrate Families of Lancaster and York* (1548). And most importantly, he also knew well and must have kept at hand Raphael Holinshed's *Chronicles of England, Scotland, and Ireland* (1587), which was his major working source.[1]

Shakespeare focuses the action of his play on the last two years of Richard's life. The narrative of Hall's *Union* probably suggested the starting point for the play; it opens near the end of Richard's reign, specifically with a conversation in which Bolingbroke complains to Mowbray about the King who, Bolingbroke says, 'little or nothing regarded the counsel of his uncles nor of other grave and sad persons but did all thing at his pleasure, setting his will and appetite instead of law and reason' (A2^r). Bolingbroke, Hall comments, 'break[s] his mind to him [i.e. Mowbray] more for dolour and lamentation than for malice or displeasure'; however, Mowbray betrays him to the King, which leads to the formal confrontation that makes up the play's first scene. A generation of critics followed E. M. W. Tillyard in supposing that *Richard II* and the second tetralogy as a whole were written expressly to elaborate Hall's reflections on harmony as a familial, civic, and theological

---

[1] Other sources that have been proposed include *Histoire du Roy d'Angleterre Richard* by Jean Créton and the anonymous *Chronicque de la Traïson et Mort de Richart Deux*. These are, however, fifteenth-century manuscript accounts that had been used by other writers that Shakespeare drew on, so there can be no strong case that he knew them directly.

virtue.[1] Shakespeare's history, however, does not run within such narrow ideological bounds, and its representation of political questions such as the argument between the benefits of civil harmony and the rights of subjects to challenge the monarch in the interests of the commonwealth cannot be prised apart from the actions, motives, and speeches of the characters. In this play, an ideal of union is a question, not an answer; and Shakespeare's attention was likely more piqued by Mowbray's public betrayal of Bolingbroke's private confidence than by Hall's condemnation of political discord.

In developing the play, in any case, Shakespeare follows Holinshed rather than Hall, borrowing many details and tracking Holinshed almost step by step: the stymied trial-by-combat and the subsequent banishment of the two would-be combatants, the seizure 'into his hands all the goods that belonged to [Gaunt]' (p. 496), the 'farming' of the realm, the King's ill-timed expedition to Ireland, the conspiracy against him by the aggrieved nobility, Bolingbroke's return before the end of his sentence, and the capture, deposition, and murder of the King.[2]

This summary might seem to suggest that the play is merely derivative of the chronicle, but in fact Shakespeare changes much. In Holinshed, Northumberland betrays the King's trust, imprisons him in Flint Castle, and hands him over to Bolingbroke; in Shakespeare, who seems to be following Hall (A6^v) and Froissart (cap. 237) at this point, Richard takes shelter at Flint Castle on his own initiative and then gives up to Bolingbroke, rejecting the sound advice of his followers to temporize and gather support. The difference is important since Holinshed's Richard is the mere victim of a treasonous ambush whereas Shakespeare's King seems to betray himself by his capitulation to Bolingbroke. Shakespeare's demoralized Richard also owes something to Hall, who describes the King, after he has been arrested by Bolingbroke, as 'for sorrow withered, broken and in manner half dead' (A8^r)—though Shakespeare's Richard, while perhaps 'broken', is far from 'half dead'. The scene of his descent to the 'base court', which is his first staging of his downfall (the second is the 'deposition scene'),

---

[1] E. M. W. Tillyard, *Shakespeare's History Plays* (London, 1944); for a recent restatement of Tillyard's view, see Nigel Saul, *Richard II* (New Haven and London, 1997), p. 2.

[2] For the verbal borrowings, see Bullough's notes, pp. 387–415.

is at once embarrassingly abject and powerfully self-assertive. A character who surrenders his kingly authority while describing the radiance of his fall—'Down, down I come like glistering Phaëton, | Wanting the manage of unruly jades' (3.3.177–8)—easily takes centre stage in the eyes of the audience, not exactly marginalizing the play's plot and theme, but encouraging us to respond to Richard's fall through our primary response to character.

7. The Fall of Phaëton, a mythological figure traditionally associated with over-reaching (by the sculptor Simone Mosca, or Moschino, first half of the sixteenth century).

Shakespeare takes phrasing as well as incident from Holinshed, but here too the differences are more important than the similarities. Holinshed recounts how the knight speaking before the King on behalf of Bolingbroke had said that Thomas of Mowbray 'hath been the occasion of all the treason that hath been contrived in your realm for the space of these eighteen years, and by his false suggestions and malicious counsel, he hath caused to die and to be murdered your right dear uncle, the Duke of Gloucester' (p. 494). In the play, the speech is given to Bolingbroke and is written as verse, which increases its energy; Shakespeare also adds a layer of meaning that joins water and blood as the coupled liquids of sacrifice and fecundity (bad fecundity in this instance), introducing what will be a major image pattern in the play; and he also introduces a telling biblical allusion:

> . . . I say and will in battle prove, . . .
> That all the treasons for these eighteen years,
> Complotted and contrivèd in this land
> Fetch from false Mowbray their first head and spring;
> Further I say and further will maintain
> Upon his bad life to make all this good,
> That he did plot the Duke of Gloucester's death,
> Suggest his soon-believing adversaries,
> And consequently, like a traitor coward,
> Sluiced out his innocent soul through streams of blood—
> Which blood, like sacrificing Abel's, cries
> Even from the tongueless caverns of the earth
> To me for justice and rough chastisement.
>
> (1.1.92–106)

This framing of the accusation against Mowbray is of a piece with the imagery of blood that, as described above (pp. 35–9), is part of how the play attempts to explain its world. It is also integral to how Bolingbroke makes his appearance in the world of the play; and it tells us at least as much about him as it tells us about the world, especially since there is not much warrant for his characterization of his murdered uncle as an innocent Abel. Ironically enough, the rough chastisement he visits on the King, who is the real target of the speech, ends up, as we have seen, sprinkling him with blood, and indeed the blood of a sacrificed king instead of a 'sacrificing Abel'.

In addition to these and other differences is the major alteration that Shakespeare fashions by dramatizing only two years of a narrative spanning the thirty-three years of Richard's life. As we noted in the section on Politics (pp. 19–20), Shakespeare cuts off the history of back-and-forth violent struggle and brutal strategizing between the King and the nobles that had been one of the most persistent features of the reign. By not beginning with the bloody history leading up to the last phase of Richard's life, Shakespeare makes the characters in the play less battle-scarred than their counterparts in the chronicle and makes the political world, at least at the start of the play, a seemingly more civil place than it is in his main source. For example, Holinshed tells us that Richard had at the lists at Coventry 'ten thousand men in armour lest some fray or tumult might rise amongst the nobles by quarrelling' (p. 495). Shakespeare emphasizes the pageantry that he found in Holinshed but ignores the evident need for armed security.

Shakespeare's compression of the story gives the play the form of a fall from high place, a pattern that was familiar to the Elizabethans, especially given the great popularity of *The Mirror for Magistrates*, whose accounts of the falls of famous figures from English history were standard reading in the period. However, the play adds a major complication to the lapsarian pattern that Shakespeare found in the *Mirror*, which is that the world that sees the fall of Richard has itself suffered a collapse into uncertainty and changeability, as if the characters had woken up the morning of the play's first day to find that they no longer knew exactly what kind of world they were in. The fall into ideological uncertainty is a constant feature of Shakespeare's representations of the historical world. In this play, as in *Hamlet* and others, the characters seem to think that sometime in the recent past the meanings and morality of actions were easily knowable; but now, they find, everything seems unfathomable. Consider the difference between Hamlet's father's decisive victory over his enemy in chivalric combat and Hamlet's own struggle to perform a similarly public, knowable act of revenge against his uncle. Or, in this play, consider the great distance from Richard's father's radiant victory over the French (2.1.173–83) to the murky, internecine argument about just who was guilty for the death of Gloucester and just how guilty they were.

It is important to note that Shakespeare draws a firm line between political analysis and moral judgement. The play provides an ample and clear political explanation for Richard's fall. Shakespeare takes up details about Richard's faults as a ruler from the chronicles, the *Mirror* and *Woodstock*. Like the King in *Woodstock*, Shakespeare's Richard is arrogant, wasteful, heedless, and capable of brutality against those that he has made his enemies. Both are said to have become 'landlords' instead of kings and to have (as Gaunt puts it) 'leased out' England 'Like to a tenement or pelting farm' (2.1.59–60).[1] More or less as in the sources, Richard's seizure of Gaunt's property is illegal, the timing of his military expedition to Ireland is ill-considered, his intelligence system operates inefficiently, he is unable to recruit or retain a military force, and he fails to cultivate the love of the people. But Shakespeare frustrates any easy condemnation of the King, especially by preventing the character from alienating altogether the esteem of the audience. Shakespeare differs from the source texts by emphasizing the steadfast loyalty to Richard of characters such as Aumerle and Isabel and by leaving out any persuasive account of Richard's degeneracy. In the play, Bolingbroke accuses the King in these terms (see 3.1.11–15 and note); but Shakespeare's Richard, while egregiously insouciant toward the nobles and the people, is a constant and loving husband, very unlike the wastrel described by Holinshed and the other chroniclers, or as a 'pleasure pricked' king (as the *Mirror* puts it), a man whose 'lecherous mind . . . must | To Venus' pleasures always be in awe' (p. 113). While Shakespeare allows that Richard is implicated in the murder of his uncle, he lets the matter drop as the action unfolds, and he provides little evidence to countenance *Woodstock*'s unhistorical depiction of the murdered Gloucester as an exemplary honourable, plain-speaking Englishman, and therefore as someone whose death ought to matter to us. Finally, Shakespeare's Richard undertakes to overturn altogether the

---

[1] See *Woodstock*, 4.1.142–7, where Richard himself catalogues his failings:

> We shall be censured strangely, when they [i.e. foreign kings] tell
> How our great father toiled his royal person
> Spending his blood to purchase towns in France;
> And we his son, to ease our wanton youth
> Became a landlord to this warlike realm,
> Rent out our kingdom like a pelting farm.

significance of his political failure by grasping for a 'new world's crown' (5.1.24) to replace the earthly one he has lost.

Richard fills the foreground of the play and commands our attention far more than he does in Holinshed's busier, more populous and more eventful chronicle history. The focus on character is also a key feature in the *Mirror*, since the stories in that work are all told by the tragically fallen figures themselves. However, while the storytelling by the dead kings and lords in the *Mirror* is intended to exemplify and teach readers about the workings of a stable moral universe, Shakespeare's Richard is a remarkably individualized character in a world whose moral order must always remain uncertain and indeed a matter of debate among the characters.

The reorientation of historical knowledge and judgement to include the authority of the feelings and thoughts of the people who are involved in history, as well as forces external to the participants, is one of Shakespeare's great achievements. It is one for which there is perhaps no fully adequate source outside Shakespeare himself, although for the new emphasis on character as well as the particular characterization of Richard, he is to some degree indebted to Marlowe and Daniel. Marlowe's *Edward II* gave him the powerful character-centred model where the doomed king alienates the affections of the audience by his arrogant misuse of power until the point where his power begins to be stripped from him. The pathos of Edward's fall, his poignant love for Gaveston, and the brutality of his murder recreate him for the audience as a sympathetic figure. Shakespeare's handling of the pattern is similar but more nuanced. Edward is a passionate and pathetic victim at the end of his story; Richard has also a dimension of his character that calls forth our pity, but he remains fiercely self-absorbed; and unarmed though he is at the end, he musters the strength to kill two of his attackers before he is killed. Edward's antagonist Mortimer emerges as a full-blown villain whereas Richard's opposite Bolingbroke becomes increasingly burdened by events and even develops a degree of remorse for the death of his adversary. Edward's queen is so badly treated by her husband on account of his love for Gaveston that she betrays him sexually and politically; Richard's Queen Isabel is a beloved and devoted wife whose separation from her husband is the most affecting scene in the play.

Shakespeare's most memorable borrowing from Marlowe in *Richard II* is not in fact from *Edward II*. When Richard contemplates his face in the mirror in the course of the deposition scene (the stage business is Shakespeare's invention), he says,

> Was this face the face
> That every day under his household roof
> Did keep ten thousand men?
>
> (4.1.281–3)

The allusion is to Doctor Faustus' famous exclamation upon seeing a figure that he takes to be Helen of Troy—'Was this the face that launched a thousand ships | And burnt the topless towers of Ilium?' (5.1.90–1). It is significant that the face Richard admires with such bitter new understanding is his own face rather than that of the most renowned woman in history. The spectacle of the King with the looking-glass is a dramatization of a mixed emblematic tradition, in which looking in a mirror can signify either truth-seeking or narcissistic self-absorption. Richard refers to the mirror as a revelatory text—'I'll read enough | When I do see the very book indeed | Where all my sins are writ, and that's myself' (4.1.273–5). Bolingbroke's dry rejoinder suggests the hollowness of Richard's gesture: 'The shadow of your sorrow hath destroyed | The shadow of your face' (292–3). The scene builds upon Richard and Bolingbroke's dispute about the meaning of the mirror, taking us into the new territory of inward characterization; after all, we can hardly decide which of the two men is right until we understand just what Richard looks for in the mirror and how he judges what he sees. Richard's culminating comment in the exchange makes explicit how the scene stimulates our engagement with the inward man:

> . . . my grief lies all within
> And these external manners of laments
> Are merely shadows to the unseen grief
> That swells with silence in the tortured soul.
>
> (4.1.295–8)

The inward turn that Richard takes by finding his own face so captivating is at once also Shakespeare's turning away from Marlowe's more outward and declamatory style of characterization. The sources of inward characterization, the hallmark of Shakespeare's dramatic style, are too many for us to be able to trace fully, but it is clear that Daniel provided Shakespeare with some valuable starting places for the innovations that he brought to fruition in *Richard II.*

There are several moments in Daniel's *Civil Wars* where the narrator conjures the inwardness of characters by tracking their gaze and recounting their thoughts as they cast their eyes from a private space onto a larger, public one. Shakespeare adapts this by turning his characters' vision inward, so that the circuit of their looking is from one to another private space. On his last morning, Daniel's Richard looks from his prison window, sees working people going about their daily tasks and contemplates the pleasures of ordinary life against the perils of greatness:

> O had not I then better been t' have stood
> On lower ground and safely lived unknown,
> And been a herdsman rather than a king,
> Which inexperience thinks so sweet a thing.
>
> (3.68)

Shakespeare follows Daniel's example but transforms the prison soliloquy into a speech that captures the harrowing restlessness of solitude. Shakespeare's Richard, a particular individual dealing with terrible loss, cannot so easily wrap himself in the comforts of worldly renunciation. In his soliloquy (5.5.1–66), the object of his gaze is a world he creates out of his own thoughts. That mental world affords him neither stability nor solace; instead he is hauled back and forth between his desire to have all the glory and pleasure of kingship back again and his equally strong wish to be able to renounce his royalty and so claim a kind of victory in the midst of failure:

> Thus play I in one person many people
> And none contented. Sometimes am I king,
> Then treasons make me wish myself a beggar
> And so I am. Then crushing penury
> Persuades me I was better when a king,
> Then am I kinged again, and by and by
> Think that I am unkinged by Bolingbroke
> And straight am nothing.
>
> (5.5.31–8)

His inability to come down on one side or another and his consequent unsuitability to appear as a figure in an exemplary action, intensify Richard's presence to us as an individualized, inward character.

Important, finally, is how Shakespeare was influenced by the character of the Queen in Daniel. The historical Isabel was a child when she was married to Richard in 1395. She is of little consequence in the chronicle sources. Daniel made her an adult of strong passions and developed her love of Richard into a poignant feature of the narrative. In an extended sequence (bk. 2, st. 70–92), we see through the Queen's eyes the scene of Bolingbroke's triumphant and Richard's humiliating entry into London, which in Shakespeare is recounted by the Duke of York. Daniel's Isabel, 'Sick of delay and longing to behold | Her long-missed love' (st. 72), watches from a window at some distance from the procession. She calls on her women to rejoice with her at the sight of a man in white riding a white horse, surrounded by cheering crowds. She thinks that it is Richard, but of course it is Bolingbroke, immediately recognizable to us by his showy courtesy to the people (st. 74–5). When she realizes her mistake, she turns from the window in anger; then she is drawn back just in time to catch sight of a single wretched figure, whom after a struggle she recognizes as her husband. He feels her gaze but doesn't see her. Her sorrow overwhelms her, and she swoons; when she recovers, she speaks to herself eloquently of her love for the fallen King: 'though thy ungrateful land | Hath left thee thus, yet I will take thy part, . . . Thou still dost rule the kingdom of my heart' (st. 89). Once in his presence and full of rehearsed words of comfort, however, she is unable to speak.[1] They stand speechless and look into each other's eyes:

> Thus both stood silent and confused so,
> Their eyes relating how their hearts did mourn,
> Both big with sorrow and both great with woe,
> In labour with what was not to be born.
> This mighty burden wherewithal they go
> Dies undelivered, perishes unborn.
> Sorrow makes silence her best orator,
> Where words may make it less, not show it more.
>
> (st. 97)

---

[1] In the parallel scene in Shakespeare (5.1), both characters speak eloquently about their love for each other.

For the characterization of his Queen, Shakespeare makes use of Daniel's focus on the movements between sight, inward feeling, and outward expression, and also the metaphor of being pregnant with grief (2.2). But he also changes the metaphor by making the unborn sorrow both a powerful feeling and a kind of urgent knowledge, an unaccountable intuition of political disaster. Since drama does not have the use of a narrator that might speak about what a character feels inside but cannot express outwardly, Shakespeare twists the Queen's language in the conversation she has with Bushy, making her difficult to understand so as to suggest the inward pressure of hard-to-articulate feelings and thoughts. Her brooding sorrow has no apparent connection to the real world; Bushy tries to cheer her out of it by insisting on the groundlessness of her anxiety. Borrowing Daniel's metaphor of pregnancy, she is able to speak about 'some unborn sorrow', as yet not present to her, not yet anything (that is, 'nothing'), but nevertheless certain to be born from 'Fortune's womb' as something far more dire than the King's temporary absence:

> . . . methinks
> Some unborn sorrow, ripe in Fortune's womb,
> Is coming towards me, and my inward soul
> With nothing trembles; at something it grieves
> More than with parting from my lord the King.
> (2.2.9–13)

The Queen's insistence on an inward feeling of sorrow that another character finds insubstantial makes her a precursor of Hamlet, who also resists the bullying cheerfulness of his interlocutors by means of riddling language.[1] The difference between the two characters is of note, however, since Hamlet's grief clearly has an answerable object (the death of his father) even if his uneasiness seems without foundation, whereas the Queen's sorrow is for a tragedy that has not happened. Her inward, nearly inexpressible sorrow is therefore a form of prophetic knowledge—

---

[1] Stanley Wells points out that the Queen 'feels about herself as T. S. Eliot felt of Hamlet: that her emotion is "in excess of the facts as they appear"' (Wells, 'Lamentable', p. 12).

information about the history of the future. In the event, the unfolding news soon proves her right. The King has left for Ireland, Bolingbroke with a small army has returned from France before the end of his banishment and the traitorous nobles are flocking to him. '[T]hou art the midwife to my woe', the Queen says to Green, who has just arrived bearing the most recent bad news,

> And Bolingbroke my sorrow's dismal heir.
> Now hath my soul brought forth her prodigy
> And I, a gasping new-delivered mother,
> Have woe to woe, sorrow to sorrow joined.
> (2.2.62–6)

As clearly indebted to Daniel as he is, Shakespeare neverthe-less parts company with him by developing the character of the Queen in relationship to his own broader interest in the nature of history. Since, in Shakespeare's view, history is as much a matter of interpretation as it is a factual record of historical events and persons, the Queen must be seen to be a major historical actor in the play.[1] As we discussed above (pp. 30–3), the Queen cannot compete with the Gardener when it comes to up-to-date information or savvy analysis of factional politics at court. But she has what no other person in the play has—the ability to feel the approach of the future and the capacity to discern its unborn shape. Her brooding anticipation of tragedy helps set the mood for the disaster to come. But her prophetic, physically sensible knowledge about one of the formative events of the English past serves the play's historiographical goal of creating a sorrowful witnessing of history among the playgoers, so memorably described by Thomas Nashe, a witnessing that is able to match the play's investment in critical historical analysis.

---

[1] In their study of gender and historiography in Shakespeare, Jean Howard and Phyllis Rackin argue that the women in *Richard II* and the second tetralogy are far less active and important than the women in the first. Their argument is per-suasive so long as one thinks about history exclusively as the record of what was done in the past. If one expands the idea of history to include interpretation as well as action, then one can begin to see how a character like Isabel is an important historical agent. See *Engendering a Nation: A Feminist Account of Shakespeare's English Histories* (London and New York, 1997), pp. 137–59.

Language

Although *Richard II* is one of only a handful of Shakespeare plays to be written entirely in verse,[1] its style is far from uniform. Highly formal and ritualistic language is matched by intimate exchange, elaborate and self-conscious rhetoric by plain speech, metaphorical density by befuddled distraction or conspiratorial indirection. Differences of style emanate from character, but are also contingent upon public life. Speech in that sense is political as well as personal, all the more so in this profoundly political play.

Northumberland's plain style, when he arrests the protesting Bishop of Carlisle, may serve as a preliminary example. It bespeaks not just his individual abruptness, his enjoyment of a certain harshness that makes him a willing 'enforcer', though it does indeed register that aspect of his personality. But it also emerges from the public space he occupies, his desire at that moment to silence Henry's opponents and to pave the way for Richard's declaration of guilt, which he pursues with equal relentlessness a few minutes later. It has, that is, a punitive public dimension. Carlisle, in one of the great prophecies of lament that dot the play, has predicted that 'The blood of English shall manure the ground . . . And in this seat of peace tumultuous wars | Shall kin with kin and kind with kind confound' (4.1.138–42). He ends, Cassandra-like, by calling for resistance and crying 'woe'. Northumberland responds sardonically:

> Well have you argued, sir, and for your pains
> Of capital treason we arrest you here.
> My lord of Westminster, be it your charge
> To keep him safely till his day of trial.

$$(4.1.151-4)$$

His retort serves not only to deflate the Bishop's rhetoric, but to indicate that the new regime means business; his style, that is, derives from a particular social context. The same tone, driven by the same political requirements, surfaces later in the scene, when he insists that Richard read aloud the accusations against him.

---

[1] The others, all early history plays, are the first and third parts of *Henry VI* and *King John*.

57

Richard, who has just finished a long speech dense with rhetorical flourishes (201–22), turns at the end to his tormentors and, on a suddenly unadorned note, asks, 'What more remains?' This shift to plain, direct speech tells us of Richard's awareness of the very real and inescapable political situation he finds himself in; he knows that rhetoric won't get him out of it. The style of Northumberland's reply carries the same recognition:

> No more, but that you read
> These accusations and these grievous crimes
> Committed by your person and your followers
> Against the state and profit of this land . . .
>
> (4.1.222–25)

While Northumberland's typically no-nonsense air comes from within, political exigency helps determine the nature of his language.

In the play's third scene, Thomas Mowbray, Duke of Norfolk, is banished for life. Surprisingly, his first reaction is to lament the loss of his 'native English' (1.3.160), the fact that his tongue will now be imprisoned in his mouth, unused inside its case, like 'an unstringèd viol or a harp' (162).[1] From this perspective, speechlessness is equivalent to death ('What is thy sentence then', Mowbray asks the king, 'but speechless death . . . ?'—172). This is the clearest statement of a theme that runs throughout the play—the importance of language as the foundation of public identity. Most prominently, the King's power is vested in his capacity to give voice to his will. When, moments after exiling Mowbray, he reduces Bolingbroke's banishment from ten to six years, the latter comments: 'How long a time lies in one little word! | Four lagging winters and four wanton springs | End in a word—such is the breath of kings' (1.3.213–15). Later, as he begins to lose ground to his adversary, Richard bemoans the fact that 'this tongue of mine, | That laid the sentence of dread banishment | On yon proud man, should take it off again | With words of sooth' (3.3.132–5). His social position is still a matter of speech, but now his weakness of status is matched by that of his words. Thus it is entirely consistent that in the deposition scene it

---

[1] The word 'tongue' occurs more often in *Richard II* than in any other Shakespeare play (26 times); *King John* and *Love's Labour's Lost* are next at 21 (if we include plural and possessive forms, the count is *R2* 31, *LLL* 26, *KJ* 24).

is through language that he dethrones himself, as he himself is aware: 'With mine own tongue [I do] deny my sacred state' (4.1.209).

The same theme is replayed in a comic vein when the Duchess of York and her son plead for pardon from King Henry for Aumerle's treason (5.3.110–35). As the Duchess realizes, 'Twice saying "pardon" doth not pardon twain, | But makes one pardon strong' (133–4). But it is not just the king whose political position is founded in speech. Throughout the play, personal identity and public language are inextricable—from the ritualized quarrel between Mowbray and Bolingbroke in Scene 1, right through to the thwarted expectations of Exton, who undertakes the murder of Richard on the basis of overheard speech (5.4.1–11) and presents himself for reward in the final scene only to be rebuffed by Henry: 'Exton, I thank thee not, for thou hast wrought | A deed of slander with thy fatal hand | Upon my head and all this famous land' (5.6.34–6). Exton's crime, that is, is one of language—a deed of slander.

One particular strain of symbolic language is especially important in informing the relation between speech and politics: the persistent linking of England with earth and gardens. Central to this motif are two sequences. The first is Gaunt's famous account of England as an Eden-like 'demi-paradise', a 'blessed plot' which, under the destructive husbandry of King Richard, has become nothing but a scrabble-earth farm, a 'tenement' leased out in shame (2.1.40–60); the second is the garden scene (3.4) in which hard-working and politically savvy gardeners carefully tend their enclosed space, and mark out the contrast between their well-ordered world and the larger enclosure that is England, the 'sea-wallèd garden' celebrated by Gaunt, which is now 'full of weeds', 'unpruned', and 'Swarming with caterpillars' (3.4.42–7). This is an element of the play's poetic texture that performance can, and often does, exploit—one noteworthy production featured a pile of rich soil on one side of the stage, handled reverently or disdainfully at different points by different characters; others work to provide visual links between Gaunt and the gardeners, through, for example, using the same bank of flowers to establish the two scenes. Such performative strategies highlight the linkage between poetry and politics since the language of gardens is really a way of talking about the functioning of the state.

Indeed, whenever issues of governance arise, we are likely to encounter the language of earth and growth. Thus when Bolingbroke returns to England he arrests 'Bushy, Bagot and their complices, | The caterpillars of the commonwealth | Which I have sworn to weed and pluck away' (2.3.164–6). When, a little later, Richard also returns, he greets the English earth sentimentally, perhaps by running it through his 'royal hands', and conjuring it to 'Yield stinging nettles to mine enemies' (3.2.11, 18). So too, Carlisle, when he prophesies the civil war to come, declares how 'The blood of English shall manure the ground . . . and this land be called | The field of Golgotha and dead men's skulls' (4.1.138, 144–5). As this last passage indicates, the language of *blood*, also prominent in the play, is closely linked to that of gardens. Blood means personal vitality, it means family heritage, and it means violence. All three meanings are joined in the opening speeches of 1.2, when the Duchess of Gloucester upbraids her brother-in-law, Gaunt, for his weakness in declining to avenge the murder of her husband:

> Hath love in thy old blood no living fire?
> Edward's seven sons, whereof thyself art one,
> Were as seven vials of his sacred blood,
> Or seven fair branches springing from one root.
> Some of those seven are dried by nature's course,
> Some of those branches by the destinies cut . . .
>
> (1.2.10–15)

Her extended comparison of the seven sons of Edward III to living branches and vials of blood establishes both the fragile link between gardens and family and the violence that threatens it; in particular, the vial and branch, which stand for her husband Thomas, are 'cracked' and 'hacked down . . . By envy's hand and murder's bloody axe' (19–21). That foundational act, engineered by Richard before the play begins (something that everyone knows but is afraid to voice), underlies both the action and the language. Whenever blood is mentioned, there is always an appeal to family and always a danger, whether explicit or implicit, to the welfare of both family and commonwealth.

Behind these associations, there is often a Christological element as well—the power of Christ's blood to redeem, however shot through with irony such comparisons always are when they appear. At the end, when Henry is at last settled on the throne, his rival resting on the bier that dominates the final moments, he protests, 'my soul is full of woe | That blood should sprinkle me to make me grow' (5.6.45–6). Exactly as Carlisle had predicted, the blood of Henry's cousin is indeed 'manur[ing] the ground' on which he strides. But we might be inclined to doubt the sincerity of his declaration of woe—does he forget that earlier on he had threatened Richard with watering 'the summer's dust with showers of blood | Rained from the wounds of slaughtered Englishmen', even while he expressed the hope that 'such crimson tempest should [not] bedrench | The fresh green lap of fair King Richard's land' (3.3.42–6)? The garden of England is, and frequently will be, stained with the blood of its most illustrious inhabitants.

Such intricate interweaving of imagistic motifs is typical of the play, which frequently displays a poetic self-consciousness, a kind of linguistic muscle-flexing or youthful delight at its author's own verbal powers, a characteristic of many of Shakespeare's earlier plays. While such verbal elaboration can strike readers as overwrought, and even impede emotional connection, in this play Shakespeare found an effective way both to flaunt his rhetorical skills and to make the language count dramatically: he conceived his protagonist as a man both capable of brilliant poetic elaboration and sharply aware of his propensity to spin a metaphor or exploit a rhetorical device. There are moments when Richard seems almost self-mocking, aware both of the effect that he is creating and of the futility or weakness associated with his verbal dexterity. He is, in other words, an ironist as well as a would-be poet, and this double sense of himself gives him a nimbleness that the other characters cannot match. Nowhere is this more brilliantly on view than in the great speech he makes mourning the death of kings:

> For God's sake let us sit upon the ground
> And tell sad stories of the death of kings,
> How some have been deposed, some slain in war,
> Some haunted by the ghosts they have deposed,
> Some poisoned by their wives, some sleeping killed—
> All murdered. For within the hollow crown
> That rounds the mortal temples of a king
> Keeps death his court, and there the antic sits,

Scoffing his state and grinning at his pomp,
Allowing him a breath, a little scene
To monarchize, be feared and kill with looks,
    . . . and humoured thus
Comes at the last and with a little pin
Bores through his castle wall—and farewell king.

(3.2.155–70)

The word 'monarchize', which Shakespeare seems to have picked up from his fellow writer Thomas Nashe,[1] epitomizes the double attitude. Richard is aware of the role he plays as monarch, and how vulnerable the prerogatives he claims in fact are; he enjoys the display as much as the reality—indeed the two are inextricable. His rhetoric makes this evident: as he very consciously weaves the dazzling metaphor that pits the mock-king, Death, against mortal kings, so he ends with the deliberate puncturing of the very illusions implied throughout the passage and registered by the theatrical metaphor. His witty irony is the pin that bursts the bubble, and 'farewell king'.

Richard's Queen tends also to speak in ornate ways, but she lacks the ironic awareness that marks his speech. Her dominant tonality is grief traversed by foreboding:[2] 'I cannot but be sad: so heavy sad, | As, though on thinking on no thought I think, | Makes me with heavy nothing faint and shrink' (2.2.30–2). Her sorrow is patent but her exact meaning remains obscure: 'For nothing hath begot my something grief, | Or something hath the nothing that I grieve— | 'Tis in reversion that I do possess— | But what it is, that is not yet known' (36–9). The delicate interplay between nothing and something, which may strike us as needlessly complicated for the expression of her anxiety, speaks more of the author's exuberance than the character's pain. It contrasts with Richard's elaboration of a similar motif as he languishes in prison:

---

[1] The earliest *OED* citations of both 'monarchize' and 'monarchizing' are from Nashe in 1592, shortly before *Richard II* was written, each of which carries a suggestion of mockery, though not so pronounced as in Richard's use of the term.

[2] Grief and lament are in fact a major element of both the play's language and its theme; almost all the main characters give way to lament at some point, though the queen is its primary exemplar. See Wells, 'Lamentable'; and Scott McMillin, 'Shakespeare's *Richard II*: Eyes of Sorrow, Eyes of Desire', *SQ* 35 (1984), 40–52.

> Then am I kinged again, and by and by
> Think that I am unkinged by Bolingbroke
> And straight am nothing. But whate'er I be,
> Nor I nor any man that but man is,
> With nothing shall be pleased till he be eased
> With being nothing.   (5.5.36–41)

Although he never entirely abandons his self-aware rhetoric (note the multiple negatives, the play on different meanings of 'nothing', and the internal rhyme of 'pleased' / 'eased'), his language also conveys a sense of tragic personhood.

The Queen, however, is capable of quite different speech when her husband falters. During their meeting on a London street as he is being led to the Tower, she upbraids him for his defeatism without elaboration: 'Hath Bolingbroke | Deposed thine intellect, hath he been in thy heart?' Later her sorrow is equally direct: 'And must we be divided, must we part?' (5.1.27–8, 81). While the play offers a variety of styles, we might hazard the generalization that as the action edges toward tragedy, the language of the principals to some extent moves inward, becoming a little suppler and less self-conscious.

The variety of styles extends even to Bolingbroke, the most consistently public voice in the play, whose matter-of-fact manner earns him the epithet 'silent King' (4.1.290), though he has more lines than anyone except Richard. His discourse arises out of the political positions he occupies, but, as with the others, it stems from his personality as well, which Shakespeare treats mostly in external terms. Near the outset, as appellant in a stately ritual, he speaks the necessary language ('Harry of Hereford, Lancaster and Derby | Am I, who ready here do stand in arms'—1.3.35–6); when later called upon to settle the quarrels of his feudal lords, he does so straightforwardly and with authority, in marked contrast to Richard: 'Lords appellants, | Your differences shall all rest under gage | Till we assign you to your days of trial' (4.1.105–7). But he too shifts to a far richer style when occasion demands, as in his invocation of the sun-like appearance of King Richard on the walls at Flint:

> See, see, King Richard doth himself appear,
> As doth the blushing discontented sun
> From out the fiery portal of the east

When he perceives the envious clouds are bent
To dim his glory and to stain the track
Of his bright passage to the occident.

(3.3.61–6)

It is harder to see this as emanating from character than from the complex pressures of the immediate situation. Bolingbroke is on a trajectory of what looks like usurpation; in order to offset that impression, his praise of Richard highlights the key metaphor of kingship, that of the sun, and his rhetoric evokes the grandeur of monarchy, implying that Richard is, in Lear's words, 'every inch a king' (4.5.107). Bolingbroke himself appears as nothing more than an 'envious cloud', a brief and insignificant impediment, though at the same time the suggestion of the imminent setting of this fiery sun in the 'occident' hints at the historical arc which Henry is tracking.

Such an elevated, elaborate style extends even to moments of intimacy, as in Henry's leave-taking from Gaunt. It is a private affair that contrasts with the ceremonious ritual that preceded it; urged by his grieving father to imagine himself out of the sorrow of banishment, he asks, 'O, who can hold a fire in his hand | By thinking on the frosty Caucasus? | Or cloy the hungry edge of appetite | By bare imagination of a feast?' (1.3.294–7). Reverting to the strain of imagery that underlies so much of the play's feeling, he parts from Gaunt on a brave note: 'Then England's ground, farewell, sweet soil, adieu, | My mother and my nurse that bears me yet' (1.3.306–7).

Hence the vaunted stylistic unity of the play, much praised by Walter Pater, the nineteenth-century essayist and aesthete, and often reiterated by critics since his time, turns out to be a first impression, one that needs to be qualified—underneath the apparent unity there is constant shifting. Even the most obvious feature of the play's poetry, the prevalence of rhyme, does not mean sameness.[1] It can be used to quite varied effect, as the following examples indicate:

---

[1] Rhyme appears in close to a quarter of the total number of lines, a higher percentage than in all but three Shakespeare plays, all early comedies (Forker, p. 57).

Grandiose formality:

> Cousin of Hereford, as thy cause is right
> So be thy fortune in this royal fight.
>
> (1.3.55–6)

> Most mighty liege, and my companion peers,
> Take from my mouth the wish of happy years.
>
> (1.3.93–4)

Witty sarcasm:

> Right, you say true. As Hereford's love, so his.
> As theirs, so mine, and all be as it is.
>
> (2.1.145–6)

Bewildered pathos:

> I should to Pleshey too,
> But time will not permit. All is uneven
> And everything is left at six and seven.
>
> (2.2.120–2)

Comic importunity:

> And if I were thy nurse, thy tongue to teach,
> 'Pardon' should be the first word of thy speech. . . .
> Speak 'pardon' as 'tis current in our land,
> The chopping French we do not understand.
>
> (5.3.112–13, 122–3)

Tender intimacy (indicated as well by the sharing of the rhyme):

> QUEEN
>   And must we be divided, must we part?
> RICHARD
>   Ay hand from hand, my love, and heart from heart.
>
> (5.1.81–2)

Intrusive bluntness (this couplet, also shared, though now the pairing is ironic, follows immediately from the one just quoted):

> QUEEN
>   Banish us both and send the King with me.
> NORTHUMBERLAND
>   That were some love but little policy.
>
> (5.1.83–4)

Callous abuse of power:

> Think what you will, we seize into our hands
> His plate, his goods, his money and his lands.
> (2.1.209–10)

Heartfelt (or, in the second couplet, questionably sincere) lament:

> Come ladies, go
> To meet at London London's king in woe.
> (3.4.96–7)

> Lords, I protest my soul is full of woe
> That blood should sprinkle me to make me grow.
> (5.6.45–6)

More examples could be adduced, but even this limited array makes clear just how various the language of the play can be, even while under the constraint of strict rhyme. Language registers feeling, speaks precisely to political positioning and reveals character. It is the fundamental constituent of this and every Shakespeare play.

Character

In considering the language we have inevitably touched on the matter of character as well, since the two are so intimately related. Like language, character is frequently defined in relation to public positioning. Even those characters whose lives seem most secluded and private, such as the Duchess of Gloucester and the Queen, cannot escape public definition. The Duchess, we might say, stands for mourning and a pent-up, unfulfilled desire for revenge, but both her sorrow and her anger derive from the fundamental fact of her husband's murder. It is an act both familial and political, effected, as everyone knows, by the King (however indirectly) and it colours everything that happens in the play. The Duchess appears only once (1.2), but her presence, like a qualm of conscience, hovers over the action. And when she weeps, it is not only for her own personal misfortune, but for the very stones of the estate that she inhabits, emblem of rank and political position: 'Alack, and what shall good old York there see [at Pleshey] | But empty lodgings and unfurnished walls, | Unpeopled offices, untrodden stones' (1.2.67–9). The Queen, while a larger presence than the Duchess, is again mostly private, unwillingly entangled in the larger political world over which she has no control. Like Cassandra in Greek mythology, part clairvoyant, part victim, she has dark forebodings, but she is enriched also by a deep and abiding love of her husband, the source of whatever joy she has felt and of the pain that dogs her throughout. These two illustrate a general feature of the history plays, where women tend to play symbolically laden roles—figures of prophecy, fury, or lament. So their characters are subject to constraints that are generic as well as political, their intensity a product of their abiding connection with family. It is primarily the men who occupy the public sphere and whose external lives more directly configure their internal dimensions.

King Richard   Richard tends to evoke strong and strongly contrasting reactions. Prone to self-pity, alternately cruel, narcissistic and ineffectual, he also has a wicked sense of humour, a witty and ironic self-awareness and a flair for the dramatic. His command of poetic speech outstrips that of everyone in the play, and he is loved, deeply and sincerely, by his Queen as by the anonymous groom of the stable who appears in 5.5, just moments before his death. Even the hesitant and vacillating York, after changing sides and declaring his allegiance to the new monarch, is overcome by the devotion that the former King can, it seems, almost effortlessly command (5.2.30–6). Those who resist his charisma, such as Northumberland, and even Bolingbroke himself, can appear harsh and stony beside their counterparts on the other side, such as the brave and upright Bishop of Carlisle or even the soft and rather weak Aumerle. Despite this, Richard can be breathtakingly nasty and insufferably whiney, so that, at least in the early stages of the play, our attitude toward him is bound to be negative, or at least ambivalent.

For all his flaunting of royal prerogative, his weakness is apparent from the outset. Unable to reconcile the quarrelling Mowbray and Bolingbroke who, despite the King's repeated commands ('throw down we bid', 'Give me his gage', 'Cousin, throw up your gage'—1.1.164, 174, 186), refuse to give in, he tries to disguise his apparent failure:

We were not born to sue, but to command,
Which, since we cannot do to make you friends,
Be ready, as your lives shall answer it,
At Coventry.   (196–9)

8. Gilt bronze effigy of Richard II in Westminster Abbey, originally commissioned in 1395 for the future tomb he would share with Anne of Bohemia; the head and hood (shown here) were cast separately from the body.

But his 'command' means little. He is unable to control the warring factions that Bolingbroke handles so adroitly in the gage throwing scene in 4.1, and his incapacity is aggravated by the awareness, shared by the whole court, that there is a cover-up going on, that Richard is primarily responsible for the murder of his uncle, the Duke of Gloucester.

The unflattering portrayal persists through the next few scenes, where his willingness to 'farm [the] royal realm' (1.4.45), his reliance on unworthy counsellors, and his callous response to the news of Gaunt's illness ('Come, gentlemen, let's all go visit him. | Pray God we may make haste and come too late'— 1.4.63–4), all tend to siphon away our sympathy. The feeling is intensified in the following scene when Richard displays nothing but contempt for the sympathetic Gaunt's justified complaints, and then appropriates his land and assets while dismissing the news of his death with barely a nod ('So much for that'— 2.1.155). His behaviour seems like a desperate attempt to assert his public identity and power, but it has disastrous consequences: the developing conspiracy in favour of Bolingbroke, which bubbles up immediately (2.1.224–300). Dramatically the conspiracy seems to emerge directly from Richard's behaviour, but the political picture is more complicated, since Bolingbroke's return seems to have been initiated well before the king's illegal confiscation of his goods and title.

Richard now leaves the stage not to reappear till 3.2. In his absence, Bolingbroke gains ground so that, once he does return, Richard is the underdog. From here to the end his character grows, gaining depth and self-awareness, and his skill with language increases. This is not to say that his self-pity entirely disappears, or that he develops the kind of rich interiority displayed by a Hamlet. But Shakespeare, without losing sight of the character's extravagance and occasional mawkishness, seems nevertheless intent on transforming a mean-spirited and immature king into something of a tragic figure, thus driving a wedge between royal identity and personal being. Richard has been a prisoner of his kingly role, so it seems fitting that, as the crown slips from him, he develops more fully as a person. His theatricality, which had seemed hollow earlier, remains an essential part of him but takes on a different tenor; while aware of his effects, he is still able to evoke genuine suffering and a commonalty with others:

> Cover your heads and mock not flesh and blood
> With solemn reverence. Throw away respect,
> Tradition, form and ceremonious duty.
> For you have but mistook me all this while,
> I live with bread like you, feel want,
> Taste grief, need friends. Subjected thus,
> How can you say to me I am a king?
>
> (3.2.171–7)

The trappings of kingship, so crucial to his self-definition earlier, here begin to fall away and he becomes, in his ruefully ironic and witty phrase, 'subjected': turned into a subject (and thus no longer a monarch) by being subjected to the sufferings of ordinary mortals.

Role and identity are difficult to disentangle from each other in his self-representations. This is abundantly clear in the deposition scene, where his mastery of both language and dramatic effect give him a theatrical advantage over Bolingbroke, even though the latter holds all the political cards. Richard controls the effects but at the same time he cannot hide his weakness—the fact that he is now 'subjected' to his rival's power. York asks him to resign and his response reveals both his alertness and his vulnerability:

> Give me the crown.
> Here, cousin, seize the crown. Here, cousin,
> On this side my hand, and on that side thine.
> Now is this golden crown like a deep well
> That owes two buckets filling one another,
> The emptier ever dancing in the air,
> The other down, unseen and full of water.
> That bucket down and full of tears am I,
> Drinking my griefs whilst you mount up on high.
>
> (4.1.181–9)

The first three lines show Richard apparently in command. Aware of his audience, he holds out the crown as a challenge to his rival, who is forced to seize it and hence play his part in the stage image that Richard is creating. Even the repeated 'cousin' has a needling effect. But the balance is soon lost in the elaborate conceit of the buckets dancing in the well, which can all too easily signal self-pity. Similarly, his play with the mirror a bit later captures both the 'brittle glory' of kingship and his personal helplessness.

The tender leave-taking scene with the Queen (5.1) and then York's description of Bolingbroke's triumph and Richard's disgrace (5.2) prepare us for the King's final moments—the scene at Pomfret Castle where death awaits. The tragic empathy that Shakespeare has been building toward here gets its fullest expression, though the verbal pyrotechnics can still be obtrusive—as with the over-elaborate clock metaphor (5.5.50–60). Even so, his long soliloquy (66 lines) brings us into contact with his innermost thoughts, the first time this has happened in the play. He is alone 'studying how I may compare | This prison where I live unto the world', a telling idea that Shakespeare would reprise in a reversed way with Hamlet ('Denmark's a prison' and 'the world . . . A goodly one'—2.2.246–8). His meditation leads him to the humbling conviction that, whether royal or 'unkinged', he, like everyone else, is essentially nothing:

> But whate'er I be,
> Nor I nor any man that but man is,
> With nothing shall be pleased till he be eased
> With being nothing.   (38–41)

This solidarity with humankind is confirmed a few minutes later with the arrival of the loyal groom and Richard's eagerness to establish a kind of equality with him ('Thanks noble peer, | The cheapest of us is ten groats too dear'—67–8). And it leads to a surprising surge of personal strength in the confrontation with Exton and the murderers when Richard, though unarmed, is able to kill two of them before falling beneath Exton's sword. Rather like Lear killing 'the slave that was a-hanging' Cordelia (*History of King Lear* 24.270), Richard redeems some of his previous folly with tragic violence.

Overall then, we might say that Richard's relation to his public role is double. Losing it gives him depth, which suggests a disjunction between public (royal) and private self, but at the same time the loss of the throne is itself a public event which propels him into a new relationship with himself and his intimates, especially his Queen. Perhaps that is why we sometimes get the impression that he seeks the very deposition that he bemoans—it means freedom from the constraints of playing the king, even though the element of playing never disappears.

Compared to the great tragic figures of Shakespeare's maturity (such as Hamlet or Macbeth), Richard remains somewhat externalized, but we can recognize as well something of the complex and elusive selfhood that marks those more famous characters, and it is this that ultimately gives him more staying power than his politic rival.

Henry Bolingbroke   Bolingbroke is clearly designed as a contrast to Richard, but he is not composed in only one key. Capable, decisive, and self-contained, where Richard is weak, vacillating, and histrionic, Bolingbroke may appear unemotional and even rigid, but he is capable of strong feeling, as when he departs from Gaunt and England (1.3), though even there his realistic rationalism prompts him to counter his father's attempts at comfort. For him imagination cannot allay the real pain of exile. He tends always to keep his intentions under wraps, so that we are never quite sure whether his return to England is motivated initially by a wish to dethrone Richard or whether his desire for the crown develops as he becomes aware of both his own advantage and his rival's increasing powerlessness. Indeed, his ambition is an example of the general point made earlier that character is to some degree a matter of public positioning: i.e. it is a result at least partly of the wrong done to him by Richard's seizure of his patrimony, which then leads to his move toward gaining restitution. Ambition is, in that sense, 'thrust upon him', as 'greatness' is on Malvolio in *Twelfth Night*, but for Bolingbroke it comes with a certain ruthlessness, necessary if he is to carry out what at first seems like a perfectly legitimate aim—to restore 'his own' (2.3.148). At the same time, the hints that he plans his treasonous return to England before Richard confiscates his father's estate suggest a deep-seated personal drive toward a goal that he has been preparing for since the initial quarrel with Mowbray.

Upon his return to his native soil (2.3), he holds his emotions carefully in check, making vague but telling promises:

> I wot your love pursues
> A banished traitor. All my treasury
> Is yet but unfelt thanks, which, more enriched,
> Shall be your love and labour's recompense.
>
> (59–62)

9. Henry Bolingbroke, as King Henry IV; the picture dates from the late sixteenth century or early seventeenth, artist unknown.

He cleverly acknowledges his 'treasonous' behaviour and the dangerous situation which his friends have embraced, but then quickly offsets this with the promise of recompense from enriched coffers, anticipating his 'infant fortune com[ing] to years' (66), and using the word 'exchequer', usually reserved for the royal treasury. He greets York in a similarly oblique way, deferential but steel-fisted underneath (105–6, 161–6). That he controls his emotions doesn't, however, mean he lacks them. Indeed, his great speech indicting Bushy and Green is thick with strong feeling (3.1.1–30). He accuses his enemies of 'divorcing' the Queen from her husband[1] and, more important, injuring him, unleashing righteous indignation on his own part and sympathy on the Queen's. But we recognize as well the astutely politic motivation behind the condemnation, as Bolingbroke clears the path toward the throne, shooting down Richard's confederates as proxies of the King.

Indeed, whenever he expresses emotion, we are led to suspect a political motive, even as we recognize the justice of the feeling. When he casts himself on his knees before Richard in 3.3, when he mourns the death of his old enemy Mowbray (4.1.102–7), and especially when he expresses remorse for the murder of Richard, an act that he at the same time admits he instigated ('They love not poison that do poison need'), it is hard to avoid the impression that he is deliberately enacting a scenario designed to advantage himself politically:

> Lords, I protest my soul is full of woe
> That blood should sprinkle me to make me grow.
> Come mourn with me for what I do lament
> And put on sullen black incontinent.
> I'll make a voyage to the Holy Land
> To wash this blood off from my guilty hand.
> March sadly after. Grace my mournings here
> In weeping after this untimely bier.
>
> (5.6.45–52)

---

[1] There is no evidence in the play beyond Bolingbroke's implication here to suggest that Richard's favourites have intruded on the Queen's relationship to Richard, but perhaps under the influence of Marlowe's *Edward II* and its overt representation of the King's homosexual desire, some modern productions have characterized Richard in such terms. By contrast, others have presented Bolingbroke, induced by Northumberland, either reading or speaking these accusations with distaste, knowing they are false. In general, Shakespeare portrays the relationship between the King and Queen as close and loving, and portrays Bushy and Green as sympathetic confidants of the Queen (2.2).

The conventional rhyming couplets that thus end the play sound a trifle flat, though Henry's guilt seems genuine, and indeed haunts him at moments in the two plays that follow and that bear his name. We perhaps get a glimpse here of an inner torment and uncertainty that shadow his brilliantly competent and exactly poised exterior.

Becoming king carries heavy burdens, as both kings in this play recognize (and as Henry's son Henry V also learns when his time comes). There is hence a parallelism between these two very different men. And it is one that performance can convey in a variety of ways. One memorable production, directed many years ago by John Barton, found an effective way to signal their doubleness. Barton had two different actors trade the two roles (see pp. 90–3). The idea was to suggest that kingship is itself a performance, one that constricts the human being who takes it on. The evening began with 'Shakespeare' coming on with a book, the actors following. 'Shakespeare' then 'selected' one of the two leads to play the King that night, the other Bolingbroke. Even though for practical reasons the selection had already been made and announced, Barton wanted to make the point that each in his different way is defined by his role and at the same time stands outside it. It was a fitting way to register the complex relations between public and private selves that the play explores.

Gaunt and York, Northumberland and Mowbray, Aumerle and Friends   Most of the other characters in the play are powerful barons, charged with self-interest and bristling with aristocratic pride. At the top of the pyramid are the brothers, Gaunt and York, the last remaining sons of the original seven born to Edward III, who are parallel but very different figures. Gaunt is fierce and prophetic in his condemnation of the present regime, though prepared, as he says to the angry Duchess of Gloucester in 1.2, to wait for God to take the revenge that he himself is unwilling to initiate. York is more conciliatory but also more vacillating and uncertain. He speaks up strongly against Richard's confiscation of Gaunt's lands after the latter's death (2.1.186–208), but despite this, immediately accepts the governorship of England which is conferred on him for the period that Richard is away in Ireland. When Bolingbroke returns, York, though governor, is at a loss how to handle the situation, finally capitulating to what he recognizes as superior strength. In the midst of the escalating bad news (capped by a report of the Duchess of Gloucester's death) comes a touching and characteristic moment: moving to comfort the distraught Queen, York makes a tiny, fully understandable mistake: 'Come, sister—cousin I would say—pray pardon me' (2.2.103–5). Just for a second he confuses the Queen, his 'cousin' by marriage, and his 'sister', the Duchess; this brief touch of intimacy captures both the stress of his bewilderment and the warmth of the love he bears the two women. As the play develops, his uncertainty does too; he participates in the deposition, asking Richard to resign, but then mourns the treatment afforded the one-time King (5.2.28–36). Within minutes after that, however, he is fiercely defending the new King against the conspiracy involving Aumerle, and rushes off to expose and condemn his son and heir. Throughout these struggles, he displays the pathos of a kind but rather ineffectual man caught in a political conflict that he can neither control nor accept.

Northumberland is, as noted above, the play's tough guy, backing Bolingbroke because he sees an opportunity for himself and his family (his son, Harry Percy, will become the fiery Hotspur of *1 Henry IV*), and doing his boss's dirty work in an uncompromising, but also spirited way. He is quick to stir up rebellion at the earliest opportunity (2.1.224–300), angry at the offences perpetrated ''Gainst us, our lives, our children and our heirs' (245), and richly persuasive in his incitement to action when news arrives of Bolingbroke's landing:

> If then we shall shake off our slavish yoke,
> Imp out our drooping country's broken wing,
> Redeem from broking pawn the blemished crown,
> Wipe off the dust that hides our sceptre's gilt
> And make high majesty look like itself,
> Away with me in post to Ravenspur.
>
> (291–6)

His boldness pays off and he quickly becomes Henry's right-hand man, the intermediary in the negotiations in 3.3, and the one who insists on Richard reading a list of crimes and misdemeanours to justify the deposition (relenting only when Bolingbroke intervenes).

Mowbray appears only in the first act, a former ally of the King who now feels himself double-crossed. He is forced to disguise both his feelings and his role in the death of Gloucester, and so he turns aggressively against his enemy Bolingbroke. Banished for life, he comes close to exposing Richard: 'A dearer merit, not so deep a maim | As to be cast forth in the common air, | Have I deservèd at your highness' hands' (1.3.156–8). But then his thoughts take a surprising turn: 'The language I have learned these forty years, | My native English, now I must forgo . . .', a theme he develops at length. Even as it wraps Mowbray in a sympathetic glow, this powerful expression of national feeling, as embedded in the English language, goes beyond the specifics of the speaker's character. Up to this point, Mowbray is not especially winning, but suddenly he begins talking about England and he becomes a spokesman for a crucial theme. This exemplifies a common Shakespearian strategy, which is to etch character in terms not only of individual personality or public voice, though both are important, but of dramatic exigency. The play, as it were, needs a timely and vibrant expression of the defining significance of English as the bedrock of the nation, and Mowbray is there to deliver it.

As for Aumerle and the rest of Richard's friends, they have often been played as self-seeking and mean-spirited cronies, Teddy boys on the loose and concerned only for their own pleasures. Often too their relationship to Richard has been given a homosexual seasoning, sometimes in rather crude or caricatured ways. And while this approach has roots in the text, most hints of bad and mercenary behaviour on their part come from their enemies, especially Bolingbroke and Northumberland. In 2.2, for example, Green and especially Bushy show themselves devoted to the Queen and compassionate about her sufferings, and there is a strong element of foreboding pathos at the end of that scene when they part from their friend Bagot, with the intuition that they 'ne'er shall meet again' (142). Aumerle, who seems closest to the King, is both allied to, and apart from, the other 'caterpillars'. As a member of the royal family, he cannot be reproached for being an upstart, and he seems deeply concerned for his cousin's welfare, especially in the scene of Richard's return (3.2). We glimpse the intimacy between them in the lovely moment when Richard, aware that he may be conceding too much to Northumberland, turns to Aumerle: 'We do debase ourselves, cousin, do we not, | To look so poorly and to speak so fair?' (3.3.126–7). So, when Aumerle joins the conspiracy against the new King, it is no surprise to see him stake his life on the loyalty that has characterized him throughout, though, when discovered, he is quick and eager to plead for the life he had risked. Like so many of the characters, then, Aumerle is complexly drawn, public affairs and private intensities both playing their part in the representation. The minor characters have often been seen as rather flat, but Aumerle, like the nobles and churchmen, and even the few commoners, who people Richard's world, emerges into dynamic personhood when played by an actor on the stage.

The Play on the Stage

Early Fortunes and Misfortunes   *Richard II* has not always been as popular on stage as it is at present. In fact, for a long period, it was rarely seen, and then only in strange guises. During Shakespeare's lifetime, however, and for a short period thereafter, it enjoyed a vibrant stage presence. There are several indications of this. One is the number of editions the play went through before the appearance of the Folio in 1623 (five different quartos)—frequent publication being a gauge of the currency of a play both on stage and off. Another is the testimony of each of these quartos that the play had lately been 'publicly acted' by Shakespeare's company. A third is the interest clearly taken in the play by the Earl of Essex and his followers, as well as by the Queen (see pp. 2–9). A fourth is the (ambiguous) record of a possible private performance at an aristocratic household in 1595: on 9 December of that year, Sir Edward Hoby, whose wife was the daughter of Baron Hunsdon, the chief patron of Shakespeare's company, wrote to Sir Robert Cecil, one of the Queen's most important advisors, inviting him to supper. As an added incentive he promised that 'K. Richard [would] present himself to your view'.[1] Though some scholars

---

[1] Chambers, ii. 320–1.

have thought Hoby may have been referring to an unknown portrait, the phrase 'present himself to your view' is much better
suited to a live theatrical performance than to an inanimate painting. But, given that, was the play Shakespeare's? We have no way
of knowing, but the connection to Hunsdon makes it not
unreasonable to suppose that it was. Still another indication of
the play's popularity in its own time is the likelihood that in 1607
it was acted on board a ship bound to the East Indies though
anchored for some time off the coast of Sierra Leone; William
Keeling, captain of the *Dragon*, had his 'companions' act out
'King Richard the Second' for Captain William Hawkins who was
visiting from a sister ship. That this was probably Shakespeare's
play is suggested by Keeling's note that *Hamlet* was also presented
on board around the same time; nor, as far as we know, did any
other play named *Richard II* then exist in print, and the amateur
actors were 'not likely to have used anything but a printed play'.[1]
Throughout this period there continued to be numerous allusions
to the text of the play on the part of other writers, editors of
anthologies, and compilers of commonplace books.[2] And in 1631
the play was still sufficiently popular to be revived for a recorded
benefit performance by the King's company at the Globe.[3]

After this, until the beginning of the twentieth century, the
play appears only sporadically, and when it does surface, it is

[1] See Chambers, i. 356, and ii. 334–5. It should be noted that the authenticity of
the Keeling document has been periodically questioned.

[2] In, for example, *Englands Parnassus*, a compilation of over 2,400 passages
from various English poets compiled by Robert Allott and published in 1600, there
are seven passages from *Richard II* (these are reprinted in Gurr, pp. 231–4). For
other instances, see *The Shakspere Allusion-Book*, ed. Clement Mansfield Ingleby
et al. (rev. edn., London, 1909); and more recently, Adam G. Hooks, *Vendible
Shakespeare* (unpublished PhD dissertation, Columbia University, 2009) and
Stanley Wells, 'A New Early Reader of Shakespeare' in *Shakespeare's Book: Essays
in Reading, Writing and Reception*, ed. Richard Meek, Jane Rickard, and Richard
Wilson (Manchester, 2008), pp. 233–40.

[3] The beneficiary was Sir Henry Herbert, Master of the Revels, who records the
amount received 'for the benefit of their summer day, upon the second day of
Richard the Second' (Black, p. 568). The phrase 'second day' had come to refer
by this time to some kind of benefit performance (Tiffany Stern, *Rehearsal from
Shakespeare to Sheridan* (Oxford and New York, 2000), pp. 116–19). So, whether
this means he had also received a 'winter' benefit, either for the same or a different
play, or whether his benefit took place at the second consecutive performance of
the play, is unclear. Whatever the case, the take was fairly substantial, so that the
play seems still to have been a reasonable 'draw'.

frequently at times of political controversy or crisis. Until the nineteenth century, the text seems on occasion to have retained some of the edginess it had in the late 1590s, able still to ignite the odd political brushfire. In 1680, the now notorious Nahum Tate (who the following year rewrote *King Lear* with a happy ending) staged his adaptation of the play, but it was quickly banned; he tried again a short while later, this time shifting the scene to Sicily and renaming it *The Sicilian Usurper*. This too was banned despite the fact that, as the new title suggests, Tate's sympathies were with the royal victim whose throne is usurped. Any dramatization of deposition or regicide was bound to be risky in the years following the Restoration of the monarchy in 1660, only a generation after the execution of Charles I in 1649. Though the play, along with many others by Shakespeare, had been licensed for performance in 1669, no one before Tate had taken up the challenge of making it palatable to nervous post-Restoration censors. Moreover, in 1680, matters of royal succession were very much in the air. Tate no doubt saw a marketing opportunity in the fact that the nation was in the throes of what came to be known as the Exclusion Crisis—the attempt by powerful factions to exclude Charles II's Catholic brother from the succession. But Tate's foray into political controversy was a trifle hot to handle. He complained in a Preface to the published version (1681) that his innocent attempt to portray a 'dissolute' and 'ignorant' age was unjustifiably suppressed as a 'libel' upon the present.[1] His cautious approach, which nevertheless did him no good, is evident in the pains he took to make Richard more finely heroic and Bolingbroke more manipulative and unsavoury, thus disrupting the balance between the original play's antagonists. Richard, for example, is reconciled with Gaunt on his deathbed, nor does he confiscate Gaunt's lands, but merely borrows them; and Bolingbroke is seen deviously 'cultivat[ing] the opinions of the rabble' (Shewring, p. 33). Tate's attempt to give the play a loyalist perspective is an indication of his awareness, despite his protestations, that he was indeed venturing into dangerous waters.

---

[1] The text of this and the other adaptations discussed in this section are available online at the Chadwyck-Healey subscription site, 'Editions and Adaptations of Shakespeare'. Quotations are from the versions reproduced there.

In 1719, Lewis Theobald, who later proved himself a careful Shakespearian editor, produced an adaptation that, in its all-out attempt to avoid political relevance, reveals its author's anxiety about over-stepping the bounds. In his prologue, he disarms possible criticism by declaring: 'Fearful of Censure, and offended Law, | The Muse presumes no Parallels to draw'. Making good on this promise, Theobald cut the first two acts altogether, thereby eliminating most of Richard's bad behaviour. He offers pathos instead of political 'Rage': 'From Richard's Ruin, only, she intends | To wound your Souls, and make you Richard's Friends'. In his preface, he excuses the many changes he made by declaring that what Shakespeare's play needed was a way to incorporate its 'many scatter'd Beauties' into a 'regular Fable'—i.e. one ordered according to eighteenth-century principles of dramatic unity. Thus he begins the action after Richard's return from Ireland and confines it to the Tower, where Richard and Bolingbroke first meet. He also 'sentimentalizes the drama unblushingly'[1] by keeping York 'steady to the Interest of the King' (Preface) instead of vacillating, and then having him die of a broken heart after his sovereign's death; in even more outrageous compliance with audience tastes, he introduces a love interest between Aumerle and Lady Piercy, the daughter of Richard's enemy Northumberland, which turns to sentimental tragedy when Aumerle is executed for the cause and his sweetheart promptly commits suicide. Ross reports the 'horror':

> The beauteous *Piercy*, with a desp'rate Hand,
> Hearing *Aumerle* was dead, a secret Dagger
> Drew from her Side, and plung'd it in her Breast.

To which the repentant Northumberland replies: 'My Daughter! Fate pursues my Guilt too fast.'[2]

This version proved rather popular and was revived seven times that season and three more times over the next two; nor did it incur censorship, despite what was a politically turbulent time.[3] Theobald's sapping of the play's political energies apparently

---

[1] Forker, p. 53.

[2] Quotations taken from the Chadwyck-Healey online version, accessed February 2010, at <http://collections.chadwyck.com/eas/htxview?template=basic.htx&content=frameset.htx>

[3] McManaway, pp. 163, 167.

worked. By contrast, a production at Covent Garden in 1738, mounted by John Rich (at the instigation of the 'Shakespeare Ladies Club'[1]) and marked by a return to Shakespeare's text, took a different tack, making its political dimensions clear enough to stir controversy. The political context was twofold; on the one hand, Robert Walpole, the prime minister, had brought in a Playhouse Bill that the opposition press mocked, by, among other things, instancing passages from old plays that would be forbidden on stage if the law were to proceed—these included a number of substantial passages from *Richard II*. Walpole was also held up to scorn for his appeasement policy toward Spain; one satirical print portrayed him 'standing by while a Spaniard removed the claws from the British lion' (*DNB*). Thus, when passages that audiences could easily link to these situations were spoken at Covent Garden, the result was that the audience 'applied almost every line that was spoken to the occurrences of the time'. The short conspiratorial dialogue between Northumberland, Ross, and Willoughby that comes immediately after Richard's confiscation of Gaunt's lands was particularly provocative. Lines such as 'The king is not himself but basely led | By flatterers' (2.1.241–2) were met by 'loud and boisterous' disruptions, 'clapping of hands and clattering of sticks', while 'The earl of Wiltshire hath the state [*sic*] in farm' (256) provoked 'the loudest shouts and huzzas I ever heard'.[2]

Even so, the performance was not halted, the tenor of the times being somewhat more liberal than in the 1680s. John Rich, the producer, no doubt knew what he was doing. Ten years earlier he had had a huge success with Gay's *The Beggar's Opera*, whose audiences 'found it easy to draw parallels between both the highwayman Macheath and the thief-taker Peachum on the one hand and Walpole on the other' (*DNB*). So, in choosing *Richard II*, Rich and the Covent Garden management were 'giving the public opportunity to echo' the attacks in the opposition press

---

[1] See Emmett L. Avery, 'The Shakespeare Ladies Club', *SQ*, 7 (1956), 153–8, and Fiona Ritchie, 'The Influence of the Female Audience on the Shakespeare Revival of 1736–38: The Case of the Shakespeare Ladies Club', in Sabor, pp. 57–69.

[2] Thomas Davies, quoted in McManaway, p. 171. Davies's report is taken from his *Dramatic Miscellanies*, published in 1784. McManaway provides a thorough account and analysis of this production, detailing its contexts and salient features. His descriptions are based on a prompt book in the Folger Library consisting of leaves taken from the Second Folio (1632) but with many handwritten changes and additions drawn from Pope and two drawings illustrating 1.3 and 4.1.

(McManaway, p. 171). As for the production itself, it followed Shakespeare's text quite closely, using Pope's edition in tandem with F2 and cutting only three short scenes (1.4, 2.4, and 5.4) plus about 285 more lines, most of which seem to have been regarded as extraneous embellishment.[1] The prompt book, which was prepared by John Roberts, includes two sketches that illustrate the stage set-up for the 'Combat' and 'Parliament' scenes (1.3 and 4.1).[2] What is remarkable about these is how traditional the stage picture was: in both, the throne occupies the centre of the stage at the back with noblemen and high churchmen symmetrically arranged in hierarchical order on either side and flanking diagonally toward the front. For the Parliament scene, which includes 'civilians' as well, a long official table is in the centre with the Chancellor at the top end; the throne behind him is empty while, of course, at the lists, it is occupied by Richard, surrounded by guards. As McManaway shows, this layout closely imitates an engraving of Queen Elizabeth presiding over Parliament published 130 years earlier. So if the production had a progressive political edge, its dramaturgical dimensions were highly conservative.

After this, the play once more faded into the background, until it was revived by the vividly romantic actor Edmund Kean in 1815, who eschewed any political application. He brought a dynamism to the role that Hazlitt thought unsuitable to a character who should be marked by 'feeling' combined with 'weakness' rather than with 'energy'. But Kean's 'passion' was contagious and audiences responded enthusiastically, despite (or perhaps because of) the depredations made to the final act of the play by its adapter, Richard Wroughton. Seeking a more emotionally saturated ending, Wroughton enhanced the role of the Queen whose pleas to Bolingbroke to visit Richard in prison are so successful that the new King repents and determines to restore his predecessor to the throne. But 'Exton and history intervene',[3] and

---

[1] As described by McManaway (pp. 161–2, 171–2) the prompt book consists of leaves of the Second Folio (1632) with manuscript deletions, emendations, and additions deriving from Pope's edition (including some but not all of the passages Pope had inserted from the quartos).

[2] McManaway reproduces these in his article (between pp. 174 and 175) as does Shewring (pp. 42–3).

[3] A. C. Sprague, *Shakespeare's Histories: Plays for the Stage* (London, 1964), p. 30.

the Queen arrives to find her husband already dead; racked by grief she holds out just long enough to accuse Bolingbroke ('You might have sav'd him—now he is lost for ever') and speak Lear's dying words over the dead Cordelia before herself succumbing to the dark angel.[1] The new reluctant King is left to mop up and promise, with suitable moral tags, a pilgrimage to the holy land and a reign attentive to his 'subjects' hearts'.

Victorian Extravagance   It was Kean's son Charles, however, who at mid-century really gave the play traction. His productions brought to its apogee the ruling pictorial style, infusing it with a taste for detailed historical, even archaeological, accuracy. For *Richard II* (1857), Kean created replicas of British sites such as Gaunt's room at Ely House (complete with frescoes and paintings based on illuminated manuscripts), the Privy Council Chamber at Westminster, Westminster Hall (for the deposition), St George's Chapel at Windsor (for the final scene), and the Gloucestershire countryside. Pageantry ruled. The combat scene featured lifelike, though inanimate, horses, and Kean invented a triumphal entry for Bolingbroke into London (based loosely on York's description in 5.2 but placed before the garden and deposition scenes), complete with over five hundred extras, including banner-wielding representatives of all the major guilds, a 'dance of itinerant fools', a vast number of well-wishers, and the new King on horseback. As the latter passed by, Richard appeared and was 'received in silence'; a pantomime ensued in which a boy points a finger at the shamed monarch, the crowd hurls insults, and a single old soldier, 'accompanied by his grandson', tries to 'pay homage . . . but is prevented by the mob and treated with contempt'.[2] Spectators were mightily impressed, but such pictorial emphasis tended to diminish the affective power of the actors, who were dwarfed by the sets; it slowed down the action (often requiring ten- or fifteen-minute breaks between scenes as stagehands shifted the scenery); and it typically led to rearrangement and

---

[1] The raging old King's words did however suffer some decorous adaptation: for example, 'pray you undo my lace' replaced 'pray you undo this button'!

[2] Shewring reproduces the entire text of this interpolated scene (pp. 193–4), and provides a full account of the painstaking historical detail of the carefully staged scenes and pageants (pp. 48–58).

deep cutting of Shakespeare's texts. In the case of Kean's *Richard II*, around forty per cent of the text was eliminated. Some whole scenes disappeared: 1.4, 2.4, 3.1, 5.2 (except for, unaccountably, York's description of Bolingbroke's triumphal entry to London which had already been represented in the pageant), and 5.3. The deposition remained but everything else in 4.1 (the gage scene, Carlisle's protests and his conspiracy) was jettisoned. Carlisle was left with only a few inconsequential lines and most of Aumerle's part was also omitted. Even more surprisingly, a large swath of Richard's prison soliloquy and more than half of Gaunt's hymn to England disappeared. There were as well dozens of internal cuts, many of which show Kean's intelligent, even judicious, attention to the text, but at the same time greatly reduce the poetic elaboration that gives the play its distinct flavour. Inevitably, subtlety of character portrayal was threatened, though Kean's wife, Ellen Tree, won high praise for her portrayal of the distraught queen, especially in the farewell scene (5.1), which was staged relatively simply at the 'Traitor's Gate' near the Tower. But for the most part the reviews at the time confined themselves to elaborate descriptions of spectacle, ignoring matters of character and political or social meaningfulness. As for Kean's own performance, it was, at least if Walter Pater's memory served him well thirty years after the fact, delicately lyrical,[1] though perhaps rather too single-mindedly touched by pathos, without the dynamism that his father had brought to the part.

Richard the Poet   Pater's praise of Kean was of a piece with his view of Richard as an 'exquisite poet'; his comments are representative of one side of a debate that went on for a good part of the nineteenth century; on the other side were those critics who saw Richard as an effeminate weakling, incapable of rule. It wasn't until century's end that an actor emerged who sought to portray both sides of this complex personality, who, as C. E. Montague wrote, was able to 'fill the same man with the attributes of a feckless wastrel . . . and with the quite distinct but

---

[1] Pater praised Kean's 'winning pathos [and] sympathetic voice' and remarked that in his hands, 'the play became like an exquisite performance on the violin' (Forker, *Critical*, p. 297).

not incompatible attributes of a typical, a consummate artist'.[1] That actor was Frank Benson, who performed the part at Stratford and on tour over a number of years beginning in 1896. For Montague, Benson transformed everything that happens to Richard, even the most dire moments of pain and self-fragmentation, into an 'idea' to seize and recreate in words; 'he runs out to meet the thought of a lower fall or a new shame as a man might go to his door to see a sunset or a storm'.[2] Responsiveness to the artistic appeal of even his darkest moments was the hallmark; nothing, says Montague, 'was finer than the King's air, during the mirror soliloquy, as of a man going about his mind's engrossing business in a solitude of his own making'.[3] Benson, as actor–manager, was still caught up in the pictorial tradition of Victorian performance, though without the archaeological fervour of Kean. But perhaps fortuitously, the production that Montague saw in Manchester in 1899 took place shortly after a fire had destroyed most of the scenery and costumes;[4] no doubt the relative poverty of the makeshift scene threw added emphasis on the acting of the central character and helped Montague develop at length his detailed and influential account.

The kind of feeling that Benson found in the play became a hallmark of productions in the twentieth century, as focus shifted more and more to the character of Richard and his tragedy. Spectacle and pageantry maintained its hold, and ingenious ways were often found to register this aspect of the text. But the dominant interest was personal. This approach traced the trajectory of a vain and self-absorbed young man, who, while convinced of his own divinely supported right, is gradually stripped of the trappings of royalty and comes face to face with his own brittle mortality. Scenes that formed the cornerstone of Montague's reading of Benson's performance, such as that at Barkloughly Castle, where Richard first faces the possibility of defeat, the carefully calibrated play with the mirror in the deposition scene, or his self-interrogation in the prison where he will soon die, became the central markers of what actors like to call his 'journey'. And in this interpretation, certain lines became

[1] Forker, *Critical*, p. 366. [2] Forker, *Critical*, p. 367.
[3] Forker, *Critical*, p. 368. [4] Shewring, p. 69.

particularly resonant: 'I live with bread like you, feel want, | Taste grief, need friends. Subjected thus, | How can you say to me I am a king?' (3.2.175–7); 'Was this face the face | That every day under his household roof | Did keep ten thousand men?' (4.1.281–3); 'Nor I nor any man that but man is, | With nothing shall be pleased till he be eased | With being nothing' (5.5.39–41). Though not every actor sought to make an artist out of the central character, most found ways to make him sympathetic and attractive; at the same time, the emphasis on loss did not ignore Richard's folly, his narcissism, or his arbitrariness. Thinking about the play as a tragedy necessarily meant thinking about the ways in which Richard's blindness to the realities around him helped seal his fate.

While Benson was impressing C. E. Montague with his sensitive portrayal, William Poel, crusader and founder of the Elizabethan Stage Society, hired a young actor named Harley Granville Barker to play Richard in a production at University College in London in 1899. Poel was an enthusiast who had launched a campaign for a return to Elizabethan stage conditions, which meant rapidly spoken, uninterrupted Shakespeare on a (relatively) bare stage. For Barker, Poel's approach was a revelation, and his performance, marked by a quick but thoughtfully lyrical rendering of the verse, suited the new theatrical style.[1] Though Poel's own productions were often amateurish, his ideas soon caught fire, partly through the initiative of Barker who became an important producer and spokesman for the new movement. Poel, and Barker after him, stressed the need for an open stage, without multiple sets, but typically with a platform that jutted out beyond the proscenium, thus freeing the language and the actors, bringing them closer to the audience and enabling easy transitions from one scene to another. As with Benson's performance in Manchester, these changes put the actors at the centre, highlighting what they had to say, and giving richer scope to the characters they portrayed.

When Harcourt Williams, the new director of the Old Vic, chose the young John Gielgud to play Richard in 1929, the

---

[1] Many years later he sent Poel a note about the time in 1899 when Poel came to see him 'and shook all my previous convictions by showing me how you wanted the first lines of *Richard II* spoken' (Dennis Kennedy, *Granville Barker and the Dream of Theatre* (Cambridge, 1985), p. 149).

company had already absorbed the lessons that Barker had been promoting for two decades. Partly by necessity, the Old Vic was committed to a 'poor' theatre, and in Gielgud they found an actor whose poetic grasp and supple voice allowed him to speak the verse quickly, naturally, and meaningfully. Gielgud made the part

10. John Gielgud as Richard (Queen's Theatre, 1937), showing something of the sensibility as well as the determination, the combined intensity and delicacy, of his performance.

his own, playing it again in a revival in the West End that he himself directed in 1937, and later still directing Paul Scofield in a production at Stratford in 1953. His Richard was a man of fine, if overwrought, sensibility, at one point savouring the aroma of an orange stuck with cloves. Petulant and weak at the outset, he grew in subtlety as his misfortunes, many self-generated, multiplied. Reviewing the 1937 revival, *The Times* found the mirror scene to be pivotal: 'all his playing is a movement toward this climax, and, after the fall, a spiritual search beyond it' (7 Sept. 1937, quoted in Shewring, p. 80). Pathos, as so often, was a dominant note, epitomized in the memorable finale to the deposition scene at the Old Vic, when, dressed in black velvet, he 'tottered down the steps . . . towards the exit, dragging his feet behind him and tilting his chin upwards in a last exhibition of majesty'.[1] But not only pathos; one can detect in this last detail a richer characterization—an element of stubbornness, perhaps, and a lingering sense of his right, together with a failure of nerve. The key thing, as Barker had insisted, and exemplified in his *Prefaces*,[2] was to seek the character in the details of the language, and that was what Gielgud did.

Richard and Bolingbroke in the Balance   Another important consequence of the simplification of scenery and staging was to highlight the symmetries of the play, which meant (among other things) focusing on the crucial balance between the two central characters, a feature that had often been missing from earlier productions. Once again Gielgud provides an example. For his 1937 production, he found the money to hire an excellent cast, including Michael Redgrave as Bolingbroke, who abandoned the traditional approaches (either a strong competent king or a ruthless schemer) for a more complex figure; combining these characteristics, this Bolingbroke was conflicted about the very gains that he sought for himself. The effort to balance the two figures has become the standard in more recent productions, where the pathos of the King's loss tends to be offset not only by

---

[1]   Eric Philips, quoted in Shewring, p. 77.
[2]   Barker's *Prefaces to Shakespeare*, a series of volumes begun in 1927, are a brilliant example of a man of the theatre reading Shakespeare's texts very closely for what they reveal about character and about the necessary work of the actor.

his own giddiness but by his opponent's bewildered conscience. In a production at Stratford's Other Place in 2000, David Troughton brought this tendency to a high point, portraying a tormented Bolingbroke, who was conscious of his tendency to fury and kept trying to stifle it; he ended the play speaking some of Richard's lines from the prison soliloquy (they had provided a kind of threnody throughout): 'Nor I nor any man that but man is, | With nothing shall be pleased till he be eased | With being nothing'.

No doubt the best known attempt to even the playing field on which the two men face each other is the 1973 version directed at Stratford by John Barton. This has been much written about and stands as one of the defining productions of the play in the twentieth century.[1] Barton, in seeking both to bring out an analogy between king and actor, and to strike a balance between Richard and Bolingbroke, made a crucial decision to cast two actors to alternate the roles of king and challenger (Richard Pasco and Ian Richardson).[2] This flagged the central theme: as Anne Barton wrote in a programme note, 'Richard's journey from king to man is balanced by Bolingbroke's progress from a single to a twin-natured being'. The idea was that kings, like actors, are 'twin-natured', their personhood and their role intricately entwined. The production found a host of emblematic ways to bring home the analogy. It began with an unscripted dumbshow in which 'Shakespeare' entered with a large book, followed by the actors in rehearsal clothes. Then, taking a mask and crown, 'Shakespeare' placed them on the book now held by the two leads, thus prefiguring the moment in the deposition scene when they would once again hold the crown between them. After a brief moment of suspension, he bowed to the actor slated to play Richard that day, making him 'King'. Amid shouts of 'Long live the King', Richard was then masked, and robed as if for a coronation, while the other actors donned their costumes in full

---

[1] See, for example, Wells, *Royal*, pp. 64–80; Shewring, pp. 120–37; Richard David, *Shakespeare in the Theatre* (Cambridge, 1978), pp. 164–73; Anthony B. Dawson, *Watching Shakespeare: A Playgoer's Guide* (Basingstoke, 1988), pp. 78–87; Page, pp. 57–68; Stredder, pp. 23–42; Lopez, pp. 137–41.

[2] It is tempting but no doubt wrong to suspect that the echoes between the names of the actors and that of the play influenced the casting. At the very least, we can note how appropriate those echoes are to the production's theme.

view of the audience. Only then did the King, removing his mask and finding his place in the proffered book, begin the play.

The mirroring of actor and king found literal representation in the production's extensive use of actual mirrors. From the opening dumbshow, where Bolingbroke held a mirror to the robed King, to Richard's final moments, the production capitalized on the central symbolic gesture during the deposition when Richard calls for a mirror and then smashes it, noting 'How soon my sorrow hath destroyed my face'. Bolingbroke's rejoinder was fraught with meaning for this production, and stressed accordingly, 'The shadow of your sorrow hath destroyed | The shadow of your face' (4.1.291–3), his words being repeated in chorus by the attendant lords. Richard did not throw the mirror down but broke through it with his fist; Bolingbroke then took the empty frame and placed it slowly and deliberately over Richard's head, so that it became a kind of mock crown and then, as Peter Thomson

11. 'Here, cousin, seize the crown': Richard Pasco (right), as Richard, reluctantly hands over the crown to his icy cousin Henry (Ian Richardson), in John Barton's production of 1973, where the two principal actors alternated the main roles.

noted,[1] a noose. The empty frame remained around his neck during the farewell scene with the Queen (5.1) and was still there at the end when, in the play's most controversial moment, the hooded groom of the stable, who in the text comes to offer sympathetic allegiance, was revealed to be Bolingbroke in disguise. Richard then took the mirror frame from his own neck and 'held it between them, so that each saw the other as though he were a reflection of himself', the implication being that 'their shared experience of the hollowness of the kingly crown draws them together more powerfully than their former rivalry sets them apart'.[2] This was a clear instance of stretching the text to fit the interpretation, but it had a powerful theatrical effect. And it fitted well with the boost that Barton sought to give to Bolingbroke throughout in order to keep the balance between the two main parts/actors. In doing so, he not only invented business but added a soliloquy for Bolingbroke in which the new King shares his tormented soul with the audience.[3] Spoken at the beginning of 5.3, this was taken largely from a speech in 2 *Henry IV*, where Henry laments his sleeplessness, but was bolstered by lines from another character in that play and even more extraordinarily, from Richard himself in this one (repeating Richard's prediction at 5.1.55–9 that the alliance between Henry and his 'ladder', Northumberland, will soon collapse). Giving Bolingbroke a tortured conscience is of course to make him more sympathetic; and consistent with that aim, the production turned Northumberland into the real villain, making him responsible for the predations upon Richard, while Bolingbroke remained a rather reluctant ally.

One effect of making Bolingbroke a more sympathetic figure is to raise the question of his motivation and the timing of his royal trajectory. In making Northumberland the chief architect of Bolingbroke's rise, Barton reduced the latter's potential

---

[1] 'Shakespeare straight and crooked: a review of the 1973 Season at Stratford', *SS* 27 (Cambridge, 1974), 143–53 (p. 153).

[2] Wells, *Royal*, p. 79.

[3] This desire to make Bolingbroke more understandable than he is in the original, to put his character on a more rational foundation, is akin to both eighteenth-century adaptations of the play and to character-centred criticism of our own time. See Paul Yachnin, 'Looking for *Richard II*', in Sabor, pp. 121–35.

ruthlessness, projecting it on to his henchman. But, perhaps indicating a discomfort with this approach, Barton also inserted an ambiguous line as the banished Henry departed: 'Now must I serve a long apprenticehood.' This rewrites an (omitted) line from a little earlier ('Must I not serve a long apprenticehood | To foreign passages'—1.3.271–2), suggesting, without actually saying so, that he will eventually 'graduate' to kingship. Bolingbroke's intentions thus remained enigmatic—and this is a feature that must be faced by any modern production. Is he already a contender for the throne before Richard banishes him, so that Richard is consciously getting rid of a major threat? Or is what he says when he does return, that he is coming only to claim his rightful inheritance, actually true? His followers, Northumberland in particular, seem to assume that he will eventually become king, and hence are positioning themselves for a role in the new regime. At the same time, they are cautious about how they express their dismay with the current one (see 2.1.262–300). As we have seen, this ambiguity has characterized the play from its earliest performances, when Essex's men read it according to their own desires and convictions. While, in the 1590s, the opposition was more between political principles (the sanctity of the king vs. the rights of subjects) than between individuals, Shakespeare locates it in character. And this is made all the plainer when the balance between the two main figures is restored, so that each is right in some ways and each wrong. This makes the politics of the play less overt but also less abstract, and hence more theatrically appealing.

Ritualism   Barton's treatment of Northumberland also illustrates his production's exploitation of the play's ritualistic elements. His emphasis on spectacle and pageantry was almost as robust as Charles Kean's, though in a symbolic rather than an archaeological vein. While the masks that were originally considered for the production ended up being discarded, the idea of masks structured the conception. Characters often spoke their lines directly to the audience, giving them an incantatory inflection. They rode 'hobby horses', some quite ominously large, which were built into their costumes to give the impression of their being on horseback. Upon his return from Ireland Richard was mounted on a large Roan Barbary, 'a mythical horse with a unicorn's horn, propelled on skis'.[1] Northumberland and his men occasionally appeared on stilts and, when he was sent to split Richard from his queen and deliver him to Pomfret (5.1.51), he was costumed as a huge plumed bird of prey, a figure of raw naked power. Such conscious stylization marked the production throughout—beginning with the ritual already described.[2] The play ended as it began, with another ritual, mirroring the first. Henry IV was crowned by 'Shakespeare' with the same ceremony accorded the former king in the prologue. As he turned to the audience, however, he showed not the golden mask from the beginning, but a skull. Then two hooded figures on either side suddenly turned and revealed themselves to be the two main actors, with between them the crowned skull-king. The 'hollow crown | That rounds the mortal temples of a king' (3.2.160–1) could hardly have been more graphically illustrated.[3]

For the British stage, at least, Barton took the play a long way into ritual. But on foreign stages, Shakespeare is often played in deliberately non-naturalistic, emblematic styles. The work of Giorgio Strehler provides an early example of this. *Richard II*, mounted at his new Piccolo Teatro in Milan in 1948, was the first of his Shakespearian productions, some of which (especially *King Lear* in 1972 and *Tempest* in 1978) made a significant international impact. Himself influenced by Brecht, Strehler brought to his theatre a strong Marxist commitment and a determination, like that of his contemporary Jean Vilar in France (who the year before had directed *Richard II* in front of the vast fourteenth-century Palais des Papes in Avignon), to bring theatre to new, wider, and more proletarian audiences. As its name indicates, the Piccolo Teatro is a small space, but Strehler and his designer, Gianni Ratto, managed to provide a sense of capaciousness by using a stylized version of an Elizabethan stage, to which he added 'a long continuous curvilinear balcony along both sides . . . and across the upstage façade';[4] he filled both stage and balcony with a

---

[1] Wells, *Royal*, p. 72.

[2] Though the extravagance of these effects was toned down somewhat when the production was revived the following year, their essence remained.

[3] Stredder, p. 42.

[4] Leiter, p. 574.

huge cast, including many silent characters—troops, heralds, bishops, or whatever suited the scene. The idea was to 'represent' history, or more precisely, to present it theatrically, using devices rooted in performative tradition;[1] hence, for example, the move to non-naturalistic visual elements, such as black-clad stage-hands carrying 'mysterious moons' through 'imaginary spaces' to suggest the passing of time. In a similar vein the elaborate pageants of extras created a 'marvelous jumble of impressions' that provided energy and scenographic density while, aurally, the production was woven together by threads of music based on popular tunes of Richard's own time.[2] As with Vilar, Strehler's aim was political in the sense that performance itself, and its potential effect on the masses, was at the centre; theirs was a 'rough celebratory theatre'[3] designed to change the way the French and Italian public understood theatrical, and ultimately political, reality.

Vilar's production, the first ever in France, was marked by what Dennis Kennedy calls a 'gigantic simplicity', its spare style designed to bring participants together in a ceremonial ritual resembling the Catholic mass (199). When Ariane Mnouchkine turned to the play more than thirty years later (at the Théâtre du Soleil in Paris in 1981), she made the ritualistic elements the core of the experience—but outside of any Christian or indeed European context. Inspired partly by Artaud's dictum that 'the theatre is oriental', she told an interviewer: 'When we decided to perform Shakespeare, a recourse to Asia became a necessity.'[4] Convinced that western acting is contaminated by 'psychological venom', she wanted to break away from realism by using Asian theatrical forms in combination with her own translation of Shakespeare's text.[6] She therefore ignored the play's specifically national resonance, instead importing movement, costumes, and a hieratic style loosely borrowed from Japanese kabuki and Noh, interlaced with Balinese and Kathakali influences, along with various styles of Asian music. Films such as Kurosawa's *Kagemusha* also influenced her style.[7] The aim was not to mimic

---

[1] Shewring, p. 163.   [2] Leiter, p. 574.   [3] Shewring, p. 165.
[4] Pavis, p. 95.   [6] Williams, p. 94.   [7] Kiernander, p. 111.

12. The deposed King Richard (Georges Bigot) is imprisoned in a web of poles and attacked by Samurai-like murderers, in Ariane Mnouchkine's highly 'orientalized'1981 production at the Théâtre du Soleil in Paris (note the King's Kabuki white-face).

Asian methods, but to reveal the play's 'sacred and ritualistic aspects'.[1] Movement was carefully controlled, sometimes solemn, sometimes fast, such as at the opening when the actors moved rapidly along a ramp and suddenly stopped in a line, with the King, holding what looked like a samurai sword, seated cross-legged on a low table (the 'throne'). The actors rarely looked at each other, often facing the audience with their knees spread and their hands held ceremoniously apart. In such a context, their words came across with great clarity, almost 'as if these were not characters but bodies traversed by a single voice'. The temperature, however, was not always cool: at the end, Bolingbroke actually kissed the lips of the murdered King, before lowering his body to the floor; he then laid himself out on a table, 'tiny and fragile, in the centre of an enormous bare carpet'.[2] Mnouchkine's

[1] Pavis, p. 96.
[2] Colette Godard, *Le Monde*, 15 Dec. 1981, cited in Williams, pp. 91–2. See also Kiernander, p. 115.

project was to avoid psychology and instead to enact what she calls 'states', a kind of inner passion without subjectivity, expressed outwardly through the disciplined bodies of the actors. She stressed the succession of such states in discontinuity, each played as forcefully as possible. The costumes and set added to this, as, for example, when Richard went from rich, multilayered 'vestments in white, red and gold' at the beginning of the deposition to a simple loin cloth, the transferring of the crown being accompanied by a ritual stripping.[1] Mnouchkine was in quest of theatrical means that would answer to what she saw as Shakespeare's 'extraordinary ability' to 'transpose everything into poetry' while at the same time speaking 'in the voice of a character'.[2] Wanting to universalize the play by wrenching it from its British roots, she translated not just the text but its history, its politics of kingship, and its connection with English nationhood, by interlinking it with Asian form.

Politics, Character, and Sequence in Modern Performance   Mnouch-kine suppressed the play's political resonances. So, in a different way, have many of the more conventional 'psychological' versions that have been the standard on English-speaking stages and indeed in films such as the BBC TV version, where Derek Jacobi's ironic, self-absorbed, brilliantly manipulative but ultimately incapable Richard was no match for the steely, unyielding but still sympathetic Bolingbroke of Jon Finch. The play becomes in such versions much more about personalities than about governance. But in its original form, it poses a crucial question about whether or not it is legitimate to overthrow a properly constituted government when that regime has lost its moral compass, and it locates that question in represented persons. Historically of course the issue of resistance to 'proper' authority concerns kingship and the matter of divine sanction. If God, as figures such as Gaunt, York, and Carlisle insist, upholds the right of the duly anointed king, then it is always wrong to unseat him. But the play's meditation on this problem is not simple. Bolingbroke has been deeply wronged and our sympathies are often with him, especially in the first half. Is he right to do

[1] Kiernander, p. 115
[2] Her own words, quoted in Williams, p. 94.

what he does? In a modern context, where the sacredness of kingship is no longer much felt, we are inclined, almost without thinking about it, to regard Henry's response as legitimate. But then of course, with the tormenting and murder of Richard, which Bolingbroke benefits from and hypocritically disavows, the balance shifts. So we are left in doubt.

Ian McKellen, who portrayed Richard as a tragic victim in a traditionally conceived production for the Prospect Theatre Company (1968), describes how a personal reading can be disrupted by a highly charged political context. When he began working on the role, he looked for a way to convey to a modern audience the significance of 'Richard's fall from the golden stardom of Godship to the obscurity of humanity' which he saw as the play's 'particular tragedy'. One model that he considered was the displaced Dalai Lama, which helped him find a gesture that started him on his way: 'a regal, priestly raising of the arms, symbolic but deeply felt' on which he 'quickly built all the rest of the character'.[1] Despite his model, he construed the role in purely personal terms—the tragedy of an individual. The play's politics remained in the background and only came home to him as 'revealingly modern' after a performance on tour in Czechoslovakia. Playing in Bratislava shortly after the overthrow of Alexander Dubcek and the events of Prague spring, he came to the great homecoming speech in 3.2 when Richard bends to salute the English earth, 'though rebels wound thee with their horses' hoofs'. Concerned about whether the audience even understood what he was saying, McKellen at first missed the urgency with which they had begun to react—'the plash, the gasp, the scuffles, the mewing'. But then he realized that they were weeping, grieving for their own land, so recently invaded, their earth 'the only symbol of a future freedom'.[2] Thus can politics enter unbeknownst through the stage door.

A more direct way to confront the play's political concerns is to present it in relation to its partners in the tetralogy which it initiates (*1 Henry IV*, *2 Henry IV*, and *Henry V*) or indeed in relation

---

[1] McKellen, p. 105. It is worth noting here the working method of the actor—finding one defining bodily move as a way into the character he wishes, almost literally, to flesh out.

[2] McKellen, p. 108.

13. Ian McKellen as Richard greets the English soil, in the Prospect Theatre Company's 1968 production, which enjoyed a memorable response from the people of Bratislava during a performance shortly after the dashing of the hopes associated with Prague spring.

to the larger cycle of Shakespeare's history plays—including the tetralogy he wrote first but which dramatizes events subsequent to, and deriving directly from, the events depicted here (the three parts of *Henry VI* and *Richard III*). In 1963–4, the RSC, under Peter Hall, presented a sequence of seven plays under the general title of 'The Wars of the Roses', dramatizing the civil violence that finds its origin in the fall of Richard. Beginning in 1963 with three plays (the *Henry VI* trilogy reduced to two and followed by *Richard III*), the company went on in the following year to mount *Richard II* and the other plays in its tetralogy. This had the effect of de-emphasizing the importance of Richard's individual loss and instead locating in his reign the seeds of bloody slaughter to come. Carlisle's prophecy that 'the blood of England shall manure the ground' could thus carry more weight than it does outside such a sequence. The violence was not confined to Richard's enemies—indeed it was epitomized in his own behaviour, such as when he repeatedly slashed the dying Gaunt with a whip. The programme spoke of Bolingbroke as 'the new man, the caring man, the man of integrity, [who] becomes a rebel almost against his will'; it is therefore right that he should displace the self-indulgent king who has built 'an elaborate artifice' that fails to meet 'the needs of the country as a whole'. Such a formulation, while it brings the play's meanings into line with the kinds of political critique gaining ground in the 1960s, also oversimplifies them. And in the event, the production itself was more complex than the flat statements in the programme. Bolingbroke may have started as a man of integrity, but the violence he let loose, quite graphically in the case of the execution of Bushy and Green, was as harsh as anything delivered by the *ancien régime*. As if to emphasize this point, in the prison scene Richard was 'tethered by a huge, noisy chain that had to be flung aside to allow movement'.[1] The general, anti-heroic idea was that politicians of whatever stripe tend to be brutalized by the exercise of power. This was reinforced by the look of the production, especially the studded metallic set designed by John Bury and held over from the *Henry VI* plays the previous year, which featured mostly dun colours with, for *Richard II*, a hint of gold. The harsh clanging of doors and the ringing of boots on the metal floor added to the atmosphere of incipient violence and helped convey the sense of 'crisis in which the nation finds itself as power changes hands'.[2]

Hall and the RSC's perspective on the plays contrasted sharply with the only earlier attempt (1951, also at Stratford) to play the whole second tetralogy in sequence. In 1951, the post-war mood of the Festival of Britain was celebratory, and Anthony Quayle's production was conceived as an appropriately vibrant and relevant English epic.[3] Accordingly, the focus was on Bolingbroke's rise, on his successful, indeed ideal, son who becomes Henry V (played by the young Richard Burton), and on the nature of kingship itself. Michael Redgrave, who played Richard with a sharply cruel and spiteful edge, was one of the first actors to make him overtly homosexual in the role, not an approach designed to win sympathy in 1951. Richard David etches a

[1] J. R. Brown, *Shakespeare's Plays in Performance* (Harmondsworth, 1966), p. 196.
[2] Shewring, p. 103.
[3] The *Henry VI* plays, and hence the darker consequences of Henry's usurpation, were not included.

memorable portrait of what he saw as Redgrave's 'wayward weakling', with 'an uncertain smile, half self-approving half placatory, that appeared whenever smiles were least in season. The indecision in the face was reflected in the nervous gestures, the handkerchief picked at and flaunted, the self conscious jauntiness of gait . . .'.[1] Such a man did not deserve to be king; indeed, within the sequence as a whole, his defects were designed, according to the programme, as the foil for 'Prince Hal's virtues . . . the perfect counterpoise and prologue'.[2]

When the RSC performed the Wars of the Roses, they took the plays in the order in which they were written; some twenty years later, the English Shakespeare Company, by contrast, played them in historical order, so that the trajectory they traced went from the fall of Richard II to the rise of Richmond (Henry VII and Elizabeth's grandfather) at the end of *Richard III*. Theirs was an even more overtly political reading of the cycle than that of the RSC. Of the seven plays eventually performed between 1986 and 1989 (and produced for television in 1989), *Richard II* was in many ways the most conservative, and certainly the most formal. In fact, the original plan was to start with *Henry IV* and leave the earlier play out altogether. But it became clear to company founders Michael Bogdanov and Michael Pennington that for the audience to understand the full sweep of the history, *Richard II*, which initiates the internecine wars, would be indispensable; so it was added in 1987. Bogdanov, who directed all the plays, saw them as directly relevant to Thatcherite Britain: 'Boardrooms may have replaced the Palace at Westminster, Chairpersons (mainly men) replaced monarchs, but the rules were the same . . . Nothing had changed in six hundred years, save the means.'[3] As a way of bringing this kind of point home, the costumes and setting were eclectic, leaping back and forth between medieval armour and the punk rockers of the 1980s but generally following a chronological development from the Victorian period for the earlier plays through to contemporary Britain. When *Richard II* was added, it

---

[1] Quoted in Page, p. 50. Some critics, by contrast, did see royal, if also rather harsh, strength in Redgrave's Richard.

[2] Quoted in Shewring, p. 98.

[3] Michael Bogdanov and Michael Pennington, *The English Shakespeare Company: the story of 'The Wars of the Roses'*, 1986–9 (London, 1990), pp. 24–5.

was accordingly given a vaguely Regency (pre-Victorian) look—remote enough to undercut the attempts at contemporary relevance. Richard's court was dressed in silken finery, while his Lancastrian opponents were sober and buttoned-up military men. Since the aim was to implicate Richard's self-absorption and wasteful extravagance as much as it was to critique the contemporary situation when, as in the play, 'the "rotten parchment bonds" of the fourteenth century were being drawn up again as Britain went into hock' (p. 24), it may seem inconsistent that Pennington's performance as Richard, while allowing for his faults, did in the end turn him into a quasi-tragic figure. For some critics at least, this showed the openness of the interpretation, which was more than willing to play the complexities and not limit itself through the imposition of heavy ideological freight. Thus David Fuller writes approvingly, 'As the prologue to a

14. Michael Pennington as a highly sympathetic Richard, holding the broken mirror (a sign of both his sensitivity and his defeat), in the English Shakespeare Company's strongly politicized version of 1987–8, directed by Michael Bogdanov.

People's *Henriad* this *Richard II* is surprisingly aristocratic in its final emphasis.'[1] And Pennington himself declared, 'Your moral judgement criticises [Richard] but your instinctive human sympathy goes out to him . . . which is exactly the sort of ambiguity you get in all Shakespeare.'[2]

These attempts to play the grand chronicle of English history in sequence clearly allow for a political perspective, whether celebratory of English nationhood as in 1951, or critical of the naked brutalities of power as in the other two. Since it takes a large dedicated acting company and a fair bit of money, the full sequence does not get played very often. When the play stands alone, the focus tends to be personal and the tonality tragic, though it can still be given a strong political colouring. In, for example, Ron Daniels's RSC production in 1991, politics put in an appearance, albeit in rather odd form. As Richard, Alex Jennings, tall and physically powerful, dominated the stage as a 'dictator' (Holland, p. 76), lording it over a rather meek and passive Bolingbroke (Anton Lesser), who clearly had *not* returned with any desire for the throne and was 'pushed unwillingly into power' by a viciously manipulative Northumberland (p. 77). There could be no tragedy when such a domineering, tyrannical Richard was reduced to a foetal position on his iron bedstead at Pomfret, nor even when he roused himself to use his chains to garrotte two of Exton's followers. That kind of leader simply had to go, even if it meant a descent into a kind of political chaos, mirrored in the set design by a gradual dismantling of the dark metal walls into 'piles of industrial scrap' (p. 77). The only tragedy here was, oddly, that of Aumerle, the young idealist bullied by Richard and reduced to near catatonia by the tide of events that overcame him.

Deborah Warner's celebrated production of 1995 at the Cottesloe,[3] with Fiona Shaw in the leading role, took the politics

---

[1] David Fuller, 'The Bogdanov Version: the English Shakespeare Company *War of the Roses*', *Literature/Film Quarterly*, 33.2 (2005), 114–37 (p. 121).

[2] Quoted in Shewring, p. 114.

[3] The Cottesloe is the small studio auditorium at the National Theatre, which, for this production, was fitted out with a narrow platform that ran between two opposing tiers of seats (Irving Wardle likened it to a 'palatial tennis court'— *Independent on Sunday*, 4 June 1995).

in a quite different direction—by playing the personal as fully as possible. If this seems paradoxical, it began with the choice to cast a woman as a man-king who so often in the past had been described as effeminate. But the intention was not to highlight gender, nor was the cross casting designed to establish a simple correspondence—quite the opposite. Rather, the point seems to have been to disrupt audience expectation—the strategy also that lay behind the move to infantilize Richard throughout (most notoriously Shaw sucked her thumb as she sat upon the ground

15. Fiona Shaw in her celebrated performance as Richard (directed by Deborah Warner at the Cottesloe, in 1995), alternately needling and pleading with her obdurate cousin during the deposition scene.

to tell sad stories of the death of kings (3.3.155 ff.)).[1] It all started
with Warner and Shaw's conception of the role—Richard as a
kind of child who adores his cousin, the two in fact sharing a
past love that is anchored in their complex mix of identity and
difference (the actor playing Bolingbroke, David Threlfall, bore an
uncanny resemblance to Shaw). Shaw saw it thus: Bolingbroke
'is the man Richard is most jealous of and the man Richard most
loves; and Richard is the one [Bolingbroke] most admires'.[2] They
had a past rooted in games in which Bolingbroke, always the
stronger, protected his cousin and allowed him to win. Theirs
was a jokey but deeply serious connection; during the lists (1.3),
for example, Richard first anointed Mowbray with holy water,
solemnly acknowledging the imminent death of one of the participants, then turning to his beloved cousin, Shaw's Richard, despite
his/her emotional investment, broke the ritual: 'she mockingly
paddled her fingers in the water and flicked it in his face'.[3] In
the deposition scene, on 'Here, cousin, seize the crown', Richard
challenged Bolingbroke to a game of paddy-whack; Bolingbroke
refused to play, but in doing so he lost the match, or, as Rutter
put it, by winning the crown, 'he'd made the prize meaningless'.[4]
The process of 'unkinging' continued the idea: Shaw sat on the
throne empty-handed as she spoke 'I give this heavy weight
from off my head | And this unwieldy sceptre from my hand'
(4.1.204–5); the tone was light, but harboured a kind of
solemnity as well, which became more pointed as the speech continued. As she finished she swept up the crown from the floor (she
had carried it in a basket) and 'rammed it painfully down on
Bolingbroke's head'. Shaw saw this as Richard's discovery that
'the whole thing' is an 'illusion'. 'There isn't anything *real*
about being a king.'[5] Thus the whole idea of kingship was de-
constructed. The gender of the actor was the means, though

---

[1] See Lopez, pp. 132–5, who points as well to Shaw's defiance of standard
modes of verse speaking as consistent with this aim.

[2] Rutter, p. 321. The Shaw quotations are from a 1995 interview with Carol
Rutter, and are cited from Rutter's article.

[3] Rutter, p. 320. Rutter consistently uses female pronouns when describing
Richard, while most male critics describing this production tend to use the
masculine.

[4] Rutter, p. 321.

[5] Rutter, p. 322.

not the focus, of the deconstruction—just because of the added irreverence unleashed by having a woman radically demystify the precious idea of kingship.[1]

Richard on the BBC   In a production like Warner's, psychology and a strong, if slightly abstract, political point can coexist, even if it bypasses the kinds of specifically theatrical values sought by someone like Mnouchkine in her attempt to break from the 'venom' of psychology. While there have been attempts in the English-speaking world to highlight other modes, if one goes to the Globe Theatre in London or any of the major repertory theatres in Britain, the US, or Canada, one will typically encounter an interpretation that puts individual character at the centre. It seems fitting therefore to end this survey with a brief account of the BBC television version, which, in keeping with the aim of the series as a whole, sought to provide a mainstream reading of the play, emphasizing the tragedy of the man Richard and the complex and enigmatic inner life of his antagonist.[2] The film begins with a long shot behind the credits, Richard (Derek Jacobi) approaching the camera in his gold and white regalia, accompanied by a few courtiers. Just before entering the presence chamber, he hikes his shoulders, takes a deep breath, and with a look in his eye that says 'here we go' he enters to where Gaunt, played by John Gielgud, awaits him. The moment establishes a great deal about the character and the interpretation. Sharply aware that he has to handle this looming confrontation right, and unsure of his capacity to meet the challenge, he knows he must play the game through. Thus emerges an interiorized Richard,

---

[1] Peter Holland's view that the production was 'an elegy for the loss of Richard and with Richard . . . a medieval world of ordered ceremony and religious mystery' (p. 247) ties dialectically to the deconstructive strategies sketched by Rutter and Lopez. For the emphasis on the diminishment of ceremony could also suggest the futility of such ceremony, the sharply political awareness that playing, whether that of the king, the president or the actor, should not really be taken all that seriously.

[2] Cedric Messina, the producer of the first two years of the six-year series, makes this aim clear in his preface to the published version of the script (London, 1978): the 'guiding principle', he says, was 'to make the plays, in permanent form, accessible to audiences throughout the world' (p. 8); this meant a straight, classical style of production and acting.

the small bodily signals, enabled especially by the opportunities of the television medium, making it possible to read the man's inner compunctions. This kind of thing is continued in the scene that follows, during which Richard modulates between public speech and softer more intimate tones, punctuated by close-ups and tracked eye movement. For an audience unfamiliar with the historical conflicts behind the scene, this makes clear how much there is at stake, even if we don't know exactly what it is. The presence of John Gielgud, the British actor most closely associated with the part of Richard, also adds a special touch. Though now playing Richard's uncle, he signals just by being there that Jacobi's Richard must somehow live up to the Gielgud standard, not deviating too far from the master's approach (hence assuring a traditional perspective) and yet establishing his own difference. (From this angle, Jacobi's hiked shoulders and the 'here we go' look speak to the actor's challenge as much as the character's.) As the scene develops, the enigma of Bolingbroke is wonderfully rendered by Jon Finch, whose face gives nothing away; unflinching, even harsh, he watches, his eyes trained, like a perfect hound on the scent. No wonder Richard, with his arch comments and slightly high pitch, is so wary.

The performance continues with alternating moments of public pronouncement and intimate exchange—Gaunt and the Duchess, the lists, then Bolingbroke showing some emotion as he takes leave of England and his father. This pattern of alternation extends to Richard as well; speeches that seem public are often spoken privately, such as the great lament spoken from the battlements of Flint Castle, 'What must the King do now?' (3.3.142 ff.). On stage, this is almost inevitably spoken, if not directly to Northumberland, at least in his presence, since he has just returned as an emissary from Henry. Here, however, it is transformed into a painful moment of intimacy, especially with Aumerle, and the two even share a rueful chuckle over the self-conscious extravagance of Richard's poetic reveries about digging a grave with tears. As he descends into the base court (the camera follows him down the stairs), Richard's wordplay on 'base' is again private and self-lacerating. These become the touchstone moments that provide the viewer with a glimpse of the bare soul of the suffering King. Meanwhile, Bolingbroke gets tougher and more unyielding, his brutal henchman Northumberland only an extension of his own obdurateness.

This double movement is marked by York (played with deep sympathy by Charles Gray), whose pain at Richard's loss and disapproval of Bolingbroke's ambitious rise are foregrounded and serve to conduct the audience's sympathies. During 4.1, for example, as Carlisle speaks his prophecy of the civil butchery to come, York remains at the front edge of the frame, his steady gaze registering his discomfort with the new King. When Northumberland arrests Carlisle, York's dismay is clear and he intervenes when Northumberland moves in response to Henry's command to fetch Richard, saying, in a low voice, 'I will be his conduct.' A moment later, in response to Richard's 'To do what service am I sent for hither?', he again speaks quietly, privately, sympathetically, to Richard: 'To do that office of thine own good will | Which tired majesty did make thee offer . . .' The scene proceeds with Richard stealing the show from the quiet Bolingbroke, though it is plainly a show, and a poor substitute for the lost crown—a fact made clear by Bolingbroke's ironic watchfulness as he sits on the throne. At the same time, the new King's troubles are far from over; he seems decisive and in control, but there are indications of the struggles to come. As the play draws to a close, he becomes slightly unwound. Immediately after pardoning Aumerle, dispatching York to Oxford, and getting rid of his importunate aunt, left alone, he allows himself a half-triumphant, half-bewildered 'Ha' as he raises his hands to his head and wrinkles his face. In the final scene, he is more volatile, shouting curses at Exton and wobbling towards the open coffin of his cousin/enemy. It appears that the disease which plagues him in the plays to come has already lodged in his seemingly invulnerable body, his triumph as empty as his repentant promise to visit the holy land.

Here, as throughout its history, *Richard II* locates its politics in the minds and bodies of the men that make the politics, and it reminds us again and again of the symbols and rituals that tend to bind the protagonists to courses of action that they would be better to avoid. Thus the emblematic and even pictorial style of so many of the productions we have looked at does in the end blend with the interest in the psychology of the main figures. If that psychology is itself an actorly one, both sustained and maimed by an awareness of its own performances, that too suits the medium, even while it complicates what it means for either a king or a player to be real. The play poses a dilemma about how we are to understand these royal performers, and it leaves in the hands and minds of the audience a central question about what constitutes a just polity. The last two scenes stake out that dilemma. In the penultimate one, we see a suffering Richard whose plaintive lament about his lonely condition modulates into sympathy with the common groom who comes to visit and then into bold action as he faces his murderers. The play then ends with a dominating Bolingbroke who accepts with relief the murder of the former King but condemns and exiles the useful murderer, Exton. Barton made the groom who comes to visit Richard into Bolingbroke in disguise, thus cementing his concept of the balanced link between them. But Shakespeare has quite deliberately kept them separate here, giving each a scene, and leaving the contrarieties for the audience to resolve if they can.

Textual Analysis[1]

While there are a number of uncertainties about the early texts of *Richard II* and their relations to each other, the overall picture is relatively clear. Most of the difficulties have only a minor effect on the final text that any editor is likely to produce. As we have already outlined in this introduction (pp. 9–11), five quarto editions of the play were published before its appearance in the First Folio (F, 1623). The first quarto (Q1) appeared in 1597, two more the following year (Q2 and Q3), a fourth in 1608, and a fifth in 1615;[2] each of these was based on the immediately previous one, meaning that the 'original' and hence most authoritative of the quartos is Q1, which was derived from either an authorial

---

[1] We have tried to keep the present discussion of the text as succinct as possible, omitting or consigning to footnotes elements that might bog down our presentation of what we regard as the key issues. Readers who want to pursue these and other issues more fully should refer to the discussions in Black, Ure, Gurr, and Forker, as well as to Richard Hasker, 'The copy for the First Folio *Richard II*', *SB* 5 (1952–3), 58–68, and to A. W. Pollard, ed., *King Richard II: A New Quarto* (London, 1916). The fullest discussion is to be found in Jowett and Taylor. Throughout this analysis, the early texts are quoted in the original spelling.

[2] There was also a sixth quarto, published in 1634 and based on the 1632 Second Folio edition.

autograph or a transcript of such. However, as also described above, Q1 lacks the so-called 'deposition scene' (4.1.155–318), which did not appear in print till 1608 (Q4), and even then in a poor text marked by omissions and mislineation. The Folio text, like the later quartos, is also derivative, but unlike them it is something of a composite. Based primarily on Q3 for most of the play, it also seems to have some fleeting connection to Q5 near the end and it restores a significant number of readings from Q1 that had suffered from errors and corruption in the move to Q2 and Q3. How it did so has been the subject of some debate; but it is clear that the copy of Q3 that was used by the F printers must have been annotated in some way. The most obvious evidence for this is the presence of the deposition scene, which does not appear in Q3. Since F's version of this scene is substantially different from, and superior to, that in Q4/Q5, and could not have been derived from them, it must have been based on a manuscript of some kind that was brought in to supplement Q3. Other evidence, such as the restoration of some of the Q1 readings, also points to the existence of a manuscript that seems to have been consulted (though on a somewhat irregular basis) by the people responsible for the editing and printing of F. What was the nature of that manuscript? Although we cannot know for sure, there is good reason to conclude that it came from the theatre, and may have been the 'book' that Shakespeare's company used to run the performance. That 'book' (what in the modern theatre is called the 'prompt book'[1]) seems to have been based on a transcription of Shakespeare's original papers.

Because Q1 stands closest to the hand of Shakespeare, all modern editors have based their texts on it. Ours is no exception. But each editor has to decide how much weight to give to certain F readings that differ from those of Q1. Do these constitute 'corruption' either from actors or from those involved in the process of publication (editors, compositors, and the like), or are they 'Shakespearean second thoughts' as G. B. Evans put it?[2] In

---

[1] The term 'prompt book' can be misleading since playhouse manuscripts from Shakespeare's period are very different from modern prompt books, often showing only the most rudimentary of markings. But they seem to have been sufficient for the players and bookkeeper to manage the performance without undue mishap—see Long.

[2] Riverside, p. 880.

weighing these readings on an individual basis as one needs to do, we have tended to admit a few more of them than in the Arden 3 (Forker) or Cambridge (Gurr) editions, but not so many as the Oxford. Why we have done so will, we hope, become clearer after a brief examination of the uncertainties surrounding the F text.

As we said, certain features of F point to a theatrical origin. Most prominent in this regard are the stage directions. On the whole, F has fuller and more precise directions than Q1 and these clearly bear the marks of the playhouse, while Q1 has several that can be regarded as 'authorial'—i.e. the kind of thing an author might set down as he is thinking his way through a scene. Some examples will help clarify the differences. At 1.4.52, Q1 has *Enter Bushie with newes*; in F, this becomes simply *Enter Bushy*, but F also adds a line 'Bushy, what newes?' The phrase '*with newes*' is readerly rather than theatrical. F's short line is much more audience-friendly, identifying a new character who has not spoken so far, and making it clear that he does have news to deliver. If Shakespeare himself did not initiate this change, he would probably have concurred with it (and so we, like most editors, follow F). A little later, when Richard and his entourage arrive to visit the sick Gaunt (2.1.68.1–2), Q1 reads: '*Enter king and Queene, &c.*', while F provides a comprehensive list of those in the King's train; this is the kind of thing that it would be necessary to specify in the theatre, but when the author is writing quickly, a simple 'etc.' will do. Similarly, the King, when he enters at 1.3.6.1–2, is accompanied by '*his nobles*' in Q1, but in F four of them are named. F also adds sound effects, mainly trumpets but also drums on two occasions, that derive from staging requirements. As, for example, the combat between Bolingbroke and Mowbray begins, F prints '*A charge sounded*' and, a few lines later '*A long Flourish*' (1.3.117.1, 122.1) while Q1 is silent. Even when Q1 does provide for sound effects, F is more complete and specific: at 3.3.60.1–3, Q has '*The trumpets sound, Richard appeareth on the walls*', while F reads '*Parle without, and answere within: then a Flourish. Enter on the Walls, Richard, Carlile, Aumerle, Scroop, Salisbury*'. A different kind of example of F's more precise awareness of theatrical exigency occurs near the end of the play, when Q1 fails to note the clearing of the stage after 5.3; it does provide an *Exeunt* for Henry and York's family, but then reads '*Manet* [i.e. *Manent*—'remain'] *sir Pierce Exton, &c.*'. This makes no sense since Exton has not been on stage. What seems to have happened is that Shakespeare or the scribe has failed to mark the break in the manuscript behind Q1, and, with the following lines given to Exton, an editor or possibly a compositor has added the incorrect direction.[1] F straightens this out by printing: '*Enter Exton and Seruants.*' At the beginning of 1.4, Q1 has: '*Enter the King with Bushie, &c. at one dore, and the Lord Aumerle at another*'. '*Bushie*' is an error, since he enters later on in the scene (52); F correctly replaces Bushy with Bagot and adds Greene (but at the same time it says nothing about their entering at different doors). F adds entry or exit directions in several other places which Q1 omits, though it leaves out one *Exeunt* that appears in Q (at the end of 1.3) and several times fails to supply missing entries or exits also absent from Q1. As Gurr remarks, 'F's systematising of the Q directions is some way from being perfect' (p. 187). Despite this, the pattern is tolerably clear and we can safely conclude that F's text owes something to the theatre. For this reason, we have tended to favour F's stage directions in our text, though we often combine the Q and F directions in some way, and provide the precise wording of each in the collation.

It is worth noting one particular example which cuts against what we have been saying. At the end of the opening scene in Q1 Gaunt exits with the others, while in F he is given an exit ten lines earlier, an entirely unmotivated exit but in keeping with the general principle of Elizabethan staging, that characters who exit at the end of a scene do not re-enter immediately for the beginning of the following one (as Gaunt does with the Duchess of Gloucester in 1.2). Most editors follow F here, though we do not. The moment is a tense one; Richard, unable to reconcile the quarrelling noblemen, is about to rule on Gaunt's son's fate; why would Gaunt leave at such a moment? It seems to us that F's '*Exit Gaunt*' is a bookkeeper's or editor's interpolation and that Q's silence on the matter does represent Shakespeare's intention, in this case, to challenge ordinary theatrical practice. As we point

---

[1] An alternative explanation was proposed by Wilson who infers that a scene has been 'cut out in . . . preparing the play for the stage', one in which, perhaps, Henry actually spoke the quoted words (Wilson, p. lxix); since having them spoken twice would greatly reduce their dramatic potency, the scene might then have been dropped, but the direction mistakenly allowed to remain until the theatrical text behind F cleared up the confusion.

out in our note to the line (1.1.195), the stage-clearing at the end of the scene could be handled by Bolingbroke and his father leaving before the others, followed by a formal exit on the part of the King and his entourage, thus providing a short interval before Gaunt's re-entry.

F also shows the effect of deliberate theatrical cutting. Several passages in 1.3 are removed, no doubt to give this long scene more dash and momentum—lines 129–33, 239–42, 268–93 all disappear. The last of these substantially reduces the rather tedious discussion between Bolingbroke and his father about coping with the pain of exile and thus helps move the scene more briskly to its conclusion. Other cuts include 3.2.29–32 (Carlisle's words are obscure and easily expendable) and 4.1.53–60, the speech by an unnamed 'Another Lord' which is dramatically clumsy and repetitive (see notes to 4.1.53 and 71–2). All of these reflect an intermittent and somewhat haphazard attempt to streamline the play.[1] Since Q1 is our control text, we have retained these passages, though performers may well want to follow F by removing them. One other feature of F points to its theatrical provenance: the wholesale substitution of 'heaven' for 'God' throughout the text.[2] These changes were made in order to conform with the Act to Restrain Abuses, enacted in 1606, which forbade the use of profanity on the stage but did not apply to printed texts. In our text we follow Q1 in all such cases.

Aside from the kinds of theatrical markers that distinguish F from Q1, there are a number of textual differences that complicate the picture of the relationship between them. Many of these are verbal substitutions, often of words with similar meanings; examples include 'iust' for 'right' (1.3.55), 'Faction' for 'party (3.2.203), and 'mock at' for 'laugh at' (3.3.170). At the same time, there are a number of instances in which F restores Q1 readings that had been corrupted in subsequent quartos (for example, 'beggar-feare' replaces Q2/Q3's 'begger-face' at 1.1.189 and 'sparkes' replaces Q2/Q3's 'sparkles' at 5.3.21).[3] This seeming

---

[1] There are also a number of single lines omitted, most of which are probably inadvertent errors rather than deliberate cuts.

[2] There are a few exceptions to this, notably at 1.3.11–25, where as Forker points out (p. 513) the ritual nature of the occasion may have meant that 'God' could be retained.

[3] *TC* provides a list of some 79 instances of such restored readings (p. 315).

paradox is best explained by postulating that the manuscript which, in addition to Q3, stands behind F derives ultimately from the same source as that behind Q1 but has been subject to some sporadic revision. This is consistent with its having been used in the theatre, where occasional verbal substitutions, some perhaps made by the author, others by actors or the bookkeeper, could easily have slipped in. We can thus infer that both Q1 and F go back to Shakespeare's original papers, but in different ways. Q1 was probably printed directly from those papers or a transcript of them,[1] while F's provenance is much more complicated. Jowett and Taylor have argued that the process went something like this: Shakespeare's original draft was both transcribed for use as a 'prompt book' and sent to the printers as copy for Q1 (though, as just stated, the Q1 manuscript may have been scribal rather than authorial); in preparation for the F printing, the prompt book was collated with a copy of Q3, which was extensively annotated by reference to it, though in an inconsistent manner. An annotator, that is, compared the manuscript version with the printed Q3 and made a number of changes which were then incorporated in F. This accounts for various features of F, though it doesn't solve all the puzzles. There are, for example, a number of instances where F introduces errors that can best be explained by a misreading of secretary hand (examples include 'soules' for 'smiles' (1.4.28), 'placed' for 'plated' (1.3.28), and the very odd 'White Beares' for 'White beards' (3.2.112). If we assume that the F compositors were working from an annotated copy of Q3, we have to ask why an annotator would have crossed out correct readings in that printed text and introduced nonsense arising from a misreading of secretary hand. This complicates Jowett and Taylor's argument and suggests the possibility that the F compositors sometimes worked directly from the playhouse manuscript.

What about the differences between F's version of the deposition scene and that contained in Q4? The latter version, as Jowett writes (*TC*, 307), bears the earmarks of a 'reported' text (one perhaps provided to the printer of Q4 by actors or a

---

[1] A transcript seems more likely, for two reasons: the relative cleanness of Q1, suggesting it was printed from a fairly readable copy (which Shakespeare's original 'foul' papers probably were not); and the scarcity of some of Shakespeare's characteristic spellings, most tellingly, 'O' for the interjection 'Oh' (the latter occurs 28 times, the former 8).

playhouse shorthand recorder), including extensive mislineation and omitted part-lines; F's fuller and more accurate version seems by contrast to derive from the playhouse manuscript (itself derived, more or less directly, from Shakespeare's papers). There is one more wrinkle in the complicated story of F's provenance; Jowett and Taylor, following and revising Richard Hasker,[1] argue that Q5, not Q3, lies behind a short passage near the end (5.5.70–118). They conjecture that a defect in the prompt book had, some time in the past, been remedied by reference to Q5, which provided the missing lines, and in the collation process a few divergences from Q3 found their way into F. The evidence for this is sparse, and to us not entirely convincing, but we mention it here to indicate the kinds of uncertainties that surround the F text.

Despite all this, there is reason to trust some of the F variants. That is because they must have been in the 'prompt book', and if they got there as a result of authorial tinkering, editors are justified in adopting them. But, since an Elizabethan playbook is the product of multiple agents—scribes, bookkeepers, actors, author—it is difficult to be sure that a particular variant originates with Shakespeare, rather than someone else. For this reason, in our edition, we have most often preferred quarto readings, except in cases where F seems to have successfully corrected Q1 error or is otherwise manifestly superior (and hence accepted by almost all editors). But in a few cases we have selected F variants not always admitted by editors, concurring with Jowett and Taylor that F manifests 'sprinklings of authority'.[2] Of these the most significant (quoted in original spelling) are:

1.3.172	addition of 'then'
1.4.59	'his' for 'the'
3.2.35	'friends' for 'power'
3.2.84	'sluggard' for 'coward'
3.2.134	'this Offence' for 'this'
3.2.178	'waile their present woes' for 'sit and waile theyre woes'

---

[1] 'The Copy for the First Folio *Richard II*', *SB* 5 (1952–3), 58–68.

[2] As we stated above, we have admitted fewer F readings than Oxford, but more than most other modern editions.

4.1.113	'of that Name the Fourth' for 'fourth of that name'
4.1.319–20	'On Wednesday next, we solemnly set downe | Our Coronation: Lords, prepare your selues' for 'Let it be so, and loe on wednesday next, | We solemnly proclaime our Coronation, | Lords be ready all.'[1]
5.1.25	'stricken' for 'throwne'
5.1.84	'*North.*' for '*King*'
5.2.81	'Sonne' for 'Aumerle'
5.5.58	'Houres, and Times' for 'times, and houres'

We have also, as editors since the eighteenth century have done, accepted the act and scene divisions in F, which probably do not have authorial warrant.[2] And we have in one instance followed F in its correction of historical fact (see textual notes and commentary to 5.6.8) and occasionally, on the same basis, provided the correct names for historical figures (see 2.1.280).

Two other areas of difference between Q1 and F remain to be discussed. The first pertains to how the play's two kings, Richard and Bolingbroke, are identified in speech prefixes and stage directions. Both texts are somewhat inconsistent, though Q1 more so. At the start, Q1 and F each have '*King Richard*' above the first line of dialogue. Following that, the prefixes in 1.1 in both texts are *King* but after that F has *Rich.* throughout (or *Ri.* or *Ric.*), while Q1 retains *King* till the end of 5.1 (except at 5.1.16 where Q's prefix is *Rich.*) and reverts to *Richard* in 5.5. As for stage directions, in Q1 he is uniformly referred to as *King*, with the exception of 5.1.6 (where '*Enter Ric.*' is squeezed into the margin) and 5.5 where he is called *Richard* in both directions where he is mentioned. In F's directions up to 2.1.68, he is called *King* but in Act 3 and thereafter he becomes *Richard*. As for Bolingbroke, he is usually designated *Bullingbrooke* (or some abbreviated form), though sometimes in both texts he is called by his title, *Duke of Hereford* (or simply *Hereford*).[3] In Act 5, after he becomes King,

---

[1] Though most editors do indeed follow F here, we include this passage in our list because of its importance to the matter of Q1's omission of the deposition scene.

[2] As previously noted, F fails to designate a new scene at 5.4; we follow Steevens by adding one and emend the two final scene numbers accordingly.

[3] This occurs at his entries in 1.3 and 2.3 in both texts and again at his entry in 3.1 in Q1.

Q1 (inconsistently but with a clear intention) refers to him as *King* or *King H⟨enry⟩*,[1] while F makes no such adjustment; there, with the exception of the two instances of *Hereford*, he is called *Bullingbrooke* all the way through in both directions and prefixes. In our text, we have regularized the names, calling the two principals, simply, Richard and Bolingbroke.[2]

Finally there is the matter of the play's quite regular metre. As noted earlier, this is one of very few Shakespeare plays that are written entirely in verse, and, because it is noteworthy for its metrical regularity, editors have often questioned the relatively few lines that do not fit the pattern, and have, as a result, sometimes sought to emend or regularize by, for example, adding a syllable to a 'defective' line (see 5.3.143 n.), or creating awkward or stretched 'pentameter' lines out of a pair of short lines (for example at 5.2.87–8 and 110–11). In general we have resisted this, since it seems to us that theatrical speech need not always follow the strict demands of pentameter. At the same time, where in many instances F, as a theatrical text, indicates syllabic elision as a means of regularizing metre and Q1 does not (substituting 'com'st' for 'comest', for example), we have tended to follow F. Our assumption in doing so is that where contractions of verb forms and the like appear in F, they represent the lines as spoken in the theatre, and would probably have had authorial approval, even though the author may not have written such contractions into his initial manuscript.

In summary, then, for all but the abdication passage in 4.1, Q1 provides us with the best and most authoritative text, though F, especially given its close proximity to the theatre, also commands a certain amount of respect. In attending as closely as we could to the many differences between the texts, we have tried to acknowledge F's intermittent authority and have adopted readings accordingly. In the end though, it has to be admitted that the many variants between the texts do not add up to anything major (again with the exception of the deposition scene). The textual story of *Richard II*, in its general outlines, is a relatively

---

[1] In the final scene in Q1 he is called *King* in the prefixes, but *Bullingbrooke* in the direction.

[2] We have made an exception for the initial entry, where, in keeping with the formal panoply of the scene, and to honour the ceremonious opening implied by both texts, we give Richard his title.

simple one, despite the complexities of detail. The play was clearly popular in its time, going through more single editions than the vast majority of Shakespeare's plays, each of which rested on the relatively firm foundation of the preceding one. The fact that it did so speaks to its textual stability but its several editions speak also to its political relevance and theatrical viability, even years after the death of Elizabeth and the execution of her former favourite, the Earl of Essex.

EDITORIAL PROCEDURES

THE present text is a modernized version of a play originally written in 1595 and printed two years later. As explained in the Textual Analysis section of the Introduction, *Richard II* first appeared in a quarto edition of 1597 (Q1) and was subsequently reprinted in four successive quartos, each based on the one preceding, before appearing in the Folio (F) of 1623. The first quarto derives from Shakespeare's original manuscript or a transcript of it, while F's version is a composite one, deriving from Q3 (1598) and a playhouse manuscript used to augment and annotate Q3. That manuscript also supplied the copy for the 'deposition scene' (4.1.155–318), which is missing in Q1–Q3, having, it appears, been subject to censorship (see pp. 9–16). Since Q1 is the base text for all those that follow it, it stands as our copy-text for this edition, except, of course, for the deposition scene, for which F serves that function. Because of F's evidently close connection to the theatre, it has also played an important role in our determination of the text as printed here.

There are hundreds of small differences between Q1 and F (of spelling, punctuation, and lineation, for example) and there are dozens of substantive differences as well (verbal substitutions, omitted lines, added or altered stage directions). It is the editors' job to adjudicate these differences and decide what to print. While we generally follow Q1, there are many instances where F seems the better choice (the grounds for such choices are outlined in the Textual Analysis section). Since these kinds of judgements are necessarily subjective, readers interested in this aspect of the play are encouraged to pay close attention to the collation (the small print below the play text on each page), which records all substantive variants between Q1 and F. While variants from the other quartos are in general not collated in this edition, we indicate in the textual notes those instances where a particular F variant first appeared in one or other of the quartos, and if so, which one; we do so by such notations as 'Q2–F' (meaning that both Q2 and F, as well as all the intervening quartos, feature

119

the variant in question) or 'Q5, F'(meaning that the variant in question first appeared in Q5 and subsequently in F). If a later quarto provides an adopted reading not in either Q1 or F, that too is indicated in the notes. For the deposition scene, we record all substantive variants between F (our copy-text for that scene) and Q4, where it was first printed.

The citations in the collation always begin with the line number and the reading adopted in this text, followed by the source of that reading. When the adopted reading is from Q1 (or Q4 for the deposition scene), the collation will then follow with the F reading (in original spelling) if that is different, and vice versa. As noted above, when the F reading is itself derived from one of the intervening quartos, that too is indicated. If the adopted reading is from another source (an eighteenth-century editor, for example, or, more rarely, a different quarto), then the rejected Q1/Q4 and F readings will follow. Occasionally, editorial emendations that have been frequently adopted by subsequent editors, and are thus well established, are included in the collation even if we have not adopted them. In identifying the source, the textual notes use short forms keyed to the Abbreviations and References below.

Reading the collation, which is written in a kind of shorthand, takes some practice. A few general points first: though modernized spelling is not generally collated in this edition, when a modernized word in our text occurs in a quite different form in the early texts, that is indicated by putting the original spelling in parentheses after the citation (if the difference is minimal it can also be indicated by placing '*subs.*', i.e. substantively, in parentheses). If an editor has made a conjecture (*conj.*) about a given reading but not printed it, that too is indicated in parentheses (e.g. *conj.* Johnson). Stage directions are indicated by decimal numbers: thus 1.2.0.1 indicates the opening direction of Act 1 Scene 2 while 1.3.6.1 indicates the first line of the direction following line 6 of 1.3. Stage directions embedded in a line are keyed to that line. Here are some examples of entries that may serve as a brief guide to an interested but potentially confused reader:

1.1.87 speak] Q1; said Q2–F
This means that our text follows Q1 in printing 'speak' while Q2 through to Q5 and F all read 'said'.

1.4.20 cousin, cousin,] F (Cosin (Cosin)); Coosens Coosin, Q1

Here our text follows F, though with different punctuation—we leave out the parentheses surrounding the second occurrence of 'Cosin' replacing them with commas; both versions indicate in different ways that the second 'cousin' is a vocative addressed to Aumerle while the first is a reference to Bolingbroke; we have not followed Q1's reading, which mistakenly makes 'Coosens' into a possessive (i.e. 'cousin's') or, possibly, a plural.

2.1.18 whose . . . feared] OXFORD; whose . . . found Q1; whose state the wise are found Q2; his state: then there are found Q3–5; his state: then there are sound F

This shows that the phrase in line 18 of 2.1 in our text ('[of] whose taste the wise are feared') is derived from an emendation first proposed by the Oxford edition and that the early texts feature different readings, in different combinations, none of which is satisfactory.

1.3.248.1] *Flourish* F; *not in* Q1
Exit] Q1c, F (*placed before* 'Flourish.'); *not in* Q1u
Richard and his train] CAPELL (*subs.*); *not in* Q1, F

These notes indicate the differences between our text and the early texts with regard to the stage direction for this line: the word 'Flourish' occurs in F but not in Q1; 'Exit' occurs in the corrected version of Q1 but not in the uncorrected (*c* and *u* refer to variants that are the result of press corrections); we have moreover reversed the order of F's direction, since the 'flourish' of the trumpets would normally precede and accompany the King's exit not follow it; and finally, the early texts are silent about who actually exits, so we follow (in substance) eighteenth-century editor Edward Capell in adding the phrase 'Richard and his train'.

2.1.186–8] *as* THEOBALD; *three lines ending* 'matter?' 'please.' 'with all,' Q1; *four lines ending* 'Vncle,' 'matter?' 'if not' 'with all:' F

This note refers to changed lineation; we have adopted Lewis Theobald's arrangement, and we indicate the differing arrangements in Q1 and F by citing the endings of the various lines.

4.1.281–3] *as* F; *two lines ending* 'vnder his', 'men?' (*omitting* 'Thou . . . me') Q4

In this instance from the deposition scene, we follow F's lineation over that of Q4 which, as noted, omits the part line 'Thou dost beguile me' and prints two lines to F's three.

Modernizing the text means bringing spelling and punctuation into conformity with modern practice, eliminating misprints and the like. As stated above, changes of this nature are not normally included in the collation; however, when punctuation affects meaning in a substantive way, it is collated (for example at 2.2.31 and 39), and occasionally significant spelling variants are recorded. Contractions are also silently emended (*nere* becomes 'ne'er', *e're* or *ere* become 'e'er', etc.) and verb forms regularized ('look'd' becomes 'looked', 'lackst' becomes 'lack'st', etc.). Our general rule has been to record significant differences (erring on the side of inclusion where there is uncertainty about significance), in order to enable the kinds of scrutiny of our text that we think important. We stress again that any edition of a Shakespeare play is a construction on the part of the editor(s), the result of hundreds of small decisions, and readers interested in how such texts are put together should have at their disposal whatever means the editors can reasonably put before them.

Of particular interest in that regard are the stage directions. As with most modern editions (though in contrast to the usual practice of Oxford editions), all editorial changes or additions to the stage directions in our text are placed in square brackets and recorded in the textual notes; so too any differences between the directions in Q1 and F are collated. In printing the directions we have bracketed anything that appears in *neither* Q1 nor F, since, though Q1 is our copy-text, F shows many signs of theatrical provenance and can therefore serve as a possible guide to early performance practice. In the text we have frequently combined Q and F SDs and recorded the exact wording of each in the notes. Adding editorial directions can be a tricky business since varying stage interpretations constantly remind us that the same text can yield very different enactments. For this reason readers should pay attention to those square brackets, since what lies within them is a product of the editors' judgement and not part of the original texts. Editorial SDs help readers make sense of the action, but they can be intrusive and restrictive. Hence, when stage action appears to be ambiguous, it seems best to us to indicate this in the commentary instead of specifying particular stage action (see, for example, notes to 1.1.195, 3.3.30, or 3.3.182.1). Our hope is that this approach will stimulate readers to imagine their own performances—reading a play is, we insist, itself a kind of theatrical enterprise.

Finally, a word about punctuation. While modernized, the punctuation in this edition is lighter than in many earlier ones. Our aim has been to punctuate for the voice as much as the eye, though the constraints of modern grammatical punctuation were always before us. Nevertheless, in an attempt to provide a feel for Elizabethan (or at times modern theatrical) styles of speech, we use more dashes and colons and fewer full stops than is usual, and frequently omit commas where they might appear in modern discourse (around vocatives for example). While it is not always possible to achieve the lightness one might desire, our hope is that readers will try to imagine the text aloud—try indeed to get their breath and voices around the words, using the punctuation as a guide but not a straitjacket.

Abbreviations and References

All citations of Shakespeare's works, except *Richard II*, are taken from the Oxford *Complete Works* (1986). Place of publication, except where otherwise specified, is London.

EDITIONS OF *RICHARD II*

Q1	The First Quarto, 1597 (Q1*u* and Q1*c* refer to uncorrected and corrected versions)
Q2	The Second Quarto, 1598
Q3	The Third Quarto, 1598
Q4	The Fourth Quarto, 1608
Q5	The Fifth Quarto, 1615
Q6	The Sixth Quarto, 1634
Qq	Quartos 1–6
F	The First Folio, 1623 (F*u* and F*c* refer to uncorrected and corrected versions)
F2	The Second Folio, 1632
F3	The Third Folio, 1663
F4	The Fourth Folio, 1685
Black	Matthew W. Black, *Richard II*, The New Variorum Shakespeare (Philadelphia, 1955)
Cambridge	W. G. Clark and W. A. Wright, *Works*, The Cambridge Shakespeare, 9 vols. (Cambridge, 1863–6), vol. 4
Capell	Edward Capell, *Plays*, 10 vols. (1767–8), vol. 5

Collier	John Payne Collier, *Works*, 8 vols. (1842–4), vol. 4
Collier ms	Manuscript emendations in Collier's copy of F2
Craig	William J. Craig, *Works* (1891)
Delius	Nicolaus Delius, *Works*, 7 vols. (1854–60), vol. 3
Dyce	Alexander Dyce, *Works*, 6 vols. (1857), vol. 3
Dyce 1864	Alexander Dyce, *Works*, 9 vols. (1864–7), vol. 4
Forker	Charles R. Forker, *Richard II*, The Arden Shakespeare (2002)
Gurr	Andrew Gurr, *Richard II*, The New Cambridge Shakespeare (Cambridge, 1984)
Hanmer	Sir Thomas Hanmer, *Plays*, 6 vols. (Oxford, 1743–4), vol. 3
Hudson	Henry N. Hudson, *Works*, 11 vols. (Boston, Mass., 1851–6), vol. 5
Hudson 1881	Henry N. Hudson, *Works*, 20 vols. (Boston, Mass., 1880–1), vol. 10
Irving	Henry Irving and Frank A. Marshall, *Works*, 8 vols. (New York, 1888–90), vol. 2
Johnson	Samuel Johnson, *The Plays of William Shakespeare*, 8 vols. (1765), vol. 4
Kittredge	G. L. Kittredge, *The Tragedy of Richard the Second* (Boston, Mass., 1941)
Malone	Edmond Malone, *Works*, 10 vols. (1790), vol. 5
Mowat and Werstine	Barbara A. Mowat and Paul Werstine, *Richard II*, The New Folger Library Shakespeare (New York, 1996)
Muir	Kenneth Muir, *Richard II*, The Signet Shakespeare (New York, 1963)
Oxford	Stanley Wells and Gary Taylor (gen. eds.), *The Complete Works*, The Oxford Shakespeare (Oxford, 1986)
Pope	Alexander Pope, *Works*, 6 vols. (1723–5), vol. 3
Rann	Joseph Rann, *Plays*, 6 vols. (Oxford, 1786–94), vol. 3
Riverside	G. Blakemore Evans, *The Riverside Shakespeare* (Boston, Mass., 1974)
Rowe	Nicholas Rowe, *Works*, 6 vols. (1709), vol. 3
Rowe 1709	Nicholas Rowe, *Works*, 6 vols. (1709, 2nd edn.), vol. 3
Rowe 1714	Nicholas Rowe, *Works*, 8 vols. (1714), vol. 3
Singer	Samuel W. Singer, *Dramatic Works*, 10 vols. (1826), vol. 5
Singer 1856	Samuel W. Singer, *Dramatic Works*, 10 vols. (1855–6), vol. 4

Sisson	C. J. Sisson, *William Shakespeare: The Complete Works* (1954)
Staunton	Howard Staunton, *Plays*, 3 vols. (1858–60), vol. 1
Steevens	Samuel Johnson and George Steevens, *Plays*, 10 vols. (1773), vol. 5
Steevens–Reed	George Steevens and Isaac Reed, *Plays*, 10 vols. (1785), vol. 5
Steevens–Reed 1793	George Steevens and Isaac Reed, *Plays*, 15 vols. (1793), vol. 8
Theobald	Lewis Theobald, *Works*, 7 vols. (1733), vol. 3
Ure	Peter Ure, *Richard II*, The Arden Shakespeare (1956)
Warburton	William Warburton, *Works*, 8 vols. (1747), vol. 4
Wells	Stanley Wells, *Richard II*, The New Penguin Shakespeare (Harmondsworth, 1969)
White	Richard Grant White, *Works*, 12 vols. (Boston, Mass., 1857–66), vol. 6
White 1883	Richard Grant White, *Works*, The Riverside Shakespeare, 3 vols. (Boston, Mass., 1883), vol. 2
Wilson	John Dover Wilson, *Richard II*, The New Shakespeare (Cambridge, 1939)

OTHER ABBREVIATIONS

(Works cited more than once in the edition are listed here, single references are included in the text)

Abbott	E. A. Abbott, *A Shakespearian Grammar* (1894). Citations are to section numbers, not pages
Bacon	*The Letters and the Life of Francis Bacon*, ed. James Spedding, 7 vols. (1862)
Barroll	Leeds Barroll, 'A New History for Shakespeare and His Time', *SQ* 39 (1988), 441–64
Bate	Jonathan Bate, *Soul of the Age* (New York, 2009)
Bible	*The Geneva Bible: A Facsimile of the 1560 Edition*, ed. Lloyd E. Berry (Madison, Wisc., 1969)
Blake	Norman Francis Blake, *A Grammar of Shakespeare's Language* (Basingstoke, 2002)
Bullough	Geoffrey Bullough, *Narrative and Dramatic Sources of Shakespeare*, vol. 3 (1960)
Chambers	E. K. Chambers, *William Shakespeare: A Study of Facts and Problems,* 2 vols. (Oxford, 1930)

Clegg	Cyndia Susan Clegg, ' "By the choise and inuitation of al the realme": *Richard II* and the Elizabethan Press Censorship', *SQ* 48 (1997), 432–48
Coleridge	Samuel Taylor Coleridge, *Coleridge's Criticism of Shakespeare: A Selection*, ed. R. A. Foakes (1989)
conj.	conjectured by
Daniel	Samuel Daniel, *The First Fowre Bookes of the Civile warres between the Two Houses of Lancaster and Yorke* (1595)
Dawson and Yachnin	Anthony Dawson and Paul Yachnin, *The Culture of Playgoing in Shakespeare's England: A Collaborative Debate* (Cambridge, 2001)
Dent	R. W. Dent, *Shakespeare's Proverbial Language: An Index* (Berkeley, Calif., 1981)
DNB	*Dictionary of National Biography*
Dutton	Richard Dutton, 'Shakespeare and Marlowe: Censorship and Construction', *Yearbook of English Studies*, 23 (1993), 24–5
Edward II	Christopher Marlowe, *Edward II*, in *Doctor Faustus and Other Plays*, ed. David Bevington and Eric Rasmussen (Oxford, 1998)
Faustus	Christopher Marlowe, *Doctor Faustus*, in *Doctor Faustus and Other Plays*, ed. David Bevington and Eric Rasmussen (Oxford, 1998)
Forker, *Critical*	Charles Forker (ed.), *Shakespeare: The Critical Tradition, Richard II* (London and Atlantic Highlands, NJ, 1998)
Hadfield	Andrew Hadfield, *Shakespeare and Republicanism* (Cambridge, 2005)
Hall	Edward Hall, *The vnion of the two noble and illustrate families of Lancastre and Yorke* (1548)
Hamilton	Donna B. Hamilton, 'The State of Law in *Richard II*', *SQ* 34 (1983), 5–17
Hammer	Paul Hammer, 'Shakespeare's *Richard II*, the Play of 7 February 1601, and the Essex Rising', *SQ* 59 (2008), 1–35
Holinshed	Raphael Holinshed, *The Chronicles of England, Scotland, and Ireland*, 2nd edn. (1587)
Holland	Peter Holland, *English Shakespeares: Shakespeare on the English Stage in the 1990s* (Cambridge, 1997)
Jowett and Taylor	John Jowett and Gary Taylor, 'Sprinklings of Authority: The Folio Text of *Richard II*', *SB* 38 (1985), 151–200

Kantorowicz	E. H. Kantorowicz, *The King's Two Bodies: A Study in Mediaeval Political Theology* (Princeton, NJ, 1957)
Kennedy	Dennis Kennedy, *Looking at Shakespeare: A Visual History of Twentieth-century Performance* (Cambridge, 2001)
Kiernander	Adrian Kiernander, *Ariane Mnouchkine and the Théâtre du Soleil* (Cambridge, 1993)
Leiter	Samuel L. Leiter, *Shakespeare Around the Globe: A Guide to Notable Postwar Revivals* (New York, Westport, Conn., and London, 1986)
Lettsom	W. N. Lettsom, 'New Readings in Shakespeare—No. 11', *Blackwood's Edinburgh Magazine*, 74 (1853)
Long	William B. Long, 'John a Kent and John a Cumber: an Elizabethan playbook and its implications', in *Shakespeare and Dramatic Tradition*, ed. W. R. Elton and William B. Long (1989), 125–43
Lopez	Jeremy Lopez, *Richard II*, The Shakespeare Handbooks (Basingstoke, 2009)
McKellen	Ian McKellen, 'The Czech Significance', in Ronald Harword, ed., *A Night at the Theatre* (London, 1982), pp. 103–8
McManaway	James McManaway, '*Richard II* at Covent Garden', *SQ* 15 (1964), 161–75
Mirror	*The Mirror for Magistrates*, ed. Lily B. Campbell (New York, 1960)
ms	manuscript
n., nn.	note, notes
Nashe	Thomas Nashe, *Pierce Penilesse his Supplication to the Divell* (1592)
Norbrook, 'Body'	David Norbrook, 'The Emperor's New Body? *Richard II*, Ernst Kantorowicz, and the Politics of Shakespeare Criticism', *Textual Practice*, 10 (1996), 329–57
Norbrook, 'Liberal'	David Norbrook, ' "A Liberal Tongue": Language and Rebellion in *Richard II*', in *Shakespeare's Universe: Renaissance Ideas and Conventions, Essays in Honour of W. R. Elton*, ed. J. M. Mucciolo (1996), 37–51
OED	*Oxford English Dictionary*
Page	Malcolm Page, *Richard II*, Text and Performance (Basingstoke, 1987)
Pavis	Patrice Pavis, *The Intercultural Performance Reader* (1996)
RSC	Royal Shakespeare Company

Ritson	Joseph Ritson, *Remarks, Critical and Illustrative, on the Text and Notes of the Last Edition of Shakespeare* (1783)
Rutter	Carol Rutter, 'Fiona Shaw's *Richard II*: the Girl as Player-King as Comic', *SQ* 48 (1997), 255–69
Sabor	Peter Sabor and Paul Yachnin, eds., *Shakespeare and the Eighteenth Century* (Aldershot, 2008)
SB	*Studies in Bibliography*
Shrewring	Margaret Shrewring, *King Richard II*, Shakespeare in Performance (Manchester, 1996)
Siemon	James Siemon, *Word against Word* (Amherst and Boston, 2002)
Spedding	James Spedding, ed., *The Works of Francis Bacon* (1857–74)
SQ	*Shakespeare Quarterly*
SS	*Shakespeare Survey*
Stredder	James Stredder, 'John Barton's Production of *Richard II* at Stratford-upon-Avon', *Shakespeare Jahrbuch* (1976), 23–42
Stubbes	John Stubbes, *The discouerie of a gaping gulf* (1579)
subs.	substantively
Tilley	M. P. Tilley, *A Dictionary of Proverbs in England in the Sixteenth and Seventeenth Centuries* (Ann Arbor, Mich., 1950)
TC	Stanley Wells and Gary Taylor, with John Jowett and William Montgomery, *William Shakespeare: A Textual Companion* (Oxford, 1987)
Wells, 'Lamentable'	Stanley Wells, 'The Lamentable Tale of "Richard II"', *Shakespeare Survey* (Japan), 17 (1982), 1–23
Wells, *Royal*	Stanley Wells, *Royal Shakespeare: Four Major Productions at Stratford-upon-Avon* (Manchester, 1977)
Williams	David Williams, *Collaborative Theatre: the Théâtre du Soleil Sourcebook* (1999)
Woodstock	*Woodstock, A Moral History*, ed. A. P. Rossiter (1946)

Richard II

THE PERSONS OF THE PLAY

KING RICHARD II

QUEEN Isabel, Richard's wife

John of GAUNT, Duke of Lancaster, Richard's uncle

Edmund of Langley, Duke of YORK, Richard's uncle

DUCHESS OF YORK, his wife

DUCHESS OF GLOUCESTER, widow of Richard's uncle, Thomas of Woodstock

Henry BOLINGBROKE, Duke of Hereford, Gaunt's son and Richard's cousin,
later King Henry IV

Duke of AUMERLE, York's son and Richard and Henry's cousin

Thomas MOWBRAY, Duke of Norfolk

BUSHY
BAGOT   } Richard's followers and counsellors
GREEN

Henry Percy, Earl of NORTHUMBERLAND
Harry PERCY, his son
Lord ROSS
Lord WILLOUGHBY   } followers of Bolingbroke
Lord FITZWATER
ANOTHER LORD

Lord BERKELEY
Earl of SALISBURY
Bishop of CARLISLE
Sir Stephen SCROOP   } allies of Richard
Duke of SURREY
Abbot of WESTMINSTER

Lord MARSHAL
A Welsh CAPTAIN
Two HERALDS
GARDENER
Gardener's SERVANTS
LADIES attending on the Queen

KEEPER of the prison at Pomfret where Richard is incarcerated

GROOM of Richard's stable

Sir Pierce EXTON, Richard's murderer

Exton's SERVANTS and fellow murderers

Other noblemen, servants, attendants, soldiers

THE PERSONS OF THE PLAY] There is no list of *Dramatis Personae* in Qq or F. Rowe was the first editor to provide a (partial) list, which has been augmented by subsequent editors. Names we have used in speech prefixes and stage directions are in small capitals.

KING RICHARD II (1367–1400, reigned 1377–99). He was the son of Edward the Black Prince, who was in turn the eldest son of Edward III. Since the prince died before his father, and Richard's older brother died young, Richard inherited the crown as a child. The action of the play takes place during the last two years of Richard's life.

QUEEN Isabel. Though the historical Queen Isabel was only a child of ten or eleven during the events of the play, Shakespeare, following Daniel, makes her a loving adult companion, conflating her with Richard's first wife, Anne of Bohemia, with whom the King shared a genuinely close romantic attachment.

John of GAUNT (1340–99). The fourth son of Edward III, and the most powerful baron in England, a skilled player on both the national and the international stage; his name, a source of some wordplay in the text, derives from modern-day Ghent in Belgium. In real life, he appears to have been more complex and ambitious, and less gracious, than in the play.

Duke of YORK (1341–1402). The fifth of Edward III's sons; though historically not very effectively involved in politics or war, the role that Shakespeare gives him in the middle of the power struggle is accurate enough. What Shakespeare adds for dramatic purposes is the painful way in which he is torn between conflicting loyalties.

DUCHESS OF YORK (1366–1434). Historically she was Aumerle's stepmother, but Shakespeare makes her into a loving and anxious mother. She was Surrey's sister and later married Lord Willoughby.

DUCHESS OF GLOUCESTER (1365–99). Widow of the Duke of Gloucester (known as Woodstock), whose murder looms large over the first few scenes of the play; she is primarily a figure of lament.

Henry BOLINGBROKE (1367–1413, reigned as Henry IV 1399–1413). Called Duke of Hereford (a title he gained in 1397 because of an inheritance through his first wife), he became Duke of Lancaster upon Gaunt's death. His name (spelled Bullingbrooke in the early texts—and Bullingbrook in some modern editions— probably reflecting Elizabethan pronunciation) derives from his birthplace.

AUMERLE (Edward, Duke of Aumale; 1373(?)–1415). He became Duke of York in 1402. Shakespeare, following Holinshed, makes him a loving and loyal follower of Richard, though there is some doubt about whether he actually joined the conspiracy against Henry. He later served the new King in various capacities and died fighting heroically on the part of Henry's son, King Henry V, at the battle of Agincourt (see *Henry V* 4.8.103).

Thomas MOWBRAY (1366–99). A relative of the King's, he had charge of the Duke of Gloucester when the latter was being held at Calais, and was, with good reason, suspected of murdering the Duke at Richard's instigation. This suspicion stands behind the accusations hurled at him in 1.1.

BUSHY Sir John (d. 1399). An active politician under Richard and much favoured by him; a member of the Regency Council overseeing England during Richard's absence in Ireland, he was captured at Bristol and beheaded soon after.

BAGOT Sir William (d. 1407). His career was similar to Bushy's but he escaped to Ireland and, though captured after he returned, was later released.

GREEN Sir Henry. Like Bushy, an active member of Parliament, regency councillor, and friend of Richard, executed at Bristol in 1399.

Earl of NORTHUMBERLAND (1341–1408). In Holinshed he lays a trap for Richard, but Shakespeare omits this detail. Henry's staunch ally, he later turned against the King and stands as the chief rebel in the later struggles dramatized in *1* and *2 Henry IV*.

Harry PERCY (1364–1403). Called Harry Percy when he appears in *Richard II*, to distinguish him from his father, Henry, we call him simply 'Percy'. In *1 Henry IV* he is surnamed Hotspur because of his fiery temperament and battle prowess and is (unhistorically) killed by Prince Hal (later Henry V). Though he was actually two years older than Bolingbroke, Shakespeare makes him the same age as Bolingbroke's son, Hal.

Lord ROSS William, seventh Baron (d. 1414). Became Lord High Treasurer under Henry.

Lord WILLOUGHBY William, fifth Baron (d. 1409). Turned against Richard despite his having been made Knight of the Garter.

Lord FITZWATER Walter Fitzwalter, fourth Baron (1368–1406). Closely associated with Woodstock, he accused Aumerle in Parliament of murdering the Duke (4.1.36 ff.). Holinshed's spelling, adopted by Shakespeare, probably indicates Elizabethan pronunciation; of three occurrences in Q1, the name twice appears as 'Fitzwaters' and once as 'Fitzwater', while of the four in F, only one has the final 's'.

Lord BERKELEY Thomas (d. 1417). Holinshed mentions that he is with York at Berkeley Castle but Shakespeare invents his role as a messenger to Bolingbroke and the rather sarcastic tone with which he greets the rebellious Henry (see 2.3.74–80). That seems to establish him as

sympathetic to Richard, though he has no further role in the play.

Earl of SALISBURY John Montagu, third Earl (*c.*1350–1400). A member of the conspiracy hatched in 4.1 and executed at Cirencester (see 5.6.8).

Bishop of CARLISLE Thomas Merk(e) (d. 1409). A close friend of Richard, and a political churchman who probably never lived in his diocese; arrested in 1399 for his part in the conspiracy and put in the friendly custody of the Abbot of Westminster, later reprieved and granted a country vicarage, though he continued to lead a fairly active public life.

Sir Stephen SCROOP (d. 1408). A famous soldier who remained loyal to King Richard, but was never executed; he later served as Henry's deputy lieutenant in Ireland.

Duke of SURREY Thomas Holland, Earl of Kent, created Duke of Surrey in 1397. He remained faithful to Richard, joined the conspiracy against Henry, and was executed with Salisbury and others in 1400 (see 5.6.8, where he is called 'Kent' having been stripped of his dukedom). He acted as Lord Marshal in the lists at Coventry (dramatized in 1.3), but Shakespeare, who makes the Marshal distinctly sympathetic to Bolingbroke, seems to have ignored that fact or been ignorant of it. The two roles could conceivably be played by the same actor.

ABBOT of Westminster William (of) Colchester (d. 1420). Shakespeare takes from Holinshed the claims that he spearheaded the conspiracy by holding a dinner party at which it was planned (4.1.331–4) and died shortly after it was foiled (5.6.19–21). In fact, after a brief imprisonment, he lived on and prospered under Henry IV and Henry V.

Sir Pierce EXTON Nothing is known of him besides what Holinshed writes and Shakespeare reiterates. There was, however, a play written about him (mentioned by theatrical entrepreneur Philip Henslowe in 1598 but no longer extant), which suggests his reputation as a regicide was well established soon after *Richard II* was written.

Richard II

1.1 *Enter King Richard, John of Gaunt with other nobles [including Lord Marshal] and attendants*

RICHARD

Old John of Gaunt, time-honoured Lancaster,
Hast thou, according to thy oath and bond,
Brought hither Henry Hereford, thy bold son,
Here to make good the boist'rous late appeal,
Which then our leisure would not let us hear,   5
Against the Duke of Norfolk, Thomas Mowbray?

GAUNT

I have, my liege.

RICHARD

Tell me moreover, hast thou sounded him
If he appeal the Duke on ancient malice
Or worthily, as a good subject should,   10
On some known ground of treachery in him?

GAUNT

As near as I could sift him on that argument,

1.1] F (*Actus Primus, Scaena Prima*); *not in* Q1   0.1–2 *including Lord Marshal*] WELLS (*subs.*); *not in* Q1, F   1 RICHARD] CAPELL (*subs.*); *King Richard* Q1, F   2 bond] Q1 (bande), F (band)   8 RICHARD] CAPELL (*subs.*); *King.* Q1, F (*so throughout scene*)

1.1 Shakespeare would have read in Holinshed about the series of violent confrontations between the King and the nobles that preceded Richard's fall. Although the history of bitter conflict is alluded to in the scene only by Richard's mention of 'ancient malice' (9) and by Mowbray's confession that he once laid an ambush for John of Gaunt's life (137), it is nevertheless there in the background. On the surface a spectacle of royal judgement, the scene is in essence a proxy attack on the King for the killing of Thomas of Woodstock that is couched as an appeal against Mowbray. That means that the various participants are saying more than they appear to be saying and that Richard is in the uncomfortable position of playing the impartial judge when he is implicitly the accused.

0.1–2 The King and his court make a formal entry which culminates with Richard taking his place, probably on a raised throne.

1 **time-honoured** Honour belongs especially to the old and those of ancient noble descent.

2 **bond** The pledge that Gaunt had made to bring his son before the court.

4 **boist'rous** violent or truculent (*OED* 9a)
   appeal formal accusation requiring proof, often of treason

5 **leisure** lack of opportunity

8 **sounded** questioned (with the sense of getting to the bottom of something)

9 **on ancient malice** on the grounds of long-standing antipathy

12 **sift** discover by examining
   argument question

On some apparent danger seen in him
Aimed at your highness, no inveterate malice.
RICHARD
    Then call them to our presence. Face to face,   15
                                        [*Exeunt attendants*]
    And frowning brow to brow, ourselves will hear
    The accuser and the accusèd freely speak.
    High-stomached are they both and full of ire,
    In rage deaf as the sea, hasty as fire.
        Enter Bolingbroke and Mowbray
BOLINGBROKE
    Many years of happy days befall   20
    My gracious sovereign, my most loving liege.
MOWBRAY
    Each day still better other's happiness,
    Until the heavens, envying earth's good hap,
    Add an immortal title to your crown.
RICHARD
    We thank you both—yet one but flatters us,   25
    As well appeareth by the cause you come,
    Namely, to appeal each other of high treason.
    Cousin of Hereford, what dost thou object
    Against the Duke of Norfolk, Thomas Mowbray?
BOLINGBROKE
    First, heaven be the record to my speech: 30
    In the devotion of a subject's love,
    Tend'ring the precious safety of my prince

---

15 presence.] POPE (*subs.*); presence‸ QI, F   15.1 *Exeunt attendants*] WHITE 1883 (*subs.*);
not in QI, F   22 other's] QI, F (others); *apostrophe* THEOBALD

13 **apparent danger** evident threat
14 **inveterate** long-established
15–17 These lines establish the form of the
    appeal where the accuser and accused
    face each other and are entitled to
    speak freely ('Face . . . brow' modifies
    'accuser and accused', not 'ourselves').
    By using the royal 'we' ('ourselves' =
    'we'), Richard represents himself as the
    impartial judge.
15 **presence** As at 34, the King's presence
    and royal aura ground the formal legal
    proceedings.
18 **High-stomached** (a) courageous; (b)
    arrogant

18 **ire** anger
19 Both similes are proverbial: see Dent
    S169.2 and F246.1.
21 **liege** Term used by subjects to express
    their allegiance to the king.
22–4 i.e. may your happiness increase until
    God, envying our good fortune (in having
    you here on earth), supplements your
    earthly crown with a heavenly one
26 **come** i.e. come to plead
27 **appeal** accuse
30 **heaven . . . speech** let heaven attest to the
    truth of what I say
32 **Tend'ring** having regard for (*OED v.*[2] 3a)

And free from other misbegotten hate,
Come I appellant to this princely presence.
Now, Thomas Mowbray, do I turn to thee,   35
And mark my greeting well; for what I speak,
My body shall make good upon this earth
Or my divine soul answer it in heaven.
Thou art a traitor and a miscreant!
Too good to be so and too bad to live—   40
Since the more fair and crystal is the sky,
The uglier seem the clouds that in it fly.
Once more, the more to aggravate the note,
With a foul traitor's name stuff I thy throat,
And wish, so please my sovereign, ere I move,   45
What my tongue speaks, my right drawn sword may prove.

MOWBRAY

Let not my cold words here accuse my zeal.
'Tis not the trial of a woman's war,
The bitter clamour of two eager tongues,
Can arbitrate this cause betwixt us twain.   50
The blood is hot that must be cooled for this,
Yet can I not of such tame patience boast
As to be hushed and naught at all to say.
First, the fair reverence of your highness curbs me
From giving reins and spurs to my free speech,   55
Which else would post until it had returned
These terms of treason doubled down his throat.

57 doubled] Q1; doubly F

39 **miscreant** villain, scoundrel
40 **good** noble in rank
41–6 The couplets may, as Coleridge suggested, indicate the premeditated nature of Bolingbroke's accusation, which contrasts with 'the vehemence and sincere irritation of Mowbray' (132).
41 **crystal** transparently bright. The metaphor is probably linked to the Ptolemaic idea that the heavenly bodies were fixed to concentric crystalline spheres.
43 **aggravate the note** add weight to the reproach
45 **move** depart
46 By defeating Mowbray in combat with his 'right drawn' (i.e. drawn in a just cause) sword, Bolingbroke will prove his charge.
47 **accuse** impugn

48–50 Mowbray recalls the traditional formula, 'women are words, men deeds'.
49 **eager** biting, sharp
50 **Can arbitrate** that can decide
51 **cooled** i.e. by death. The reference is to the medical practice of blood-letting, which was thought to cool the overheated body.
54–6 **curbs . . . reins and spurs . . . post** The series of equestrian metaphors conveys Mowbray's struggle between the need to restrain his emotions in the presence of the king and his desire to give free rein to his anger.
56 **post** gallop
returned driven back
57 **down his throat** Responding to Bolingbroke's earlier threat (44).

Setting aside his high blood's royalty,
And let him be no kinsman to my liege,
I do defy him and I spit at him,   60
Call him a slanderous coward and a villain,
Which to maintain I would allow him odds
And meet him, were I tied to run afoot
Even to the frozen ridges of the Alps
Or any other ground inhabitable,   65
Wherever Englishman durst set his foot.
Meantime, let this defend my loyalty:
By all my hopes most falsely doth he lie.

BOLINGBROKE

Pale trembling coward, there I throw my gage,
Disclaiming here the kindred of the King,   70
And lay aside my high blood's royalty,
Which fear, not reverence, makes thee to except.
If guilty dread have left thee so much strength
As to take up mine honour's pawn, then stoop.
By that and all the rites of knighthood else   75
Will I make good against thee, arm to arm,
What I have spoke or thou canst worse devise.

MOWBRAY [*taking up the gage*]

I take it up, and by that sword I swear
Which gently laid my knighthood on my shoulder,
I'll answer thee in any fair degree   80
Or chivalrous design of knightly trial.

---

70 the King] Q1; a King Q2–F   73 have] Q1; hath F   77 spoke . . . devise] Q1; spoken, or thou canst deuise F

58–9 **high . . . kinsman** Referring to the fact that Bolingbroke is the King's first cousin.
62 **odds** an advantage (*OED n.* 5a)
63 **tied . . . afoot** obliged to run on foot
65 **inhabitable** uninhabitable (cf. 4.1.75–7)
66 **durst** dares
67 **defend** attest to
69 **gage** Token thrown down as a challenge to knightly combat, most often a glove (cf. 4.1.26 ff.).
70–2 Bolingbroke responds to Mowbray's lines at 58–9, agreeing to set aside his blood relationship with the king, which, he says, Mowbray 'excepts' (claims is an obstacle) out of fear rather than devotion to the royal family.

74 **pawn** gage. See 69 n.
stoop Both the demeaning act of bending down and the rapid descent of a falcon on its prey.
77 **or . . . devise** While the meaning is uncertain, Bolingbroke seems to say that he will 'prove Mowbray the author of any crimes, even worse than the ones with which Bolingbroke has already charged him' (Ure).
78 **that sword** i.e. the king's sword
80–1 I will respond to you in any orderly process of combat sanctioned by the laws of chivalry.

And when I mount, alive may I not light
If I be traitor or unjustly fight.

RICHARD

What doth our cousin lay to Mowbray's charge?
It must be great that can inherit us   85
So much as of a thought of ill in him.

BOLINGBROKE

Look what I speak, my life shall prove it true:
That Mowbray hath received eight thousand nobles
In name of lendings for your highness' soldiers,
The which he hath detained for lewd employments,   90
Like a false traitor and injurious villain.
Besides I say and will in battle prove,
Or here or elsewhere to the furthest verge
That ever was surveyed by English eye,
That all the treasons for these eighteen years,   95
Complotted and contrivèd in this land
Fetch from false Mowbray their first head and spring;
Further I say and further will maintain
Upon his bad life to make all this good,
That he did plot the Duke of Gloucester's death,   100
Suggest his soon-believing adversaries,
And consequently, like a traitor coward,
Sluiced out his innocent soul through streams of blood—

---

87 speak] Q1; said Q2–F   97 Fetch] Q1; Fetcht Q2–F (Fetch'd)   101 soon-believing] *hyphen*
POPE   102 traitor] Q1 (taitour), F (Traitor)

82 **light** alight, dismount
85 **inherit us** put me in possession (*OED* 1, quoting this line)
88 **nobles** Gold coins worth approximately a third of a pound.
89 **lendings** money advanced to soldiers when the regular pay cannot be given (*OED n.*² 2b)
90–1 As in Holinshed (p. 494), Mowbray is said to have diverted to his own use the money intended for the soldiers ('lewd' = base, unprincipled).
93 **Or . . . or** either . . . or
   furthest verge utmost bounds (cf. 65–6)
95 **eighteen years** The figure is taken from Holinshed, who uses it without explanation. Clarendon points out that it was the time from the Peasants' Revolt in

1381 to the present day of the play (Black, p. 23).
96 **Complotted** plotted in concert with others
97 **Fetch** derive
   head source
100 The Duke of Gloucester, uncle of Bolingbroke and King Richard, was murdered while in Mowbray's custody. Bolingbroke carefully omits mentioning that Richard may have been involved in the murder. See headnote and Introduction, pp. 19, 37.
101 **Suggest . . . adversaries** prompt Gloucester's easy-to-convince opponents (to join the conspiracy)
103 **Sluiced** let flow ('sluice' = a dam or embankment with an adjustable gate)
   streams of blood Cf. 1.2.11–20.

Which blood, like sacrificing Abel's, cries
Even from the tongueless caverns of the earth   105
To me for justice and rough chastisement.
And by the glorious worth of my descent,
This arm shall do it or this life be spent.

RICHARD

How high a pitch his resolution soars!
Thomas of Norfolk, what sayst thou to this?   110

MOWBRAY

O let my sovereign turn away his face
And bid his ears a little while be deaf,
Till I have told this slander of his blood
How God and good men hate so foul a liar.

RICHARD

Mowbray, impartial are our eyes and ears.   115
Were he my brother, nay, my kingdom's heir,
As he is but my father's brother's son,
Now by my sceptre's awe, I make a vow
Such neighbour nearness to our sacred blood
Should nothing privilege him nor partialize   120
The unstooping firmness of my upright soul.
He is our subject, Mowbray, so art thou.
Free speech and fearless I to thee allow.

MOWBRAY

Then, Bolingbroke, as low as to thy heart,
Through the false passage of thy throat, thou liest.   125
Three parts of that receipt I had for Calais

---

104 Abel's, cries] Q4; Abel's‸ cries Q1, F   116 my kingdom's] Q1; our kingdomes F
118 by my] F; by Q1

104 **sacrificing Abel's** Abel sacrificed animals from his flock to God, which were preferred to Cain's offering of grain, so Cain slew Abel out of jealousy. Gloucester is compared to Abel, whose blood cried out from the ground for justice (Genesis 4: 10).

106 **To me** Since the demand for justice applies equally to Richard, Bolingbroke's phrase is an implicit rebuke of the King. **chastisement** correction, punishment

107 **descent** lineage

109 **pitch** the highest point of a falcon's flight. In performance, this line is often spoken with an ironic edge.

113 **slander of his blood** i.e. Bolingbroke's very being slanders the royal blood

116 **my kingdom's heir** A fairly obvious foreshadowing of the ouster of Richard by his cousin.

119 **neighbour nearness** extreme closeness ('neighbour' functions as an intensifier)

120 **nothing** in no way **partialize** prejudice

124–5 Varying the metaphor of jamming words down throats (44, 57), Mowbray imagines Bolingbroke's lies rising from his false heart through his equally false throat.

126 **receipt** money received

Disbursed I duly to his highness' soldiers;
The other part reserved I by consent,
For that my sovereign liege was in my debt
Upon remainder of a dear account   130
Since last I went to France to fetch his queen.
Now swallow down that lie. For Gloucester's death,
I slew him not, but to my own disgrace
Neglected my sworn duty in that case.
For you, my noble lord of Lancaster,   135
The honourable father to my foe,
Once did I lay an ambush for your life,
A trespass that doth vex my grievèd soul;
But ere I last received the sacrament
I did confess it and exactly begged   140
Your grace's pardon, and I hope I had it.
This is my fault. As for the rest appealed,
It issues from the rancour of a villain,
A recreant and most degenerate traitor,
Which in myself I boldly will defend   145
And interchangeably hurl down my gage
Upon this overweening traitor's foot
To prove myself a loyal gentleman
Even in the best blood chambered in his bosom.
       [*He throws down his gage. Bolingbroke takes it up*]

127 duly] Q1; *not in* Q2–F   133 not, but] Q2; not but Q1; not; but F my] Q1; mine Q2–F
137 did I] Q1; I did F   139 But] Q1*c*, F; Ah but Q1*u*   149.1] IRVING (*after* 146); *not in* Q1, F

128 **by consent** by agreement (with the King)
130 **remainder of a dear account** outstanding part of a significant debt
131 In 1395 Mowbray and Aumerle arranged Richard's marriage to the French King's daughter Isabel and spent large sums negotiating the match.
132–4 **For . . . case** Mowbray is being intentionally ambiguous about the real cause of Gloucester's death; he must protect not only himself but the King (in 1.2.37–9 Gaunt says the King 'caused' Gloucester's death). Mowbray suggests that he is responsible only because he failed to prevent Gloucester's murder while under his protection. His phrasing, however, might also suggest that he failed in his duty by *not* killing the Duke.
132 **For** as for

138 **grievèd** troubled, grieving
139 **sacrament** Eucharist
140 **confess** i.e. in a formal rite of confession in church
    exactly in precise terms
144 **recreant** faithless (or perhaps a noun = one who breaks faith)
145 **Which** The antecedent is ambiguous: it is either 'the rest' (142), in which case he is saying that he will defend himself in his own person ('in myself') against Bolingbroke's accusation, or it refers to Mowbray's charge against Bolingbroke in the previous two lines, which charge he will make good with his life.
146 **interchangeably** in exchange
147 **overweening** presumptuous
149 **Even . . . chambered** by shedding the best (i.e. royal) blood that is housed

In haste whereof most heartily I pray   150
Your highness to assign our trial day.

RICHARD

Wrath-kindled gentlemen, be ruled by me,
Let's purge this choler without letting blood.
This we prescribe, though no physician—
Deep malice makes too deep incision.   155
Forget, forgive, conclude and be agreed,
Our doctors say this is no month to bleed.
[*To Gaunt*] Good uncle, let this end where it begun,
We'll calm the Duke of Norfolk, you your son.

GAUNT

To be a make-peace shall become my age.   160
Throw down, my son, the Duke of Norfolk's gage.

RICHARD

And Norfolk, throw down his.

GAUNT   When, Harry, when?
Obedience bids I should not bid again.

RICHARD

Norfolk, throw down, we bid, there is no boot.

MOWBRAY [*kneeling*]

Myself I throw, dread sovereign, at thy foot: 165
My life thou shalt command, but not my shame.
The one my duty owes, but my fair name,
Despite of death, that lives upon my grave,
To dark dishonour's use thou shalt not have.
I am disgraced, impeached and baffled here,   170

---

152 gentlemen] F; gentleman Q1   157 month] Q1; time F   162–3 When . . . bids]
POPE; When Harry? when obedience bids. | Obedience bids Q1; When *Harrie* when?
Obedience bids, | Obedience bids F   165 *kneeling*] WELLS (*subs.*); *not in* Q1, F

152–7 Richard's slightly flippant tone in
this speech may be seen to cover up
his discomfort in the face of the proxy
attack being launched against him by
Bolingbroke.
153 Choler, or yellow bile, was traditionally
thought to be the physiological cause
of anger. Richard suggests that the antagonists should eliminate their mutual
anger without resorting to combat
('bloodletting'), but he does not specify
how. For the medical metaphor, see 51 n.

157 **no month to bleed** Medieval physicians
would consult almanacs to determine the
most favourable times for bloodletting.
This astrological practice had fallen into
disrepute by Shakespeare's time.
162 **When** An expression of impatience.
164 **boot** alternative
167–8 **my fair . . . grave** my noble name
(that like an epitaph) lives after me in
despite of death
170 **impeached and baffled** accused of a
felony and formally stripped of knighthood

Pierced to the soul with slander's venomed spear,
The which no balm can cure but his heart-blood
Which breathed this poison.

RICHARD   Rage must be withstood.
Give me his gage. Lions make leopards tame.

MOWBRAY
Yea, but not change his spots. Take but my shame   175
And I resign my gage. My dear dear lord,
The purest treasure mortal times afford
Is spotless reputation; that away,
Men are but gilded loam or painted clay.
A jewel in a ten-times-barred-up chest   180
Is a bold spirit in a loyal breast.
Mine honour is my life, both grow in one—
Take honour from me and my life is done.
Then, dear my liege, mine honour let me try;
In that I live and for that will I die.   185

RICHARD
Cousin, throw up your gage. Do you begin.

BOLINGBROKE
O, God defend my soul from such deep sin!
Shall I seem crestfallen in my father's sight,
Or with pale beggar fear impeach my height
Before this out-dared dastard? Ere my tongue   190

---

178 reputation;] F (*subs.*); Reputation, Q1   186 up] Q1; downe F   187 God] Q1; heauen F
deep] Q1; foule F

171–2 The imagery here draws oddly on the
    story of the crucifixion of Christ and the
    redeeming power of his blood. Mowbray
    recalls the piercing of Christ's side but
    imagines the redemptive blood issuing
    from the slanderer (Bolingbroke) rather
    than the sacrificial victim (himself).
174 **Lions . . . tame** Richard believes in the
    natural order that guarantees the dom-
    inance of the superior over the inferior
    creature, an assumption that maps
    unevenly onto the world of politics.
175–6 **Take . . . gage** only if you take my
    shame upon yourself will I surrender my
    gage
178 **spotless reputation** Dedication to good
    reputation was an abiding passion of
    Shakespeare's culture.
179 **gilded loam or painted clay** mere earth

    with a decorative coating of gold leaf or
    paint
180–1 Usual word order is inverted: the
    tenor ('a bold spirit') would normally
    precede the vehicle ('a jewel').
184 **try** test in combat
185 **that** i.e. his honour
186 **throw up** surrender or give up. The
    phrase perhaps indicates a staging in
    which Bolingbroke is asked to throw
    Mowbray's gage up to Richard on his
    raised dais; F's 'throw down' might
    derive from a different staging.
188 **crestfallen** humbled
189 **pale . . . height** i.e. disgrace my noble
    birth ('height') with low-born cowardice
190 **out-dared dastard** Bolingbroke asserts
    that he has surpassed the base coward
    ('dastard') Mowbray in daring.

Shall wound my honour with such feeble wrong,
Or sound so base a parley, my teeth shall tear
The slavish motive of recanting fear
And spit it bleeding in his high disgrace,
Where shame doth harbour, even in Mowbray's face.   195

RICHARD
We were not born to sue, but to command,
Which, since we cannot do to make you friends,
Be ready, as your lives shall answer it,
At Coventry, upon Saint Lambert's Day.
There shall your swords and lances arbitrate   200
The swelling difference of your settled hate.
Since we cannot atone you, we shall see
Justice design the victor's chivalry.
Lord Marshal, command our officers-at-arms
Be ready to direct these home alarms.   *Exeunt*   205

---

191 my] Q1; mine F   192 parley] Q1 (parlee); parle F   195 face.] Q1; face. | *Exit Gaunt.* F
202 we shall] Q1; you shall Q2–F   205 *Exeunt*] F; *Exit* Q1

---

192 **sound** call (as with a trumpet)
parley negotiations
193 **motive** moving limb or organ, specifically here the 'tongue' (190). Bolingbroke's threat recalls the climax of Kyd's *The Spanish Tragedy*, where Hieronymo bites off his own tongue in defiance (ed. J. R. Mulryne, New Mermaids (1989), 4.4.191–4).
recanting fear fear that would cause me to recant
194 **in his high disgrace** as a sign of Mowbray's extreme disgrace. Some commentators suggest that 'his' = its, i.e. the tongue's, which produces a contorted and unlikely sense.
195 F has Gaunt exit at this point, presumably to prepare for his entrance with the Duchess of Gloucester in 1.2. Because early modern staging required each scene to follow the preceding one without a pause, convention dictated that characters on stage at the end of one scene would not appear at the beginning of the next. Since Q1's mass exit at the end of this scene would require Gaunt to exit and immediately re-enter at the start of 1.2, most editors follow F. But the Duke's exit at 195 is difficult to account for in

both theatrical and psychological terms, since it seems unmotivated, especially given that the King is about to rule on his son's fate. One fairly simple way to deal with the apparent problem would be to separate Gaunt and his son's exit from that of the other characters at the end of the scene; they could perhaps go off first, followed by a formal exit on the part of the King and his entourage.
196 **sue** plead
198 **Be . . . it** (a) be prepared upon pain of death; (b) be prepared to defend your cause with your lives
199 **Saint Lambert's Day** 17 September
201 **swelling difference** growing antagonism
202 **atone** set at one, bring into concord (*OED* 1)
203 **design . . . chivalry** 'designate the winner in a chivalrous combat' (Ure). The trial by combat was based on the idea that divine justice would assure that the victor was indeed in the right. In Shakespeare's time duelling of any kind was no longer a sanctioned form of determining justice.
205 **home alarms** call to arms here in our native country

I.2 *Enter John of Gaunt with the Duchess of Gloucester*

GAUNT

Alas, the part I had in Woodstock's blood
Doth more solicit me than your exclaims
To stir against the butchers of his life.
But since correction lieth in those hands
Which made the fault that we cannot correct,   5
Put we our quarrel to the will of heaven
Who, when they see the hour's ripe on earth,
Will rain hot vengeance on offenders' heads.

DUCHESS

Finds brotherhood in thee no sharper spur?
Hath love in thy old blood no living fire?   10
Edward's seven sons, whereof thyself art one,

1.2] F (*Scaena Secunda*); *not in* Q1   0.1 *Enter ... Gloucester*] Q1; *Enter Gaunt, and Duchesse of Gloucester.* F   1 Woodstock's] Q1 (Woodstockes); Glousters F   7 hour's] Q4 (hower's); houres Q1–3, F

1.2 This short scene, which is not in Holinshed, provides the crucial piece of information that is missing from 1.1: that the King was responsible, though whether 'wrongfully' (39) or not is left uncertain, for the killing of his uncle Gloucester, Thomas of Woodstock. The scene's intimacy contrasts strongly with the public quality of the preceding and following scenes and throws into relief how public, courtly speaking tends to obscure rather than reveal the truth. It also introduces the note of women's grieving, which will be forcefully elaborated by the Queen later in the play.

1 **part . . . blood** Gaunt was Woodstock's brother; 'part' = share. This is the only instance in the play where the name Woodstock is used; F regularizes to 'Glousters'.

2 **solicit** entreat or petition (*OED* 2a)

3 **stir** act

4–5 **correction . . . correct** the right to punish the wrongdoer lies with him who is responsible for the crime which we cannot ourselves punish

6 **Put we** let us refer

6–7 **heaven . . . they** The shift from singular noun 'heaven' to plural pronoun 'they' is unusual; presumably, Gaunt is thinking of an entity such as 'heavenly powers'.

7 **see . . . earth** decide that the time for retribution has come

8 **rain hot vengeance** The metaphor recalls the divine punishment of Sodom and Gomorrah (Genesis 19: 24–5) and looks ahead to the play's elaboration of rain as both bloodshed and nurture (see 3.3.42–6, 5.6.45–6).

9–36 The Duchess's speech is an artful expression of grieving and also an argument for action. It combines a general appeal to Gaunt's family pride; an ethical argument about the duties of individuals to their siblings, their mothers, and especially the memory of their fathers; and a politically savvy reminder that Gaunt's failure to act will put his own life in danger.

9 **spur** provocation

10 **old . . . fire** According to humoral theory, the blood of the old was cooler and less plentiful than the blood of the young, with its 'living fire'.

11–21 This image of branches containing the blood of the seven sons of Edward III, of which Gaunt and Thomas are two, draws on the tradition of the genealogical tree, and especially the biblical Tree of Jesse, whose topmost branch was the Messiah. See Isaiah 11: 1.

Were as seven vials of his sacred blood,
Or seven fair branches springing from one root.
Some of those seven are dried by nature's course,
Some of those branches by the destinies cut,   15
But Thomas, my dear lord, my life, my Gloucester,
One vial full of Edward's sacred blood,
One flourishing branch of his most royal root,
Is cracked and all the precious liquor spilt,
Is hacked down and his summer leaves all faded,   20
By envy's hand and murder's bloody axe.
Ah Gaunt, his blood was thine! That bed, that womb,
That mettle, that self mould that fashioned thee,
Made him a man; and though thou liv'st and breath'st,
Yet art thou slain in him. Thou dost consent   25
In some large measure to thy father's death
In that thou seest thy wretched brother die,
Who was the model of thy father's life.
Call it not patience, Gaunt, it is despair.
In suff'ring thus thy brother to be slaughtered   30
Thou show'st the naked pathway to thy life,
Teaching stern murder how to butcher thee.
That which in mean men we entitle patience
Is pale cold cowardice in noble breasts.
What shall I say? To safeguard thine own life   35
The best way is to venge my Gloucester's death.

---

24 liv'st and breath'st] F; liuest and breathest Q1   31 show'st] F (*subs.*); shewest Q1

12 **vials** glass vessels (often associated in Christian iconography with sacred, restorative blood)

15 **the destinies** the three fates (one of whom wielded shears to cut the thread of human life)

16–21 In contrast to the natural deaths of some of the sons of Edward III, Gloucester died by violence. Note that 19 follows from 17 as 20 continues 18.

21 **envy's** malevolence's

22–4 The obligation that binds Gaunt and Gloucester is founded on the fact that they were conceived of a single married couple ('bed') and formed in the womb of the same woman.

23 **mettle** Both the substance out of which they were formed and the character or disposition (*OED* 1) that they inherited. **self mould** 'selfsame mould (as in casting metal), i.e. the womb' (Forker)

27 **seest** watch passively

28 **model** smaller copy (*OED n.* 2a)

30–2 **In . . . thee** In passively enduring your brother's murder, you invite his murderers to murder you.

31 **naked** open, defenceless

33 **mean** low-born

34 **pale cold cowardice** Cowardice is associated with a humoral deficit—a lack of blood (making the complexion 'pale') and a corresponding deficiency of heat.

GAUNT

God's is the quarrel, for God's substitute,
His deputy anointed in his sight,
Hath caused his death, the which if wrongfully
Let heaven revenge, for I may never lift   40
An angry arm against his minister.

DUCHESS

Where then, alas, may I complain myself?

GAUNT

To God, the widow's champion and defence.

DUCHESS

Why then I will. Farewell, old Gaunt.
Thou goest to Coventry, there to behold   45
Our cousin Hereford and fell Mowbray fight.
O, sit my husband's wrongs on Hereford's spear
That it may enter butcher Mowbray's breast!
Or if misfortune miss the first career,
Be Mowbray's sins so heavy in his bosom   50
That they may break his foaming courser's back
And throw the rider headlong in the lists,
A caitiff recreant to my cousin Hereford.
Farewell, old Gaunt. Thy sometimes brother's wife
With her companion, grief, must end her life.   55

---

37 God's . . . God's] QI (Gods); Heauens . . . heauens F   42 alas] QI*c*, F; *not in* QI*u* complain] QI; complaint F   43 God] QI; heauen F and] QI; to F   47 sit] F; set QI
48 butcher] QI*c*, F; butchers QI*u*

37–41 Gaunt reminds the Duchess that
avenging Gloucester's death would mean
challenging God's lieutenant, who was
'anointed' (38) with holy oil in the
coronation ceremony, and therefore
defying divine authority.

37 God's . . . quarrel the dispute is in God's
hands

39 the . . . wrongfully if the killing of
Gloucester was indeed unjust

41 minister representative or proxy, here the
King

42 Where to whom
complain myself complain

43 widow's champion The idea is commonplace; cf. Psalm 68: 5.

44 The Duchess says farewell here but
extends the parting for a further 30 lines.

46 fell fierce, ruthless

47 sit . . . spear may the weight of my
husband's murder be fixed on Bolingbroke's lance (adding force to the blow)

49 miss . . . career should miss Mowbray
during the first charge
career charge of the horses toward one
another in a joust

51 foaming courser steed frothing at the
mouth with exertion

52 lists fencing that surrounded a tilting
ground

53 caitiff recreant captive and villainous
coward

54 sometimes i.e. deceased

GAUNT

  Sister, farewell. I must to Coventry.

  As much good stay with thee as go with me.

DUCHESS

  Yet one word more. Grief boundeth where it falls,

  Not with the empty hollowness, but weight.

  I take my leave before I have begun,   60

  For sorrow ends not when it seemeth done.

  Commend me to thy brother, Edmund York.

  Lo, this is all. Nay, yet depart not so;

  Though this be all, do not so quickly go.

  I shall remember more. Bid him—ah what?—   65

  With all good speed at Pleshey visit me.

  Alack, and what shall good old York there see

  But empty lodgings and unfurnished walls,

  Unpeopled offices, untrodden stones,

  And what hear there for welcome but my groans?   70

  Therefore commend me; let him not come there

  To seek out sorrow that dwells everywhere.

  Desolate, desolate will I hence and die.

  The last leave of thee takes my weeping eye.   *Exeunt*

---

58 it] Q2–F; is Q1   59 empty] Q1c, F; emptines, Q1u   60 begun] Q2–F; begone Q1
62 thy] Q1; my Q2–F   65 ah] Q1; Oh F   70 hear] Q1c, F; cheere Q1u

---

58–9 **Grief . . . weight** The metaphor of grief, an important and recurrent motif in the play, as a heavy, bouncing ball (*boundeth* = rebounds) is odd but conveys well how expressions of sorrow do not alleviate the sorrow but arouse the need to give voice to it again. The poignancy of the Duchess's reluctance to let Gaunt part from her registers her need to keep talking about her loss.

60 **before . . . begun** almost before I have started (to lament)

65–71 Sorrow makes the Duchess vacillate about inviting her brother-in-law York to Pleshey (the Gloucester country home in

Essex). At 71 she decides that he should not visit.

68 **unfurnished** i.e. without tapestries

69 **Unpeopled offices** duties with no one to perform them

70 **hear** Q1's presumably uncorrected reading, 'cheere' (= welcome), is possible, though the parallel with 'what . . . see' (67) suggests that 'hear' is correct.

71 **commend me** extend my greetings (to York)

74 **The . . . eye** The syntax is inverted: 'eye' is the subject of 'takes'. The Duchess has a premonition of her own death as well perhaps of Gaunt's.

1.3 *Enter Lord Marshal and the Duke Aumerle*

LORD MARSHAL

My lord Aumerle, is Harry Hereford armed?

AUMERLE

Yea, at all points, and longs to enter in.

LORD MARSHAL

The Duke of Norfolk, sprightfully and bold,

Stays but the summons of the appellant's trumpet.

AUMERLE

Why then, the champions are prepared and stay   5

For nothing but his majesty's approach.

> *The trumpets sound and [Richard] enters with his nobles,*
> *Gaunt, Bushy, Bagot, Green and others. When they*
> *are set, enter Mowbray, the Duke of Norfolk, in arms,*
> *defendant, [with a] herald*

RICHARD

Marshal, demand of yonder champion

The cause of his arrival here in arms.

Ask him his name and orderly proceed

To swear him in the justice of his cause.   10

1.3] F (*Scena Tertia*); *not in* Q1   0.1 *Enter . . . Aumerle*] Q1; *Enter Marshall, and Aumerle* F
1 LORD MARSHAL] OXFORD; *Mar.* Q1, F (*so throughout scene*)   6.1 *The . . . nobles*] Q1; *Flourish.*
| *Enter King* F   6.1 *Richard*] Q1 (*the King*)   6.2 *Gaunt . . . others*] F; *not in* Q1   6.2–4 *When*
. . . defendant] Q1 (*omitting 'Mowbray'*); *Then Mowbray in Armor* F   6.4 *with a herald*] F (*and*
Harrold); *not in* Q1   7 RICHARD] F (*Rich.*); *King* Q1 (*so until* 5.1)

1.3 The scene condenses the four-day tournament described by Holinshed but retains its rich chivalric detail. Since Shakespeare's playhouse did not use stage scenery, the performance would have conveyed to the audience a sense of the organized, ceremonial space of the 'lists' (with its enclosing fence, lengthwise barrier, and tents for the combatants) by means of the formalistic placement, movement, and speech of the elaborately costumed actors. The text indicates that the King presides from a raised platform or throne (54), so that kind of stage property can be assumed; at 120 the King orders Bolingbroke and Mowbray back to their 'chairs' so those properties are also probably on the stage.

2 **at all points** completely (armed)
enter in enter the lists (see headnote)
3 **sprightfully** in good spirits
4 **Stays** awaits
appellant's accuser's (Bolingbroke's)
6.1–2 *The trumpets . . . others* The King's entry is marked by a fanfare of trumpets, instruments appropriate for a trial-by-combat. The stage directions of the early texts pay careful attention to sound and spectacle in this scene.
6.3–4 *enter Mowbray . . . defendant* According to the normal rules of combat, the defendant, Mowbray, would wait for the appellant's trumpet, but in this case he enters before his accuser.
10 **swear him in** have him swear an oath as to

LORD MARSHAL [*to Mowbray*]
  In God's name and the King's, say who thou art,
  And why thou com'st thus knightly clad in arms,
  Against what man thou com'st, and what thy quarrel.
  Speak truly on thy knighthood and thy oath,
  As so defend thee heaven and thy valour.   15
MOWBRAY
  My name is Thomas Mowbray, Duke of Norfolk,
  Who hither come engagèd by my oath—
  Which God defend a knight should violate—
  Both to defend my loyalty and truth
  To God, my King and my succeeding issue,   20
  Against the Duke of Hereford that appeals me,
  And by the grace of God and this mine arm
  To prove him, in defending of myself,
  A traitor to my God, my King, and me—
  And as I truly fight, defend me heaven.   25
     The trumpets sound. Enter [Bolingbroke,] Duke of
     Hereford, appellant, in armour [with a] herald
RICHARD
  Marshal, ask yonder knight in arms
  Both who he is and why he cometh hither
  Thus plated in habiliments of war,
  And formally, according to our law,
  Depose him in the justice of his cause.   30
LORD MARSHAL [*to Bolingbroke*]
  What is thy name, and wherefore com'st thou hither
  Before King Richard in his royal lists?

---

11 *to Mowbray*] WELLS; *not in* Q1, F   13 what thy] Q1; what's thy Q2–F   14 thy oath]
Q1; thine oath F   15 thee] Q1 (the), F   17 come] Q1; comes F   18 God] Q1; heauen F
20 my succeeding] Q1; his succeeding F   25.1–2 *The . . . armour*] Q1; *Tucket. Enter Hereford*
F   25.1 *Bolingbroke*] ROWE; *not in* Q1, F   25.2 *with a herald*] F (*and Harold*); *not in* Q1
28 plated] Q1; placed F   29 formally] Q1; formerly Q5, F   31 *to Bolingbroke*] WELLS; *not in*
Q1, F

---

15 **As . . . valour** let heaven and your valour
  attest to the truth of your oath (the word
  order is inverted)
18 **defend** forbid
20 **my succeeding issue** my heirs. F has
  'his' (i.e. the King's) issue, which is
  also possible. Johnson thought that
  'Mowbray's issue was, by this accusation,

in danger of an attainder, and therefore
he might come among other reasons for
their sake'.
21 **appeals** accuses
28 **plated** armoured
  habiliments accoutrements
30 **Depose him in** take his deposition
  concerning

Against whom com'st thou, and what's thy quarrel?
Speak like a true knight, so defend thee heaven.

BOLINGBROKE

Harry of Hereford, Lancaster and Derby 35
Am I, who ready here do stand in arms
To prove by God's grace and my body's valour
In lists, on Thomas Mowbray, Duke of Norfolk,
That he is a traitor foul and dangerous
To God of heaven, King Richard and to me; 40
And as I truly fight, defend me heaven.

LORD MARSHAL

On pain of death, no person be so bold
Or daring-hardy as to touch the lists,
Except the Marshal and such officers
Appointed to direct these fair designs. 45

BOLINGBROKE

Lord Marshal, let me kiss my sovereign's hand
And bow my knee before his majesty,
For Mowbray and myself are like two men
That vow a long and weary pilgrimage;
Then let us take a ceremonious leave 50
And loving farewell of our several friends.

LORD MARSHAL

The appellant in all duty greets your highness
And craves to kiss your hand and take his leave.

RICHARD

We will descend and fold him in our arms.
[*He descends and embraces Bolingbroke*]
Cousin of Hereford, as thy cause is right 55
So be thy fortune in this royal fight.

---

33 com'st] F; comes Q1   39 he is] Q1; he's F   43 daring-hardy] THEOBALD; daring, hardy
Q1; daring hardie F   54.1 *He . . . Bolingbroke*] OXFORD (*subs.*); *not in* Q1, F   55 right]
Q1; iust F

43 **daring-hardy** rash
   touch interfere with
45 **fair designs** formal proceedings (i.e. the
   trial-by-combat)
51 **several** various

54 Richard's descent here indicates the presence of a raised platform.
55–6 **as . . . fortune** if your cause is just, may
   you succeed
56 **royal fight** The duel is 'royal' because of
   Richard's presence.

Farewell, my blood—which if today thou shed
Lament we may, but not revenge thee dead.

BOLINGBROKE

O, let no noble eye profane a tear
For me, if I be gored with Mowbray's spear.   60
As confident as is the falcon's flight
Against a bird do I with Mowbray fight.
[*To Lord Marshal*] My loving lord, I take my leave of you,
[*To Aumerle*] Of you, my noble cousin, Lord Aumerle,
Not sick although I have to do with death,   65
But lusty, young and cheerly drawing breath.
Lo, as at English feasts, so I regreet
The daintiest last to make the end most sweet.
[*To Gaunt*] O thou, the earthly author of my blood,
Whose youthful spirit in me regenerate,   70
Doth with a twofold vigour lift me up
To reach at victory above my head,
Add proof unto mine armour with thy prayers,
And with thy blessings steel my lance's point
That it may enter Mowbray's waxen coat   75
And furbish new the name of John of Gaunt
Even in the lusty haviour of his son.

---

63 *To Lord Marshal*] MALONE; *not in* Q1, F   64 *To Aumerle*] WELLS; *not in* Q1, F   69 *To Gaunt*]
COLLIER; *not in* Q1, F   earthly] Q1; earthy F   71 vigour] Q1; rigor F   76 furbish]
Q1; furnish F   of Gaunt] CAPELL; a Gaunt Q1, F

57–8 Richard says farewell to his 'blood' relation, Bolingbroke, and then, playing on the literal meaning of blood, declares that if Bolingbroke dies, Richard will not revenge his death (since the trial-by-combat is assumed to yield a divinely sanctioned judgement).

59 **profane a tear** i.e. it would be impious to weep if he is killed since his defeat would prove him a liar

63 While Bolingbroke could be speaking to Aumerle here, in which case 64 would simply repeat the leave-taking, it is more likely that he is addressing the Lord Marshal, who is a close ally (see 251–2), though the latter's position demands that he remain impartial during the combat.

65–6 **Not . . . breath** Addressed both to Aumerle and more generally to the assembled company.

67–8 Turning to his father he declares that he has saved the best till last (*regreet* =

salute). Gurr quotes Francis Bacon: 'Let not this Parliament end, like a Dutch feast, in salt meats, but like an English feast, in sweet meats' (Bacon, 3.215).

69 **earthly author** i.e. the creator of Bolingbroke on earth, as opposed to his divine 'author'

69–70 **blood . . . spirit** In humoral theory, the substances of blood and spirit could be allied rather than opposed (*OED n.* 16a); Gaunt's 'spirit' is therefore of a piece with the earthly blood he authored in his son.

70 **regenerate** reborn
71 **twofold** both father's and son's
73 **proof** impenetrability
74 **steel** harden
75 **waxen** i.e. as if it were made of wax (rather than chain-mail)
76 **furbish** polish
77 **lusty haviour** vigorous deportment

GAUNT

God in thy good cause make thee prosperous!
Be swift like lightning in the execution
And let thy blows, doubly redoubled,   80
Fall like amazing thunder on the casque
Of thy adverse pernicious enemy.
Rouse up thy youthful blood, be valiant and live.

BOLINGBROKE

Mine innocence and Saint George to thrive!

MOWBRAY

However God or Fortune cast my lot,   85
There lives or dies, true to King Richard's throne,
A loyal, just and upright gentleman.
Never did captive with a freer heart
Cast off his chains of bondage and embrace
His golden uncontrolled enfranchisement   90
More than my dancing soul doth celebrate
This feast of battle with mine adversary.
Most mighty liege, and my companion peers,
Take from my mouth the wish of happy years.
As gentle and as jocund as to jest   95
Go I to fight. Truth hath a quiet breast.

RICHARD

Farewell my lord. Securely I espy
Virtue with valour couchèd in thine eye.
Order the trial, Marshal, and begin.

LORD MARSHAL

Harry of Hereford, Lancaster and Derby,   100
Receive thy lance, and God defend the right.

78 God] Q1; Heauen F   82 adverse] Q1; amaz'd F   85, 101 God] Q1; heauen F
86 King] Q1; Kings F   101 the] Q1; thy Q2–F

81 **amazing** stupefying
  casque helmet
84 **Mine . . . thrive** May the truth of my
  cause and Saint George (the patron saint
  of England) help me succeed.
85 **God or Fortune** Mowbray introduces a
  note of doubt into the proceeding by
  suggesting that the outcome might be
  the result of either divine judgement or
  chance.
90 **golden . . . enfranchisement** precious
  unrestrained freedom

95 **As . . . jest** as mildly and cheerfully as
  I would were I going merely to amuse
  myself (see *OED*, jest, *v*. 4b)
97 **Securely** with confidence (a 'squinting'
  adverb that may modify *espy* or *couchèd*)
98 **couchèd** lodged
100–16 The lances are formally handed to
  the combatants, and then the Heralds,
  speaking for Bolingbroke and Mowbray,
  officially reiterate the charges.

BOLINGBROKE

Strong as a tower in hope, I cry amen.

LORD MARSHAL [*to an attendant*]

Go bear this lance to Thomas, Duke of Norfolk.

FIRST HERALD

Harry of Hereford, Lancaster and Derby

Stands here for God, his sovereign and himself,   105

On pain to be found false and recreant,

To prove the Duke of Norfolk, Thomas Mowbray,

A traitor to his God, his King and him,

And dares him to set forward to the fight.

SECOND HERALD

Here standeth Thomas Mowbray, Duke of Norfolk,   110

On pain to be found false and recreant,

Both to defend himself and to approve

Henry of Hereford, Lancaster and Derby

To God, his sovereign and to him disloyal,

Courageously and with a free desire,   115

Attending but the signal to begin.

LORD MARSHAL

Sound, trumpets, and set forward, combatants!

    A charge sounded

Stay. The King hath thrown his warder down.

RICHARD

Let them lay by their helmets and their spears

And both return back to their chairs again.   120

Withdraw with us and let the trumpets sound

---

103 *to an attendant*] CAPELL (*subs.*); *not in* Q1, F   104 FIRST HERALD] F (*subs.*); *Herald* Q1
108 his God] Q1*c*, F; God Q1*u*   109 forward] Q1; forwards Q2–F   110 SECOND HERALD] Q1
(*Herald* 2), F (2. *Har.*)   117.1 *A charge sounded*] F (*after* 116); *not in* Q1; *placed here* RANN

102 **Strong . . . hope** Cf. Psalm 61: 3: 'For thou hast been my hope and a strong tower against the enemy'.

112 **approve** prove

117–20 This moment poses a problem of staging, since horses seem required but were probably not used. It is likely that the Marshal's command to 'set forward' would be an invitation for Bolingbroke and Mowbray, who have presumably been either sitting or standing in front of their 'chairs' (120), to make their way to the lists (which may be imagined as occupying the downstage platform, the space of the yard, or, perhaps, some unspecified space behind the stage). But before that happens, while the 'charge' is being 'sounded' (i.e. while the trumpet is calling the two men to the fight), the King interrupts the proceedings, throwing down a ritual truncheon ('warder'). This is a moment of calculated disappointment for the antagonists, the on-stage onlookers and the audience, since it breaks the dramatic arc that has been building toward the fight.

While we return these dukes what we decree.
   A long flourish. [Richard confers apart with Gaunt and
    other nobles]
Draw near,
And list what with our council we have done.
For that our kingdom's earth should not be soiled   125
With that dear blood which it hath fosterèd,
And for our eyes do hate the dire aspect
Of civil wounds ploughed up with neighbour's sword,
And for we think the eagle-wingèd pride
Of sky-aspiring and ambitious thoughts,   130
With rival-hating envy, set on you
To wake our peace, which in our country's cradle
Draws the sweet infant breath of gentle sleep,
Which so roused up with boist'rous untuned drums,
With harsh resounding trumpets' dreadful bray   135
And grating shock of wrathful iron arms,
Might from our quiet confines fright fair peace,
And make us wade even in our kindred's blood:

122.1 *A long flourish*] F; *not in* Q1   122.1–2 *Richard . . . nobles*] WELLS (*subs.*); *not in* Q1, F
123–4 Draw near, | And list what] *as* THEOBALD; Draw neere and list | What Q1, F
128 civil] Q1*c*, F; cruell Q1*u* sword] Q1; swords F   129–33 And for . . . sleep] Q1; *not
in* F   133 Draws] Q1*c*; Draw Q1*u*   136 wrathful iron] Q1*c*, F; harsh resounding Q1*u*

122 **While we return** until we 'state by way
of a report or verdict' (*OED v.* 16a)
122.1–2 The performers must decide how
much stage-time to give to this consultation. Holinshed, whom Shakespeare is
following and condensing, says that the
council withdrew for 'two long hours'
while Bolingbroke and Mowbray remained in their chairs, cooling their heels
(p. 495). Shakespeare transforms the
conference into a mimed discussion that
must, given the necessities of the stage,
be brief. The '*long flourish*' (extended
trumpeting) no doubt helped to cover
the consultation, as well perhaps as some
business involving the combatants, who
might, for example, be conferring with
their subordinates or taking off some of
their armour. However this is handled, it
is clear from 123–4 that a decision has
been taken, even though, realistically,
such a momentous verdict could never
be thrashed out in such a short time.

What we get is therefore a kind of re-
capitulation or symbolic replay.
123–38 The King's accusation that the two
men have been fomenting civil war is
startling, especially given the respectful
tone of the exchanges leading up to this
point as well as the formality of the trial-
by-combat itself. The vehemence of the
speech in part gives vent to the discomfort Richard must have experienced
in the face of both the veiled attack made
on him by Bolingbroke in 1.1 and the two
adversaries' refusal to back down from
their quarrel.
124 **list** listen to
125 **For that** so that
127, 129 **for** since
129 **eagle-wingèd** high flying, with perhaps
a glance at the idea that such pride
belongs properly only to the king (eagle =
king of birds)
131 **set on** prompted
136 **shock** collision

Therefore we banish you our territories.
You, cousin Hereford, upon pain of life,   140
Till twice five summers have enriched our fields
Shall not regreet our fair dominions,
But tread the stranger paths of banishment.

BOLINGBROKE
Your will be done. This must my comfort be:
That sun that warms you here shall shine on me   145
And those his golden beams to you here lent
Shall point on me and gild my banishment.

RICHARD
Norfolk, for thee remains a heavier doom,
Which I with some unwillingness pronounce.
The sly slow hours shall not determinate   150
The dateless limit of thy dear exile;
The hopeless word of 'never to return'
Breathe I against thee, upon pain of life.

MOWBRAY
A heavy sentence, my most sovereign liege,
And all unlooked for from your highness' mouth.   155
A dearer merit, not so deep a maim
As to be cast forth in the common air,
Have I deservèd at your highness' hands.

---

140 life] Q1; death F

140 **of life** i.e. of losing your life
142 **regreet** return to
143 **stranger** foreign
144–7 'Bolingbroke's ambitious hope,' Coleridge commented, 'not yet shaped into definite plan, [is] beautifully contrasted with Mowbray's desolation' (p. 133).
144 **Your . . . done** Bolingbroke echoes the Lord's Prayer, probably with some irony.
146–7 Bolingbroke's acerbic comment implies that the sun's 'golden beams' are merely lent to the King, while Bolingbroke will retain on his person the gold provided by the foreign sun.
148 **doom** judgement
149 **with some unwillingness** 'Richard here makes his only concession to the debt which Mowbray has been hinting he owes' (Gurr).

150 **sly** stealthy
determinate put an end to
151 **dateless** without end
dear painful, deeply felt
155 As someone who has served the King's design and kept his counsel, Mowbray is understandably surprised by the harshness of the sentence. Holinshed tells us that '[Mowbray] was in hope, as writers report, that he should have been borne out [supported] in the matter by the King, which when it fell out otherwise, it grieved him not a little' (p. 495).
156 **dearer merit** greater reward
maim wound
157 **cast . . . air** i.e. cast out of England into a place where there are no meaningful distinctions of individual merit (*common* = 'belonging to all mankind alike' (*OED a.* 1b))

The language I have learned these forty years,
My native English, now I must forgo, 160
And now my tongue's use is to me no more
Than an unstringèd viol or a harp,
Or like a cunning instrument cased up
Or, being open, put into his hands
That knows no touch to tune the harmony. 165
Within my mouth you have enjailed my tongue,
Doubly portcullised with my teeth and lips,
And dull unfeeling barren ignorance
Is made my jailer to attend on me.
I am too old to fawn upon a nurse, 170
Too far in years to be a pupil now.
What is thy sentence then but speechless death,
Which robs my tongue from breathing native breath?

RICHARD

It boots thee not to be compassionate.
After our sentence, plaining comes too late. 175

MOWBRAY

Then thus I turn me from my country's light
To dwell in solemn shades of endless night.

RICHARD

Return again and take an oath with thee.
    [*To both Mowbray and Bolingbroke*]

---

172 sentence then] F; sentence Q1   178.1 *To . . . Bolingbroke*] WELLS (*subs.*; *before* 178)

159–73 The anachronism of a fourteenth-century English noble not knowing at least French in addition to English is of a piece with Shakespeare's elaboration of an Anglocentric history. The speech itself plays off its copious poetic invention (as if Mowbray were relishing his last chance *to speak*) against its message of despair.

161–5 Once Mowbray is exiled from the community of English speakers, his tongue will be like a musical instrument without strings, a skilfully-made ('cunning') instrument locked in a case, or put in the hands of one with no musical training.

166–9 The image of an instrument shut in a case leads to the idea of the 'enjailed'

tongue, 'Doubly portcullised' behind the teeth and lips and guarded by a personified 'ignorance' (a portcullis is an iron grille that could be lowered across a castle gateway).

170 **nurse** servant in charge of a child in its first years, and thus likely to teach it to speak

172 **sentence** verdict (punning on the grammatical sense)

173 **breathing native breath** speaking English as well as breathing English air

174 **boots** helps, avails
compassionate sorrowful (*OED a.* 1c)

175 **plaining** making a formal complaint

178 **take . . . thee** i.e. swear an oath and carry its force with you into exile

Lay on our royal sword your banished hands:
Swear by the duty that you owe to God—   180
Our part therein we banish with yourselves—
To keep the oath that we administer:
You never shall, so help you truth and God,
Embrace each other's love in banishment,
Nor never look upon each other's face,   185
Nor never write, regreet, nor reconcile
This louring tempest of your home-bred hate,
Nor never by advisèd purpose meet
To plot, contrive or complot any ill
'Gainst us, our state, our subjects or our land.   190

BOLINGBROKE
  I swear.
MOWBRAY
  And I, to keep all this.
BOLINGBROKE
  Norfolk, so far as to mine enemy:
  By this time, had the King permitted us,
  One of our souls had wandered in the air,   195
  Banished this frail sepulchre of our flesh,
  As now our flesh is banished from this land.
  Confess thy treasons ere thou fly the realm—
  Since thou hast far to go, bear not along
  The clogging burden of a guilty soul.   200
MOWBRAY
  No, Bolingbroke, if ever I were traitor,

---

180 you owe] F; y'owe Q1   180, 183 God] Q1; heauen F   185, 186, 188 never] Q1; euer F
186 nor] Q1; or F   193 far] F2 (farre); fare Q1, F   198 the] Q1; this F

---

179 The hilt of a sword forms the shape of
  a cross, making it an appropriate object
  upon which to swear an oath.
181 Richard allows that he can no longer
  expect loyalty (the 'duty' of the previous
  line) from Bolingbroke and Mowbray
  now that they are banished.
185 **Nor never** The double negative (repeated
  in 186 and 188) is an intensifier.
186 **regreet** meet again
187 **louring** threatening

188 **advisèd** deliberate
189 **complot any ill** collaborate in any evil
  design
193 **so . . . enemy** I will say this to you even
  though we are enemies.
196 **Banished . . . flesh** banished from the
  flesh which is its tomb. The body as the
  'sepulchre' of the soul is a commonplace.
200 **clogging** encumbering; clog = weight
  fastened to a prisoner's leg to prevent
  escape.

My name be blotted from the book of life
And I from heaven banished as from hence.
But what thou art, God, thou and I do know,
And all too soon, I fear, the King shall rue.   205
Farewell, my liege. Now no way can I stray;
Save back to England, all the world's my way.   *Exit*

RICHARD
Uncle, even in the glasses of thine eyes
I see thy grievèd heart. Thy sad aspect
Hath from the number of his banished years   210
Plucked four away. [*To Bolingbroke*] Six frozen winters
    spent,
Return with welcome home from banishment.

BOLINGBROKE
How long a time lies in one little word!
Four lagging winters and four wanton springs
End in a word—such is the breath of kings.   215

GAUNT
I thank my liege that in regard of me
He shortens four years of my son's exile.
But little vantage shall I reap thereby,
For ere the six years that he hath to spend
Can change their moons and bring their times about,   220
My oil-dried lamp and time-bewasted light
Shall be extinct with age and endless night.
My inch of taper will be burnt and done
And blindfold death not let me see my son.

RICHARD
Why, uncle, thou hast many years to live.   225

204 God] Q1; heauen F   211 *To Bolingbroke*] JOHNSON; *not in* Q1, F   222 night] Q4–F;
nightes Q1

202 **My name be** let my name be
    book of life In Revelation 3: 5, a promise
    is made to those who are saved that their
    names will not be blotted out of the book
    of life. Those whose names are blotted
    will suffer damnation.
205 **rue** regret
206–7 **Now . . . way** 'I can never go astray
    now, except in returning to England; I
    am free to wander anywhere in the
    world' (Ure).
208 **glasses** windows
209 **sad aspect** sorrowful look

214 **wanton** bountifully growing, sprightly
220 **bring . . . about** can cycle through the
    seasons
221 **oil-dried** empty of oil
    time-bewasted exhausted by age (cf. time-
    honoured, 1.1.1)
222 **extinct** extinguished
223 **taper** candle
224 **blindfold death** The phrase refers to
    both the traditional image of death as an
    unseeing skull and the blindness of the
    dead.

GAUNT

But not a minute, King, that thou canst give.
Shorten my days thou canst with sullen sorrow
And pluck nights from me, but not lend a morrow.
Thou canst help time to furrow me with age
But stop no wrinkle in his pilgrimage.   230
Thy word is current with him for my death,
But dead, thy kingdom cannot buy my breath.

RICHARD

Thy son is banished upon good advice,
Whereto thy tongue a party-verdict gave.
Why at our justice seem'st thou then to lour?   235

GAUNT

Things sweet to taste prove in digestion sour.
You urged me as a judge, but I had rather
You would have bid me argue like a father.
O, had it been a stranger, not my child,
To smooth his fault I should have been more mild;   240
A partial slander sought I to avoid
And in the sentence my own life destroyed.
Alas, I looked when some of you should say
I was too strict to make mine own away,
But you gave leave to my unwilling tongue   245
Against my will to do myself this wrong.

RICHARD

Cousin, farewell, and uncle, bid him so.
Six years we banish him, and he shall go.

Flourish. Exit [*Richard and his train*]

227 sullen] Q1; sudden F   239–42 O . . . destroyed.] Q1; *not in* F   239 had it] THEOBALD;
had't Q1   241 sought] Q1C; ought Q1U   248.1 *Flourish*] F; *not in* Q1 *Exit*] Q1C, F (*placed
before* '*Flourish.*'); *not in* Q1U *Richard and his train*] CAPELL (*subs.*); *not in* Q1, F

226–8 Gaunt comments on the limitations
of royal power: the King can take time
away from his subjects by causing them
to die, but he cannot give them even a
minute of additional time.
226 **King** Gaunt's lack of decorum under-
scores his sorrowful anger; the effect
is intensified by his use of the second
person ('thou'), to which compare the
more formal third-person address of
216–17.
230 **his** its (time's)
231–2 **Thy . . . breath** Your word is currency

that can buy my death, but once I am
dead, nothing can buy my life back.
234 **party-verdict** i.e. Gaunt supported the
banishment of his son; *party-verdict* =
one person's part of a joint verdict (*OED*,
party, *n.* C1b).
237 **urged me** pressed me for my opinion
241 **partial slander** accusation of bias
243–4 **I looked . . . away** i.e. Gaunt hoped
that the other lords would compensate
for his strict impartiality by voting
against banishment.
245 **gave . . . tongue** accepted my reluctant
advice

AUMERLE

   Cousin, farewell. What presence must not know,

   From where you do remain let paper show.   [*Exit*]   250

LORD MARSHAL

   My lord, no leave take I, for I will ride

   As far as land will let me by your side.

GAUNT

   O, to what purpose dost thou hoard thy words

   That thou return'st no greeting to thy friends?

BOLINGBROKE

   I have too few to take my leave of you,   255

   When the tongue's office should be prodigal

   To breathe the abundant dolour of the heart.

GAUNT

   Thy grief is but thy absence for a time.

BOLINGBROKE

   Joy absent, grief is present for that time.

GAUNT

   What is six winters? They are quickly gone.   260

BOLINGBROKE

   To men in joy, but grief makes one hour ten.

GAUNT

   Call it a travel that thou tak'st for pleasure.

BOLINGBROKE

   My heart will sigh when I miscall it so,

   Which finds it an enforcèd pilgrimage.

---

250 *Exit*] *after* WILSON (*who has 'following' preceding* 249); *not in* Q1, F   254 return'st]
F; returnest Q1   262 travel] Q1 (trauaile), F

249–50 **What . . . show** tell me in letters what I cannot learn from you in person

250 *Exit* Though not called for in the early texts, Aumerle's exit is implied by the Lord Marshal's next lines. For him to be present for the final, rather intimate, moments among Gaunt, Marshal, and Bolingbroke also seems inappropriate since his feelings for the latter are hardly congenial.

251–2 Since it suggests widespread sympathy, the Lord Marshal's evident affection for Bolingbroke helps prepare for his welcome return to England.

256 **office** duty
   prodigal profuse

257 **dolour** grief

258 **but . . . time** i.e. only temporary

259 Joy being absent, grief is necessarily present; Bolingbroke counters his father's attempt at comfort.

262 **Call it a travel** imagine it is a journey (with a possible pun on 'travail')

GAUNT

The sullen passage of thy weary steps   265
Esteem as foil wherein thou art to set
The precious jewel of thy home return.

BOLINGBROKE

Nay, rather every tedious stride I make
Will but remember me what a deal of world
I wander from the jewels that I love.   270
Must I not serve a long apprenticehood
To foreign passages and in the end,
Having my freedom, boast of nothing else
But that I was a journeyman to grief?

GAUNT

All places that the eye of heaven visits   275
Are to a wise man ports and happy havens.
Teach thy necessity to reason thus—
There is no virtue like necessity—
Think not the King did banish thee
But thou the King. Woe doth the heavier sit   280
Where it perceives it is but faintly borne.
Go, say I sent thee forth to purchase honour
And not the King exiled thee; or suppose
Devouring pestilence hangs in our air
And thou art flying to a fresher clime.   285
Look what thy soul holds dear, imagine it

---

266 as foil] Q1; a foyle Q2; a soyle Q3–5, F   268–93 BOLINGBROKE . . . light] Q1; *not in* F

265–7 Think of ('Esteem') the misery of your exile ('sullen . . . steps') as a setting ('foil') for the 'jewel' of your happy return.
269 **remember me** remind me of
  deal of world distance
271–4 i.e. My enforced exile will serve only to make me an accomplished artisan of sorrow. An 'apprentice' had to serve in the shop of a master tradesman before being granted the 'freedom' to work on his own as a 'journeyman'. Bolingbroke puns on 'journey', which refers to 'day' labour (Fr. *journée*) and to his impending journeys in exile. The word 'passages', picked up from Gaunt (265), connects

with 'travel' in 262 and draws out its secondary meaning, 'travail' = labour.
277 Gaunt concedes the truth of his son's negative characterization of exile; he suggests that Bolingbroke nevertheless should see things more positively simply because it is necessary to do so.
280–1 **Woe . . . borne** Unhappiness weighs heavier when it observes that the bearer is weak.
284 **pestilence . . . air** Plague was thought to be caused by miasma, noxious clouds of bad air.
285 **clime** region, climate
286–7 Imagine all that you hold dear to be where you are heading, not where you came from.

To lie that way thou go'st, not whence thou com'st.
Suppose the singing birds musicians,
The grass whereon thou tread'st the presence strewed,
The flowers fair ladies and thy steps no more   290
Than a delightful measure or a dance,
For gnarling sorrow hath less power to bite
The man that mocks at it and sets it light.

BOLINGBROKE
O, who can hold a fire in his hand
By thinking on the frosty Caucasus?   295
Or cloy the hungry edge of appetite
By bare imagination of a feast?
Or wallow naked in December snow
By thinking on fantastic summer's heat?
O no, the apprehension of the good   300
Gives but the greater feeling to the worse.
Fell sorrow's tooth doth never rankle more
Than when he bites but lanceth not the sore.

GAUNT
Come, come, my son, I'll bring thee on thy way.
Had I thy youth and cause I would not stay.   305

BOLINGBROKE
Then England's ground farewell, sweet soil adieu,
My mother and my nurse that bears me yet.
Where'er I wander, boast of this I can:
Though banished, yet a true born Englishman.   *Exeunt*

---

302 never] Q1; euer F   303 he] Q1; it Q2–F   307 that] Q1; which F   309 *Exeunt*] Q1; *not in* F

---

289 **presence strewed** king's royal presence
chamber, with rushes strewn on the floor
292 **gnarling** snarling (like a dog; an image
Bolingbroke picks up in 302–3)
293 **sets it light** regards it lightly
295 **Caucasus** Caucasus Mountains
296 **cloy** allay
299 **fantastic** imagined
300 **apprehension** grasping of the idea
302 **Fell** fierce
rankle gall, irritate

303 **lanceth** surgically punctures, drains
(and so heals)
305 **cause** the charge that you've made and
the grievance that you harbour (perhaps
with a hint of how Bolingbroke will act
upon that 'cause')
306–7 **England's . . . yet** farewell to the
English soil, my mother and nurse, which
still sustains me

1.4 *Enter [Richard] with Green and Bagot at one door, and*
  Aumerle at another

RICHARD

  We did observe.—Cousin Aumerle,
  How far brought you high Hereford on his way?

AUMERLE

  I brought high Hereford, if you call him so,
  But to the next highway, and there I left him.

RICHARD

  And say what store of parting tears were shed?   5

AUMERLE

  Faith, none for me, except the north-east wind
  Which then blew bitterly against our faces
  Awaked the sleeping rheum, and so by chance
  Did grace our hollow parting with a tear.

RICHARD

  What said our cousin when you parted with him?   10

AUMERLE

  'Farewell.'
  And for my heart disdainèd that my tongue

1.4] F (*Scoena Quarta*); *not in* Q1   0.1–2 Enter . . . another] *Enter the King with Bushie, &c
at one dore, and the Lord Aumarle at another.* Q1; *Enter King, Aumerle, Greene, and Bagot.* F
7 blew] Q1; grew F   faces] Q1; face Q3–F   8 sleeping] Q1; sleepie Q3–F   11–12] POPE; *one
line* Q1, F

1.4 This scene keeps up the pattern of
alternating large public scenes and
smaller private ones. Here we see Richard
and his friends in an unguarded moment,
often highlighted in performance by
the use of an intimate setting. Their
conversation reveals their contempt for
Bolingbroke, feelings that were carefully
hidden in the previous scene.

0.1–2 The scene opens with Richard, Green,
and Bagot entering in mid-conversation.
Aumerle enters to them from having
seen Bolingbroke on his way out of
England.

1 **We did observe** At this point it is not
clear what it is that Richard and the
others have observed; we learn at 23 ff.
that they have been discussing Bolingbroke and 'his courtship to the common
people'.

2 **high** The word suggests Bolingbroke's
nobility but especially his pride.

3–4 Aumerle's mocking, resentful tone
contrasts sharply with his affectionate
overture to Bolingbroke at 1.3.249–50. In
retrospect, it begins to look as if he was
seeking to cultivate a correspondence
with his cousin in order to gather intelligence about him. His wordplay on 'high'
and 'highway' conveys his conspiratorial
intimacy with the King.

5 **store** quantity

6 **for** by

8 **rheum** moist discharge of the nose and
eyes

9 **hollow** empty, insincere

11 **Farewell** A flat, emotionless leave-taking.

12–15 Aumerle did not want to utter the
word 'farewell' since his heart told him
that the word would be profaned (defiled)
if it were spoken to Bolingbroke, so he
pretended that he was rendered speechless by grief.

Should so profane the word, that taught me craft
To counterfeit oppression of such grief
That words seemed buried in my sorrow's grave.   15
Marry, would the word 'farewell' have lengthened hours
And added years to his short banishment,
He should have had a volume of farewells,
But since it would not, he had none of me.

RICHARD

He is our cousin, cousin, but 'tis doubt,   20
When time shall call him home from banishment,
Whether our kinsman come to see his friends.
Ourself and Bushy, Bagot here and Green,
Observed his courtship to the common people,
How he did seem to dive into their hearts   25
With humble and familiar courtesy,
What reverence he did throw away on slaves,
Wooing poor craftsmen with the craft of smiles
And patient underbearing of his fortune,
As 'twere to banish their affects with him.   30
Off goes his bonnet to an oyster-wench,
A brace of draymen bid God speed him well
And had the tribute of his supple knee,
With 'Thanks, my countrymen, my loving friends',

---

15 words] Q1; word F   20 cousin, cousin,] F (Cosin (Cosin)); Coosens Coosin, Q1
23 Bushy, Bagot here and Green] Q6; Bushie Q1; *Bushy:* heere *Bagot* and *Greene* F
27 What] Q1*c*, F; With Q1*u*   28 smiles] Q1; soules F

13 **craft** craftiness
16 **Marry** A mild oath; from Mary, mother of Christ.
   would . . . have if . . . could have
18 **volume** whole book
20–2 **'tis . . . friends** it is doubtful, when Bolingbroke returns to England at the end of his banishment, that he will be coming home in order to see his noble friends; 'friends' is ironic, given Bolingbroke's hostility toward Richard and his followers and their contempt for him.
23–36 Richard's disdainful account of Bolingbroke's relationship with the common people is of a piece with contemporary discussions of the aristocratic cultivation of 'popularity', which Francis Bacon calls 'a good thing in itself', though it must 'be handled tenderly' (Bacon, 2.44).

27 **slaves** i.e. commoners; the word reveals the depth of Richard's contempt
28 **craftsmen . . . craft** The wordplay modulates from artisanal skill to political duplicity as if, in Richard's view, craft in the political realm were necessarily a form of hypocrisy.
29 **underbearing** endurance
30 **As . . . him** as if to take their affections with him into banishment
31 **bonnet** soft cloth cap; unsuitable headgear for a nobleman
   oyster-wench girl who sells oysters (a food of the poor)
32 **brace of draymen** pair of cart drivers
33 **had . . . knee** i.e. Bolingbroke bowed to them. The courtly bow involves a bending of the knee.

As were our England in reversion his,   35
And he our subjects' next degree in hope.

GREEN

Well, he is gone, and with him go these thoughts.
Now for the rebels which stand out in Ireland,
Expedient manage must be made, my liege,
Ere further leisure yield them further means   40
For their advantage and your highness' loss.

RICHARD

We will ourself in person to this war,
And, for our coffers with too great a court
And liberal largesse are grown somewhat light,
We are enforced to farm our royal realm,   45
The revenue whereof shall furnish us
For our affairs in hand. If that come short,
Our substitutes at home shall have blank charters
Whereto, when they shall know what men are rich,
They shall subscribe them for large sums of gold   50
And send them after to supply our wants,
For we will make for Ireland presently.
          Enter Bushy
Bushy, what news?

BUSHY

Old John of Gaunt is grievous sick, my lord,
Suddenly taken, and hath sent post haste   55
To entreat your majesty to visit him.

RICHARD

Where lies he?

52.1 *Enter Bushy*] F; *Enter Bushie with newes* Q1   53 Bushy, what news?] F; *not in* Q1
54 grievous] Q1; verie F

---

35 **in reversion his** legally to revert to him after Richard's death
36 **our . . . hope** successor to the throne in whom the confidence of the English people rests
38 **stand out** resist, make a stand
39 **Expedient manage** efficient conduct of the operation
40 **leisure** allowed time
43 **for** because
   coffers treasury
44 **liberal largesse** bountiful generosity
45 **farm . . . realm** apportion regions of the

kingdom to tax collectors, who pay the king a set fee and then keep whatever taxes they are able to extract from the locals
48 **substitutes** deputies
   blank charters documents authorizing agents to seize unspecified amounts of money
50 **subscribe them** i.e. complete the blank charters by entering names of donors and the amounts of their required contributions
51 **supply our wants** satisfy our needs
52 **presently** immediately

BUSHY

At Ely House.

RICHARD

Now put it, God, in his physician's mind
To help him to his grave immediately.   60
The lining of his coffers shall make coats
To deck our soldiers for these Irish wars.
Come, gentlemen, let's all go visit him.
Pray God we may make haste and come too late.

[ALL]

Amen.   *Exeunt*   65

2.1 *Enter John of Gaunt, sick, with the Duke of York [and attendants]*

GAUNT

Will the King come that I may breathe my last
In wholesome counsel to his unstaid youth?

59 God] Q1; heauen F his] F; the Q1   64 God] Q1; heauen F   65 ALL] STAUNTON; *not in* Q1, F Amen] Q1; *not in* F   Exeunt] Q1; *Exit* F
2.1] F (*Actus Secundus. Scena Prima.*); *not in* Q1   0.1 Enter . . . York] Q1; *Enter Gaunt, sicke with Yorke.* F   0.1–2 *and attendants*] CAPELL (*subs.*); *not in* Q1, F

58 **Ely House** The Bishop of Ely's house in London.
61 **lining** contents (with a pun on the lining of a garment)
65 **Amen** Q1 prints this word at the end of Richard's speech without a separate speech prefix. Staunton's prefix gives it to Richard's followers (in performance Richard may or may not join in). The moment is a wicked parody of a congregation's response to a prayer in church.
2.1 Though he drew important details from Holinshed and *Woodstock*, Shakespeare invented this deathbed confrontation between the King and John of Gaunt. The scene marks Richard's moral low-point; his abuse of his uncle—a man who is both a dying 'prophet' (31) and a witness to England's former glory—darkens the impression we have of him both in this scene and through his extended absence from the play (2.1.223–3.2.1). Two elements of the organization of the scene alleviate somewhat the harm that the King does to himself. One is that Richard enters after Gaunt's prophecy of England's ruin (40–68), so that at least he is not seen mocking a dying

Duke's magnificent tribute to his native country. The other is that the conspiracy of Northumberland, Ross, and Willoughby, which serves as an epilogue to the scene, reveals that Bolingbroke has been waiting only for the King's departure to Ireland before launching an invasion, a fact that contradicts Bolingbroke's later claim that he returned before the end of his sentence because the King had taken away his 'rights and royalties' (2.3.119) in the wake of the death of his father.
0.1–2 **Enter . . . attendants** Gaunt might be carried on stage in a chair or litter, as many editors suggest, though he could walk on with the help of York or one of his servants. However he enters, his forceful speaking coupled with his enfeebled condition suggests his seniority and moral authority in relation to the King.
2 **wholesome counsel** The counsel is wholesome even though the breath that utters it is not; the contrast between physical debility and moral strength is elaborated throughout the scene.
unstaid uncontrolled

YORK

Vex not yourself nor strive not with your breath,
For all in vain comes counsel to his ear.

GAUNT

O, but they say the tongues of dying men   5
Enforce attention like deep harmony.
Where words are scarce they are seldom spent in vain
For they breathe truth that breathe their words in pain;
He that no more must say is listened more
Than they whom youth and ease have taught to gloze;   10
More are men's ends marked than their lives before;
The setting sun and music at the close,
As the last taste of sweets, is sweetest last,
Writ in remembrance more than things long past.
Though Richard my life's counsel would not hear,   15
My death's sad tale may yet undeaf his ear.

YORK

No, it is stopped with other flatt'ring sounds,
As praises, of whose taste the wise are feared,
Lascivious metres, to whose venom sound
The open ear of youth doth always listen,   20

---

12 at] Q1; is F   17 flatt'ring] F; flattering Q1   18 whose ... feared] OXFORD; whose ...
found Q1; whose state the wise are found Q2; his state: then there are found Q3–5; his state:
then there are sound F

3 **nor . . . breath** nor strive by words
   ('breath') to counsel the King
5–6 A variation on the proverb 'Dying men
   speak true' (Tilley M514).
6 Harmonious music can seize the attention of men and even of beasts, like
   the 'youthful and unhandled colts' in
   Merchant of Venice, whose 'savage eyes
   [are] turned to a modest gaze | By the
   sweet power of music' (5.1.71–9).
9 **must** can
   listened more listened to more closely
10 **gloze** veil with specious comments (*OED
   v.*[1] 2)
11 **More . . . before** People attend more
   closely to a man's death than to the life
   that preceded it.
12 **close** closing phrase
13 **sweetest last** i.e. sweetest because it is
   tasted last
14 **Writ in remembrance** inscribed in
   memory
15 **my life's counsel** the counsel I gave while
   I lived

16 **death's sad tale** Richard will later tell 'sad
   stories of the death of kings' (3.2.156) as
   well as the 'lamentable tale' of himself
   (5.1.44).
18 **feared** wary of. Oxford's emendation is
   preferable to either Q1's 'found' or F's
   'sound', neither of which makes much
   sense, and the more usual emendation
   'fond', which makes ironic sense only
   (i.e. even the wise are fond of praises;
   and Richard is far from wise). Q1's
   'found' might have been a misreading of
   'feared', especially if the compositor's eye
   slipped to 'ſound' at the end of the line
   immediately following.
19 **Lascivious metres** lewd poems or rhymes
   venom poisonous. The idea that lewd
   words and music were poisons that could
   gain entry to the body by way of the ear
   was a commonplace in the antitheatrical
   writing of the period.

Report of fashions in proud Italy,
Whose manners still our tardy-apish nation
Limps after in base imitation.
Where doth the world thrust forth a vanity—
So it be new there's no respect how vile—   25
That is not quickly buzzed into his ears?
Then all too late comes counsel to be heard
Where will doth mutiny with wit's regard.
Direct not him whose way himself will choose,
'Tis breath thou lack'st and that breath wilt thou lose.   30

GAUNT

Methinks I am a prophet new inspired
And thus, expiring, do foretell of him:
His rash fierce blaze of riot cannot last
For violent fires soon burn out themselves.
Small showers last long, but sudden storms are short;   35
He tires betimes that spurs too fast betimes;
With eager feeding, food doth choke the feeder;
Light vanity, insatiate cormorant,
Consuming means, soon preys upon itself.
This royal throne of kings, this sceptered isle,   40

---

22 tardy-apish] *hyphen* DYCE   27 Then] Q1; That F

---

22 **tardy-apish** belatedly and foolishly
imitative
24 **vanity** worthless thing
25 **there's no respect** it does not matter
26 **buzzed** whispered frivolously
28 **will . . . regard** passion rebels against
rationality
29 **whose . . . choose** who will determine his
own course
32 **expiring** dying, and also exhaling. Gaunt
is playing on 'inspired' in the previous
line, which has both a physical connotation (the act of breathing), which extends
the scene's emphasis on breath, and a
theological one (the infusing of the
prophet with God's spirit).
33 **riot** dissolute behaviour
34–9 Gaunt ushers in his eloquent speech
with a series of distinctly uninspired
sententiae, based on proverbial wisdom
(e.g. 'Nothing violent can be permanent'
and '[Untimely] spurring [spoils] the
steed': Tilley N321 and S794). His claim
to be capable of inspired prophecy seems

convincing only when he begins to praise
England.
35 **sudden** taking place or appearing all at
once (*OED* 1a)
36 **betimes . . . betimes** early . . . at the outset (of a race)
37 **With . . . feeder** one who feeds too eagerly
will choke on his food
38–9 **Light . . . itself** Frivolous indulgence,
like a voracious bird of prey ('cormorant'), will exhaust its means of support
and then eat up itself.
40–66 Gaunt's England has four main
characteristics: (1) it is royal: both a
nation invested with regal authority
(a 'sceptered isle') and a fertile birthplace
of monarchs; (2) it is blessed by God
and Nature in its Edenic fertility, internal
peacefulness, and fortress-like geog-
raphy; (3) it is a divine, warrior nation,
led by its kings and dedicated to the
prosecution of holy wars outside its own
borders; and (4) it is famous, arousing
both envy and admiration in other lands.

This earth of majesty, this seat of Mars,
This other Eden, demi-paradise,
This fortress built by Nature for herself
Against infection and the hand of war,
This happy breed of men, this little world,   45
This precious stone set in the silver sea,
Which serves it in the office of a wall
Or as a moat defensive to a house
Against the envy of less happier lands,
This blessèd plot, this earth, this realm, this England,   50
This nurse, this teeming womb of royal kings,
Feared by their breed and famous by their birth,
Renownèd for their deeds as far from home
For Christian service and true chivalry
As is the sepulchre in stubborn Jewry   55
Of the world's ransom, blessèd Mary's son;
This land of such dear souls, this dear, dear land,
Dear for her reputation through the world,
Is now leased out—I die pronouncing it—
Like to a tenement or pelting farm.   60
England, bound in with the triumphant sea,
Whose rocky shore beats back the envious siege

---

42 demi-paradise] *hyphen* STEEVENS-REED 1793   48 a moat] Q4–5, F; moate Q1–3
52 famous by] Q1; famous for F

---

41 **earth of majesty** (a) majestical land; (b) place and birthplace of monarchs, a sense that anticipates 'this teeming womb of royal kings' at line 51 and connects with the numerous images of earthly fertility that culminate in the 'garden scene' at 3.4.
  seat of Mars official residence of the god of war

42 **demi-paradise** Not 'half-paradise', but rather a place that mixes the divine and terrestrial, as in the word 'demigod'.

44 **infection . . . war** i.e. the seas shelter Britain from foreign aggression and disease. Shakespeare's audience would have been mindful that stormy seas had helped save the nation from the Spanish Armada in 1588, and that each new wave of bubonic plague, the most recent in 1593–4, landed on England's shore only when ship-borne disease managed

to breach the watery barrier of the English Channel.

45 **little world** Forker points out that England as a world unto itself was a common Elizabethan idea.

47 **office** intended function (*OED n.* 4a)

51 **nurse** nurturer or care-giver; originally a wet-nurse (*OED n.*[1] 1a)
  teeming fertile

52 **Feared . . . breed** 'held in awe for their hereditary valor' (Riverside)

54 **Christian service** military service in the Crusades

55 **sepulchre** Christ's tomb
  Jewry The land of the Jews, said to be 'stubborn' because its inhabitants resist the Christian gospel.

56 **world's ransom** i.e. Christ

60 **tenement** property that is rented, rather than owned, by the occupant
  pelting paltry

Of watery Neptune, is now bound in with shame,
With inky blots and rotten parchment bonds.
That England that was wont to conquer others   65
Hath made a shameful conquest of itself.
Ah, would the scandal vanish with my life,
How happy then were my ensuing death!
>   *Enter [Richard], Queen, Aumerle, Bushy, Green, Bagot,*
>   *Ross, and Willoughby*

YORK

The King is come. Deal mildly with his youth,
For young hot colts, being reined, do rage the more.   70

QUEEN

How fares our noble uncle Lancaster?

RICHARD

What comfort, man? How is't with agèd Gaunt?

GAUNT

O, how that name befits my composition!
Old Gaunt indeed and gaunt in being old.
Within me grief hath kept a tedious fast,   75
And who abstains from meat that is not gaunt?
For sleeping England long time have I watched;
Watching breeds leanness; leanness is all gaunt.
The pleasure that some fathers feed upon
Is my strict fast—I mean my children's looks—   80
And therein fasting hast thou made me gaunt.

68.1–2 *Enter . . . Willoughby*] F (*subs.*); *Enter king and Queene, &c* Q1 (*after 70*)   70 reined]
SINGER 1856 (*conj.* Ritson); ragde Q1; rag'd F

63–4 Instead of ensuring that England
remain 'bound in with the triumphant
sea' (61), Richard has 'bound' the nation
with shame, signified by dishonourable
paperwork (like the 'blank charters'
mentioned at 1.4.48).

70 **reined** Q1's 'ragde' has been taken by
some editors to mean 'enraged' though
OED records no similar uses. Ritson's
conjecture, which has been widely
adopted, makes far better sense: York's
point is that Gaunt should not restrain
Richard since to do so will only make him
wilder.

73–83 Gaunt's bitter wordplay on his own
name marks a change in tone from his
expansive 'this England' speech and prepares for his recriminations against the
King. He is 'gaunt' in person as well as in
name, he says, because he is old, he is
grieving for his absent son, he is wakeful,
being on guard for a nation that drowses
under its careless King, and he is ready-
ing himself for the grave.

73 **composition** condition

76 **meat** food

77 **watched** kept awake, stood on guard

80 **strict fast** i.e. the thing I do without
children's Gaunt in fact had children other
than Bolingbroke, but the plural here is
merely incidental.

Gaunt am I for the grave, gaunt as a grave
Whose hollow womb inherits naught but bones.

RICHARD

Can sick men play so nicely with their names?

GAUNT

No, misery makes sport to mock itself.   85
Since thou dost seek to kill my name in me,
I mock my name, great King, to flatter thee.

RICHARD

Should dying men flatter with those that live?

GAUNT

No, no, men living flatter those that die.

RICHARD

Thou now a-dying sayst thou flatt'rest me.   90

GAUNT

O no, thou diest, though I the sicker be.

RICHARD

I am in health, I breathe, and see thee ill.

GAUNT

Now he that made me knows I see thee ill:
Ill in myself to see, and in thee seeing ill.
Thy deathbed is no lesser than thy land   95
Wherein thou liest in reputation sick,
And thou, too careless patient as thou art,
Commit'st thy anointed body to the cure
Of those physicians that first wounded thee.

---

88 with] Q1; *not in* Q2–F   92 and] Q1; I Q2–F   95 thy land] Q1; the Land Q2–F

---

83 **womb** The grave's operation is like child-bearing in reverse.
84 **nicely** wittily, daintily
85 This line confirms that 'punning in the play can frequently be a symptom of genuine pain' (Forker).
86 **Since . . . me** because you seek to eradicate my family's name and honour (by banishing my son). Gaunt's concern about the loss of his name and therefore of his honourable reputation beyond his death anticipates the long harrowing of the King as his titles are taken from

him—'even that name was given me at the font . . . [is] usurped' (4.1.256–7).
91 **thou diest** i.e. in reputation, as Gaunt explains at 95–6
94 Gaunt puns on 'ill' as (a) 'sick' and (b) 'wrongly' or 'blamefully'. I might see you as sick, he says to the King, because I am sick myself, but I also see you as sick because you perceive (and treat) your land wrongfully.
95 **lesser** less
97 **careless patient** careless a patient
99 **physicians** i.e. the King's flatterers, who harm rather than heal

A thousand flatterers sit within thy crown,   100
Whose compass is no bigger than thy head,
And yet, encagèd in so small a verge,
The waste is no whit lesser than thy land.
O, had thy grandsire with a prophet's eye
Seen how his son's son should destroy his sons,   105
From forth thy reach he would have laid thy shame,
Deposing thee before thou wert possessed,
Which art possessed now to depose thyself.
Why cousin, wert thou regent of the world
It were a shame to let this land by lease,   110
But, for thy world, enjoying but this land,
Is it not more than shame to shame it so?
Landlord of England art thou now, not king,
Thy state of law is bondslave to the law,
And thou—
RICHARD   —a lunatic, lean-witted fool,   115
Presuming on an ague's privilege,
Dar'st with thy frozen admonition

102 encagèd] F (incaged); inraged Q1   109 wert] Q1; were F   110 this] Q1; his F
113 now, not king] THEOBALD; now not, not King Q1; and not King F   115 thou—]
CAPELL; thou˯ Q1; And— F

100–3 The image moves between the actual
    crown on Richard's head, the crown as a
    symbol of the royal court, and the crown
    as a symbol of the nation. Flatterers
    occupy the space within the court, which
    is likened to the circumference (*compass*)
    of the King's head, yet even though
    they take up 'so small a verge', the waste
    (both 'wasteland' and 'extravagance')
    they create is as great as the whole
    nation (*verge* = the sphere or scope of
    something; specifically, the area extend-
    ing twelve miles around the king (*OED*
    n.[1] 10a)).
104 **grandsire** Edward III
105 This is as close as Gaunt has so far come
    to accusing Richard to his face of the
    murder of Woodstock. Gaunt has already
    said that Richard is killing him (81) by
    taking away his son, and he unleashes a
    full-scale accusation at 124–34.
107 **Deposing** dethroning. Gurr and Forker
    suggest 'disinheriting', as if Gaunt were
    being careful with his words, but Gaunt
    is angry and forthright.

107–8 **possessed . . . possessed** in possession
    of . . . possessed by an evil spirit
109 **regent** ruler
111 **for . . . land** since you have only this
    land to enjoy as your world
113 **Landlord** The word and the negative
    meaning evoked here are borrowed from
    Woodstock, 'And thou no king, but land-
    lord now become' (5.3.106).
114 **Thy . . . the law** i.e. your kingdom, once
    characterized by its devotion to lawful-
    ness, has now become a slave to the law
    (likely the latter use of 'law' refers to con-
    tract or property law). See Introduction,
    pp. 17–18.
115 **a lunatic** Richard interrupts the Duke
    and turns the invective against him.
    lean-witted i.e. the Duke's wit is as
    'gaunt' as his body
116 **Presuming . . . privilege** taking advan-
    tage of the fact that you are sick (*ague* =
    violent fever)
117 **Dar'st** do you dare
    frozen cold and hostile

Make pale our cheek, chasing the royal blood
With fury from his native residence.
Now, by my seat's right royal majesty,   120
Wert thou not brother to great Edward's son
This tongue that runs so roundly in thy head
Should run thy head from thy unreverent shoulders.

GAUNT

O spare me not, my brother Edward's son,
For that I was his father Edward's son.   125
That blood already, like the pelican,
Hast thou tapped out and drunkenly caroused.
My brother Gloucester, plain well-meaning soul—
Whom fair befall in heaven 'mongst happy souls—
May be a precedent and witness good   130
That thou respect'st not spilling Edward's blood.
Join with the present sickness that I have,
And thy unkindness be like crookèd age
To crop at once a too-long-withered flower.

---

118 chasing] Q1; chafing F   124 brother] Q2; brothers Q1, F   127 Hast thou] Q1; Thou
hast F   128 well-meaning] *hyphen* POPE

118–19 The image of Richard's blood fleeing
   from his face ('native residence') connects
   with other images of the young King's
   sudden fluctuations between blushing
   and ashen paleness. Cf. 3.2.76–9 and
   3.3.61–2.
120 **seat's** throne's (the emblem of his
   kingship)
121 **Edward's son** Richard's father and
   Gaunt's elder brother, the Black Prince
   (the eldest son of Edward III)
122 **roundly** outspokenly, glibly
123 **unreverent** disrespectful
124–5 **Edward's . . . Edward's** Edward the
   Black Prince's . . . Edward III's. Gaunt
   picks up Richard's phrase, 'Edward's son'
   (121), reminding the King that he is a
   member of a family as well as a monarch.
126–7 The pelican was traditionally believed
   to peck its own breast so that its hatch-
   lings might be nourished by its blood
   and thus was viewed as a type of Christ.
   Here, Gaunt twists the emblem to suggest
   filial ingratitude rather than parental

solicitude, since it is Richard who, by
   killing Gloucester, has 'tapped' Edward
   III's sacred blood.
127 **tapped out** drawn off (like liquor from a
   cask fitted with a spout)
128 **plain . . . soul** According to Holinshed,
   Gloucester was 'fierce of nature, hasty,
   wilful, and given more to war than to
   peace' (p. 489). Gaunt's description likely
   comes from *Woodstock*, where the hero is
   called 'plain Thomas' and is contrasted
   with the extravagant King.
129 **Whom . . . befall** may good happen to
   him
130 **precedent . . . witness** Legal terms
   linked to the 'state of law' (114) that the
   King has forgone.
131 **respect'st not** are indifferent to
132 **Join** may you join
133 **unkindness** (a) cruelty; (b) unnaturalness
134 **crop . . . flower** pick at once an ageing
   flower (himself) that has withered on the
   stalk

Live in thy shame but die not shame with thee— 135
These words hereafter thy tormentors be.
Convey me to my bed, then to my grave.
Love they to live that love and honour have.

Exit [*with attendants*]

RICHARD
And let them die that age and sullens have,
For both hast thou and both become the grave. 140

YORK
I do beseech your majesty, impute his words
To wayward sickliness and age in him.
He loves you, on my life, and holds you dear
As Harry Duke of Hereford, were he here.

RICHARD
Right, you say true. As Hereford's love, so his. 145
As theirs, so mine, and all be as it is.

Enter Northumberland

NORTHUMBERLAND
My liege, old Gaunt commends him to your majesty.

RICHARD
What says he?

NORTHUMBERLAND   Nay, nothing. All is said—
His tongue is now a stringless instrument.
Words, life, and all, old Lancaster hath spent. 150

YORK
Be York the next that must be bankrupt so;
Though death be poor, it ends a mortal woe.

138.1 *with attendants*] Capell (*subs.*); *not in* Q1, F   146.1 *Enter Northumberland*] F; *not in* Q1

135 **die . . . thee** may your ignominy outlive
you
139–40 Inverting the rhymes of Gaunt's last
couplet (Gurr), the King counters
Gaunt's emphasis on 'love' and 'honour'
by accusing him of senility ('age') and ill
humour ('sullens').
140 **become** are suited to
145 **As . . . his** Richard twists York's words
to mean, 'Gaunt loves me as much as his
son Harry loves me (i.e. not very much)'.
146 **As . . . mine** my love to them will be as
theirs is to me

146.1 Wells suggests that Northumberland
enters with Gaunt at the start of the
scene, exits with him at 138.1, and
returns here with news of his death. This
would make Northumberland a silent
witness to Gaunt's speech about England
as well as to the bitter exchange between
the Duke and the King.
149 **stringless instrument** The image
appears also at 1.3.161–2.
151 **bankrupt** Playing off 'spent' in the previous line.

RICHARD

The ripest fruit first falls and so doth he.
His time is spent—our pilgrimage must be.
So much for that. Now for our Irish wars: 155
We must supplant those rough rug-headed kerns,
Which live like venom where no venom else,
But only they, have privilege to live.
And for these great affairs do ask some charge,
Towards our assistance we do seize to us   160
The plate, coin, revenues and movables
Whereof our uncle Gaunt did stand possessed.

YORK

How long shall I be patient? Ah, how long
Shall tender duty make me suffer wrong?
Not Gloucester's death nor Hereford's banishment,   165
Nor Gaunt's rebukes nor England's private wrongs,
Nor the prevention of poor Bolingbroke
About his marriage, nor my own disgrace,
Have ever made me sour my patient cheek
Or bend one wrinkle on my sovereign's face.   170

---

156 rug-headed] F; rugheaded Q1 kerns] Q1c, F; kerne Q1u   161 coin] Q1c, F; coines Q1u
163 Ah] Q1; Oh F   168 my] Q1c, F; his Q1u

---

154 **pilgrimage** Though treated dismissively
here by Richard (who blithely cites the
platitude 'Life is a pilgrimage': Tilley
L249), pilgrimage is a recurrent motif in
the play and in the two that follow it (*1*
and *2 Henry IV*). Bolingbroke ends this
play and begins the next one by promis-
ing to make a pilgrimage to 'the Holy
Land | To wash this blood off from my
guilty hand' (5.6.49–50).
must be is still to be made
156 **supplant** root out (*OED v.* 4)
rug-headed kerns shaggy-haired Irish
foot soldiers. Some editions retain 'kern',
which is the reading in the uncorrected
version of Q1, on the grounds that the
word could be a collective plural.
157 **venom** serpents (a synecdoche). Ireland
famously was purged of snakes by St
Patrick; Richard suggests that the kerns
have taken their place.
159 **ask some charge** entail some costs
160 **seize** expropriate

161 **plate** gold or silver utensils
movables 'any kind of property not fixed,
as opposed to real or fixed property (such
as land, a house, etc.)' (*OED n.* 1). Richard does not seize the estate itself, but
only its 'revenues' and whatever else can
be converted into ready money.
166 **Gaunt's rebukes** Richard's rebuke of
Gaunt
private wrongs the wrongs suffered by
private citizens
167–8 **prevention . . . marriage** Richard
denied Bolingbroke permission to marry
a cousin of the French king during his
exile, an historical detail not otherwise
mentioned in the play.
168 **my own disgrace** There is no known historical disgrace to which York might be
referring, unless he is ashamed of his
role in Richard's misgovernment.
169 **sour . . . cheek** blemish my patient
countenance with a sour look
170 **bend one wrinkle on** (a) direct one
frown at; (b) cause a frown to appear on

I am the last of noble Edward's sons,
Of whom thy father, Prince of Wales, was first.
In war was never lion raged more fierce,
In peace was never gentle lamb more mild
Than was that young and princely gentleman.   175
His face thou hast, for even so looked he,
Accomplished with the number of thy hours;
But when he frowned, it was against the French
And not against his friends. His noble hand
Did win what he did spend and spent not that   180
Which his triumphant father's hand had won.
His hands were guilty of no kindred blood
But bloody with the enemies of his kin.
O Richard! York is too far gone with grief,
Or else he never would compare between—   185
RICHARD
 Why uncle, what's the matter?
YORK   O my liege,
Pardon me if you please; if not, I, pleased
Not to be pardoned, am content withal.
Seek you to seize and gripe into your hands
The royalties and rights of banished Hereford?   190
Is not Gaunt dead, and doth not Hereford live?
Was not Gaunt just, and is not Harry true?
Did not the one deserve to have an heir?
Is not his heir a well-deserving son?

---

177 the] F; a Q1   182 kindred] Q1; kindreds F   185 between—] HANMER; betweene. Q1, F
186 RICHARD … O] Q1c, F; *not in* Q1u   186–8] *as* THEOBALD; *three lines ending* 'matter?'
'please.' 'with all,' Q1; *four lines ending* 'Vncle,' 'matter?' 'if not' 'with all:' F   194 well-
deserving] F; well deseruing Q1

173 **was . . . raged** did . . . rage
177 **Accomplished . . . hours** (when he was)
    as old as you are now
180 **win** earn
182 **guilty . . . blood** Alluding to Gloucester's
    murder.
184–5 **York … between—** Some editors
    treat this as a complete sentence and
    punctuate accordingly, but it is more
    likely that York breaks down and does
    not finish his sentence. Indeed, Richard
    responds as if to someone overcome by
    emotion.

187 **Pardon me** More than a feature of polite
    conversation (where one apologizes in
    advance for saying what might offend),
    York's request for 'pardon' reminds us
    that what he is about to say is tanta-
    mount to treason.
189 **gripe** grasp
190 **royalties** The rights or prerogatives of
    jurisdiction granted by a king.
192 **Harry** Henry Bolingbroke

Take Hereford's rights away and take from time   195
His charters and his customary rights,
Let not tomorrow then ensue today,
Be not thyself—for how art thou a king
But by fair sequence and succession?
Now, afore God—God forbid I say true—   200
If you do wrongfully seize Hereford's rights,
Call in the letters patents that he hath
By his attorneys-general to sue
His livery, and deny his offered homage,
You pluck a thousand dangers on your head,   205
You lose a thousand well-disposèd hearts
And prick my tender patience to those thoughts
Which honour and allegiance cannot think.

RICHARD
Think what you will, we seize into our hands
His plate, his goods, his money and his lands.   210

YORK
I'll not be by the while. My liege, farewell.
What will ensue hereof there's none can tell,
But by bad courses may be understood
That their events can never fall out good.   *Exit*

---

201 rights] Q1; right Q2–F   202 the] Q1; his F   203 attorneys-general] *hyphen* ROWE
206 lose] Q2; loose Q1, F   well-disposèd] F; well disposed Q1

195–7 **Take . . . today** i.e. if you deprive
  Bolingbroke of his rights by violating
  the legal principle of inheritance, you
  are undoing time itself, disrupting the
  natural succession of days
197 **ensue** follow
200 **say** Though this is the reading in all
  extant copies of Q1, the facsimile of
  1890, based on the Huntington copy, has
  'lay', which has misled some editors.
202–4 Using legal terms that Shakespeare
  borrowed from Holinshed, York warns
  Richard against revoking the documents ('letters patents'), which granted
  Bolingbroke the right to appoint
  'attorneys-general' able to claim his
  inheritance ('livery') in his absence. York

also cautions the King against denying
  Bolingbroke the right to pay what Holinshed calls a 'reasonable fine' (p. 496) in
  lieu of his in-person profession of allegiance to the monarch, which was part
  of the procedure of inheritance and
  which Bolingbroke could not have performed during his banishment. The
  phrase 'offered homage' (204) seems to
  conflate the act of homage and the fine.
209–10 The act of seizure (see 160–2) now
  includes the lands themselves as well as
  the movable property.
213–14 **by . . . good** we know from con-
  sidering 'bad courses' of action that
  good outcomes ('events') never issue
  from them

178

RICHARD

Go, Bushy, to the Earl of Wiltshire straight,   215

Bid him repair to us to Ely House

To see this business. Tomorrow next

We will for Ireland, and 'tis time I trow.

And we create in absence of ourself

Our uncle York lord governor of England,   220

For he is just and always loved us well.

Come on, our Queen, tomorrow must we part.

Be merry, for our time of stay is short.

> *Flourish. Exeunt [Richard] and Queen, [Aumerle, Bushy,*
> > *Green, and Bagot.]*
> > *Northumberland, Willoughby and Ross remain*

NORTHUMBERLAND

Well lords, the Duke of Lancaster is dead.

ROSS

And living too, for now his son is Duke.   225

WILLOUGHBY

Barely in title, not in revenues.

NORTHUMBERLAND

Richly in both if justice had her right.

ROSS

My heart is great, but it must break with silence

Ere't be disburdened with a liberal tongue.

223.1 *Flourish*] F; *not in* Q1 *Exeunt . . . Queen*] Q1 (subs.); *not in* F   223.2 *Aumerle . . . Bagot*]
CAPELL; *not in* Q1, F   223.3 *Northumberland . . . remain*] F (subs.); *Manet North.* Q1
226 revenues] Q1; reuennew F

---

215 **Earl of Wiltshire** One of Richard's four
favourites (with Bushy, Bagot, and
Green), he does not appear in the play.
216 **repair** come
217 **see this business** manage the matter
(the confiscation of Gaunt's property)
218 **trow** believe
219 **create . . . ourself** appoint in our
absence. It is a remarkable instance of
foolhardiness that Richard deputizes York
as regent immediately after his uncle has
so categorically denounced his treatment
of Bolingbroke.
222 **our Queen** The Queen has said nothing
throughout this whole sequence. Her
reactions in performance could be

important in establishing audience per-
ceptions and judgement of Richard's
behaviour, negative or positive.
224–31 The closing section of the scene
dramatizes the immediate consequences
of Richard's rashness. The three nobles
at first pronounce their disaffection
warily but are soon assured that they can
speak their treasonous thoughts without
fear of betrayal. Their mutual trust suggests how outrageous the King's actions
have been and how solidly the aristocracy has joined ranks against him.
228 **great** full of emotion
229 **disburdened . . . tongue** relieved by
speaking freely

NORTHUMBERLAND

Nay, speak thy mind, and let him ne'er speak more   230
That speaks thy words again to do thee harm.

WILLOUGHBY

Tends that thou wouldst speak to the Duke of Hereford?
If it be so, out with it boldly, man—
Quick is mine ear to hear of good towards him.

ROSS

No good at all that I can do for him   235
Unless you call it good to pity him,
Bereft and gelded of his patrimony.

NORTHUMBERLAND

Now, afore God, 'tis shame such wrongs are borne
In him, a royal prince, and many more
Of noble blood in this declining land.   240
The King is not himself but basely led
By flatterers; and what they will inform
Merely in hate 'gainst any of us all,
That will the King severely prosecute
'Gainst us, our lives, our children and our heirs.   245

ROSS

The commons hath he pilled with grievous taxes
And quite lost their hearts. The nobles hath he fined
For ancient quarrels and quite lost their hearts.

WILLOUGHBY

And daily, new exactions are devised,
As blanks, benevolences, and I wot not what.   250
But what in God's name doth become of this?

---

232 thou wouldst ... the Duke] Q1; thou'dst ... th'Du. F   238 God] Q1; heauen F
251 in] This edition; a Q1; o' F

232 **Tends . . . to** does what you have to say
     relate to
234 **Quick** attentive
237 **gelded** deprived. The literal meaning,
     'castrated', is also pertinent given the
     strong connection between the inherit-
     ance of title and property and the possi-
     bility of having a legitimate successor.
238–9 **borne . . . him** permitted (by others)
     in his case
241–2 **The King . . . flatterers** A con-
     ventional way of accusing the ruler and
     also absolving him of direct blame for
     wrong-doing; the same charge is central
     in *Woodstock*.

242 **inform** charge
243 **Merely in hate** from utter hatred
244 **prosecute** avenge
246 **pilled** despoiled
248 **For ancient quarrels** Holinshed reports
     that Richard 'caused seventeen shires . . .
     to pay no small sums of money for
     redeeming their offences, that they had
     aided the Duke of Gloucester, the Earls
     of Arundel and Warwick when they rose
     in armour against him' (p. 496).
250 **blanks** blank charters (see 1.4.48
     and n.)
     benevolences forced loans

NORTHUMBERLAND

Wars hath not wasted it, for warred he hath not,
But basely yielded upon compromise
That which his noble ancestors achieved with blows.
More hath he spent in peace than they in wars.   255

ROSS

The Earl of Wiltshire hath the realm in farm.

WILLOUGHBY

The King's grown bankrupt like a broken man.

NORTHUMBERLAND

Reproach and dissolution hangeth over him.

ROSS

He hath not money for these Irish wars,
His burdenous taxations notwithstanding,   260
But by the robbing of the banished Duke.

NORTHUMBERLAND

His noble kinsman—most degenerate King!
But lords, we hear this fearful tempest sing
Yet seek no shelter to avoid the storm.
We see the wind sit sore upon our sails   265
And yet we strike not but securely perish.

ROSS

We see the very wreck that we must suffer
And unavoided is the danger now
For suffering so the causes of our wreck.

NORTHUMBERLAND

Not so. Even through the hollow eyes of death   270
I spy life peering; but I dare not say
How near the tidings of our comfort is.

WILLOUGHBY

Nay, let us share thy thoughts as thou dost ours.

254 noble] Q1; *not in* F   257 King's] Q3–F (Kings); King Q1   262 kinsman—most]
ROWE; kinsman most Q1; Kinsman, most F

252–4 **warred . . . blows** Referring in particular to Richard's ceding of the town
  of Brest in France to the Duke of Brittany
  in 1397.
256 **farm** See 1.4.45 and note.
263 **sing** See *Tempest* 3.3.97: 'The winds did
  sing it to me'.
265 **sit sore upon** press hard against
266 **strike** lower our sails (as a precaution
  against the wind: *OED v.* 17)

266 **securely perish** are lost because of our
  false sense of security
267–9 **We . . . wreck** We see our imminent
  destruction ('wreck'), but the danger is
  unavoidable because we have for so long
  allowed the King's misgovernment.
270 **hollow . . . death** empty eye sockets of
  death (imagined as a skull)

ROSS

    Be confident to speak, Northumberland.

    We three are but thyself, and speaking so   275

    Thy words are but as thoughts; therefore, be bold.

NORTHUMBERLAND

    Then thus: I have from Le Port Blanc,

    A bay in Brittany, received intelligence

    That Harry Duke of Hereford, Rainold Lord Cobham,

    Thomas, son and heir to the Earl of Arundel,   280

    That late broke from the Duke of Exeter,

    His brother, Archbishop late of Canterbury,

    Sir Thomas Erpingham, Sir Thomas Ramston,

    Sir John Norbery, Sir Robert Waterton and Francis Coint,

    All these, well furnished by the Duke of Brittany   285

    With eight tall ships, three thousand men of war,

    Are making hither with all due expedience

    And shortly mean to touch our northern shore.

    Perhaps they had ere this, but that they stay

    The first departing of the King for Ireland.   290

    If then we shall shake off our slavish yoke,

    Imp out our drooping country's broken wing,

    Redeem from broking pawn the blemished crown,

    Wipe off the dust that hides our sceptre's gilt

    And make high majesty look like itself,   295

---

277 Le Port Blanc] Q1 (le Port Blan); Port *le Blan* F   278 Brittany] Q2 (Brittannie); Brittaine
Q1; *Britaine* F   280 Thomas . . . Arundel] RIVERSIDE; *not in* Qq, F; The son of Richard Earl
of Arundel, MALONE   283 Thomas Ramston] MUIR; Iohn Ramston Q1; Iohn *Rainston* F
284 Coint] F (*Quoint*); Coines Q1   285 Brittany] COLLIER ms (Britainie); Brittaine
Q1; *Britaine* F

275 **We . . . thyself** i.e. we are of one mind
    with you
277–88 This conflates two differing accounts
    of Bolingbroke's force as Shakespeare
    found them in Holinshed: in the first
    Bolingbroke is accompanied by all those
    named here, but 'few else were there, for
    (as some write) he had not past fifteen
    lances'; in the other, we hear that the
    Duke of Brittany 'delivered unto him
    three thousand men of war to attend
    him, and that he had eight ships well
    furnished for the war' (p. 498).
280 This line, not in Q1 or F, is Riverside's
    reconstruction of a detail that was likely

    skipped by the Q1 compositor. It was not
    Cobham who 'broke [escaped] from . . .
    Exeter' (281), but Arundel, described by
    Holinshed as 'Thomas Arundel, son and
    heir to the late Earl of Arundel' (p. 498).
287 **expedience** speed
289 **had** would have (landed)
    stay await
292 **Imp out** mend (a term from falconry
    meaning to repair broken feathers by
    grafting)
293 **from broking pawn** from the custody of
    pawnbrokers
294 **gilt** thin covering of gold (with a glance
    at 'guilt', as the word is spelled in Q1)

Away with me in post to Ravenspur.
But if you faint, as fearing to do so,
Stay and be secret, and myself will go.

ROSS

To horse! To horse! Urge doubts to them that fear.

WILLOUGHBY

Hold out my horse and I will first be there.　　　*Exeunt*　300

2.2 *Enter the Queen, Bushy and Bagot*

BUSHY

Madam, your majesty is too much sad.
You promised when you parted with the King
To lay aside life-harming heaviness
And entertain a cheerful disposition.

QUEEN

To please the King I did, to please myself　　　5
I cannot do it. Yet I know no cause
Why I should welcome such a guest as grief,
Save bidding farewell to so sweet a guest
As my sweet Richard. Yet again, methinks
Some unborn sorrow, ripe in Fortune's womb,　　　10

2.2] F (*Scena Secunda.*); *not in* Q1　0.1 *Enter . . . Bagot*] *Enter the Queene, Bushie, Bagot.*
Q1; *Enter Queene, Bushy, and Bagot.* F　3 life-harming] Q1; selfe-harming F

---

296 **in post** with speed
　Ravenspur Then a harbour on the
　Humber in Yorkshire.
297 **faint** are afraid, hesitate
299 **Urge . . . fear** speak of doubts to the
　fearful
300 **Hold . . . horse** if my horse endures
2.2 This scene, Shakespeare's invention,
　gives us a Queen whose language is
　difficult but very powerful, and whose
　intuition of disaster, downplayed at first
　by the courtly Bushy, proves to be only
　too true once the bad news starts to pour
　in. The Queen's prophetic knowledge,
　which takes life in 'Fortune's womb' (10)
　and in her own 'inward soul' (11) and
　which seems remarkably personal, is a
　variation on Gaunt's national prophecy
　in the previous scene and helps prepare
　us to respond sympathetically to the
　tragedy of her husband.

3 **heaviness** both 'oppressed condition of
　the body' and 'dejectedness of mind'
　(*OED* d, e). Another meaning, the con-
　dition of pregnancy, is also relevant since
　both Fortune and the Queen are 'heavy'
　with 'some unborn sorrow' (10).
4 **entertain** cultivate. A secondary mean-
　ing, 'to receive as a guest' (*OED v.* 13),
　is pertinent since the Queen speaks of
　'such a guest as grief' at line 7.
5–13 The Queen considers the possibility
　that saying goodbye to her husband has
　stricken her with grief, but rejects that
　idea, suggesting instead that her sorrow
　comes from her intuition of approaching
　disaster.
5–6 **To please . . . it** I promised to be cheerful
　in order to please the King, but I am
　unable to do so to please myself.
10 **ripe** ready to be born

Is coming towards me, and my inward soul
With nothing trembles; at something it grieves
More than with parting from my lord the King.
BUSHY
Each substance of a grief hath twenty shadows
Which shows like grief itself but is not so.   15
For sorrow's eyes, glazed with blinding tears,
Divides one thing entire to many objects,
Like perspectives, which rightly gazed upon
Show nothing but confusion—eyed awry,
Distinguish form. So your sweet majesty,   20
Looking awry upon your lord's departure,
Find shapes of grief more than himself to wail
Which, looked on as it is, is nought but shadows
Of what it is not. Then, thrice-gracious Queen,
More than your lord's departure weep not. More's
          not seen,   25

12 With] Q1*c*, F; At Q1*u*   16 eyes] Q1; eye F   19 Show] Q1*c*, F; Shews Q1*u*   24 thrice-
gracious Queen] F; thrice (gracious Queene) Q1   25 More's] F; more is Q1

11–13 **my . . . King** i.e. the cause of my
sense of doom might seem like nothing,
but it is nevertheless something more
than my parting from my husband. By
introducing the word 'nothing' ironically, the Queen anticipates and counters
Bushy's dismissal of her sense of fore-
boding (20–4).
14–15 **Each . . . so** For every substantial
grief there are many delusive images of
sadness, which merely seem to be real.
The distinction between the thing itself
and false images is a favourite one with
Shakespeare, as at the end of *1 Henry IV*,
where the rebels are beset with 'many of
his shadows . . . And not the very King'
(5.4.29–30); here 'shadows' as that
which fools the eyes of the beholder leads
to Bushy's extended comparison of the
Queen's grief to 'perspective' paintings.
17 **Divides . . . objects** Tears, like multiple
mirrors or lenses (called 'perspectives' in
the next line), divide the object of sight
into many images.
18 **perspectives** Bushy confuses two separate
meanings of the word: (a) glass instruments whose multi-prism lenses show
the viewer multiple images of an object;
(b) a particular kind of painting whose
true image or deeper meaning can be

discerned only when it is looked at
obliquely. The most famous is Holbein's
The Ambassadors, a handsome likeness of
two accomplished young men that looks
at first to be marred by a large grey blur
at their feet; when 'eyed awry' (19) the
blur resolves into a skull, a stealthy
reminder of mortality.
18 **rightly** from directly in front
19–20 **eyed . . . form** looked at obliquely,
reveal their true form
21–4 **Looking . . . not** When you look at
your husband's departure obliquely,
you see many sorrowful images of the
King to grieve at, which, looked at
straightforwardly, reveal themselves to
be nothing but false images. Bushy's
witty use of the double negative (the
Queen, he says, sees false images of what
is not real) and his clever play with the
idea of perspective do not obscure the
fact that he is confused about how
'perspectives' work (if the Queen were
looking awry, she would see the true
image of her husband's departure) and
that he is wrong about the disaster that is
coming toward them.
25 **More . . . weep not** Do not weep for anything other than the King's departure.

Or if it be, 'tis with false sorrow's eye
Which for things true weeps things imaginary.

QUEEN

It may be so, but yet my inward soul
Persuades me it is otherwise. Howe'er it be
I cannot but be sad: so heavy sad,   30
As, though on thinking on no thought I think,
Makes me with heavy nothing faint and shrink.

BUSHY

'Tis nothing but conceit, my gracious lady.

QUEEN

'Tis nothing less. Conceit is still derived
From some forefather grief. Mine is not so,   35
For nothing hath begot my something grief,
Or something hath the nothing that I grieve—
'Tis in reversion that I do possess—
But what it is, that is not yet known; what
I cannot name, 'tis nameless woe I wot.   40

    Enter Green

---

27 weeps] Q1; weepe F   31 As, though] THEOBALD; As thought Q1; As though F on think-
ing on] Q1, F; on thinking, on POPE; in thinking, on CAPELL (*conj.* Johnson)   33 'Tis . . . lady]
Q1c, F; *not in* Q1u   34 QUEEN] Q1c, F; *not in* Q1u (*because of omission of* 33; *see previous
note*)   37 something hath] Q1; something, hath F   37–8 grieve— . . . possess—]
RIVERSIDE; grieve, . . . possess, Q1, F   39 is, that . . . known;] CAPELL; is that . . . knowen͵
Q1; is, that . . . knowne, F   40.1 *Enter Green*] F; *not in* Q1

---

27 **weeps** laments
30–2 **so heavy . . . shrink** (I am) so sad that,
   although I am dwelling on no thought
   (since I have no legitimate cause for
   sorrow and therefore no clear idea of
   why I should be sorrowful), my sadness,
   even if baseless, nevertheless enfeebles
   and diminishes me. 'I think' (31) is
   mostly superfluous, meaning merely
   that the thought she is not thinking is
   her thought. 'It' is understood at the
   beginning of line 32. The whole passage
   is difficult, the difficulty exacerbated by
   the multiple possible ways of punctuat-
   ing l. 31 and the difference between Q1's
   'thought' and 'though' (Q2–F) as the
   second word in l. 31. We have punctuated lightly and have followed F by
   adopting 'though', thereby making the
   line concessive in meaning.

33 **conceit** imagination
34 **'Tis nothing less** By suggesting that there
   could be something less than what is
   merely imagined, the Queen continues to
   insist on the substance of her apparently
   groundless sorrow.
   Conceit imagined sorrow
   still always
36 **something** substantial, real (not just felt)
37 **Or . . . grieve** or something real has begot
   the nothing for which I lament. The word
   'begot' from the previous line is
   understood.
38 **'Tis . . . possess** I will eventually come
   into full possession of my grief. To possess
   'in reversion' means to possess as an
   inheritor who will come into the property
   upon the death of the owner.
40 **wot** know

GREEN

God save your majesty, and well met, gentlemen.
I hope the King is not yet shipped for Ireland.

QUEEN

Why hop'st thou so? 'Tis better hope he is,
For his designs crave haste, his haste good hope.
Then wherefore dost thou hope he is not shipped?   45

GREEN

That he, our hope, might have retired his power
And driven into despair an enemy's hope,
Who strongly hath set footing in this land:
The banished Bolingbroke repeals himself,
And with uplifted arms is safe arrived   50
At Ravenspur.

QUEEN   Now God in heaven forbid!

GREEN

Ah madam, 'tis too true and, that is worse,
The Lord Northumberland, his son young Harry Percy,
The lords of Ross, Beaumont and Willoughby
With all their pow'rful friends are fled to him.   55

BUSHY

Why have you not proclaimed Northumberland
And all the rest revolted faction, traitors?

GREEN

We have, whereupon the Earl of Worcester
Hath broke his staff, resigned his stewardship,
And all the household servants fled with him   60
To Bolingbroke.

---

41 God] Q1; Heauen F   43 hop'st] F; hopest Q1   50–1 And . . . Ravenspur] F; *one line* Q1
52 Ah] Q1; O F   53 son young] Q1; yong sonne Q2–F Harry] Q1 (H.), F (*Henrie*)   54 lords]
Q1c, F; lord Q1*u*   55 pow'rful] F (powreful); powerful Q1   57 all the rest] Q1; the rest of
the Q2–F   59 broke] Q2–F; broken Q1   60–1] POPE; *one line* Q1, F

---

43 **better hope** better to hope
46 **retired** withdrawn (from the Irish
expedition)
49 **repeals himself** revokes his own
banishment
50 **uplifted arms** raised weapons
52 **that** what
59 **broke his staff** By breaking the staff
which is the symbol of his high office as

the King's steward, Worcester, brother
of Northumberland and uncle of Harry
Percy, symbolically renounces his allegiance to Richard.
60 **household servants** the retainers, noblemen, and attendants of Richard's court.
In the deposition scene, Richard says that
'under his household roof' he kept 'ten
thousand men' (4.1.282–3).

QUEEN

So, Green, thou art the midwife to my woe,
And Bolingbroke my sorrow's dismal heir.
Now hath my soul brought forth her prodigy
And I, a gasping new-delivered mother,   65
Have woe to woe, sorrow to sorrow joined.

BUSHY

Despair not, madam.

QUEEN   Who shall hinder me?
I will despair and be at enmity
With cozening hope. He is a flatterer,
A parasite, a keeper-back of death,   70
Who gently would dissolve the bonds of life,
Which false hope lingers in extremity.

       Enter York

GREEN

Here comes the Duke of York.

QUEEN

With signs of war about his agèd neck.
O, full of careful business are his looks!   75
Uncle, for God's sake, speak comfortable words.

YORK

Should I do so, I should belie my thoughts.
Comfort's in heaven, and we are on the earth
Where nothing lives but crosses, cares and grief.

---

62 to] Q1; of Q2–F   65 new-delivered] *hyphen* POPE   70 keeper-back] *hyphen* CAPELL
71 bonds] Q1, F (bands)   72 hope lingers] Q1; hopes linger F   72.1 *Enter York*] F; *not in* Q1
76 God's] Q1; heauens F   77] Q1; *not in* F   78 on] Q1c, F; in Q1u   79 cares] Q1; care
Q2–F

62–6 **So . . . joined** These lines give form to
   the Queen's embryonic expressions of
   feeling 'heavy sad' (30) with some
   approaching sorrow.
63 **heir** Bolingbroke is the child born of the
   Queen's grief and also the grief itself.
64 **prodigy** monstrous offspring
65–6 The Queen's birth pains are exacerbated by the monstrousness of her
   offspring.
69 **cozening** deceitful
   He hope (and anyone who counsels her
   to be hopeful)

71 **Who** death
72 **lingers in extremity** causes to linger at
   the point of death
74 **signs . . . neck** York is perhaps wearing a
   gorget, a piece of armour used to protect
   the throat, which could be worn with
   civilian dress.
75 **careful** anxious (full of care)
76 **comfortable** comforting. Note the Queen's
   change of heart, as she shifts from despair to hopefulness.
77 **belie** misrepresent
79 **crosses** vexations

Your husband, he is gone to save far off   80
Whilst others come to make him lose at home.
Here am I left to underprop his land
Who, weak with age, cannot support myself.
Now comes the sick hour that his surfeit made,
Now shall he try his friends that flattered him.   85

  Enter a Servant

SERVANT

My lord, your son was gone before I came.

YORK

He was? Why so, go all which way it will.
The nobles they are fled, the commons they are cold
And will, I fear, revolt on Hereford's side.
Sirrah, get thee to Pleshey, to my sister Gloucester,   90
Bid her send me presently a thousand pound—
Hold, take my ring.

SERVANT

My lord, I had forgot to tell your lordship,
Today as I came by, I callèd there—
But I shall grieve you to report the rest.   95

YORK

What is't, knave?

SERVANT

An hour before I came the Duchess died.

YORK

God for his mercy, what a tide of woes

---

81 lose] Q1, F (loose)   85.1 *Enter a Servant*] F; *not in* Q1   88 they are cold] Q1, F; cold POPE
93–4] *as* Q1; My . . . forgot | To . . . there F   94 as I came] Q1; I came Q2–F   98 God]
Q1; Heau'n F

---

80 **to . . . off** i.e. to put down the rebellion in
 Ireland
82 **underprop** support
84 **surfeit** excess
85 **try** test (his false friends will fail the
 test)
86 York has sent for help to his son,
 but Aumerle has evidently left to join
 Richard in Ireland; Holinshed reports
 that the Duke accompanied the King on
 his expedition, but Shakespeare leaves
 the matter ambiguous. When the King
 and Aumerle enter together at the
 beginning of 3.2, Aumerle asks Richard
 about how he feels after his voyage across

the Irish Sea; this could suggest that
Aumerle has remained in England,
although an audience might easily infer
that he has been with the King all along.
87 **go . . . will** let all happen as it will
88 **cold** unreceptive (to Richard's cause)
90 **sister** i.e sister-in-law
91 **presently** immediately
92 **take my ring** York's ring will confirm
 that the request comes from him.
97 In fact, the Duchess died several months
 after these events. The addition of her
 death to the news of Aumerle's departure
 heightens the impression of overwhelm-
 ing, multiple sorrows.

Comes rushing on this woeful land at once!
I know not what to do. I would to God,   100
So my untruth had not provoked him to it,
The King had cut off my head with my brother's.
What, are there no posts dispatched for Ireland?
How shall we do for money for these wars?
Come, sister—cousin I would say—pray pardon me.   105
Go, fellow, get thee home, provide some carts
And bring away the armour that is there.

            Exit Servant

Gentlemen, will you go muster men?
If I know how or which way to order these affairs,
Thus disorderly thrust into my hands,   110
Never believe me. Both are my kinsmen:
Th'one is my sovereign, whom both my oath
And duty bids defend; th'other again
Is my kinsman, whom the King hath wronged,
Whom conscience and my kindred bids to right.   115
Well, somewhat we must do. [*To Queen*] Come, cousin,
I'll dispose of you.
Gentlemen, go muster up your men
And meet me presently at Berkeley Castle.

---

99 Comes] Q1; Come F 100 God] Q1; heauen F 103 no posts] Q1; postes F 107.1 *Exit Servant*] CAPELL; *not in* Q1, F 108 go muster] Q1; muster F 116 *To Queen*] IRVING; *not in* Q1, F 117–19] *as* OXFORD; *two lines ending* 'men,' 'Barkly;' Q1; *two lines ending* 'men,' 'Castle:' F 119 Castle] F; *not in* Q1

100–2 **I would . . . brother's** I would have preferred, as long as I had done nothing dishonourable to deserve it, that the King had executed me along with my brother Gloucester.

103 **are . . . Ireland?** i.e. has the King not been informed of Bolingbroke's rebellion? This further indication of a lack of preparedness on the King's side and of York's agitation was likely suggested by Holinshed, who reports that bad weather prevented news from reaching the King in Ireland for six weeks (p. 499).

105 **sister** Preoccupied by grief, York confuses the Queen with his sister-in-law, about whose death he has just learned.

106–7 York is reduced to rummaging for armaments from his own estate.

111–15 **Both . . . right** York is caught between his sworn duty to the King and the demands of justice on Bolingbroke's side. That the first is primarily outward ('oath and duty') and the second mostly inward ('conscience') helps us understand his subsequent shift of allegiance.

116 **somewhat** something

117 **dispose of** make arrangements for

119 **Berkeley Castle** A fortress in Gloucestershire. As Forker remarks, the name might have resonated ominously for Shakespeare's playgoers as the place where Edward II (in Marlowe's play of the same name) was gruesomely murdered.

I should to Pleshey too,   120
But time will not permit. All is uneven
And everything is left at six and seven.

Exeunt York and Queen

BUSHY
The wind sits fair for news to go for Ireland
But none returns. For us to levy power
Proportionable to the enemy is all unpossible.   125

GREEN
Besides, our nearness to the King in love
Is near the hate of those love not the King.

BAGOT
And that's the wavering commons, for their love
Lies in their purses, and whoso empties them
By so much fills their hearts with deadly hate.   130

BUSHY
Wherein the King stands generally condemned.

BAGOT
If judgement lie in them then so do we,
Because we ever have been near the King.

GREEN
Well, I will for refuge straight to Bristol Castle.
The Earl of Wiltshire is already there.   135

120–2] *as* POPE; I should . . . permit: | All is . . . seauen Q1, F   122.1 *Exeunt York and Queen*]
ROWE; *Exeunt Duke, Qu man. Bush. Green,* Q1; *Exit* F   123 go for] Q1; go to F
125 unpossible] Q1; impossible F   128 that's] F; that is Q1   133 ever have been] Q1; haue
beene euer F

---

120 **I should to Pleshey** No doubt York
wishes to pay his respects at the Duchess's
funeral.
122 **at six and seven** in disorder
123–4 **The wind . . . returns** A good easterly
wind allows messengers to reach the King
in Ireland but prevents messages from
Ireland reaching us.
124 **power** military forces
126–7 **our . . . King** our love for the King
earns us the hatred of his enemies
128–30 **that's . . . hate** i.e. the fickle common people are so in love with their
own money that they hate anyone who
empties their purses. Richard's severe
taxation of the commons has already

been mentioned (2.1.246–7). Note the
contradiction between Bagot's charge
of inconstancy against the commons
and his understanding of the invariable
relationship between high taxes and
popular discontent.
132 **If . . . we** i.e. if the commons have the
power to judge, they will condemn us (as
well as the King).
134–5 In Holinshed, Bushy, Green and the
Earl of Wiltshire are arrested by Bolingbroke at Bristol Castle. In Shakespeare,
the Earl never appears on stage and is not
mentioned when Bushy and Green are
taken and killed at 3.1.1–35.

BUSHY

Thither will I with you, for little office
Will the hateful commons perform for us,
Except, like curs, to tear us all to pieces.
Will you go along with us?

BAGOT

No, I will to Ireland, to his majesty.   140
Farewell. If heart's presages be not vain,
We three here part that ne'er shall meet again.

BUSHY

That's as York thrives to beat back Bolingbroke.

GREEN

Alas, poor Duke, the task he undertakes
Is numb'ring sands and drinking oceans dry.   145
Where one on his side fights, thousands will fly.
Farewell at once—for once, for all and ever.

BUSHY

Well, we may meet again.

BAGOT   I fear me never.   *Exeunt*

2.3 *Enter Bolingbroke and Northumberland [with soldiers]*

BOLINGBROKE

How far is it, my lord, to Berkeley now?

137 commons] Q1, F; commoners OXFORD   138 to pieces] Q1; in pieces Q2–F   147] *as*
Q1; *assigned to Bushy* F; *assigned to Bagot* WHITE   148 *Exeunt*] ROWE; *Exit*. F; *not in* Q1
    2.3] F (*Scaena Tertia.*); *not in* Q1   0.1 *Bolingbroke and*] Q1 (*Hereford*,); *the Duke of Hereford,*
and F   *with soldiers*] CAPELL (*subs.*); *not in* Q1, F

136 **office** service
137 **hateful** (a) hated; (b) full of hate
140 At 3.2.122, Richard seems not to know
    where Bagot is, so perhaps he failed to
    join the King (see note to that line). In
    4.1, Bagot, at that point a prisoner, is
    called on by Bolingbroke to provide
    evidence about the murder of Gloucester.
141 **presages** premonitions
145 **numb'ring . . . dry** Two proverbial
    expressions for doing the impossible
    (Tilley S91 and O9).
146 **Where . . . fights** for every man who
    fights on his side

2.3 In contrast to the stasis and despair that
    mark the previous scene, this one is full
    of movement, desire and aspiration.
    Shakespeare makes even busier Holin-
    shed's account of the busy travels of
    those who are flocking to Bolingbroke's
    cause. At the start of the scene, Boling-
    broke and Northumberland are journey-
    ing through the Cotswolds (near Shake-
    speare's home town of Stratford) from
    Ravenspur (near present-day Hull) to
    Berkeley Castle in Gloucestershire. The
    ease of Bolingbroke's political ascend-
    ancy is sealed by his confrontation with
    York, who, after a bout of ineffectual
    verbal resistance, ends up inviting the
    rebels to spend the night at Berkeley
    Castle.

NORTHUMBERLAND

   Believe me, noble lord,
   I am a stranger here in Gloucestershire.
   These high wild hills and rough uneven ways
   Draws out our miles and makes them wearisome,   5
   And yet your fair discourse hath been as sugar,
   Making the hard way sweet and delectable.
   But I bethink me what a weary way
   From Ravenspur to Cotswold will be found
   In Ross and Willoughby, wanting your company,   10
   Which I protest hath very much beguiled
   The tediousness and process of my travel.
   But theirs is sweetened with the hope to have
   The present benefit which I possess,
   And hope to joy is little less in joy   15
   Than hope enjoyed. By this the weary lords
   Shall make their way seem short, as mine hath done
   By sight of what I have, your noble company.

BOLINGBROKE

   Of much less value is my company
   Than your good words.

       Enter Harry Percy

                 But who comes here?   20

NORTHUMBERLAND

   It is my son, young Harry Percy,

---

6 your] Q1; our F   9 Cotswold] Q1 (Cotshall), F (Cottshold)   14 which] Q1; that Q2–F
20 *Enter Harry Percy*] *placed as in* OXFORD; *after* 'here?' Q1, F

4 **hills** the Cotswolds. Northumberland, from the Scottish border regions in the north, is unfamiliar with the countryside of south-west England. It is surprising that he would characterize the Cotswolds as 'high wild', given the towering roughness of the more remote Pennines in his native region.

6–18 Northumberland's cloying flattery of Bolingbroke (he uses the words 'sugar', 'sweet', and 'sweetened', not to mention 'delectable', in the space of eight lines) seems to be illustrating a principle of monarchical rule, which is that everyone lies to the king (or the person likely to become king) almost all the time. The dying Gaunt and the distraught York are notable exceptions. Earlier, the usually plain-spoken Northumberland professed to be disgusted by Richard's flatterers (2.1.241–2).

10 **In** by

11 **beguiled** relieved, charmed

12 **tediousness and process** tedious progression (an example of hendiadys)

15–16 **hope to . . . enjoyed** The anticipation of joy is only a little less joyous than joy itself.

16 **this** this hope of enjoying your company

21 **young Harry Percy** The historical Harry was in fact two years older than Bolingbroke.

Sent from my brother Worcester whencesoever.
Harry, how fares your uncle?
PERCY
I had thought, my lord, to have learned his health of you.
NORTHUMBERLAND
Why, is he not with the Queen?   25
PERCY
No, my good lord. He hath forsook the court,
Broken his staff of office and dispersed
The household of the King.
NORTHUMBERLAND   What was his reason?
He was not so resolved when last we spoke together.
PERCY
Because your lordship was proclaimed traitor.   30
But he, my lord, is gone to Ravenspur
To offer service to the Duke of Hereford,
And sent me over by Berkeley to discover
What power the Duke of York had levied there,
Then with directions to repair to Ravenspur.   35
NORTHUMBERLAND
Have you forgot the Duke of Hereford, boy?
PERCY
No, my good lord, for that is not forgot
Which ne'er I did remember. To my knowledge,
I never in my life did look on him.
NORTHUMBERLAND
Then learn to know him now. This is the Duke.   40
PERCY
My gracious lord, I tender you my service,

28–9 What was . . . together] F; What . . . resolude, | When . . . togither Q1   29 last we]
Q1; we last F   30 lordship] Q2–F; Lo: Q1   35 directions] Q1; direction F   36 Hereford,
boy] Q3–F (*subs.*); Herefords boy Q1

22 **whencesoever** from wherever Worcester
   may be
26–35 Harry Percy repeats the news
   reported at 2.2.56–61 with the addition
   of an account of his own travels.
34 **power** forces
35 **repair** go
36 Northumberland rebukes his son for not
   offering Bolingbroke a proper greeting.

As he makes clear in the following lines,
however, Percy has never met Bolingbroke. The misunderstanding, which can
get a laugh in performance, provides a
character note for the irreverent Percy.
41–4 Harry Percy conceives of the service
   that he offers ('tenders') to Bolingbroke as
   a young 'tender' plant that he hopes will
   'ripen' into something tested ('approvèd')
   and deserving.

Such as it is, being tender, raw and young,
Which elder days shall ripen and confirm
To more approvèd service and desert.

BOLINGBROKE

I thank thee, gentle Percy, and be sure   45
I count myself in nothing else so happy
As in a soul rememb'ring my good friends;
And as my fortune ripens with thy love
It shall be still thy true love's recompense.
My heart this covenant makes, my hand thus seals it.   50

NORTHUMBERLAND

How far is it to Berkeley, and what stir
Keeps good old York there with his men of war?

PERCY

There stands the castle by yon tuft of trees,
Manned with three hundred men, as I have heard,
And in it are the lords of York, Berkeley and Seymour,   55
None else of name and noble estimate.

     Enter Ross and Willoughby

NORTHUMBERLAND

Here come the lords of Ross and Willoughby,
Bloody with spurring, fiery red with haste.

BOLINGBROKE

Welcome, my lords. I wot your love pursues

---

53 yon] Q1; yond F   56.1 *Enter . . . Willoughby*] F; *not in* Q1

45–50 In *1 Henry IV* (1.3.247), Hotspur (i.e.
Harry Percy) angrily recalls this speech
as 'a candy deal of courtesy'.

47 **in . . . remem'ring** i.e. in having a soul
that remembers

48–9 **as . . . recompense** as my fortune
(success; material wealth) improves
along with (or because of) your love, that
fortune will serve to reward you. As Black
points out, there is 'a touch of politic
vagueness in the phrasing'.

48 **ripens** improves. Horticultural images
are commonly used as a way of bracket-
ing off the violence attendant upon
characters' political ambitions. It is a
feature of Bolingbroke's language that

appears again in his speech before Flint
Castle (3.3.41–7) and at the end of the
play (5.6.45–6).

50 **thus** To provide outward confirmation of
his professed inward commitment to the
Percies, Bolingbroke offers to shake
Harry Percy's hand or claps his own
hand to his breast.

51–2 **what . . . York** what is York doing
(York is the subject of the clause)

58 **Bloody with spurring** bloody with the
blood of the horses they have spurred in
hard pursuit of Bolingbroke. Holinshed
tells us that Ross and Willoughby joined
Bolingbroke at Ravenspur.

59 **wot** believe

A banished traitor. All my treasury 60
Is yet but unfelt thanks, which, more enriched,
Shall be your love and labour's recompense.

ROSS

Your presence makes us rich, most noble lord.

WILLOUGHBY

And far surmounts our labour to attain it.

BOLINGBROKE

Evermore thanks—the exchequer of the poor, 65
Which, till my infant fortune comes to years,
Stands for my bounty.

Enter Berkeley

But who comes here?

NORTHUMBERLAND

It is my lord of Berkeley as I guess.

BERKELEY

My lord of Hereford, my message is to you.

BOLINGBROKE

My lord, my answer is to 'Lancaster', 70
And I am come to seek that name in England,
And I must find that title in your tongue
Before I make reply to aught you say.

---

65 thanks—the] Q5, F (thankes, the); thanke's the Q1   67 *Enter Berkeley*] *placed as in*
OXFORD; *after* 'here?' F; *not in* Q1

60 **treasury** repository of wealth. Watt
comments that 'Bolingbroke speaks as if
he already were king' (Black, p. 160),
though 'treasury' can also refer to a private person's treasure-house; nevertheless, the word is a move toward an
increasingly royal vocabulary, which is
supplemented when Bolingbroke uses
'exchequer' (65), although even there he
uses the word metaphorically.

61 **unfelt** intangible, unrealized

61–2 **enriched . . . recompense** Bolingbroke
speaks more frankly than he does at 48–9
about the material rewards he is willing
to promise his supporters.

63 **presence** The word might have reminded
an Elizabethan of the phrase 'the royal
presence', the space around the person
of the monarch.

64 **far . . . it** i.e. your company is more

precious than the exertions we take to
enjoy it

65 **thanks . . . poor** i.e. thanks is all the poor
can give as a reward
exchequer royal or national treasury
(*OED n.* 5)

66–7 **till . . . bounty** A child could not take
possession of his inheritance until he
attained the age of majority.

67 *Enter Berkeley* In Holinshed (p. 498),
Berkeley and York confront Bolingbroke
together. Shakespeare changes his source
in order to create two separate encounters between Henry and those still
loyal to the King.

70 **Lancaster** Bolingbroke insists that
Berkeley use the title he assumed on the
death of his father, Duke of Lancaster.
Gurr notes that he did not object when
Northumberland called him 'Hereford'
at l. 36.

BERKELEY

Mistake me not, my lord, 'tis not my meaning
To raze one tittle of your honour out.   75
To you, my lord, I come—what lord you will—
From the most gracious regent of this land,
The Duke of York, to know what pricks you on
To take advantage of the absent time
And fright our native peace with self-borne arms.   80
    Enter York [with attendants]

BOLINGBROKE

I shall not need transport my words by you.
Here comes his grace in person. My noble uncle!
    [*He kneels*]

YORK

Show me thy humble heart and not thy knee,
Whose duty is deceivable and false.

BOLINGBROKE

My gracious uncle—   85

YORK

Tut, tut, grace me no grace, nor uncle me no uncle.
I am no traitor's uncle and that word 'grace'
In an ungracious mouth is but profane.

---

75 raze] Q1 (race), F tittle] Q1, F (title)   77 gracious regent] Q1; glorious Q2 (*subs.*)–F
80.1 *Enter York*] F; *not in* Q1   *with attendants*] CAPELL; *not in* Q1, F   82.1 *He kneels*] ROWE
(*subs.*); *not in* Q1, F   86 no uncle] Q1; *not in* F

75 **raze** erase, scrape away
   tittle small stroke or point in writing
   (*OED n.* 1), with a pun on 'title'. Q1, F's
   'title' is an alternative spelling, and thus
   registers the play on words.
76 **what . . . will** whatever title you might
   choose
78 **pricks** spurs
79 **absent time** time of the King's absence
80 **native peace** naturally peaceful state.
   'Berkeley implies that Bolingbroke is
   behaving like a foreign invader' (Forker).
   self-borne arms weapons carried for self-
   interested rather than patriotic reasons.
   Gurr suggests that there is a pun on birth
   (i.e. born from itself), implying the
   unnaturalness of the rebellion.
81 I do not need you to carry my message.
83–4 York's scepticism about his nephew's
   formal act of deference to him as regent
   and elder kinsman can also put in

question Bolingbroke's earlier gestural
performance of inward dedication (50).
84 **deceivable** able to deceive
86–104 York's speech, which teeters between
   a powerful rebuke from a position of
   monarchical principle and an expression
   of abject helplessness in the face of
   Bolingbroke's overwhelmingly superior
   force, sets the stage for the King's more
   elaborately expressed anguish in the face
   of the same contradiction in 3.2.
86 **grace me . . . no uncle** York chides
   Bolingbroke as if he were a bad child.
   Malone points out the parallel with
   Romeo and Juliet: Capulet uses the same
   phrasing to upbraid his daughter: 'Thank
   me no thankings, nor proud me no
   prouds' (3.5.152).
88 **ungracious** (a) insolent; (b) without
   God's grace (hence 'profane')

Why have those banished and forbidden legs
Dared once to touch a dust of England's ground?   90
But then, more why—why have they dared to march
So many miles upon her peaceful bosom,
Frighting her pale-faced villages with war
And ostentation of despisèd arms?
Com'st thou because the anointed King is hence?   95
Why, foolish boy, the King is left behind,
And in my loyal bosom lies his power.
Were I but now the lord of such hot youth
As when brave Gaunt, thy father, and myself
Rescued the Black Prince, that young Mars of men,   100
From forth the ranks of many thousand French,
O then how quickly should this arm of mine,
Now prisoner to the palsy, chastise thee
And minister correction to thy fault.

BOLINGBROKE

My gracious uncle, let me know my fault.   105
On what condition stands it and wherein?

YORK

Even in condition of the worst degree:
In gross rebellion and detested treason.
Thou art a banished man and here art come,

---

89 those] Q1; these F   91 then, more] Q1 (then more); more than Q2–4;   more then Q5,
F   why—] CAPELL; why? Q1; why, F   98 now the] F; now Q1

---

90 **dust** an iota of dust
92–3 In York's bizarrely anthropomorphic
account, England is a woman whose
bosom Bolingbroke marches across,
frightening the villages, which are faces
blanched with fear.
94 **ostentation** brandishing
despisèd despised because they are
carried by traitors
95–7 **the anointed . . . power** i.e. Richard
might be absent but his authority is
present, vested in his deputy.
99–101 There is no historical basis for this
evocative anecdote, which reiterates the
ideal of family and national solidarity
against a foreign enemy that was given
such memorable expression in Gaunt's
'this England' speech (2.1.40–66). It

is worth noting that, of the present
generation, Richard is fighting a foreign
enemy in Ireland while Bolingbroke is
waging a domestic campaign that has
been equipped by the Duke of Brittany.
103 **palsy** paralysis or weakness, sometimes
with tremor (*OED n.* 1a)
105–6 Bolingbroke   repositions   York's
moralist language in a legalistic register,
pulling York's 'fault' (= defect in moral
character) toward 'default' (= 'failure to
perform some legal requirement or obligation' (*OED n.* 3a)) through association
with 'condition' (= stipulation).
107 **condition** circumstance. York quibbles
on 'condition' in order to restore a strong
sense of 'fault' as moral failing.

Before the expiration of thy time,   110
In braving arms against thy sovereign.
BOLINGBROKE
As I was banished, I was banished Hereford;
But as I come, I come for Lancaster.
And, noble uncle, I beseech your grace,
Look on my wrongs with an indifferent eye.   115
You are my father, for methinks in you
I see old Gaunt alive. O then, my father,
Will you permit that I shall stand condemned
A wandering vagabond, my rights and royalties
Plucked from my arms perforce and given away   120
To upstart unthrifts? Wherefore was I born?
If that my cousin King be king in England,
It must be granted I am Duke of Lancaster.
You have a son, Aumerle, my noble cousin.
Had you first died and he been thus trod down,   125
He should have found his uncle Gaunt a father
To rouse his wrongs and chase them to the bay.
I am denied to sue my livery here
And yet my letters patents give me leave.
My father's goods are all distrained and sold   130
And these and all are all amiss employed.
What would you have me do? I am a subject
And I challenge law. Attorneys are denied me

---

122 in] Q1; of Q2–F   124 cousin] Q1; Kinsman F   133 I] Q1; *not in* F

111 **braving** defiant, boastful
112–13 **As . . . Lancaster** I was banished as the Duke of Hereford; I return to claim my inheritance as Duke of Lancaster.
115 **indifferent** unbiased. Note, however, that Bolingbroke immediately asks York to regard him as his son.
119–20 **rights . . . perforce** prerogatives and privileges due to me as the Duke of Lancaster ('arms' = coat of arms) taken away by force ('perforce'). Bolingbroke unknowingly echoes York's attempt to persuade the King not to seize Bolingbroke's 'royalties and rights' at 2.1.190 (Gurr).
121 **upstart unthrifts** presumptuous spendthrifts
122–3 As at 119, Bolingbroke is repeating

the argument for lawful succession that York used on his behalf when speaking to the King (2.1.195–9).
125 **first died** died before Gaunt
127 to ferret out any wrongs done to him and chase them to a standstill (where they will be defeated). The image is of hunted animals being driven from their lairs by hounds and being forced to turn and fight (see *OED*, bay, *n.*[4] 3).
128–9 **sue my livery . . . letters patents** further echoes of York (see 2.1.202–4 and nn.). Bolingbroke has been deprived of his right to claim his inheritance.
130 **distrained** seized
131 **amiss employed** wrongfully used
133 **challenge law** claim my rights under the law

And therefore personally I lay my claim
To my inheritance of free descent.   135

NORTHUMBERLAND
The noble Duke hath been too much abused.

ROSS
It stands your grace upon to do him right.

WILLOUGHBY
Base men by his endowments are made great.

YORK
My lords of England, let me tell you this:
I have had feeling of my cousin's wrongs   140
And laboured all I could to do him right.
But in this kind to come—in braving arms
Be his own carver and cut out his way
To find out right with wrong—it may not be.
And you that do abet him in this kind   145
Cherish rebellion and are rebels all.

NORTHUMBERLAND
The noble Duke hath sworn his coming is
But for his own, and for the right of that
We all have strongly sworn to give him aid.
And let him ne'er see joy that breaks that oath.   150

YORK
Well well, I see the issue of these arms.
I cannot mend it, I must needs confess,
Because my power is weak and all ill-left.
But if I could, by him that gave me life,

144 wrong] Q1; Wrongs F   150 ne'er] Q3–F (ne're, neu'r); neuer Q1   153 ill-left] *hyphen*
HANMER

135 **of free descent** i.e. according to the laws
of inheritance
137 **It . . . upon** it is incumbent upon your
grace
138 **endowments** bequeathed property
(which should be Bolingbroke's by right)
142 **kind** manner
143–4 **Be . . . wrong** cut his own meat
greedily at table and slice his way
(through the law and those loyal to the
King), using unjust means to achieve
('find out') just ends
147–50 Northumberland makes it plain that
the lords' support of the rebellion is not
a matter for debate, as York might have

supposed, but rather a *fait accompli*,
sealed by a collective oath. There is also
an element of threat intended to enforce
the lords' support of Bolingbroke.
148 **his own** his rights and properties (not
the King's)
151 **issue of these arms** result of this taking
to arms
152–3 Holinshed (p. 498) provides a different reason for York's failure to resist
the rebellion, which is that, while York
had in fact deployed a strong force,
the soldiers refused to fight against
Bolingbroke.

I would attach you all and make you stoop   155
Unto the sovereign mercy of the King.
But since I cannot, be it known unto you
I do remain as neuter. So fare you well,
Unless you please to enter in the castle
And there repose you for this night.   160

BOLINGBROKE

An offer, uncle, that we will accept;
But we must win your grace to go with us
To Bristol Castle, which they say is held
By Bushy, Bagot and their complices,
The caterpillars of the commonwealth   165
Which I have sworn to weed and pluck away.

YORK

It may be I will go with you—but yet I'll pause,
For I am loath to break our country's laws.
Nor friends nor foes, to me welcome you are,
Things past redress are now with me past care.   170

Exeunt

---

157 unto] Q1; to Q2–F

---

155 **attach** arrest
    stoop bow
158 **neuter** neutral. Unwilling to acknow-
    ledge that he has definitively changed
    sides, York's struggle between his loyalty
    to the King and his sympathy for the
    rights of Bolingbroke is nevertheless put
    to rest by a declaration of neutrality that
    is tantamount to his joining the
    rebellion.
159–60 **Unless . . . night** York's surprising
    offer of hospitality to the rebels confirms
    both his *de facto* shift of allegiance and his
    inability to acknowledge it.
162 **win** convince. Gurr observes that
    Henry 'does not hesitate to push York
    further once he has begun to weaken'.
    Bolingbroke's deferential-seeming ma-
    nipulation of his uncle, whose presence
    at Bristol will lend legitimacy to the
    'weeding away' of the King's favourites,

anticipates how he will assume a
reverential pose while taking charge of
Richard's movements after the King's
arrest at the end of 3.3.
164 **complices** accomplices
165 **caterpillars** parasites, which destroy
    the garden of England (see 3.4). The
    metaphor has biblical origins (see Isaiah
    33: 4) and was a commonplace in early
    modern English homily and satire.
166 **weed** remove (vermin, noxious animals)
    (*OED v.* 3b)
169 **Nor . . . are** you are welcome as neither
    friends nor foes. The unresolved sense
    of the sentence mirrors York's situation
    and state of mind, since he knows that
    his presence with Bolingbroke at Bristol
    will be a form of participation in the
    rebellion.
170 **Things . . . care** i.e. I can do nothing
    more about things that are past redress.

2.4 *Enter Earl of Salisbury and a Welsh Captain*

CAPTAIN

My lord of Salisbury, we have stayed ten days
And hardly kept our countrymen together,
And yet we hear no tidings from the King;
Therefore we will disperse ourselves. Farewell.

SALISBURY

Stay yet another day, thou trusty Welshman,   5
The King reposeth all his confidence in thee.

CAPTAIN

'Tis thought the King is dead. We will not stay.
The bay trees in our country are all withered
And meteors fright the fixèd stars of heaven.
The pale-faced moon looks bloody on the earth   10
And lean-looked prophets whisper fearful change.
Rich men look sad and ruffians dance and leap,
The one in fear to lose what they enjoy,
The other to enjoy by rage and war.

2.4] F (*Scoena Quarta.*); *not in* Q1   0.1 *Enter ... Captain*] Q1; *Enter Salisbury, and a Captaine.* F   1, 7 CAPTAIN] F (*Capt.*); *Welch.* Q1   8 are all] Q1; all are Q2–F

2.4 This short scene, which takes place somewhere in Wales, is based on Holinshed's report that the Earl of Salisbury, having been sent by the King to gather soldiers, succeeded in mustering an army but could not prevent it from disbanding as a result of Richard's prolonged absence: 'there were to the number of forty thousand men assembled, ready to march with the King against his enemies if he had been there himself in person' (p. 499). Holinshed also reports that Richard could not return to England in a timely way because of bad weather and bad planning. Shakespeare omits mention of this, although he does adopt stormy weather as a metaphor for the dangers Richard now faces (22). The Welsh captain, though unnamed, speaks of supernatural portents in a manner very like his counterpart Glendower (Glyndŵr) in *1 Henry IV* (who is mentioned at l. 43 of the next scene).

1 **stayed** waited

1 **ten days** Holinshed reports that the force, which included 'Welshmen and others', was willing to wait fourteen days for the King's arrival. Shakespeare adapts his source material for the metre and for focus.

2 **hardly** with difficulty

8 Holinshed reports that English bay trees withered and grew green again before Richard departed for Ireland (p. 496). Shakespeare relocates the trees to Wales and excises the detail about their regeneration so as to make the observation more ominous. The bay laurel was classically the symbol of victory.

9 **meteors . . . stars** Meteors and comets were thought to be harbingers of cataclysmic change; their ability to 'fright the fixèd stars', symbols of permanence, heightens the impression of impending doom.

10 **The . . . earth** The moon, usually pale white, looks red, as if to foretell the shedding of blood on the earth.

11 **lean-looked** thin-faced

These signs forerun the death or fall of kings—   15
Farewell, our countrymen are gone and fled,
As well assured Richard their King is dead.   *Exit*
SALISBURY
Ah, Richard, with the eyes of heavy mind
I see thy glory like a shooting star
Fall to the base earth from the firmament.   20
Thy sun sets weeping in the lowly west,
Witnessing storms to come, woe and unrest.
Thy friends are fled to wait upon thy foes
And crossly to thy good all fortune goes.   *Exit*

3.1 *Enter Bolingbroke, York, Northumberland, Ross, Percy,*
    Willoughby [and soldiers], with Bushy and Green prisoners
BOLINGBROKE
Bring forth these men.
Bushy and Green, I will not vex your souls,
Since presently your souls must part your bodies,
With too much urging your pernicious lives,
For 'twere no charity. Yet to wash your blood   5
From off my hands, here in the view of men

---

15 or fall] Q1; *not in* Q2–F   17 *Exit*] F; *not in* Q1   18 the] Q1; *not in* Q2–F   24 *Exit*] F; *not in* Q1

3.1] F (*Actus Tertius. Scena Prima.*); *not in* Q1   0.1–2 *Enter . . . prisoners*] F; *Enter Duke of Hereford, Yorke, Northumberland, Bushie and Greene prisoners.* Q1   0.2 *and soldiers*] CAPELL (*Officers behind*); *not in* Q1, F

15 **forerun** precede
18–24 Salisbury becomes something of a prophet himself. His image, 'thy sun sets weeping', anticipates Bolingbroke's variation of the 'sun–king' metaphor at 3.3.61–6, where Richard's rising and setting is emphasized rather than his god-like brightness; and the fall of the 'shooting star . . . to the base earth' looks ahead to the King's Phaëton-like descent to 'the base court' at 3.3.177–81.
19 **shooting star** Salisbury recalls the 'meteor' at l. 9.
22 **Witnessing** portending
23 **wait upon** serve
24 **crossly** adversely
3.1 Holinshed includes the Earl of Wiltshire in this episode, though Shakespeare leaves him out. Bolingbroke is moving to establish his power and from here the momentum of his rise begins to build,

leading inexorably to his triumph over Richard. At the same time, the summary executions of Richard's followers suggest a ruthlessness on Bolingbroke's part that might easily compromise audience feelings about his growing control.
3 **presently** very soon, immediately
  part depart from
4 **urging** alleging, affirming (*OED v.* 1)
5 **no charity** Though, on the basis of 'charity', Bolingbroke disclaims any detailing of his opponents' crimes, he goes on immediately to offer a full account.
5–6 **wash . . . hands** a fleeting and not entirely appropriate allusion to Christ's passion, with a reference to Pilate washing his hands
6 **in the view of men** in an explicitly public setting. As in 1.1 and 1.3, there is a formal, judicial element to the proceedings.

I will unfold some causes of your deaths:
You have misled a prince, a royal king,
A happy gentleman in blood and lineaments,
By you unhappied and disfigured clean.   10
You have in manner with your sinful hours
Made a divorce betwixt his queen and him,
Broke the possession of a royal bed
And stained the beauty of a fair queen's cheeks
With tears drawn from her eyes by your foul wrongs.   15
Myself—a prince by fortune of my birth,
Near to the King in blood and nea'er in love
Till you did make him misinterpret me—
Have stooped my neck under your injuries
And sighed my English breath in foreign clouds,   20
Eating the bitter bread of banishment
Whilst you have fed upon my signories,
Disparked my parks and felled my forest woods,

---

15 by] Q1; with Q2–F   17 nea'er] This edition (*conj.* Wells); neere Q1, F   20 sighed]
Q3–F; sigh't Q1   22 Whilst] Q1; While Q2–F

9 **happy** fortunate
  blood noble blood (as so often in the play)
  lineaments distinctive features (especially
  of the face, though the word also implies
  more general attributes and talents)
10 **unhappied . . . clean** rendered miserable
  and utterly debased
11–15 The suggestion here of homosexual
  interest between Richard and some of his
  followers, leading to tension and unhappiness in the relationship between the
  King and Queen, is a feature frequently
  exploited in modern productions, though
  it is not in fact borne out by the rest of
  the play. Holinshed says that the King's
  indulgence in 'the filthy sin of lechery
  and fornication' led God to 'shred him
  off from the sceptre of his kingdom'
  (p. 508), but he does not accuse Richard
  of sodomy. While the Queen is clearly
  unhappy (see 2.2.1–72), her sadness does
  not seem to derive from Richard's being
  drawn to 'sinful hours', but rather from
  her being physically separated from him
  and anxious about his fortunes; nor does
  she appear at all resentful toward Bushy
  and Green, in whom she confides. In
  5.1, Richard treats her very tenderly.

12 **Made a divorce** driven a wedge (not
  caused an actual divorce)
13 **possession** i.e. the right of each marriage
  partner to possess the other
16 **Myself** After dealing first with Bushy and
  Green's supposed moral crimes, Bolingbroke turns, as though to a secondary
  matter, to the offences against himself.
  prince Bolingbroke is entitled to the
  designation since he is a member of the
  royal family, but the title nevertheless
  signals his ambition since it frequently
  means 'monarch' or 'sovereign ruler'.
17 **nea'er** Since QF's 'neere' can, as elsewhere in the play, be the comparative
  form, we have so interpreted it here, thus
  giving more punch to Bolingbroke's
  complaint.
20 Bolingbroke's language recalls that of
  Mowbray when both are banished
  (1.3.160–73).
22 **signories** feudal estates
23 **Disparked my parks** converted my land
  to other, possibly commercial, uses
  ('parks' = land set aside for hunting or
  other aristocratic pursuits)

From my own windows torn my household coat,
Razed out my imprese, leaving me no sign   25
Save men's opinions and my living blood
To show the world I am a gentleman.
This and much more, much more than twice all this
Condemns you to the death. See them delivered over
To execution and the hand of death.   30

BUSHY

More welcome is the stroke of death to me
Than Bolingbroke to England. Lords, farewell.

GREEN

My comfort is that heaven will take our souls
And plague injustice with the pains of hell.

BOLINGBROKE

My lord Northumberland, see them dispatched.   35

[*Exeunt Northumberland and others
with the prisoners*]

Uncle, you say the Queen is at your house—
For God's sake fairly let her be intreated,
Tell her I send to her my kind commends.
Take special care my greetings be delivered.

YORK

A gentleman of mine I have dispatched   40
With letters of your love to her at large.

BOLINGBROKE

Thanks, gentle uncle. Come lords, away,

---

24 my own] Q1; mine owne Q3–F   25 Razed] Q1 (Rac't), F   32 Lords, farewell] Q1; *not in* F
35.1–2 *Exeunt . . . prisoners*] CAPELL; *not in* Q1, F   37 God's] Q1; Heauens F

---

24 **coat** coat of arms (set in a stained-glass
window)
25 **Razed . . . imprese** destroyed my
emblem(s); 'imprese' is the plural form
of Italian *impresa*, a device combining
pictorial and verbal elements expressive
of family distinction (though here the
word is apparently used as a singular
noun of two syllables).
   sign External markers of aristocratic
status and value were as important in
Shakespeare's time as in the fourteenth
century; Bolingbroke's complaint that
he has been deprived of such signs is a
serious one.

26 **men's opinions** i.e. reputation. The importance of noble reputation and honour
is recurrent in the play: see, for example,
1.1.177–9, 182–3, 190 ff.
34 **plague injustice** punish the unjust (i.e.
Bolingbroke)
35 **dispatched** sent off, executed
36 At 2.2.117, York has told the Queen
that he will 'dispose of' her, i.e. make
arrangements for her accommodation;
he has presumably given her shelter at
one of his estates.
37 **intreated** treated
38 **commends** greetings, regards
41 **at large** in full

To fight with Glendower and his complices—
A while to work, and after, holiday.   *Exeunt*

3.2 *Drums, flourish, and colours. Enter Richard, Aumerle,*
      Carlisle, and soldiers

RICHARD
Barkloughly Castle call they this at hand?
AUMERLE
Yea, my lord. How brooks your grace the air
After your late tossing on the breaking seas?
RICHARD
Needs must I like it well. I weep for joy
To stand upon my kingdom once again;   5
Dear earth, I do salute thee with my hand
Though rebels wound thee with their horses' hoofs.

---

43 Glendower] Q1 (Glendor), F (*Glendoure*); Glyndŵr OXFORD
  3.2] F (*Scena Secunda.*); *not in* Q1   0.1–2 *Drums . . . soldiers*] F; *Enter the King Aumerle,*
Carleil, &c. Q1   1 Barkloughly] Q1, F; Harlechly OXFORD   they] Q1; you Q2–F

---

43 **Glendower** A Welsh chieftain (the name
    is disyllabic, as suggested by the Q and F
    spellings); he has a prominent role in *1
    Henry IV* but plays no other part in this
    play, unless the 'Welsh Captain' who
    appears in 2.4 is to be identified with
    Glendower. That this line both refers to
    an episode that is not mentioned else-
    where, and interrupts a rhyming couplet,
    has led to the supposition (originating
    with Theobald) that it may have been
    inserted at a later time, perhaps to link
    the skirmishes here with the war in *1
    Henry IV*.
3.2 Richard has been absent from the stage,
    and from England, since 2.1.223.
    Immediately upon his departure at that
    point, the conspiracy against him began
    to build. Bolingbroke's presence in 2.3
    and 3.1 gives him a theatrical as well
    as a political advantage, which we have
    just seen him exploit. So when Richard
    now appears, he seems already at a dis-
    advantage, a sense that is augmented by
    his somewhat maudlin and self-pitying
    reaction to the series of escalating mis-
    fortunes which mark the scene; and of
    course, by its end, he is on the ropes.

0.1 *colours* flags (carried in by extras)
  1 **Barkloughly** i.e. Harlech. Shakespeare
    derives the name from Holinshed, who
    calls it 'Barclowie', though the real name
    of the castle was Hertlowie (modernized
    to Harlechy by Oxford). Berkeley ('Barkly'
    or 'Barkely') Castle, mentioned in
    2.2.119, is a different place altogether,
    though Shakespeare's spelling here may
    have been influenced by it.
  2 **brooks** likes
  4 **Needs must** A common phrase meaning
    simply 'must', but rather odd in this con-
    text since it usually implies unwillingness
    or inescapability of some sort, whereas
    Richard is apparently delighted to be
    back on his native soil.
  6 **earth . . . hand** He stoops to touch the
    ground; earth is a persistent feature
    of the text's imagery, one that was
    graphically represented in a production
    at Stratford's Other Place in 2000
    through the presence of a large mound
    of actual soil on the stage which at this
    point Richard sifted lovingly through his
    hands.

As a long-parted mother with her child
Plays fondly with her tears and smiles in meeting,
So weeping, smiling, greet I thee, my earth,   10
And do thee favours with my royal hands.
Feed not thy sovereign's foe, my gentle earth,
Nor with thy sweets comfort his ravenous sense,
But let thy spiders that suck up thy venom
And heavy-gaited toads lie in their way,   15
Doing annoyance to the treacherous feet
Which with usurping steps do trample thee.
Yield stinging nettles to mine enemies
And when they from thy bosom pluck a flower,
Guard it, I pray thee, with a lurking adder,   20
Whose double tongue may with a mortal touch
Throw death upon thy sovereign's enemies.
Mock not my senseless conjuration, lords.
This earth shall have a feeling and these stones

---

8 long-parted] *hyphen* POPE   11 favours] Q1; fauor Q2–F   20 pray thee] Q1; prethee F

8–11 **As . . . hands** An extended simile in
which Richard compares his feelings
to those of a loving mother who has
been separated ('parted') from her child
and now enjoys a tearful reunion, sad
and happy at once. (This contrasts
with Bolingbroke's characterization of
the earth as his mother or nurse at
1.3.306–7.)

13 **sense** appetite, desire

14 **spiders . . . venom** Referring to a sup-
position of natural history, that spiders
absorbed poison from the earth; E. K.
Chambers (Falcon edn., 1891) cites
Edward III, where the King compares
himself to 'a poison-sucking envious
spider' who 'turn(s) the juice I take to
deadly venom' (2.1.284–5). For other
instances of 'venom' in *Richard II,* see
1.1.171, and 2.1.19 and 157.

15 **heavy-gaited** slow-moving. Edward Top-
sell tells us: 'Toads do not leap as frogs do,
but because of their . . . short legs, their
pace is . . . soft [and] creeping' (*History
of Serpents* (1608, p. 191)); like spiders,
toads were regarded as venomous.

16 **annoyance** injury

16 **treacherous feet** i.e. the feet of the

soldiers whose 'usurping steps' (17)
support the traitor, Bolingbroke

17 **thee** i.e. the earth, which Richard is
addressing throughout this passage

20 **adder** A species of snake, the only
poisonous kind in Great Britain; Richard
adds yet another venomous, earth-bound
creature to his list. Lady Macbeth uses
the same metaphor (1.5.65–6); Black
points to the proverb 'a snake in the
grass' (Tilley S585).

21 **double** forked. Shakespeare's con-
temporaries thought the poison of the
adder resided in the tongue, whose
'mortal touch', Richard hopes, will bring
death to his enemies (22).

23 Richard, characteristically aware of his
propensity to self-dramatization, brings
himself up short, calling his extensive
apostrophe to the earth a 'senseless
conjuration'; i.e. a solemn appeal or
incantation that seems 'senseless' (foolish) in that it is addressed to a 'senseless'
(unfeeling) object: the earth.

24–6 An example of Richard's magical
thinking: his tendency to believe that his
kingship alone will spark both natural
and supernatural forces to come auto-
matically to his aid.

Prove armèd soldiers ere her native king   25
Shall falter under foul rebellion's arms.

CARLISLE

Fear not, my lord. That power that made you king
Hath power to keep you king in spite of all.
The means that heavens yield must be embraced
And not neglected; else heaven would   30
And we will not: heaven's offer we refuse,
The proffered means of succours and redress.

AUMERLE

He means, my lord, that we are too remiss
Whilst Bolingbroke, through our security,
Grows strong and great in substance and in friends.   35

RICHARD

Discomfortable cousin, know'st thou not
That when the searching eye of heaven is hid
Behind the globe and lights the lower world,
Then thieves and robbers range abroad unseen
In murders and in outrage boldly here;   40
But when from under this terrestrial ball
He fires the proud tops of the eastern pines

---

26 rebellion's] Q1; Rebellious Q3–F   29–32 The means . . . redress] Q1; *not in* F   31 will]
Q1–2; would Q3–5   32 succours] Q1 (succors); succour POPE   35 friends] F; power Q1
38 and] HANMER; that Q1, F   40 boldly] HUDSON (*conj.* Collier); bouldy Q1; bloody F

27 **power** i.e. that of God (a reference to the
  divine right of kings)
29–32 Carlisle modifies what he says in the
  previous two lines, reminding Richard
  that magical thinking is not enough; the
  king must embrace the material means
  available to fight his enemies, not just
  rely on God. These four lines are omitted
  in F, perhaps because of their relative
  obscurity, but their omission erases the
  point of Aumerle's simpler, more direct,
  and perhaps slightly comic, translation
  (33–5).
30–1 **heaven . . . refuse** i.e. we turn our wills
  against that of heaven, refusing heaven's
  offer which, as explained in the following
  line, is the military support needed to
  'redress' the situation (see next note).
32 **succours and redress** military reinforce-
  ments (*OED*, succour, 3) and assistance;
  the plural form, 'succours', was common
  until the early 17th century; hence

Pope's emendation, accepted by most
  editors, is unnecessary.
34 **security** overconfidence (resulting in
  inaction)
36 **Discomfortable** causing discomfort. For
  variations on the theme of comfort in
  the scene, see ll. 13, 65, 75, 82, 144, 206,
  and 208.
37 **searching eye** sun. The phrase initiates
  an extended, and common, analogy between sun and king ('searching' = keenly
  observant, penetrating).
38 **lower world** the other side of the world,
  the 'antipodes' (49)
40 **murders** Though Richard is here speaking in general, the audience might be led
  to recall the murder of Gloucester as well
  as the execution of Bushy and Green in
  3.1 (Forker).
41 **this terrestrial ball** the earth
42 The reference is to a bright dawn when
  the sun lights up the tree-tops.

And darts his light through every guilty hole,
Then murders, treasons and detested sins,
The cloak of night being plucked from off their backs,   45
Stand bare and naked trembling at themselves.
So when this thief, this traitor Bolingbroke,
Who all this while hath revelled in the night
Whilst we were wandering with th'antipodes,
Shall see us rising in our throne, the east,   50
His treasons will sit blushing in his face,
Not able to endure the sight of day
But, self-affrighted, tremble at his sin.
Not all the water in the rough rude sea
Can wash the balm off from an anointed king.   55
The breath of worldly men cannot depose
The deputy elected by the Lord;
For every man that Bolingbroke hath pressed
To lift shrewd steel against our golden crown,
God for his Richard hath in heavenly pay   60
A glorious angel. Then if angels fight,
Weak men must fall, for heaven still guards the right.

---

43 light] Q1; Lightning F   49] Q1; *not in* F   55 off] Q1; *not in* F   60 God] Q1; Heauen F

---

43 **every guilty hole** the places where the guilty have been hiding

47–53 Having spun out the sun analogy for eleven lines, Richard now applies it to the immediate situation: Bolingbroke is the night-lurking thief, Richard the bright sun who will expose his crimes to the 'sight of day' (52).

49 **antipodes** those who live in the 'lower world' as well as that nether region itself (see 38 n.). Richard of course has been in Ireland, not the antipodes, but in terms of his extended simile he, like the sun at night, has been under the earth.

51–2 **His . . . day** i.e. Bolingbroke's treasons will make him blush with shame when they are rendered visible by Richard's dawn

53 **self-affrighted** frightened by the sudden revelation of his own crimes. The syntax is compressed, 'he shall' being understood.
tremble Repeating the idea of thieves 'trembling' from l. 46, with specific reference to Bolingbroke.

54–62 Once again Richard reverts to magical thinking; see 24–6 n.

54 **rude** stormy, turbulent

55 **balm** holy oil with which the King is 'anointed' during the coronation ceremony (cf. 1.2.38 and 4.1.128)

56 **breath** words. Speech and breath are frequently linked in the play: see 1.3.215, 3.4.82, and 4.1.129.

58–61 The wordplay on 'crown' and 'angel', both also Elizabethan coins, suggests the economic basis of Richard's grandiose opposition of 'shrewd steel' against 'golden crown' and Bolingbroke's 'pressed' (= conscripted) soldiers against God's 'glorious angel[s]'. There may also be an allusion to Matthew 26: 53, where Jesus tells his disciples that, if he wanted to escape death, God would send legions of angels to defend him.

59 **shrewd** sharp

62 **still guards** always protects

Enter Salisbury

Welcome, my lord. How far off lies your power?

SALISBURY

Nor nea'er nor farther off, my gracious lord,

Than this weak arm. Discomfort guides my tongue   65

And bids me speak of nothing but despair.

One day too late, I fear me, noble lord,

Hath clouded all thy happy days on earth.

O call back yesterday, bid time return,

And thou shalt have twelve thousand fighting men;   70

Today, today, unhappy day too late,

O'erthrows thy joys, friends, fortune and thy state—

For all the Welshmen, hearing thou wert dead,

Are gone to Bolingbroke, dispersed and fled.

AUMERLE

Comfort, my liege. Why looks your grace so pale?   75

RICHARD

But now the blood of twenty thousand men

Did triumph in my face and they are fled;

And till so much blood thither come again

Have I not reason to look pale and dead?

All souls that will be safe fly from my side,   80

For time hath set a blot upon my pride.

AUMERLE

Comfort, my liege, remember who you are.

RICHARD

I had forgot myself. Am I not king?

---

63 Welcome] F; *King* Welcome Q1 (*repeating prefix from* 36)   64 nea'er] OXFORD; near Q1,
F; near' HUDSON 1881   67 me, noble lord] Q1 (*subs.*); (my Noble Lord) F   72 O'erthrows]
F; Ouerthrowes Q1

63 **power** army
64 **Nor nea'er** no nearer
65 **Discomfort** pain (that I feel)
67 **One day** having arrived one day
68 **clouded** Continuing the sun–king analogy; the idea of 'envious clouds' (3.3.64) obscuring the sun is recurrent in the play.
72 **state** high rank or position (*OED n.* 15)
76 Richard identifies the blood which has drained from his face, leaving him 'pale' (75), with the actual blood of the Welsh

soldiers. The King's self-conscious despair has made him exaggerate the numbers of the soldiers he has lost from twelve (70) to twenty thousand (F, at l. 85, increases the number still higher, to forty thousand).
76 **But now** just now
80 **will** want to
81 **pride** glory, grandeur. Richard ignores the implications of the word's more sinister meaning as the first of the deadly sins.

Awake, thou sluggard majesty, thou sleep'st.
Is not the king's name twenty thousand names?   85
Arm, arm, my name! A puny subject strikes
At thy great glory. Look not to the ground,
Ye favourites of a king. Are we not high?
High be our thoughts. I know my uncle York
Hath power enough to serve our turn.
> *Enter Scroop*

But who comes here?   90

SCROOP

More health and happiness betide my liege
Than can my care-tuned tongue deliver him.

RICHARD

Mine ear is open and my heart prepared,
The worst is worldly loss thou canst unfold.
Say, is my kingdom lost? Why, 'twas my care   95
And what loss is it to be rid of care?
Strives Bolingbroke to be as great as we?
Greater he shall not be: if he serve God,
We'll serve him too and be his fellow so.
Revolt our subjects? That we cannot mend;   100
They break their faith to God as well as us.
Cry woe, destruction, ruin and decay—
The worst is death, and death will have his day.

SCROOP

Glad am I that your highness is so armed
To bear the tidings of calamity.   105

---

84 sluggard] F; coward Q1 sleep'st] CAPELL; sleepest Q1, F   85 twenty] Q1; fortie F
90 Hath ... here?] Q1; *two lines ending* 'turne.' 'here?' F *Enter Scroop*] *placed as in*
OXFORD; *after* 'here?' Q1, F   102 and] Q1; Losse F

84 **sluggard** lazy. F's emendation of Q1's
'coward' (see textual notes), which could
hardly be a misreading and must have
been a deliberate revision, fits better with
'Awake' and 'sleep'st'.
88–9 **Are ... thoughts** i.e. since we are of
high rank, our thoughts should be lofty
90 **serve our turn** tip the balance in our
favour
91 **betide** be the lot of, befall
92 **care-tuned tongue** voice that is tuned to
the note of care (both 'woe' and 'concern')
95, 96 **care** Richard picks up on Scroop's
word, adding the sense of 'responsibility'.

99 **him** i.e. God
  his fellow i.e. Bolingbroke's equal
100 **mend** remedy
102 **Cry** proclaim
  and F prints 'Losse' as a fifth term in the
  series of potential disasters, but the word
  is rather colourless beside the others in
  the line.
103 **death ... day** Perhaps a variation on
  the proverb, 'Every dog has his day'
  (Tilley D464); cf. *Hamlet* 5.1.289: 'The
  cat will mew, and dog will have his day'.
105 **bear ... calamity** endure calamitous
  news

Like an unseasonable stormy day,
Which makes the silver rivers drown their shores
As if the world were all dissolved to tears,
So high above his limits swells the rage
Of Bolingbroke, covering your fearful land 110
With hard bright steel and hearts harder than steel.
Whitebeards have armed their thin and hairless scalps
Against thy majesty; boys with women's voices
Strive to speak big and clap their female joints
In stiff unwieldy arms against thy crown; 115
The very beadsmen learn to bend their bows
Of double-fatal yew against thy state;
Yea, distaff-women manage rusty bills
Against thy seat. Both young and old rebel,
And all goes worse than I have power to tell. 120

RICHARD

Too well, too well thou tell'st a tale so ill.
Where is the Earl of Wiltshire, where is Bagot,
What is become of Bushy, where is Green,
That they have let the dangerous enemy
Measure our confines with such peaceful steps? 125

---

107 makes] Q1; make F   110 covering] Q1, Fc; coueting Fu   112 Whitebeards] Q1 (White beards); White Beares F   113 boys] Q1; and Boyes Q2–F   117 double-fatal] *hyphen* WARBURTON

109–11 So . . . steel Scroop applies the analogy of an overflowing river (107–8) to Bolingbroke (*So* = thus) whose rage 'swells' above its proper 'limits' flooding ('covering') the land with steel and hard hearts.
113 women's i.e. high, shrill
114 clap press, enclose (with a suggestion of hurry; see *OED v.* 10)
115 arms armour
116 beadsmen pensioners paid to pray for others. Here it is their advanced age that is stressed: as in l. 112, even the old have taken up arms against Richard.
117 double-fatal yew Yew wood was used to make bows; 'double', while it may be simply an intensifier, probably refers to the fact that the yew can kill with its poisonous berries, as well as by providing the material to make deadly weapons.
118 distaff-women women who spin thread bills weapons (long-handled, with a blade and sometimes a spike or spear-head)

119 seat throne
122 Bagot There is some confusion about Bagot in the text. At the end of 2.2, he presumably departs for Ireland to join the King (2.2.140), but Shakespeare appears to have forgotten that here. Scroop's response to Richard's enquiry (128) would seem to include him and would therefore suggest that, like the other three, he too has 'made peace' and been executed. But he is not among the accused in 3.1, and at 141 of this scene, Aumerle does not name him, nor does Scroop's reply suggest that he is among those killed. Later, at the beginning of 4.1, he appears as a prisoner but apparently escapes execution (the historical Bagot lived on until 1407). The confusion is augmented by the fact that the Earl of Wiltshire, while frequently mentioned, does not actually appear in the play.
125 Measure . . . steps travel our land without resistance

If we prevail, their heads shall pay for it.
I warrant they have made peace with Bolingbroke.

SCROOP

Peace have they made with him indeed, my lord.

RICHARD

O villains, vipers, damned without redemption,
Dogs easily won to fawn on any man,   130
Snakes in my heart-blood warmed that sting my heart;
Three Judases, each one thrice worse than Judas,
Would they make peace? Terrible hell make war
Upon their spotted souls for this offence.

SCROOP

Sweet love, I see, changing his property,   135
Turns to the sourest and most deadly hate.
Again uncurse their souls, their peace is made
With heads and not with hands. Those whom you curse
Have felt the worst of death's destroying wound
And lie full low, graved in the hollow ground.   140

AUMERLE

Is Bushy, Green and the Earl of Wiltshire dead?

SCROOP

Ay, all of them at Bristol lost their heads.

AUMERLE

Where is the Duke my father with his power?

RICHARD

No matter where. Of comfort no man speak—
Let's talk of graves, of worms and epitaphs,   145
Make dust our paper and with rainy eyes

---

131 heart-blood] *hyphen* F3   133–4] *as* F; *lines ending* 'hel,' 'this.' QI   134 this offence]
F; this QI   136 hate.] F (*subs.*); hate, QI   139 wound] QI; hand F   142 Ay] QI; Yea
Q2–F

---

129 **vipers, damned** Cf. Matthew 23: 33: 'O
serpents, the generation of vipers, how
should ye escape the damnation of hell?'
131 **Snakes . . . heart** The King alludes to
Aesop's fable of a man who warmed a
frozen snake against his chest only to
be bitten for his trouble. The idea of
treacherous snakes and vipers (129) was
proverbial (Tilley V68).
132 **Three Judases** Judas was the betrayer
of Christ; this is the first of many comparisons that Richard makes between

himself and Jesus. He says 'three' when
he had asked about four of his supporters
earlier; see 122 n.
134 **spotted** tainted, sinful
135 **his property** its essential quality
138 **With . . . hands** by surrendering their
heads not by shaking hands (with
Bolingbroke)
146–7 Richard develops an extravagant
metaphor in which the dust of the earth
becomes paper on which he and his
companions will write with their tears.

Write sorrow on the bosom of the earth.
Let's choose executors and talk of wills—
And yet not so, for what can we bequeath
Save our deposèd bodies to the ground?   150
Our lands, our lives and all are Bolingbroke's,
And nothing can we call our own but death
And that small model of the barren earth
Which serves as paste and cover to our bones.
For God's sake let us sit upon the ground   155
And tell sad stories of the death of kings,
How some have been deposed, some slain in war,
Some haunted by the ghosts they have deposed,
Some poisoned by their wives, some sleeping killed—
All murdered. For within the hollow crown   160
That rounds the mortal temples of a king
Keeps death his court, and there the antic sits,
Scoffing his state and grinning at his pomp,
Allowing him a breath, a little scene
To monarchize, be feared and kill with looks,   165
Infusing him with self and vain conceit,
As if this flesh which walls about our life

155 God's] Q1; Heauens F

150 **deposèd** removed from the throne (see 157 and 158), but also buried. The latter meaning applies to the others on stage as well as Richard himself. The first person plural in these lines (145–54) is not the 'royal we' but rather indicates that Richard, as he does later as well (175–6), is thinking of himself as one with his companions.

153 **model . . . earth** i.e. our flesh, made from dust and hence a kind of miniature or microcosm ('model') of the earth

154 **paste and cover** 'A metaphor, not of the most sublime kind, taken from a *pie*' (Johnson). The flesh, made from earth, is like a pastry covering the bones.

155 **sit upon the ground** Sitting on the earth was emblematic of sadness and human mortality. It is not clear if his followers join him, or indeed if Richard himself sits on the stage at this moment.

158 **ghosts** i.e. the ghosts of the kings

160–70 **For within . . . farewell king** In Richard's wonderfully elaborated conceit, the space within the crown becomes Death's 'court' or presence chamber, and Death a mock-king, an 'antic' or court fool, who both controls and derides the life of the actual king. Death allows the king time and space to play at being a monarch ('monarchize'), all the while 'scoffing' at the ceremonious attention he receives ('state' and 'pomp'). Thus is the king 'infused' with vanity, to the point that he becomes persuaded of his own invincibility, until Death comes along with a tiny pin to prick out his life.

160 **hollow crown** Note the parallelism with the 'hollow ground' or grave in 140.

164 **scene** The word establishes the theatrical nature of the process of 'monarchizing'.

167 **flesh which walls** The king's body is likened to a seemingly 'impregnable' fortress (168), only to be penetrated by the 'pin' that breaches the 'castle wall' (169–70).

Were brass impregnable, and humoured thus
Comes at the last and with a little pin
Bores through his castle wall—and farewell king.   170
Cover your heads and mock not flesh and blood
With solemn reverence. Throw away respect,
Tradition, form and ceremonious duty.
For you have but mistook me all this while,
I live with bread like you, feel want,   175
Taste grief, need friends. Subjected thus,
How can you say to me I am a king?

CARLISLE
My lord, wise men ne'er wail their present woes,
But presently prevent the ways to wail.
To fear the foe, since fear oppresseth strength,   180
Gives in your weakness strength unto your foe,
And so your follies fight against yourself.
Fear and be slain, no worse can come to fight,
And fight and die is death destroying death,
Where fearing dying pays death servile breath.   185

AUMERLE
My father hath a power: inquire of him,
And learn to make a body of a limb.

---

170 through] Q2–F; thorough Q1 wall] Q1; walls Q2–F   178 wail . . . woes] F; sit and
waile theyr woes Q1   182] Q1; *not in* F

168 **humoured** indulged. Death gratifies the
king's fantasy of invulnerability; a kind
of absolute construction, referring to the
king.

171–3 **mock . . . duty** do not treat me with
the exaggerated respect normally offered
to kings, since I am only 'flesh and
blood'. In a paradoxical figure, 'solemn
reverence' is redefined as mockery.

174–7 **For . . . king** Richard for the first time
stresses his common humanity, what
he shares with other people rather than
what differentiates him from them.

176 **Subjected** (a) made into a subject (not a
monarch); (b) subjugated, overawed

178 **wail . . . woes** The F reading, which
is clearly a revision, plays wittily with
'presently' in the next line.

179 **presently . . . wail** immediately move to
avoid the courses that lead to grief

180–1 **To . . . foe** i.e. fearing the enemy only
weakens you and thus strengthens your
foe

182 **so . . . yourself** hence your foolish fears
are self-destructive

183–5 Carlisle's speech is once again somewhat gnomic (cf. 29–32 above), but his
general point is clear: the worst that can
happen is death in battle, but that is a
way to defeat death, while to fear is to
offer slavish homage ('servile breath') to
death.

184–97 The persistent rhyming in this
section, as frequently elsewhere in the
play, is characteristic of its style. The
rhymes maintain a formal tone, but
can be suggestive of a wide range of
meanings and feelings; see Introduction,
pp. 64–6.

186 **power** army

187 **make . . . limb** turn what we at first
thought was only an arm into the whole
body of our army

RICHARD

    Thou chid'st me well. Proud Bolingbroke, I come
    To change blows with thee for our day of doom.
    This ague fit of fear is over-blown,   190
    An easy task it is to win our own.
    Say, Scroop, where lies our uncle with his power?
    Speak sweetly, man, although thy looks be sour.

SCROOP

    Men judge by the complexion of the sky
    The state and inclination of the day—   195
    So may you by my dull and heavy eye
    My tongue hath but a heavier tale to say.
    I play the torturer by small and small
    To lengthen out the worst that must be spoken:
    Your uncle York is joined with Bolingbroke   200
    And all your northern castles yielded up
    And all your southern gentlemen in arms
    Upon his party.

RICHARD   Thou hast said enough.

    [*To Aumerle*] Beshrew thee, cousin, which didst lead
        me forth
    Of that sweet way I was in to despair.   205
    What say you now, what comfort have we now?
    By heaven, I'll hate him everlastingly
    That bids me be of comfort any more.
    Go to Flint Castle, there I'll pine away—

---

190 over-blown] F; ouerblowne Q1   203 party] Q1; Faction F   204 *To Aumerle*] THEOBALD; *not in* Q1, F

188 **well** appropriately
189 **change** exchange
    doom judgement (recalling the tournament (see 1.3.148 n.) as well as doomsday, the last judgement)
190 **ague** fever
    is over-blown has passed
191 **An . . . own** What he had earlier seen as impossible, Richard now regards as easy: to win the hearts of his people.
194 **complexion** appearance
195 **state . . . day** condition and tendency of the weather
198 **by small and small** little by little (modifying 'lengthen' in the next line)

203 **Upon his party** i.e. on Bolingbroke's side
204 **Beshrew** curse
204–5 **which . . . despair** who led me off the pleasant path to despair that I was on
206, 208 **comfort** See l. 36 n.
209 **Flint Castle** At this point in Holinshed, Richard steals away to Conwy Castle, though the marginal note mistakenly mentions Flint, to which Richard later repairs; perhaps Shakespeare seized on 'Flint' because of the connotation of the word, which signifies a very hard stone, and thus suggests an appropriate refuge for a despairing king.

A king, woe's slave, shall kingly woe obey.   210
That power I have, discharge, and let them go
To ear the land that hath some hope to grow,
For I have none. Let no man speak again
To alter this, for counsel is but vain.

AUMERLE

My liege, one word.

RICHARD   He does me double wrong   215
That wounds me with the flatteries of his tongue.
Discharge my followers, let them hence away
From Richard's night to Bolingbroke's fair day.

                                        Exeunt

3.3 *Enter with drum and colours, Bolingbroke, York,*
       Northumberland, attendants [and soldiers]

BOLINGBROKE

So that by this intelligence we learn
The Welshmen are dispersed and Salisbury
Is gone to meet the King, who lately landed
With some few private friends upon this coast.

---

211 them] Q1; 'em F   218.1 *Exeunt*] F; *not in* Q1
3.3] F (*Scaena Tertia*); *not in* Q1   0.1–2 *Enter . . . attendants*] F; *Enter Bull. Yorke, North.* Q1
0.2 *and soldiers*] CAPELL (*subs.*); *not in* Q1, F

210 **A king . . . obey** Turning back to the idea of the king who is a plaything of death and woe (155–70), Richard lapses into self-indulgence: kings are inevitably the slaves of sorrow.

211 **discharge** release from military obligation

212 **ear the land** till the soil (i.e. support Bolingbroke who is now, as Richard was, identified with the English earth)

215–16 **double . . . tongue** The image recalls the adder that poisons with double tongue (21 and n.).

218 **night . . . day** The traditional association of sun and king, developed earlier with regard to Richard, is now applied to Bolingbroke (see 37 n. and 47–53 n.).

3.3 This is the play's pivotal scene, in which Richard's downward trajectory crosses Bolingbroke's rising one. Shakespeare takes the events at Flint Castle primarily from Holinshed but inflects them with a visual symbolic dimension, most especially by having Richard first appear *on the walls*, i.e. on the upper stage (60.2), and then dramatically descend ('Down, down I come like glistering Phaëton', 177), although, given the exigencies of the Elizabethan playhouse, his descent would probably take place out of sight of the audience, behind the back wall. He emerges on to the main stage and wearily acknowledges his defeat, while Bolingbroke establishes control. For the way the stage is used, see also the note to l. 30 below.

1 **intelligence** news (which, presumably, he has just received from one of the attendants). Bolingbroke's efficient intelligence network contrasts with the way Richard receives a series of bad reports from a succession of messengers in the previous scene.

NORTHUMBERLAND

The news is very fair and good, my lord.　　　　　　5

Richard not far from hence hath hid his head.

YORK

It would beseem the lord Northumberland

To say 'King Richard'. Alack the heavy day

When such a sacred king should hide his head!

NORTHUMBERLAND

Your grace mistakes: only to be brief　　　　　　10

Left I his title out.

YORK　　　　　　　　　　The time hath been,

Would you have been so brief with him, he would

Have been so brief with you to shorten you,

For taking so the head, your whole head's length.

BOLINGBROKE

Mistake not, uncle, further than you should.　　　　　15

YORK

Take not, good cousin, further than you should,

Lest you mistake. The heavens are o'er our heads.

BOLINGBROKE

I know it, uncle, and oppose not myself

Against their will.

　　　　Enter Percy

　　　　　　　　But who comes here?

Welcome Harry. What, will not this castle yield?　　　20

PERCY

The castle royally is manned, my lord,

Against thy entrance.

11–13 The time . . . so brief with you to shorten you,] F; The time . . . him, | He would . . . so brief to shorten you, QI　17 o'er] F; ouer QI　our heads] QI; your head F　22–3] *as* OXFORD; Against thy entrance. | Royally . . . King. | Yes . . . Lord,) QI, F (*subs.*)

7–8 **It . . . Richard** York's sympathy for Richard and reluctant support of Bolingbroke are revealed by his insistence on proper protocol (*beseem* = befit).

11–14 **The . . . length** There was a time when, if you had been so short with him by thus omitting his title, he would have been quick to shorten you by the length of your head (i.e. by beheading you); 'taking . . . the head' means 'omitting the title', but it also conveys the ideas of 'taking the lead' and 'acting in a headstrong manner' (Black). York's sardonic

wordplay once again bespeaks his ambivalence.

15–17 **Mistake . . . Take . . . mistake** More wordplay: 'mistake' carries with it not just the idea of misconstruing but also of transgressing, while York's 'Take' warns against Bolingbroke's seizing more than he is allowed (i.e. not just his dukedom but the crown).

20 **this castle** Flint, in north Wales (where, we learn at 3.2.209, Richard has planned to take refuge and where he has now arrived)

22 **Against** as a bar to

BOLINGBROKE   Royally?
  Why, it contains no king.
PERCY   Yes, my good lord,
  It doth contain a king. King Richard lies
  Within the limits of yon lime and stone   25
  And with him are the Lord Aumerle, Lord Salisbury,
  Sir Stephen Scroop, besides a clergyman
  Of holy reverence, who, I cannot learn.
NORTHUMBERLAND
  O, belike it is the Bishop of Carlisle.
BOLINGBROKE [*to Northumberland*]
  Noble lord,   30
  Go to the rude ribs of that ancient castle,
  Through brazen trumpet send the breath of parley
  Into his ruined ears, and thus deliver:
  Henry Bolingbroke,
  On both his knees doth kiss King Richard's hand   35
  And sends allegiance and true faith of heart
  To his most royal person, hither come
  Even at his feet to lay my arms and power,
  Provided that my banishment repealed

25 yon] Q1; yond F   26 are] Q1; *not in* Q2–F   30 *to Northumberland*] ROWE; *not in* Q1,
F lord] F; Lords Q1   32 parley] Q1 (parlee); Parle F   34–7] *as* MALONE; *three lines
ending* 'hand,' 'heart' 'come' Q1; *three lines ending* 'kisse' 'allegeance' 'come' F   34 Henry
Bolingbroke] Q1 (H. Bull.), F (*Henry Bullingbrooke*)   35 On both] Q1; vpon F   37 most royal]
Q1; Royall F

29 **belike** no doubt
30 Here begins a series of movements that
  illustrates the flexibility of the Elizabethan stage. The back (or 'tiring house')
  wall represents the castle walls, which
  Bolingbroke's army is approaching; he
  stops a certain distance away and sends
  Northumberland as an emissary (48);
  the latter crosses the stage, and though
  he only takes a few steps, we understand
  that he covers a fair distance, since
  Bolingbroke, marching on the 'grassy
  carpet of this plain' (49), does not hear
  his conversation with Richard (71–125);
  at 125, Northumberland returns to con-
  fer with the Duke, 'comes back' to the
  King at 141, and once again returns to
  report to his leader what is going on
  (182.1). Bolingbroke's question at 183,
  'What says his majesty?' indicates that
  he is still out of earshot, though he has
  clearly approached the 'base court' (175)

in which the two adversaries eventually
meet face to face (185 ff.).
31 **rude ribs** rugged walls. The comparison
  of a castle to the human body recalls
  Richard's similar image of the king's
  body as a vulnerable castle (3.2.167–70);
  see also 5.5.20.
32 **brazen** made of brass
33 **ruined** Bolingbroke clearly knows that
  Richard has lost, though he claims to be
  bent on nothing more than the restitution of his land and titles; some commentators read 'ruined ears' as a metaphor
  for the crenellations of the castle, continuing the body analogy established by
  'rude ribs' (31), but it seems more likely
  that Bolingbroke is confiding his strong
  sense of his own advantage to his chief
  ally, Northumberland.
39–40 **Provided . . . granted** provided (Richard) grant that my banishment be
  repealed and my lands restored without
  condition

And lands restored again be freely granted. 40
If not, I'll use the advantage of my power
And lay the summer's dust with showers of blood
Rained from the wounds of slaughtered Englishmen;
The which, how far off from the mind of Bolingbroke
It is such crimson tempest should bedrench 45
The fresh green lap of fair King Richard's land,
My stooping duty tenderly shall show.
Go signify as much while here we march
Upon the grassy carpet of this plain.
Let's march without the noise of threatening drum, 50
That from this castle's tottered battlements
Our fair appointments may be well perused.
Methinks King Richard and myself should meet
With no less terror than the elements
Of fire and water when their thundering shock 55
At meeting tears the cloudy cheeks of heaven.
Be he the fire, I'll be the yielding water,
The rage be his whilst on the earth I rain

---

51 tottered] Q1; tatter'd Q3–F   55 shock] Q1; smoake Q2–F   58 whilst] Q1; while F
58–9 rain | My] F; raigne. | My Q1

41 ff. Like the proverbial iron fist in the velvet glove, the threat follows immediately upon the apparent submission of the previous lines.

42 **lay** allay (*OED* v.¹ 7), i.e. through moistening, perhaps the idea is 'showers of blood'

44–7 Inverted syntax: my 'stooping duty' (bowing in submission) shall show how far it is from my mind that a 'crimson tempest' of blood should drench the green land.

44 **The which** as to which (referring back to the threat of blood, which is then repeated in 45). See Abbott 272.

51 **tottered** jagged, irregularly segmented; a variant spelling of F's 'tatter'd', which carries the same meaning. Since, however, either word can also mean battered or ruinous, perhaps the idea is that the castle is in a state of advanced disrepair (though why Richard would then have chosen to take refuge there is not clear). The latter meaning would, like 'ruined' (see 33 n.), apply to Richard as well.

52 **fair   appointments** fine   military

appearance (with perhaps a hint of the threat eschewed in 50)

55–6 Weather theory held that the clash ('meeting') of the two elements of 'fire and water' (i.e. lightning and rain) within a cloud led to a kind of explosion ('thundering shock'), the lightning being the escaping fire.

57 **Be he** let him be
yielding Bolingbroke is hardly yielding (submissive), though his claims of 'stooping duty' (47) are meant to make him seem so; he also knows that water will put out fire.

58–9 **The rage . . . waters** Since he (Richard) is the 'fire', let him possess the rage while I will rain my fertile waters on the land. The figure is deceptive: it seems to promise allayment and submission, but this is belied by the suggestion of Bolingbroke's water bringing fertility to a barren land (cf. the 'garden scene', 3.4) and by the pun on 'rain', which a theatre audience is likely to hear first as 'reign' and then have to adjust to 'rain' once the following words are absorbed.

My waters—on the earth and not on him.
March on, and mark King Richard how he looks.   60
> *The trumpets sound [a] parley without and answer*
> *within. Then a flourish. Enter on the walls Richard,*
> *Carlisle, Aumerle, Scroop, Salisbury*
See, see, King Richard doth himself appear,
As doth the blushing discontented sun
From out the fiery portal of the east
When he perceives the envious clouds are bent
To dim his glory and to stain the track   65
Of his bright passage to the occident.

YORK

Yet looks he like a king: behold, his eye,
As bright as is the eagle's, lightens forth
Controlling majesty. Alack, alack for woe
That any harm should stain so fair a show!   70

RICHARD [*to Northumberland*]

We are amazed, and thus long have we stood

---

59 waters—on] WILSON; water's on Q1; Waters on F   60.1–3 *The trumpets . . . Salisbury*]
The trumpets sound, Richard appeareth on the walls Q1; *Parle without, and answere within: then a*
Flourish. Enter on the Walls, Richard, Carlile, Aumerle, Scroop, Salisbury F   61 See] F; *Bull.* See
Q1 (*repeating prefix from 30*)   65 track] Q1; tract F   71 *to Northumberland*] ROWE (*after 72*);
not in Q1, F

59 **not on him** What exactly Bolingbroke
means by this is not clear: he will not
shed tears for, or on, Richard? He
will bring fertility to the land but leave
Richard parched? It looks as if he is
trying to promise deference but his real
intentions keep poking through his
masked language.

60.1–3 The symbolic splendour of Richard's
royal appearance on the walls above the
platform where the others are stationed is
underscored by the sound of trumpets,
and then by Bolingbroke and York's awed
commentary on his majesty.

61 **See, see** Like York's 'behold' (67), this
seems a directive to the audience as well
as to those on stage.

62 **discontented sun** Another example of the
analogy between sun and king; here the
sun is said to be discontented because (as
explained in 64–6) clouds are determined
to dim his glory, as Bolingbroke threatens
Richard's grandeur.

66 **occident** west. Since that is where the
sun sets, the phrasing glances at
Richard's overthrow.

68 **eagle's** Like the sun, another common
metaphor for the king (the eagle being traditionally ranked as
the 'king' of birds).

68–9 **lightens . . . majesty** illuminates his
monarchical power (*lightens* = 'sends
down as lightning': *OED v.*[2] 7, citing this
passage)

70 **stain** York repeats Bolingbroke's word
(65), with just a hint of reproof.

71 As Bolingbroke (with an ironic edge) and
York have been marvelling at Richard's
dazzling appearance, Northumberland
has crossed the stage to stand below the
King. There may be a studied silence
before Richard speaks, since he says that
he has 'stood' for a long time, waiting for
Northumberland to show his obedience
as a subject by kneeling (72), or their
wordless interchange may be covered by
the two previous speeches. Richard's
use of the royal plural is pointed and
deliberate, underlining his sense of
divinely granted privilege.

To watch the fearful bending of thy knee,
Because we thought ourself thy lawful king.
And if we be, how dare thy joints forget
To pay their awful duty to our presence?   75
If we be not, show us the hand of God
That hath dismissed us from our stewardship,
For well we know no hand of blood and bone
Can gripe the sacred handle of our sceptre
Unless he do profane, steal or usurp.   80
And though you think that all—as you have done—
Have torn their souls by turning them from us
And we are barren and bereft of friends,
Yet know my master, God omnipotent,
Is mustering in his clouds on our behalf   85
Armies of pestilence, and they shall strike
Your children yet unborn and unbegot
That lift your vassal hands against my head
And threat the glory of my precious crown.
Tell Bolingbroke, for yon methinks he stands,   90
That every stride he makes upon my land
Is dangerous treason. He is come to open

85 mustering] Q1; mustring F   90 yon] Q1; yond F   stands] Q1; is F   92 open] Q1; ope F

72 **fearful** awestruck, full of reverence
74 **joints** i.e. knees
75 **awful** reverential. Referring, as with 'fearful' (72), to the awe which it is a subject's duty to display to his monarch. **presence** The word carries with it a sense of the aura of royalty; see 1.1.15 n. and 1.1.34.
76 **hand** signature (as well as the usual figurative sense). The contrast is with the human 'hand' referred to in l. 78.
77 **stewardship** The notion of the king being God's 'steward', or representative on earth, was traditional. See Kantorowicz and Introduction, pp. 17–18.
79 **gripe** to seek to get a hold (*OED v.*[1] 1; different from 'grip' which means simply 'hold')
79–80 **sacred . . . profane** Once again Richard insists on the idea of sacral kingship, so that any move against him is an act of profanity or blasphemy, a conviction that he reiterates in various ways in the succeeding lines.
82 **torn** destroyed

83 **bereft** devoid, stripped
85 **mustering** gathering (a term used specifically of troops)
86 **pestilence** plague. The reference is no doubt to the plagues visited on the Egyptians by God, as outlined in chapters 7 to 11 of Exodus, especially (as the mention of 'unborn children' (87) suggests) the final one, which dooms 'all the first born in the land' (11: 5). If earlier Richard expected military aid from God's 'glorious angel[s]' (3.2.61) to preserve his kingship, he now hopes only for vengeance against those that threaten it.
88 **That** The antecedent is 'you' implied by 'Your' in the previous line; see Abbott 218. **vassal** subject
90 **yon . . . stands** Bolingbroke remains distant from the exchange between Richard and Northumberland (see 30 n.).
92–3 **open . . . war** Bolingbroke will open the 'testament' (i.e. will) of war to see what it will bequeath to himself (Steevens–Reed); the adjectives 'purple' and 'bleeding' indicate Richard's view of the bloody legacy.

The purple testament of bleeding war,
But ere the crown he looks for live in peace,
Ten thousand bloody crowns of mothers' sons   95
Shall ill become the flower of England's face,
Change the complexion of her maid-pale peace
To scarlet indignation and bedew
Her pastures' grass with faithful English blood.
NORTHUMBERLAND
The king of heaven forbid our lord the King   100
Should so with civil and uncivil arms
Be rushed upon. Thy thrice noble cousin,
Harry Bolingbroke, doth humbly kiss thy hand,
And by the honourable tomb he swears,
That stands upon your royal grandsire's bones,   105
And by the royalties of both your bloods,
Currents that spring from one most gracious head,
And by the buried hand of warlike Gaunt,
And by the worth and honour of himself,
Comprising all that may be sworn or said,   110
His coming hither hath no further scope
Than for his lineal royalties and to beg

---

99 pastures'] CAPELL; pastors Q1, F; pastor's POPE; Pasture's THEOBALD

94, 95 **crown, crowns** Playing on the double sense of royal symbol and crown of the head.

95–9 Richard develops a complex interplay of heads and faces: the bloodied heads of young Englishmen will in no way befit the flowering British countryside, which is normally white and peaceful like the face of a maiden, but which will be transformed to 'scarlet indignation' as the green pastures are watered, not with dew, but with that same blood.

99 **pastures'** Q1 and F read 'pastors' (capitalized in F), and some editors have printed 'pastor's', as a reference to Richard as the shepherd of his land, tending sheep as they graze. But Capell's reading which recognizes that 'pastor' is a variant spelling of 'pasture' (see *OED*), fits better with the developing metaphor of the

fertile soil of England being blasted with the blood of war.

101 **civil . . . arms** the weapons of the King's own citizens wielded uncivilly

104 **tomb** i.e. that of Edward III in Westminster Abbey

107 **Currents** The metaphor is of a river of royal blood, arising from its source ('head') in Edward III (compare the Duchess of Gloucester's similar images in 1.2.11–21).

109 **himself** Bolingbroke

111 **scope** aim, purpose

112 **lineal royalties** hereditary prerogatives. The echoing of the word 'royalty' through this speech suggests that Bolingbroke is thinking beyond his rights as a member of the royal family, to include the rights of a sovereign, but this is carefully disguised by Northumberland's circumspection.

Enfranchisement immediate on his knees,
Which on thy royal party granted once,
His glittering arms he will commend to rust,   115
His barbèd steeds to stables and his heart
To faithful service of your majesty.
This swears he, as he is a prince and just,
And as I am a gentleman, I credit him.
RICHARD
Northumberland, say thus the King returns: 120
His noble cousin is right welcome hither,
And all the number of his fair demands
Shall be accomplished without contradiction.
With all the gracious utterance thou hast
Speak to his gentle hearing kind commends.   125
    [*Northumberland returns to Bolingbroke*]
[*To Aumerle*] We do debase ourselves, cousin, do we not,
To look so poorly and to speak so fair?
Shall we call back Northumberland and send
Defiance to the traitor and so die?
AUMERLE
No, good my lord, let's fight with gentle words   130
Till time lend friends and friends their helpful swords.
RICHARD
O God, O God, that e'er this tongue of mine,
That laid the sentence of dread banishment

---

118 a prince and just] SISSON; princesse iust Q1–2; a Prince iust Q3–5; a Prince, is iust F
125.1 *Northumberland . . . Bolingbroke*] OXFORD (*subs.*); *not in* Q1, F 126 *To Aumerle*] ROWE;
not in Q1, F We] F; *King* We Q1 ourselves] Q1; our selfe F

---

113 **Enfranchisement** Literally 'liberation'
(i.e. from the sentence of banishment)
but also, as Holinshed has Bolingbroke
say directly to Richard, 'restitution of my
person, my lands and heritage' (p. 501).
114 **party** part
116 **barbèd** fitted with an ornamental,
armoured covering over the breast and
flanks (*OED*, barb, *n.*²). Holinshed
(p. 495) uses 'barded' (the 'proper' term
according to *OED*) in describing Mowbray's horse during the preparations for
the tournament (Black, p. 416).
118 **as . . . just** Sisson's emendation (see

textual notes) yields the smoothest syntax and best sense. Q1 is clearly in error
since, for all that may be said of him,
Bolingbroke is no 'princesse'; F's reading
is plausible but awkward.
119 **credit** believe
120 **returns** responds
126–7 As Northumberland crosses trium-
phantly back to his leader, Richard
catches himself in the very process of
capitulation; his keen awareness of the
emotional implications of his situation
('poorly' = abjectly) is characteristic.

On yon proud man, should take it off again
With words of sooth! O that I were as great   135
As is my grief or lesser than my name
Or that I could forget what I have been
Or not remember what I must be now!
Swell'st thou, proud heart? I'll give thee scope to beat
Since foes have scope to beat both thee and me.   140

AUMERLE

Northumberland comes back from Bolingbroke.

RICHARD

What must the King do now? Must he submit?
The King shall do it. Must he be deposed?
The King shall be contented. Must he lose
The name of king? In God's name let it go.   145
I'll give my jewels for a set of beads,
My gorgeous palace for a hermitage,
My gay apparel for an almsman's gown,
My figured goblets for a dish of wood,
My sceptre for a palmer's walking staff,   150
My subjects for a pair of carvèd saints
And my large kingdom for a little grave,
A little, little grave, an obscure grave;
Or I'll be buried in the king's highway,
Some way of common trade where subjects' feet   155
May hourly trample on their sovereign's head,
For on my heart they tread now whilst I live,

---

134 yon] Q1; yond F   145 In] This edition; a Q1; o' F

---

135 **sooth** appeasement, flattery (*OED n.* 8)
136 **name** title (as king)
138 **what . . . now** Richard seems already to be accepting defeat.
139–40 **Swell'st . . . me** Richard, with elaborate wordplay, addresses his own heart, which he says has the 'scope' (latitude) to 'swell' and 'beat', since his enemies have the 'scope' (purpose and ability) to 'beat' (thrash) both his heart and himself.
141 For the stage action here, see note to l. 30.
146–53 Richard spins out a list of antitheses that set the lavish accoutrements of

royalty against the meagre, though spiritually valuable, possessions of religious ascetics.
146 **beads** prayer beads, rosary
148 **gay apparel** splendidly adorned clothing
almsman's gown robe of one who lives off alms or charity
149 **figured** embossed, richly patterned
150 **palmer's** pilgrim's
151 **carvèd saints** i.e small statues used for devotion
154 **king's highway** public thoroughfare (a witty bit of irony)
155 **trade** commerce

And buried once, why not upon my head?
Aumerle, thou weep'st, my tender-hearted cousin.
We'll make foul weather with despisèd tears.   160
Our sighs and they shall lodge the summer corn
And make a dearth in this revolting land.
Or shall we play the wantons with our woes
And make some pretty match with shedding tears?
As thus: to drop them still upon one place   165
Till they have fretted us a pair of graves
Within the earth and, therein laid, 'There lies
Two kinsmen digged their graves with weeping eyes'.
Would not this ill do well? Well, well, I see
I talk but idly and you laugh at me.   170
Most mighty prince, my lord Northumberland,
What says King Bolingbroke—will his majesty
Give Richard leave to live till Richard die?
You make a leg and Bolingbroke says 'Ay'.

NORTHUMBERLAND
My lord, in the base court he doth attend   175
To speak with you. May it please you to come down.

RICHARD
Down, down I come like glistering Phaëton,

167–8 'There . . . eyes'] *quotation marks added by* CRAIG   170 laugh] Q1; mock F

158 **buried once** once I am buried (Abbott 378)
160 **We'll . . . tears** i.e. our tears may be despised by our enemies, but we'll use them to make destructively bad weather
161 **lodge** flatten
162 **dearth** famine
163 **play the wantons** behave capriciously or flirtatiously
164 **match** game
165 **still** continuously
166 **fretted us** dug for us, with a suggestion also of worry or anxiety
167 **therein laid** once we are laid therein (the same construction as at 158)
167–8 **'There . . . eyes'** i.e. their epitaph
169 **ill do well** evil event make a clever impression
172–3 **will . . . die** A double-edged question since the timing and means of Richard's death are left unspecified.

174 **make a leg** bow, or kneel in deference. Northumberland apparently makes a gesture that Richard deliberately, perhaps mockingly, interprets as a sign of compliance, i.e. that Bolingbroke will grant the 'leave' that Richard has just asked for.
175 **base court** The lower courtyard of the castle; Richard plays on the name in ll. 179–81.
177 **Phaëton** Son of Apollo, the sun-god, Phaëton borrowed his father's chariot but, like a modern teenager with the family car, lost control and almost collided with the earth, till Zeus stepped in to avert disaster by striking him with a lightning bolt. The image is a telling one for Richard, whose emblem was the sun and who frequently compares himself to it.

225

Wanting the manage of unruly jades.
In the base court? Base court where kings grow base
To come at traitors' calls and do them grace.   180
In the base court come down: down court, down king,
For night-owls shriek where mounting larks should sing.
                              [*Exeunt from above*]

BOLINGBROKE
What says his majesty?

NORTHUMBERLAND   Sorrow and grief of heart
Makes him speak fondly like a frantic man,
    [*Enter Richard and his attendants below*]
Yet he is come.

BOLINGBROKE   Stand all apart   185
And show fair duty to his majesty.
    He kneels down
My gracious lord.

RICHARD
Fair cousin, you debase your princely knee
To make the base earth proud with kissing it.
Me rather had my heart might feel your love   190
Than my unpleased eye see your courtesy.
Up, cousin, up. Your heart is up, I know,
Thus high at least [*pointing to his crown*], although your
    knee be low.

---

179 court?] F; court, Q1   182.1 *Exeunt from above*] CAPELL; *not in* Q1, F   184.1 *Enter . . .
below*] CAPELL; *not in* Q1, F   186.1 *He kneels down*] Q1; *not in* F   188] *as* Q1; *two lines in* F
(Cousin, | You)   193 *pointing to his crown*] HUDSON (*subs.*); *not in* Q1, F

---

178 **Wanting the manage** lacking the ability
    to manage
    jades horses (usually with a negative
    connotation)
182 **night-owls . . . larks** i.e. dark birds of
    ominous foreboding intrude on those
    that should herald a bright morning
182.1 See headnote to 3.3. Exactly how
    Richard is to descend is a challenge to
    modern staging, though in the Eliza-
    bethan playhouse, where there was no
    external staircase in front of the back
    wall, he must necessarily have exited and
    then re-entered below through one of the

main doors. In a famous RSC production
in 1973, Richard first appeared above
on a wide platform, which, as he spoke
of coming down, descended to the stage
floor and the waiting Bolingbroke, thus
creating a striking theatrical image for
the rising and falling action (see Introduction, pp. 90–3).
184 **fondly . . . man** foolishly like a madman
190 **Me rather had** I would rather that
191 **courtesy** (a) bent knee ('curtsy'); (b)
    politeness. This ambiguous performance
    of deference reprises Bolingbroke's kneel-
    ing to York at 2.3.82.1.

BOLINGBROKE

My gracious lord, I come but for mine own.

RICHARD

Your own is yours and I am yours and all.   195

BOLINGBROKE

So far be mine, my most redoubted lord,

As my true service shall deserve your love.

RICHARD

Well you deserve. They well deserve to have

That know the strong'st and surest way to get.

[*To York*] Uncle, give me your hands. Nay, dry your eyes;   200

Tears show their love but want their remedies.

[*To Bolingbroke*] Cousin, I am too young to be your father

Though you are old enough to be my heir.

What you will have, I'll give, and willing too,

For do we must what force will have us do.   205

Set on towards London, cousin, is it so?

BOLINGBROKE

Yea, my good lord.

RICHARD   Then I must not say no.

Flourish. Exeunt

198] *as* Q1; *two lines in* F (deseru'd: | They) you deserve] Q1; you deseru'd F   200 *To York*]
HANMER; *not in* Q1, F hands] Q1; Hand F   202 *To Bolingbroke*] HANMER; *not in* Q1, F
206] *as* Q1; *two lines in* F (London: | Cousin)   207.1 *Flourish. Exeunt*] F; *not in* Q1

196 **So far be mine** Responding to Richard's
  declaration that all is now his, Bolingbroke demurs, saying 'may it be mine
  only in so far as I offer you "true service"'
  (197).
  redoubted feared, respected (frequently
  used to address monarchs)
198–9 **They . . . get** A statement of realpolitik, quite out of keeping with Richard's
  earlier insistence on divine right.
200 **hands** F has 'Hand' which seems like a
  normalization, and an unnecessary one,
  since the stage action of the weary King

grasping both his distraught uncle's
hands to comfort him can carry a much
stronger emotional charge.
201 **their love** i.e. the love of those who weep
  want their remedies fail to provide a
  remedy for the tears (i.e. for what made
  them flow in the first place)
204–7 It is noteworthy that throughout
  this section, as indeed in the whole
  conversation in the 'base court' (175),
  Richard capitulates before he is asked, as
  though he were orchestrating his own
  fall.
204 **will have** desire to have

3.4 *Enter the Queen and two Ladies*

QUEEN

What sport shall we devise here in this garden
To drive away the heavy thought of care?

LADY

Madam, we'll play at bowls.

QUEEN

'Twill make me think the world is full of rubs
And that my fortune rubs against the bias.   5

LADY

Madam, we'll dance.

QUEEN

My legs can keep no measure in delight
When my poor heart no measure keeps in grief.
Therefore no dancing, girl—some other sport.

LADY

Madam, we'll tell tales.   10

QUEEN

Of sorrow or of joy?
LADY   Of either, madam.

3.4] F (*Scena Quarta.*); *not in* Q1   0.1 *Enter . . . Ladies*] F; *Enter the Queene with her attendants* Q1   3, 6, 10, 11, 19, 21 LADY] Q1, F; 1. L⟨*ady*⟩. CAPELL; *divided between* 1 *and* 2 Lady WELLS   11 joy] ROWE 1709; griefe Q1, F (Griefe)

3.4 This remarkable scene, almost unique in Shakespeare for its largely symbolic function, provides a theatrical centre for the play's recurrent language of soil, earth and plants, and the ongoing comparison between England and a garden, developed at length by Gaunt in 2.1.40–60. The sorrowful Queen, who has taken refuge at one of the Duke of York's estates (see 2.2.117 and 3.1.36 and notes), encounters the gardeners as they go about tending their enclosure and discussing the parallel tending of the 'sea-wallèd garden' of England. Richard has been careless, while Bolingbroke has busied himself 'pluck[ing] up' the weeds that threaten to choke the land (43–53). The gardeners are labourers capable of reasoned political judgements, as well as being emblematic figures who do not speak the usual salty prose of Shakespeare's rustics, but an elegant and refined verse designed to bring home the point that the space they rule is a metaphorical 'model' (42) for the kingdom itself. See Introduction, pp. 30–3.

3 LADY Here and throughout the scene the early texts do not specify which of the two ladies speaks the lines assigned simply to 'Lady'; in the theatre then as now, they would no doubt be assigned in a convenient way. While some editors divide the lines between the women, we have left the matter open.
    bowls lawn-bowling

4–5 **full . . . bias** full of obstacles that cause my fortune to run against its normal course. A 'rub' was an impediment in a game of bowls (and thus by extension any obstacle), while *bias* = the lead weight in the bowl that determined its oblique course.

7, 8 **measure, measure** (a) series of dance steps (with perhaps also a hint of 'musical bar'); (b) limit

QUEEN

Of neither, girl.
For if of joy, being altogether wanting,
It doth remember me the more of sorrow;
Or if of grief, being altogether had,   15
It adds more sorrow to my want of joy.
For what I have I need not to repeat,
And what I want it boots not to complain.

LADY

Madam, I'll sing.

QUEEN   'Tis well that thou hast cause,
But thou shouldst please me better wouldst thou weep.   20

LADY

I could weep, madam, would it do you good.

QUEEN

And I could sing, would weeping do me good,
And never borrow any tear of thee.

Enter a Gardener and two Servants

But stay, here come the gardeners.
Let's step into the shadow of these trees;   25
My wretchedness unto a row of pins
They'll talk of state, for every one doth so
Against a change. Woe is forerun with woe.

[Queen and Ladies move away]

23.1 *Enter . . . Servants*] F; *Enter Gardeners.* Q1   24 come] Q1; comes F   26 pins] F; pines
Q1   27 They'll] F; They will Q1   28.1 *Queen . . . away*] POPE (*subs.*); *not in* Q1, F

---

13 **wanting** missing (i.e. from her heart)
17–18 **what . . . complain** I don't need to
  hear repeated more of what I already
  have (grief) and it's no help ('boots not')
  to lament what I do not have (joy)
22–3 **And . . . thee** 'And I could even sing for
  joy if my troubles were only such as
  weeping could alleviate, and then I would
  not ask you to weep for me' (Cambridge).
  The Queen's speech, as so often, is cryptic
  and condensed.
23.1 The directions in F, here and at the
  start of the scene, establish a suitably
  formal symmetry (two trios: one female,
  one male).
26 **My . . . pins** i.e. I'll stake my (great)

unhappiness against the most trivial of
things. The metaphor is from betting,
and the odds lop-sided.
27 **state** politics
28 **Against** when they anticipate
  is forerun . . . woe is the precursor of
  further woe. Exactly what she means
  is once again in doubt: she could be
  speaking of her own unhappiness being
  the harbinger of further misery or of the
  unhappy predictions made by those who
  'talk of state', which come to fruition in
  unlucky events.
28.1 The ladies withdraw to a part of the
  stage within earshot but where they
  cannot be seen by the gardeners.

GARDENER [*to one of the Servants*]
> Go bind thou up yon dangling apricots
> Which like unruly children make their sire   30
> Stoop with oppression of their prodigal weight;
> Give some supportance to the bending twigs.
> [*To the other Servant*] Go thou and like an executioner
> Cut off the heads of too-fast-growing sprays
> That look too lofty in our commonwealth—   35
> All must be even in our government.
> You thus employed, I will go root away
> The noisome weeds which without profit suck
> The soil's fertility from wholesome flowers.

SERVANT
> Why should we in the compass of a pale   40
> Keep law and form and due proportion,
> Showing as in a model our firm estate,
> When our sea-wallèd garden, the whole land,
> Is full of weeds, her fairest flowers choked up,
> Her fruit trees all unpruned, her hedges ruined,   45
> Her knots disordered and her wholesome herbs
> Swarming with caterpillars?

---

29 *to one of the Servants*] WILSON (*subs.*); *not in* Q1, F   29 yon] Q2; yong Q1; yond F apricots] Q1 (Aphricokes), F (Apricocks)   33 *To the other Servant*] WILSON (*subs.*); *not in* Q1, F   34 too-fast-growing] *hyphens* THEOBALD too] F; two Q1   38 which] Q1; that Q2–F   40, 67 SERVANT] F (*Ser.*); Man. Q1; 1 S⟨*ervant*⟩ CAPELL

29–39 **Go . . . flowers** By giving his assistants their tasks and also setting to work himself, the Gardener provides an instance of hierarchical, collaborative labour.

29 **apricots** An example of how modernized spelling can reduce the range of allusion; Q1's 'Aphricokes' and F's 'Apricocks', along with 'dangling', carry a bawdy suggestion, which contrasts with the stately quality of the language the Gardener normally uses.

34 **sprays** small branches

35 **commonwealth** The first explicit indication in the scene of the analogy between the garden and the nation (see headnote); this is followed by 'government' (36), 'sea-wallèd garden' (43), and a series of direct comparisons between the

gardeners' activities and the actions of Richard and Bolingbroke (43–66).

38 **noisome** harmful

40 **compass of a pale** within an enclosed space; 'pale' originally meant stakes used for fencing (cf. 'palisade') and then by extension came to signify the enclosure itself: *OED n.*[1] 3a.

42 **firm estate** the well-ordered nature of our domain

43–7 The relation between England and a garden is elaborated through a series of specific images; 'sea-wallèd' recalls Gaunt's image of England as a fortress (2.1.61–3) while 'caterpillars' is the term used by Bolingbroke to describe Bushy et al. (2.3.165).

46 **knots** flower beds of intricate design (*OED n.*[1] 7)

GARDENER   Hold thy peace.
He that hath suffered this disordered spring
Hath now himself met with the fall of leaf.
The weeds which his broad-spreading leaves did shelter   50
That seemed in eating him to hold him up
Are plucked up root and all by Bolingbroke—
I mean the Earl of Wiltshire, Bushy, Green.

SERVANT
What, are they dead?

GARDENER   They are, and Bolingbroke
Hath seized the wasteful King. O what pity is it   55
That he had not so trimmed and dressed his land
As we this garden! We at time of year
Do wound the bark, the skin of our fruit trees,
Lest being over-proud in sap and blood
With too much riches it confound itself.   60
Had he done so to great and growing men
They might have lived to bear and he to taste
Their fruits of duty. Superfluous branches
We lop away that bearing boughs may live.
Had he done so, himself had borne the crown   65
Which waste of idle hours hath quite thrown down.

SERVANT
What, think you the King shall be deposed?

50 which] Q1; that Q2–F   52 plucked] Q1; puld Q3–F (pull'd)   54–7] *as* CAPELL; *five lines ending* 'dead?' 'are.' 'king,' 'trimde,' 'yeare' Q1, F   54 SERVANT] F (*Ser.*); *Man.* Q1; 1 *S⟨ervant⟩* CAPELL; 2 *Man* WELLS   57 garden! We at] CAPELL; garden at Q1, F (Garden, at)   58 Do] Q1; And F   59 in] Q1; with Q2–F   66 of] Q1; and F   67 you the] Q1, F; you then the POPE

48 **He** i.e. Richard
   suffered allowed (secondarily, 'endured')
49 i.e. has now come to his own autumn (with reference to 'spring' in the previous line); the garden analogy is extended to Richard's own person.
51 That seemed to support him while in reality they were devouring him
57 **time of year** appropriate times of the year
58–60 The comparison between trees and the human body includes as well the idea of the body politic, which ought to have been surgically bled, as doctors do to patients and as the gardeners do to trees in order to prevent too abundant and potentially self-destructive growth (cf. 1.1.152–7). The Gardener makes the symbolism explicit by identifying 'bark' with 'skin' and 'sap' with 'blood'.
60 **confound** destroy
61–6 The Gardener applies the analogy directly to Richard; the 'great and growing men' that he could have pruned probably include Bolingbroke and his allies as well as Bushy, Green, and Wiltshire, though the image of 'Superfluous branches' applies specifically to the latter group.
62 **bear** bear fruit (as the pruned trees do)
63–4 **Superfluous . . . live** we strip away the unproductive branches so that those that bear fruit will prosper
66 **waste of** wasteful

GARDENER

  Depressed he is already, and deposed

  'Tis doubt he will be. Letters came last night

  To a dear friend of the good Duke of York's   70

  That tell black tidings.

QUEEN

  O, I am pressed to death through want of speaking!

    [*She comes forward*]

  Thou, old Adam's likeness, set to dress this garden,

  How dares thy harsh rude tongue sound this unpleasing

    news?

  What Eve, what serpent, hath suggested thee   75

  To make a second fall of cursèd man?

  Why dost thou say King Richard is deposed?

  Dar'st thou, thou little better thing than earth,

  Divine his downfall? Say where, when and how

  Cam'st thou by this ill tidings? Speak, thou wretch!   80

GARDENER

  Pardon me, madam, little joy have I

  To breathe this news, yet what I say is true—

  King Richard, he is in the mighty hold

  Of Bolingbroke. Their fortunes both are weighed:

  In your lord's scale is nothing but himself   85

---

69 doubt] Q1; doubted F   70 the good] Q1; the Q3–F   72.1 *She comes forward*] CAPELL
(*subs., in the middle of* 73); *not in* Q1, F   80 Cam'st] Q2–F; Canst Q1   82 this] Q1; these
Q2–F   85 lord's] F (Lords); Lo. Q1

68 **Depressed** (a) reduced (in status or
fortune); (b) dejected

69 **'Tis doubt** it is to be feared

69–71 **Letters . . . tidings** The Gardener's
knowledge of court news indicates that,
despite his primarily emblematic status,
he participates in a real world of political
manoeuvring and the circulation of
information.

72 **pressed** crushed, oppressed (as though
under a type of torture where huge
weights were placed on an accused
person who chose to remain silent
and refuse to enter a plea). The Queen
echoes, though with a different sense,
the Gardener's 'Depressed' (68).

73 **old Adam's likeness** the image of Adam,
the first gardener

75 The Queen, in her impatience, conflates

the two stories from Genesis wherein
Satan as a serpent first prompts Eve to
eat the forbidden fruit and she then
convinces Adam to join her.

75 **suggested** tempted, seduced (frequently
used by Shakespeare in this sense: see,
e.g., *Love's Labour's Lost* 5.2.762, *All's
Well That Ends Well* 4.5.45)

76 **second fall** She compares the fall of
Richard with that of mankind generally:
a bit of exaggeration worthy of Richard
himself.

79 **Divine** guess at, foretell

84 **weighed** i.e. measured against one
another. As the next five lines indicate,
the Gardener is thinking of a pair of
scales in which Bolingbroke's alliances
give him the 'odds' (89) over Richard
who has only light 'vanities' (86) on his
side of the balance.

And some few vanities that make him light,
But in the balance of great Bolingbroke,
Besides himself, are all the English peers,
And with that odds he weighs King Richard down.
Post you to London and you will find it so,   90
I speak no more than everyone doth know.

QUEEN
Nimble mischance that art so light of foot,
Doth not thy embassage belong to me
And am I last that knows it? O thou think'st
To serve me last that I may longest keep   95
Thy sorrow in my breast. Come, ladies, go
To meet at London London's King in woe.
What, was I born to this, that my sad look
Should grace the triumph of great Bolingbroke?
Gardener, for telling me these news of woe,   100
Pray God the plants thou graft'st may never grow.

          [Exeunt Queen and Ladies]

GARDENER
Poor Queen, so that thy state might be no worse,
I would my skill were subject to thy curse.
Here did she fall a tear; here in this place
I'll set a bank of rue, sour herb of grace.   105
Rue, even for ruth, here shortly shall be seen
In the remembrance of a weeping queen.   *Exeunt*

---

90 you will] Q1; you'l F   94 think'st] F; thinkest Q1   100 these] Q1; this F   101 Pray
God] Q1; I would F   101.1 *Exeunt . . . Ladies*] POPE (*subs.*); *Exit* Q1, F   104 fall] Q1; drop
Q2–F   106 even] Q1; eu'n F   107 *Exeunt*] Q1; *Exit.* F

86 **light** Playing on the meanings 'of little
   weight' and 'frivolous'.
90 **Post** go, hurry
92–4 **Nimble . . . it?** The Queen chastises
   misfortune ('mischance') which, though
   fleet of foot (in that it moves quickly into
   people's lives), has been slow to carry its
   report ('embassage') to her.
95 **serve me** offer me service (by delivering
   the message of ill news)
96 **Thy sorrow** i.e. the sorrow that 'mischance' (92) brings to her
99 **grace the triumph** be a trophy in Bolingbroke's victory procession

102–3 **so that . . . curse** if it could keep your
   situation from getting worse, I would
   wish that my gardening skill were susceptible to your curse (as articulated in
   the Queen's parting line about grafting,
   the epitome of the Gardener's art).
104 **fall** let fall, drop
105 **rue** A bitter herb associated with both
   sadness and repentance; Ophelia also
   calls it 'herb-grace' and makes the same
   associations (*Hamlet* 4.5.179–82).
106 **ruth** pity (playing on the phonic link
   with 'rue')
107 **In the remembrance** as a memorial

4.1 *Enter as to the Parliament Bolingbroke, Aumerle,*
  Northumberland, Percy, Fitzwater, Surrey, [Bishop of]
  Carlisle, Abbot of Westminster, [Another Lord,] Herald,
  Officers and Bagot

BOLINGBROKE
  Call forth Bagot.
  Now Bagot, freely speak thy mind
  What thou dost know of noble Gloucester's death,
  Who wrought it with the King and who performed
  The bloody office of his timeless end?   5

BAGOT
  Then set before my face the Lord Aumerle.

BOLINGBROKE
  Cousin, stand forth and look upon that man.

4.1] F (*Actus Quartus. Scoena Prima.*); *not in* Q1   0.1–4 *Enter . . . Bagot*] F; *Enter Bulling-*
brooke with the Lords to parliament. Q1   0.2 *Bishop of*] ROWE; *not in* F   0.3 *Another Lord*]
CAPELL; *not in* F   1 Bagot.] F; Bagot. *Enter Bagot.* Q1

4.1 The dynamic process of Richard's fall
and Bolingbroke's ascent to the throne
comes to completion now, in a series of
moves that include the off-stage abdication of the King (reported by York at
108–13), his rival's formal acceptance
of regal power (114), and the richly
dramatic deposition itself, when Richard,
unwillingly but with great theatrical flair,
hands over the crown. In doing so, he
seeks to outflank his rival, mocking him
as a 'silent King' (290) and dominating
the scene through his brilliant rhetoric
and clever manipulation of the crown
and the mirror, though his theatricality
can also seem forced. The scene begins
with the quarrels of the nobles, alternately deadly and comic, and ends with
the conspiracy of the Abbot of Westminster, clear indications that Henry's
reign will not be peaceful—a sense that is
augmented by Carlisle's bitter prophecy
that 'The blood of English shall manure
the ground' (138). While the basic
material is taken from Holinshed,
Shakespeare has once again compressed
and rearranged it, pressing incidents
from diverse times into a single day and

adding elements such as the mirror
scene, the roles of York and Northumberland, and the attempt to make Richard
formally confess his faults (the 'articles'
are reproduced in Holinshed, pp. 502–3,
but Richard is not made to acknowledge
them).

0.4 *Bagot* See 3.2.122 n. Bagot departed
from the other favourites (2.2.140 ff.)
and thus escaped the capture and
execution that they suffered (3.1.1 ff.).
His entrance follows that of the King and
courtiers, perhaps in response to Bolingbroke's opening line (which might be
called out as he enters), as some recent
editors have stipulated; but F's direction
might also allow for a massed entry,
with Bagot on stage at the back, and
then pushed forward after the command
comes.

4 **wrought it with** (a) worked upon (i.e.
persuaded him to the murder); (b)
brought it about with (the help or
knowledge of). *Wrought* is here the
'largely obsolete past tense' of 'work'
(Ure).

5 **office** undertaking
  timeless untimely

234

BAGOT

My lord Aumerle, I know your daring tongue
Scorns to unsay what once it hath delivered;
In that dead time when Gloucester's death was plotted   10
I heard you say 'Is not my arm of length
That reacheth from the restful English court
As far as Calais, to mine uncle's head?'
Amongst much other talk, that very time
I heard you say that you had rather refuse   15
The offer of an hundred thousand crowns
Than Bolingbroke's return to England,
Adding withal how blest this land would be
In this your cousin's death.

AUMERLE

Princes and noble lords,   20
What answer shall I make to this base man?
Shall I so much dishonour my fair stars
On equal terms to give him chastisement?
Either I must, or have mine honour soiled
With the attainder of his sland'rous lips.   25
There is my gage, the manual seal of death

9 once it hath] Q1; it hath once F   13 mine] Q1; my F   17–19] *as* CAPELL; *two lines ending* 'withall,' 'death.' Q1, F   23 him] Q3–F; them Q1

9 **unsay** deny
10 **dead** (a) past; (b) dark and deadly
11 **of length** long enough
12 **restful** quiet, untroubled. The remark has a 'grim playfulness' (Steevens): the court is restful with Gloucester away, but it can kill at a distance.
17 **Than . . . return** i.e. than accept Bolingbroke's return. Such elliptical phrasing is common in Shakespeare (see Abbott 390).
19 **this your cousin's** i.e. Bolingbroke's
21 **base** Aumerle emphasizes the matter of rank; for a duke of the royal family to propose a duel with a member of the gentry such as Bagot would be a considerable self-debasement.
22 **fair stars** i.e. the fair fortune of my noble birth
23 **chastisement** rebuke, punishment
24–5 **Either . . . lips** The stain ('soiled') to his honour threatened by the accusation if it goes unanswered is greater than the dishonour associated with challenging him.

25 **attainder** demeaning accusation
26 **gage** pledge, usually a glove (thrown down as part of a chivalric challenge; see 1.1.69 ff.). Thus begins what threatens to become a comic routine of multiple gages cast down and taken up. But the issues are deadly serious, and the aristocratic pride involved is fierce and unyielding. A production might include an element of grim comedy to balance or even augment the seriousness, though most would want to avoid turning it into a routine like that with the hats in *Waiting for Godot*. Because the flavour of the scene depends on how it is handled in performance, we have omitted various stage directions as to the throwing and picking up of gages that some recent editors have included, preferring to let readers, directors, and actors work out a suitable scheme for themselves.
manual seal seal affixed by hand (that of death, with wordplay on the glove used as gage)

That marks thee out for hell. I say thou liest,
And will maintain what thou hast said is false
In thy heart-blood, though being all too base
To stain the temper of my knightly sword.   30

BOLINGBROKE

Bagot, forbear, thou shalt not take it up.

AUMERLE

Excepting one, I would he were the best
In all this presence that hath moved me so.

FITZWATER

If that thy valour stand on sympathy,
There is my gage, Aumerle, in gage to thine.   35
By that fair sun which shows me where thou stand'st,
I heard thee say, and vauntingly thou spak'st it,
That thou wert cause of noble Gloucester's death.
If thou deny'st it twenty times, thou liest,
And I will turn thy falsehood to thy heart   40
Where it was forgèd, with my rapier's point.

AUMERLE

Thou dar'st not, coward, live to see that day.

FITZWATER

Now, by my soul, I would it were this hour.

AUMERLE

Fitzwater, thou art damned to hell for this.

---

27 I say] Q1; *not in* Q2–F   29 heart-blood] *hyphen* THEOBALD   34 sympathy] Q1; sympathize F   36 which] Q1; that Q2–F   39 deny'st] F4; deniest Q1, F   42 that] Q1; the F
44 Fitzwater] F; Fitzwaters Q1

29 **In thy heart-blood** by spilling the blood of
  your innermost being
30 **temper** high quality of metal, with an
  implication of moral as well as social
  superiority; Bagot's 'base' blood will be a
  blot on the perfectly tempered steel of
  Aumerle's sword.
31 **thou . . . up** The new King insists on
  proper protocol: Bagot is not of high
  enough status to take up the challenge
  (see 21 n.).
32–3 **Excepting . . . so** i.e. Aumerle would be
  ready to fight the person highest in rank
  ('best'), except 'one' (Bolingbroke), who
  might have angered him ('moved me')

  with such accusations as Bagot has
  levelled.
34 **stand on sympathy** depends on equality
  of station. Fitzwater, though not of
  princely blood, is nevertheless a nobleman and steps in as a proxy for Bagot.
35 **in gage** i.e. in answer
37 **vauntingly** boastfully
40–1 Fitzwater plays on the literal and
  metaphorical meanings of 'heart': his
  rapier will pierce Aumerle's breast
  which crafted ('forged') the lie in the first
  place.
43 **it** i.e. the projected combat

PERCY

Aumerle, thou liest. His honour is as true   45
In this appeal as thou art all unjust,
And that thou art so, there I throw my gage
To prove it on thee to th'extremest point
Of mortal breathing. Seize it if thou dar'st.

AUMERLE

An if I do not, may my hands rot off   50
And never brandish more revengeful steel
Over the glittering helmet of my foe!

ANOTHER LORD

I task the earth to the like, forsworn Aumerle,
And spur thee on with full as many lies
As may be halloed in thy treacherous ear   55
From sun to sun: there is my honour's pawn.
Engage it to the trial if thou dar'st.

AUMERLE

Who sets me else? By heaven, I'll throw at all!
I have a thousand spirits in one breast
To answer twenty thousand such as you.   60

SURREY

My lord Fitzwater, I do remember well
The very time Aumerle and you did talk.

53–60 I task ... you] Q1; *not in* F   55 As may] JOHNSON; As it may Q1 halloed] Q1
(hollowed)   56 sun to sun] CAPELL; sinne to sinne Q1   57 dar'st] Q2; darest Q1   61–2] *as*
Q1; *three lines ending* 'Fitz-water:' 'time' 'talke.' F

48–9 **to . . . breathing** to the death
50 **An if** if
53 **ANOTHER LORD** Who exactly this other
lord is is unclear; F cuts him out
altogether, perhaps to save a speaking
part, perhaps because his presence,
which seems mainly a strategy for
increasing the odds against Aumerle,
could cause either confusion or laughter.
If he is cut, the action moves more
sharply and economically, with Surrey's
rejoinder following immediately upon
Percy's support of Fitzwater (see 71–2 n.).
53 **task** encumber (by throwing down
another gage)
54 **spur thee on** i.e. to the brandishing of
'revengeful steel' Aumerle has promised
in l. 51

54 **lies** avowals that you lie
55 **halloed** shouted (with perhaps a pun on
'hollowed' (Q1's spelling), suggested by
the hollow shape of the ear)
56 **From sun to sun** from sunrise to sunset
(Malone); from one day to another
(Steevens)
pawn pledge
57 **Engage . . . trial** take it up as a pledge to
meet me in combat
58 **sets . . . throw** Terms used in playing dice
(Black, citing Collier).
59 **thousand spirits** the courage of a
thousand (which, he goes on to say, is
enough to defeat twenty thousand such
puny spirits as his accusers)

FITZWATER

  'Tis very true, you were in presence then

  And you can witness with me this is true.

SURREY

  As false, by heaven, as heaven itself is true.   65

FITZWATER

  Surrey, thou liest.

SURREY   Dishonourable boy,

  That lie shall lie so heavy on my sword

  That it shall render vengeance and revenge

  Till thou the lie-giver and that lie do lie

  In earth as quiet as thy father's skull.   70

  In proof whereof, there is my honour's pawn,

  Engage it to the trial if thou dar'st.

FITZWATER

  How fondly dost thou spur a forward horse!

  If I dare eat or drink or breathe or live,

  I dare meet Surrey in a wilderness   75

  And spit upon him whilst I say he lies

  And lies and lies. There is my bond of faith

  To tie thee to my strong correction.

  As I intend to thrive in this new world,

---

63 'Tis] Q1; My Lord, | 'Tis F   65] *as* Q1; *two lines ending* 'by heauen,' 'true.' F   66–7 Dishonourable ... sword] F; *one line* Q1   71 my] Q1; mine Q2–3, F   77 my bond] Q3–F; bond Q1

---

66 **boy** A contemptuous term, implying weakness and cowardice; Surrey was in fact younger than Fitzwater.

68 **vengeance and revenge** The redundancy adds an element of bitter intensity.

71–2 **there ... dar'st** Surrey's phrase is an exact repetition of the unnamed lord's (56–7); since Surrey is responding to Fitzwater and not to the lord, the repetition lacks force; it may indeed be an indication that even in Q1, the passage given to the lord was marked for deletion (see 53 n.) and included by error; Shakespeare, that is, perhaps decided to cut the lord's speech and reuse this part of it here.

73 **How ... horse** how foolish it is for you to spur a horse (= Fitzwater's desire to

fight) that is already eager ('forward') to run

74 Q1 has commas after 'eat', 'drink', and 'breathe', perhaps suggesting a rhetorical weighting of each verb; we follow F here because it offers the actor more interpretive scope.

75 **in** even in (see 1.1.63–5)

76–7 As in 74, Q1 has commas after the first two 'lies'.

77 **There** Fitzwater presumably throws yet another glove into the ring.

78 **tie ... correction** bind you to me for severe punishment

79 **new world** That of Bolingbroke's reign; Fitzwater makes both his loyalty and his pragmatic self-interest clear.

Aumerle is guilty of my true appeal.   80
Besides, I heard the banished Norfolk say
That thou, Aumerle, didst send two of thy men
To execute the noble Duke at Calais.

AUMERLE

Some honest Christian trust me with a gage—
That Norfolk lies, here do I throw down this,   85
If he may be repealed to try his honour.

BOLINGBROKE

These differences shall all rest under gage
Till Norfolk be repealed. Repealed he shall be
And, though mine enemy, restored again
To all his lands and signories. When he is returned,   90
Against Aumerle we will enforce his trial.

CARLISLE

That honourable day shall ne'er be seen.
Many a time hath banished Norfolk fought
For Jesus Christ in glorious Christian field,
Streaming the ensign of the Christian cross   95
Against black pagans, Turks and Saracens,
And, toiled with works of war, retired himself

90 he is] Q1; hee's F   92 ne'er] F; neuer Q1   94 Jesus] Q1, F (Iesu)

84–5 **trust . . . this** By now, Aumerle has
apparently run out of gloves (the first is
cast at 26, the second either to Percy
(50), or to the unnamed lord (58): see
26 n.). Someone, perhaps Surrey, thus
gives him a glove which he casts down in
defiance of the banished Mowbray.

87–91 Bolingbroke wisely brings an end to
the quarrelling, showing a mastery and
ease noticeably absent from King Richard's attempt to manage a parallel situation (1.1.152 ff.). He also shows political
acumen in offering to repeal his enemy,
Norfolk, though it is possible that, as Wilson suggests, he has already heard of the
latter's death and makes the offer in
order to look magnanimous. He might
also wish to show that he has honoured
his oath not to have any contact with
Mowbray (1.3.179–91). Whatever his
motivations, it is clear that he wants to
avoid destructive conflict among his
nobles, as is evident from his willingness

to forgive Aumerle for his treason later in
the play.

87 **rest under gage** remain in force but be
suspended

90 **signories** estates

91 **enforce his trial** ensure that the trial by
combat takes place

94 **Christian field** i.e. in the Holy Land,
during the crusades. Shakespeare seems
to have invented this colourful bit of
Mowbray's history, though Stow (quoted
in Black) remarks that he had been in
Jerusalem; Holinshed says only that he
died in Venice (p. 495).

95 **Streaming** flying

96 **black** Perhaps a racial epithet, perhaps
merely a moral one, more likely both.
Certainly the 'Turks' and 'Saracens'
(= Arabs) were regarded as not only
infidels but also as burnt by the scorching
sun of their middle-eastern homeland.

97 **toiled** exhausted

To Italy, and there at Venice gave
His body to that pleasant country's earth
And his pure soul unto his captain Christ,   100
Under whose colours he had fought so long.

BOLINGBROKE

Why, Bishop, is Norfolk dead?

CARLISLE

As surely as I live, my lord.

BOLINGBROKE

Sweet peace conduct his sweet soul to the bosom
Of good old Abraham. Lords appellants,   105
Your differences shall all rest under gage
Till we assign you to your days of trial.

   Enter York

YORK

Great Duke of Lancaster, I come to thee
From plume-plucked Richard who with willing soul
Adopts thee heir and his high sceptre yields   110
To the possession of thy royal hand.
Ascend his throne, descending now from him,
And long live Henry, of that name the fourth!

BOLINGBROKE

In God's name I'll ascend the regal throne.

---

102 Bishop] Q1 (B.), F   103 surely] Q1; sure Q2–F   104–6] *as* Q1; *lines ending* 'Soule' '*Abraham.*' 'gage,' F   113 of . . . fourth] F; fourth of that name Q1

---

100 **captain Christ** Carlisle's image of a militant Christ is markedly different from the suffering figure that Richard compares himself to later in the scene (171–2, 239–42).

102 See 87–91 n.

104–5 **Sweet . . . Abraham** The phrase 'Abraham's bosom', deriving from Luke 16: 22, became a proverbial name for heaven. Once again, Bolingbroke's tone is elusive; 'sweet soul' seems excessive even for a friend, not to mention a sworn enemy.

106–7 Bolingbroke, repeating his command of 87, again asserts his regal authority (see 87–91 n.).

109 **plume-plucked** stripped of finery. The image calls to mind decorative feathers, as on a helmet, which have been rudely plucked away.

112 **descending . . . him** following him as his heir

114–15 **God's . . . God** Bolingbroke invokes God's sanction of his ouster of Richard, while Carlisle appeals to the traditional notion of divine right: that God has anointed Richard and he alone can dethrone him. Whether Bolingbroke does actually now sit in the 'regal throne', which no doubt occupies a dominant place on the stage, is uncertain. He knows he has the power to do so, but since he has still to confront Richard (and does so not from the throne but on equal footing (see 182–9)), he is probably speaking metaphorically. He has a keen sense of public relations and wants to preserve as much as he can of what modern politicians call 'optics'.

CARLISLE

Marry, God forbid.   115
Worst in this royal presence may I speak,
Yet best beseeming me to speak the truth.
Would God that any in this noble presence
Were enough noble to be upright judge
Of noble Richard. Then true noblesse would   120
Learn him forbearance from so foul a wrong.
What subject can give sentence on his king,
And who sits here that is not Richard's subject?
Thieves are not judged but they are by to hear,
Although apparent guilt be seen in them,   125
And shall the figure of God's majesty,
His captain, steward, deputy elect,
Anointed, crownèd, planted many years,
Be judged by subject and inferior breath,
And he himself not present? O, forfend it God   130
That in a Christian climate souls refined
Should show so heinous, black, obscene a deed.
I speak to subjects and a subject speaks,
Stirred up by God thus boldly for his king.
My lord of Hereford here, whom you call king,   135
Is a foul traitor to proud Hereford's king
And if you crown him, let me prophesy

---

115 God] Q1; Heauen F   120 noblesse] Q1; Noblenesse Q2–F   130 forfend] Q1; forbid F
134 God] Q1; Heauen F

115–50 Carlisle's speech, while derived from Holinshed, is given a prominence it doesn't have in the chronicle, and is directed specifically against the deposition, rather than against a proposed public decree declaring Richard's guilt, as in Holinshed.

116 **Worst** i.e. lowest in rank

117 **best beseeming me** most suitable that I (as a man of the church)

118–20 Carlisle plays on various meanings of 'noble' (honourable, aristocratic, morally upstanding, regal).

121 **Learn him forbearance** teach him to keep away

122–30 Carlisle's first argument (122–3) is an appeal to divine right: that Richard is above the judgement of his subjects and cannot be prosecuted by them; he then appeals to the legal principle that forbids

prosecutions of accused who are not present. Even thieves who are clearly guilty are allowed their day in court and shall a crowned king not be afforded such a basic right? The two points are then joined in the idea of mere subjects passing sentence on the king while he is absent (129–30).

126 **figure** model, image. The basic notion, explained in the following line, is that the king is a deputy, who represents God on earth.

128 **many** for many. The recurrent image of planting and gardens is invoked here and continued in ll. 138–9.

130 **forfend** forbid

131 **climate** region
   refined purified (by baptism)

132 **obscene** repugnant

241

The blood of English shall manure the ground
And future ages groan for this foul act.
Peace shall go sleep with Turks and infidels   140
And in this seat of peace tumultuous wars
Shall kin with kin and kind with kind confound.
Disorder, horror, fear and mutiny
Shall here inhabit and this land be called
The field of Golgotha and dead men's skulls.   145
O, if you raise this house against this house
It will the woefullest division prove
That ever fell upon this cursèd earth.
Prevent it, resist it, let it not be so,
Lest child, child's children, cry against you 'woe!'   150

NORTHUMBERLAND

Well have you argued, sir, and for your pains
Of capital treason we arrest you here.
My lord of Westminster, be it your charge
To keep him safely till his day of trial.
May it please you, lords, to grant the commons' suit.   155

BOLINGBROKE

Fetch hither Richard, that in common view

139 this] Q1; his Q2–F   146 you] F; yon Q1 raise] Q1; reare F   149 let] Q1; and let Q2–F
155–318] Q4–F; *not in* Q1–3   155 commons'] F (Commons); common Q4   156 BOLING-
BROKE] F; *not in* Q4 (*speech continued to Northumberland*)

138 **manure** fertilize. Bolingbroke uses a
similar figure at 5.6.46: 'That blood
should sprinkle me to make me grow'.
140–1 'Peace' is both personified and identified with England, her 'seat' (= abode).
142 **kin** kinsfolk, blood relatives
kind natural group, clan
confound destroy
145 **Golgotha** Where Jesus was crucified, a
'place of dead men's skulls' (Mark 15:
22).
146 **house** England is envisioned as a single,
divided household (Mark 3: 25: 'if a
house be divided against itself, that
house cannot continue'). There is also a
prophetic glance toward the ensuing
wars between the 'houses' of Lancaster
and York (already dramatized by Shakespeare in the *Henry VI* plays).
148 **cursèd** i.e. doomed by the fall of Adam
and Eve
151–2 Northumberland's almost comic
bluntness makes it clear where the power

sits, despite Carlisle's eloquent plea. Still,
Carlisle is allowed to remain on stage
in Westminster's custody, and is thus
present to join the latter's conspiracy
hatched at the end of the scene.
155 Here begins the sequence that is missing
from Q1–Q3. The cut no doubt resulted
from official censorship; see Introduction, pp. 9–16.
commons' suit The request of the House
of Commons, which was that Richard
'might have judgement decreed against
him so . . . that the causes of his deposing might be published [i.e. publicly
declared] through the realm for satisfying
of the people' (Holinshed, p. 512).
156–8 Bolingbroke, despite having Carlisle
arrested, seems to acknowledge the
justice of the Bishop's complaint that to
judge Richard while he is absent would
be wrong, though it is also true that he
wants a public declaration from Richard
to legitimate his seizure of power.

He may surrender—so we shall proceed
Without suspicion.

YORK   I will be his conduct.   *Exit*

BOLINGBROKE
Lords, you that here are under our arrest,
Procure your sureties for your days of answer.   160
Little are we beholding to your love
And little looked for at your helping hands.
    Enter Richard and York

RICHARD
Alack, why am I sent for to a king
Before I have shook off the regal thoughts
Wherewith I reigned? I hardly yet have learned   165
To insinuate, flatter, bow and bend my knee.
Give sorrow leave a while to tutor me
To this submission. Yet I well remember
The favours of these men—were they not mine,
Did they not sometime cry 'all hail' to me?   170
So Judas did to Christ, but he in twelve
Found truth in all but one, I in twelve thousand none.
God save the King! Will no man say 'amen'?

157–8 He . . . suspicion] F; *one line* Q4   158 *Exit*] F; *not in* Q4   159 here are] F; are here, are Q4   162 looked] F; looke Q4   162.1 *Enter . . . York*] F; *Enter king Richard.* Q4   166 knee] F; limbes Q4   167–71] *as* F; *four lines ending* 'submission:' 'men,' 'hayle' 'twelue,' Q4   170 sometime] F; sometimes Q4

159 **under our arrest** bound to the trial we have set (referring back to 106–7). The lords who have thrown down their gages are formally subject to the King's judgement.

160 Arrange for someone who will guarantee your attendance on the day when you must 'answer' the challenges.

161 **beholding** indebted. The word is common in Shakespeare, though some editors 'modernize' to 'beholden' (a word Shakespeare never uses); *OED* indicates that both were current till the 18th century, when 'beholding' went out of use.

162 **And . . . for** which I hardly expected from. Bolingbroke's phrasing, together with the sarcasm of 'helping', reveals a sharp political awareness of the self-interest that underlies aristocratic support, an awareness that Richard clearly lacks.

163–318 What Richard wants in political astuteness he makes up for in scene management and image manipulation. Throughout this sequence he consistently outmanoeuvres Bolingbroke with theatrical flair, though Bolingbroke has only to wait silently and patiently, if at times a bit irritatedly, in order to emerge the winner.

165 **Wherewith** with which
166 **insinuate** curry favour
169 **favours** faces, looks
171–2 Another of Richard's overwrought comparisons of himself with Christ. The reference is to the betrayal of Jesus by Judas, one of his twelve apostles.

173 **God . . . King** A fraught comment, applying to both himself and, mockingly, his rival.

Am I both priest and clerk? Well then, amen.
God save the King although I be not he,   175
And yet amen, if heaven do think him me.
To do what service am I sent for hither?

YORK

To do that office of thine own good will
Which tired majesty did make thee offer—
The resignation of thy state and crown   180
To Henry Bolingbroke.

RICHARD   Give me the crown.
Here, cousin, seize the crown. Here, cousin,
On this side my hand, and on that side thine.
Now is this golden crown like a deep well
That owes two buckets filling one another,   185
The emptier ever dancing in the air,
The other down, unseen and full of water.
That bucket down and full of tears am I,
Drinking my griefs whilst you mount up on high.

---

181 Henry] F; *Harry* Q4   181–3 Give . . . thine.] *as* WELLS; *two lines ending* 'seize the
Crown:' 'thine.' F; Sease the Crowne. | Heere Coosin, on this side my hand, and on that side
yours: Q4   189 griefs] F; *griefe* Q4

---

174 **clerk** A minor cleric or, after the
Reformation, a layman, who read out
the responses in church services.

178 **office** task, but also, in response to
Richard's multiple 'amens' and his use of
'service' (177), playing on the meaning
'authorized form of divine worship' (*OED
n.* I).

good will free will

179 **tired majesty** weariness resulting from
the stress of kingship

180 **resignation** As announced by York at
ll. 109–11.

182 **seize the crown** A strikingly emblematic
gesture: Richard challenges Henry to
share the visible symbol of kingship, and
the latter, in most productions, does grip
the other side of the crown; for a
moment a balance is struck, but a brief
one, as is made clear by Richard's image
of the full and empty buckets (184 ff.).
At some point during or immediately
following the speech, Bolingbroke
relinquishes his hold on the crown.

184–9 **Now . . . high** Richard's fervid
imagination turns the 'hollow crown'
(3.2.160) into a well, with buckets
moving up and down, the lower one
identified with himself and heavy with
the water of tears, the upper one identified with Bolingbroke and, tellingly,
'empty'. The image is somewhat confused by the phrase 'filling one another'
(185), which seems to denote that as the
full bucket is raised it conveys the empty
one down to be filled; such reciprocity
between the buckets is not what Richard
means to suggest. So too the idea that
the 'down' bucket is 'unseen' is clearly
not apposite, since Richard at this point is
highly visible. Despite its tendency to
incoherence, Richard's tortured metaphor, with its focus on the value of
suffering over that of political power,
counters the Gardener's image of the
scale in which Richard is high and light
with 'some few vanities' and Bolingbroke
weighty with the support of 'the English
peers' (3.4.86–8).

BOLINGBROKE

I thought you had been willing to resign.   190

RICHARD

My crown I am, but still my griefs are mine.
You may my glories and my state depose
But not my griefs; still am I king of those.

BOLINGBROKE

Part of your cares you give me with your crown.

RICHARD

Your cares set up do not pluck my cares down.   195
My care is loss of care, by old care done,
Your care is gain of care, by new care won.
The cares I give I have, though given away,
They tend the crown yet still with me they stay.

BOLINGBROKE

Are you contented to resign the crown?   200

RICHARD

Ay, no; no, ay, for I must nothing be:
Therefore no no, for I resign to thee.
Now mark me how I will undo myself:
I give this heavy weight from off my head
And this unwieldy sceptre from my hand,   205
The pride of kingly sway from out my heart,

---

201 Ay . . . ay] F (I, no; no, I), Q4 (I, no no I)

190 Bolingbroke's reply is even more laconic
than normal; he seems, both here and
throughout the scene, to be deliberately
marking the contrast between his style of
governance and that of his predecessor.
195 **Your . . . down** the fact that you have
the extra cares of kingship does not make
my cares any less
196–7 **My care . . . won** My pain is the loss
of kingly care, exhausted as I
am by the care (= attentiveness) I had
to expend as king; your worries are
occasioned by having to take over kingly
responsibility, a position you have
achieved by taking careful steps.
Richard's wordplay, always lively and
alert, here begins to sound obsessive and
desperate.
199 **tend** (a) attend; (b) serve
200 Again, Bolingbroke is brutally direct.

201 **Ay . . . ay** 'Ay' and 'I' are indistinguish-
able both in speech and, frequently, on
paper, since 'ay' was often spelt 'I', as it is
in Q4 and F. Hence one way that the first
phrase could be spoken is 'I? No!' in
response to Bolingbroke's query; the
second could similarly be voiced in a
variety of ways, even including a denial
of selfhood ('I can't say "I" since I am
nothing').
202 **no no** Richard's logic is obscure, though
his ambivalence is clear. Apparently he
means that there will be no saying no,
since, being 'nothing' (without the
identity conferred by the crown), he has
no authority to speak; he both can and
cannot 'resign'. Despite all this he goes
on quite explicitly to 'undo' himself
(203), surrendering both crown and
sceptre (204–5).
206 **sway** power

With mine own tears I wash away my balm,
With mine own hands I give away my crown,
With mine own tongue deny my sacred state,
With mine own breath release all duteous oaths,   210
All pomp and majesty I do forswear,
My manors, rents, revenues I forgo,
My acts, decrees and statutes I deny.
God pardon all oaths that are broke to me,
God keep all vows unbroke are made to thee.   215
Make me that nothing have with nothing grieved,
And thou with all pleased that hast all achieved.
Long mayst thou live in Richard's seat to sit
And soon lie Richard in an earthy pit.
God save King Henry, unkinged Richard says,   220
And send him many years of sunshine days.
What more remains?
NORTHUMBERLAND   No more, but that you read
  These accusations and these grievous crimes
  Committed by your person and your followers
  Against the state and profit of this land,   225
  That by confessing them, the souls of men
  May deem that you are worthily deposed.

---

210 duteous oaths] F; duties rites Q4   215 are made] F; that sweare Q4   220 Henry]
F; *Harry* Q4

207–13 The formal, incantatory language
   marks the ceremonial nature of what
   is taking place; it is an anti-ritual
   orchestrated by Richard himself, who
   retains a kind of 'sway' even as he
   abdicates.
207 **balm** oil with which he was anointed
   during the coronation (see 3.2.55)
210 **duteous oaths** oaths of allegiance made
   as a matter of duty (by his subjects)
212 **revenues** Accented, as frequently in
   Shakespeare, on the second syllable.
213 **acts** laws
215 **are** that are
216 **Make . . . grieved** May I, who have
   nothing, be grieved by nothing (or 'be
   grieved by the fact of having nothing',
   a deliberately paradoxical wish, but
   one well-tuned to Richard's divided
   sensibility).
217 **with all** who have all (i.e. the throne)

220 **unkinged** Though the first citation in
   OED is to this line, the word seems to
   have been invented by John Stubbes who
   uses it with specific reference to Richard
   who 'was quite unkinged by Henry of
   Lancaster' (*The discouerie of a gaping gulf
   . . .* , 1579, C5^(r–v)).
222–7 Northumberland, taking a harsher
   stand than his master (see 156–8 n.),
   insists on the humiliating ritual of public
   confession. Holinshed lists a number of
   'articles' that were drawn up enumerat-
   ing Richard's 'misgovernance' but does
   not mention any demand that he read
   them out in public.
225 **state and profit** profitable condition (an
   example of hendiadys); 'state', which
   here carries a special reference to welfare
   or prosperity (*OED n.* 1b), keeps recur-
   ring with various shades of meaning.
227 **worthily** justly

RICHARD

Must I do so? And must I ravel out
My weaved-up follies? Gentle Northumberland,
If thy offences were upon record, 230
Would it not shame thee in so fair a troop
To read a lecture of them? If thou wouldst,
There shouldst thou find one heinous article
Containing the deposing of a king
And cracking the strong warrant of an oath, 235
Marked with a blot, damned in the book of heaven.
Nay, all of you that stand and look upon me
Whilst that my wretchedness doth bait myself,
Though some of you with Pilate wash your hands,
Showing an outward pity, yet you Pilates 240
Have here delivered me to my sour cross
And water cannot wash away your sin.

NORTHUMBERLAND

My lord, dispatch, read o'er these articles.

RICHARD

Mine eyes are full of tears, I cannot see,
And yet salt water blinds them not so much 245
But they can see a sort of traitors here.

---

229 follies] F; Folly Q4   237 all of . . . upon me] F; of . . . vpon Q4   241 delivered]
F; deliuer Q4

228 **ravel out** undo, unravel (linked to the image of weaving in the next line)
229 **Gentle** 'the bitterest epithet in this play' (Newbolt, quoted in Black, p. 270)
230 **upon record** written down (emphasis on second syllable: recòrd)
231 **so fair a troop** such august company (with more than a hint of sarcasm)
232 **read a lecture** perform a public reading
232–3 **wouldst . . . shouldst** In modern English these auxiliaries would normally be reversed, but in Shakespeare 'would' in a conditional clause typically expresses 'hypothetical volition' and 'should' in a main clause sometimes expresses simple 'futurity' (see Blake, pp. 124, 127, and cf. 3.4.20).
233 **heinous article** Richard throws Northumberland's accusation back at him; the phrase is adapted from Holinshed's account of the King's faults but Shakespeare gives it to the accused as a weapon of retaliation.

235 **oath** i.e. the oath of allegiance Northumberland has 'cracked'
236 The line refers back to the 'article' (233), a tainted one that threatens damnation to those who framed it; the 'book of heaven' may be the 'book of life' in Revelation 3: 5 and 21: 27.
238 **bait** attack (as dogs assail a bear or bull; 'wretchedness' is thus compared to the aggressive dogs in a bear-baiting ring)
239–42 Another comparison of himself to Christ; Pilate, the Roman functionary in Palestine, famously washed his hands in front of the crowd who called for Christ's crucifixion (Matthew 27: 24–6), supposedly exculpating himself (though it could hardly be said that he showed an 'outward pity'; rather a calculated indifference).
246 **sort** mob, gang

Nay, if I turn mine eyes upon myself
I find myself a traitor with the rest,
For I have given here my soul's consent
T'undeck the pompous body of a king,   250
Made glory base and sovereignty a slave,
Proud majesty a subject, state a peasant.

NORTHUMBERLAND

My lord—

RICHARD

No lord of thine, thou haught insulting man,
Nor no man's lord. I have no name, no title—   255
No, not that name was given me at the font—
But 'tis usurped. Alack the heavy day
That I have worn so many winters out
And know not now what name to call myself.
O that I were a mockery king of snow,   260
Standing before the sun of Bolingbroke
To melt myself away in water-drops.
Good King, great King, and yet not greatly good,
An if my word be sterling yet in England,
Let it command a mirror hither straight   265
That it may show me what a face I have
Since it is bankrupt of his majesty.

BOLINGBROKE

Go some of you and fetch a looking-glass.

                                    [*Exit an attendant*]

---

250 T'undeck] F; To vndecke Q4   251 base,] Q4; base; F and sovereignty] Q4; a Souer-
aigntie F   255 Nor] Q4; No, nor F   264 word] F; name Q4   268.1 *Exit an attendant*]
Capell; *not in* Q4, F

250 **undeck . . . pompous** strip the regalia
     from the richly decked out; 'pompous'
     (from 'pomp') has no negative connota-
     tion.
251–2 Richard deploys several personified
     images of debasement to describe his own
     cooperation with the effort to depose
     him.
252 **state** high estate, kingly splendour (see
     225 n.)
254 **haught** haughty, arrogant
256 **at the font** at baptism

260 **mockery** mock, imitation
261 **sun** As at 221, Richard here extends the
     regal sun imagery, previously associated
     with himself, to his enemy.
263 Richard plays on 'good' (= moral)
     and 'great' (= powerful) to suggest that
     Bolingbroke is powerful but immoral.
265 **hither straight** to be brought here
     immediately
267 **bankrupt** emptied
     his its

NORTHUMBERLAND

Read o'er this paper while the glass doth come.

RICHARD

Fiend, thou torments me ere I come to hell! 270

BOLINGBROKE

Urge it no more, my lord Northumberland.

NORTHUMBERLAND

The commons will not then be satisfied.

RICHARD

They shall be satisfied. I'll read enough
When I do see the very book indeed
Where all my sins are writ, and that's myself. 275

Enter one with a glass

Give me that glass and therein will I read.
No deeper wrinkles yet? Hath sorrow struck
So many blows upon this face of mine
And made no deeper wounds? O flatt'ring glass,
Like to my followers in prosperity 280
Thou dost beguile me. Was this face the face
That every day under his household roof
Did keep ten thousand men? Was this the face
That like the sun did make beholders wink?

275.1 *Enter . . . glass*] F; *not in* Q4   276–80] *as* F; *four lines ending* 'yet?' 'vpon this'
'woundes?' 'prosperitie!' (*omitting* 'and . . . read') Q4   276 that] F; the Q4 and . . . read]
F; *not in* Q4   279 flatt'ring] F; flattering Q4   281–3] *as* F; *two lines ending* 'vnder his'
'men?' (*omitting* 'Thou . . . me') Q4   281 Thou . . . me] F; *not in* Q4   face the face] F; the face
Q4   283–4 Was this . . . wink?] F; *not in* Q4

270 **torments** Though we might expect
'torment'st', this is in fact a fairly common form of the second person in verbs
that end with 't' or 'st', done for euphony
(see Blake, p. 89, and Abbott 340).

271 Bolingbroke once again takes the
politically sensible, even sensitive, course,
reining in the obdurate Northumberland.

273, 276 **read** expound, interpret. Richard
plays on the demand that he read the
articles aloud, saying that he will
expound the meaning of the book that
is his face.

276–89 On the complex theatrical symbolism of the mirror, see Introduction,
pp. 52–3.

280 **in prosperity** i.e. when I was in my
former prosperous state

281 **beguile** deceive

281–6 **Was . . . Bolingbroke** An unmistak-
able reminiscence of Marlowe's famous
lines about Helen of Troy, 'Was this the
face that launched a thousand ships |
And burnt the topless towers of Ilium?'
(*Faustus* 5.1.90–1); but the whole idea is
turned inward, so that unlike Faustus,
whose soul is 'sucked forth', Richard is
narcissistically engaged with his own
image and its past glories.

284 **wink** shut their eyes

Is this the face which faced so many follies,   285
That was at last outfaced by Bolingbroke?
A brittle glory shineth in this face;
As brittle as the glory is the face,
  [*He throws down the glass*]
For there it is cracked in a hundred shivers.
Mark, silent King, the moral of this sport: 290
How soon my sorrow hath destroyed my face.

BOLINGBROKE
  The shadow of your sorrow hath destroyed
  The shadow of your face.
RICHARD   Say that again.
  The shadow of my sorrow—ha, let's see—
  'Tis very true, my grief lies all within   295
  And these external manners of laments

---

285 Is . . . which] F; Was . . . that Q4   286 That] F; And Q4   288.1 *He . . . glass*] THEOBALD
(*subs.*); *not in* Q4, F   289 a] Q4; an F   293–300] *as* F; *seven lines* (*with omissions*), *ending*
'face.' 'sorrow;' 'my griefe' 'manners' 'vnseene,' 'soule:' 'giuest' Q4   296 manners]
Q4; manner F

---

285 **Is . . . which** The F text has Richard shift
to the present tense, while Q4 continues
the rhetorical pattern ('Was this the face
that . . .'). F's version brings Richard
emphatically into the present moment
and prepares for the smashing of the
mirror, his attempt to obliterate himself.
Q4's reading may be a result of over-
regularization on the part of an editor or
could conceivably have originated from a
different performance.
  faced confronted, met face to face (*OED v.*
4) (?). Most editors gloss as either
'countenanced' or 'adorned' (face = to
cover part of a garment with different
material), but it seems unlikely that
Richard is here admitting his follies.
286 **outfaced** outdone, defeated
287 **brittle** fragile. The fragility of kingly
glory, as represented by Richard's
reflected face, is echoed by that of the
glass itself.
288.1 The action of dashing the mirror to
the floor captures in a telling theatrical
gesture both Richard's uneasy relationship with his own royal identity and the
status of kingship as a matter of image,
something reflected, like the face in a
mirror.

289 **shivers** tiny fragments
290 **silent King** Richard shows his awareness
of the contrast between his own histrionic display and Bolingbroke's deliberate,
watchful restraint, not to mention the
latter's menacing, or at least contemptuous, self-containment.
292–3 **The . . . face** The acting out of your
sorrow has destroyed the external image
of your face (i.e. its mirrored reflection);
Bolingbroke is keenly aware of the
theatricalism of Richard's performance;
one meaning of 'shadow' was 'actor',
as in Puck's 'If we shadows have
offended' (*Midsummer Night's Dream*,
Epilogue 1).
294–8 Richard, with his characteristic
alertness to language, not only accepts
Bolingbroke's metaphor, but extends it,
giving it a more positive spin; like
Hamlet's, his grief is 'all within' and
external gestures of 'laments' are only
shadows of the real thing (cf. *Hamlet*
1.2.76–86); in contrast to Hamlet,
Richard declares that his inward sorrow
increases ('swells') if it does not find outward expression.

Are merely shadows to the unseen grief
That swells with silence in the tortured soul.
There lies the substance, and I thank thee, King,
For thy great bounty, that not only giv'st   300
Me cause to wail but teachest me the way
How to lament the cause. I'll beg one boon
And then be gone and trouble you no more.
Shall I obtain it?

BOLINGBROKE   Name it, fair cousin.

RICHARD
'Fair cousin'? I am greater than a king,   305
For when I was a king my flatterers
Were then but subjects. Being now a subject,
I have a king here to my flatterer—
Being so great, I have no need to beg.

BOLINGBROKE
Yet ask.   310

RICHARD
And shall I have?

BOLINGBROKE
You shall.

RICHARD
Then give me leave to go.

BOLINGBROKE
Whither?

RICHARD
Whither you will, so I were from your sights.   315

BOLINGBROKE
Go some of you, convey him to the Tower.

---

299 There . . . substance] F; *not in* Q4   300 For . . . bounty] F; *not in* Q4   giv'st] F; giuest Q4
304 Shall . . . it?] F; *not in* Q4   305 cousin'?] F; Coose, why? Q4   306–9] *as* F; *three
lines ending* 'but subiects,' 'heere' 'beg.' Q4   311 have] F; haue it Q4   313 Then] F; Why
then Q4

---

297 **to** compared to
299 **There** i.e. within the soul
301 **teachest . . . way** i.e. by reminding him
that his real sorrow is within and cannot
be adequately represented externally.
The tone, of course, is bitingly ironic.
302 **boon** favour

308 **to** as
313 Richard's surprisingly simple request
may derive from a sudden weariness with
his own self-display; or it could, as Wells
suggests, be a 'calculated deflation' of the
new King's status and power.

RICHARD

O, good—'convey'. Conveyors are you all
That rise thus nimbly by a true king's fall.

[*Exit Richard under guard*]

BOLINGBROKE

On Wednesday next we solemnly set down
Our coronation. Lords, prepare yourselves.   320

Exeunt [all but Abbot of] Westminster,
Carlisle, [and] Aumerle

WESTMINSTER

A woeful pageant have we here beheld.

CARLISLE

The woe's to come—the children yet unborn
Shall feel this day as sharp to them as thorn.

AUMERLE

You holy clergymen, is there no plot
To rid the realm of this pernicious blot?   325

WESTMINSTER

My lord,
Before I freely speak my mind herein
You shall not only take the sacrament
To bury mine intents, but also to effect
Whatever I shall happen to devise.   330
I see your brows are full of discontent,
Your hearts of sorrow and your eyes of tears.
Come home with me to supper, I'll lay a plot
Shall show us all a merry day.   *Exeunt*

318.1 *Exit . . . guard*] CAPELL (*subs.*); *not in* Q4–F   319–20 On Wednesday . . . yourselves]
Q4–F; Let it be so, and loe on wednesday next, | We solemnly proclaime our Coronation, |
Lords be ready all. Q1   320.1–2 *Exeunt . . . Aumerle*] ROWE (*subs.*); Exeunt. | Manent West.
Caleil, Aumerle. Q1; Exeunt. F   326 My lord] Q1; *not in* Q3–F   326–7 My lord, | Before . . .
herein] *as* CAMBRIDGE; *one line* Q1   332 hearts] Q1; hart Q2–F (Heart)   333–4] *as* POPE;
lines ending 'plot', 'daie' Q1, F

317 **convey** Once again, Richard seizes on
   Henry's words and wittily re-deploys
   them; here he plays on 'convey' as a
   euphemism for stealing (*OED v.* 6b), and
   'conveyor' as a 'nimble' thief (*OED n.* 2).
319–20 Here the Q1 text resumes, with what
   appears to be an awkward transition
   occasioned by the large cut: the addition
   of 'Let it be so, and loe' (see textual
   notes). Q1's 'proclaime' and 'be ready all',
   however, may well derive from Shake-

speare's original but were changed in the
theatrical version that lies behind F.
321 **pageant** Westminster is well aware of
   the theatrical dimensions of the preceding action.
328 **sacrament** Eucharist (as a pledge)
329 **bury mine intents** keep my intentions
   hidden
331–4 **I see . . . day** Spoken to both the
   others, though the first part of the speech
   (326–30) is directed to Aumerle only.

5.1 *Enter Queen and Ladies*
QUEEN
This way the King will come. This is the way
To Julius Caesar's ill-erected tower
To whose flint bosom my condemnèd lord
Is doomed a prisoner by proud Bolingbroke.
Here let us rest, if this rebellious earth   5
Have any resting for her true king's queen.
    Enter Richard and Guard
But soft, but see, or rather do not see
My fair rose wither. Yet look up, behold,
That you in pity may dissolve to dew
And wash him fresh again with true-love tears.   10
Ah thou, the model where old Troy did stand,

5.1] F (*Actus Quintus. Scena Prima.*); *not in* Q1   0.1 *Enter . . . Ladies*] F; *Enter the Queene with her attendants.* Q1   6.1 *Enter . . . Guard*] F; *Enter Ric.* Q1

5.1 This tender scene of leave-taking between Richard and his queen has no parallel in any of the chronicles. The Queen, having left York's protection to go meet her husband (see 3.4.96–7), has now come to London in order to intercept him as he is escorted to the Tower. The intimacy of their meeting and the pathos of their enforced separation contrasts with the public spectacle of the previous scene, and Richard's tendency to self-conscious theatricalizing, so evident when he faces his enemies, is here almost entirely absent. The sequence opens a window on to Richard's private feelings, preparing us for the more far-reaching exploration of his inwardness in 5.5. While largely Shakespeare's invention, this meeting of King and Queen draws on a sequence from Daniel's *Civil Wars*, in which the Queen first watches from a window as Bolingbroke enters London in triumph with Richard as captive, and later contrives to join him in his cell, where, speechless with grief, the two face each other until Richard offers words of comfort. Though Daniel's scene takes place before the deposition, the touching devotion of the lovers and their mutual compassion are similar in both texts. See Introduction, pp. 54–6.

2 **ill-erected** constructed for evil ends
  tower The Tower of London, built, according to legend, by Caesar; there is a similar allusion in *Richard III* 3.1.69–71.

3 **flint** Both (a) hard-hearted, and (b) made of flint, a hard stone.

5 **rebellious earth** i.e. England (now in the hands of rebels), as well as the tiny patch of it on which they stand

7 **soft** 'an exclamation with imperative force, either to enjoin silence or deprecate haste' (*OED adv.* 8a). Here the former signification seems intended: 'shh'.
  see . . . see Daniel's *Civil Wars* depicts Isabel as similarly in conflict about looking and not looking: 2.77–8, 83.

9 **dew** tears (as clarified in the following line)

11 **Ah thou** Up to this point, the Queen has been at a certain distance from Richard; now she addresses him directly, perhaps because he has come close enough to enable conversation, though it is equally likely, especially given the somewhat impersonal nature of the metaphors she weaves over the next four lines, that he remains out of earshot till near the end of her speech.
  model . . . stand i.e. Richard's broken person is like the ruined city of Troy. British mythology held that Brut, the founder of Britain, had Trojan ancestry, being the great grandson (or in some versions the grandson) of Aeneas, the Trojan prince who fled the burning city and went on to found Rome. Thus Richard represents the ruins of Britain as well as Troy.

Thou map of honour, thou King Richard's tomb,
And not King Richard. Thou most beauteous inn,
Why should hard-favoured grief be lodged in thee
When triumph is become an alehouse guest?   15

RICHARD

Join not with grief, fair woman, do not so
To make my end too sudden. Learn, good soul,
To think our former state a happy dream
From which awaked, the truth of what we are
Shows us but this. I am sworn brother, sweet,   20
To grim necessity, and he and I
Will keep a league till death. Hie thee to France,
And cloister thee in some religious house—
Our holy lives must win a new world's crown,
Which our profane hours here have stricken down.   25

QUEEN

What, is my Richard both in shape and mind
Transformed and weakened? Hath Bolingbroke
Deposed thine intellect, hath he been in thy heart?
The lion dying thrusteth forth his paw
And wounds the earth if nothing else with rage   30
To be o'erpowered, and wilt thou pupil-like
Take thy correction mildly, kiss the rod

---

16 RICHARD] Q1 (*Rich.*), F   25 stricken] F; throwne Q1   32 thy correction mildly,] F; the
correction, mildly, Q1

12 **map** embodiment, representation
(parallel to 'model' in the preceding line),
though here, as Forker suggests, the
sense seems to be 'mere image' (all that
is left of 'former grandeur').
   tomb i.e. Richard's body is the tomb of
his essential being, his royal identity
13–15 **Thou . . . guest** Richard is compared
to a 'beauteous inn' that, incongruously
and wrongly, harbours ugly ('hard-
favoured') grief, while Bolingbroke is a
cheap tavern ('alehouse') that, equally
incongruously, welcomes 'triumph' as a
guest.
17 **make . . . sudden** bring me too quickly to
my end
20 **this** i.e. this misery (probably with a
gesture to indicate their ruined state)

21 **necessity** destiny, unavoidable circumstance (personified as an unwelcome
companion)
22 **league** alliance
   Hie thee hurry
   to France Richard directs his wife, the
daughter of Charles VI, to return home.
24–5 The holiness of our lives from now on
must win us a heavenly crown since our
'profane' (= wasteful, irreligious) use of
time has lost us our earthly one.
29 **lion** Once again the correspondence
between king of beasts and king of men is
asserted, and reiterated at the end of the
speech (34); cf. 1.1.174 and 2.1.173.
32 **correction** punishment
   rod i.e. the stick wielded by the school-
master who disciplines his submissive
'pupil'. The expression was proverbial
(Tilley R156).

And fawn on rage with base humility,
Which art a lion and the king of beasts?

RICHARD

    A king of beasts indeed—if aught but beasts   35
I had been still a happy king of men.
Good sometimes Queen, prepare thee hence for France.
Think I am dead and that even here thou tak'st
As from my death-bed thy last living leave.
In winter's tedious nights sit by the fire   40
With good old folks and let them tell thee tales
Of woeful ages long ago betid.
And ere thou bid good night, to 'quite their griefs,
Tell thou the lamentable tale of me
And send the hearers weeping to their beds;   45
For why the senseless brands will sympathize
The heavy accent of thy moving tongue
And in compassion weep the fire out,
And some will mourn in ashes, some coal-black,
For the deposing of a rightful king.   50

    Enter Northumberland [and others]

NORTHUMBERLAND

    My lord, the mind of Bolingbroke is changed,
You must to Pomfret, not unto the Tower.
And madam, there is order ta'en for you,
With all swift speed you must away to France.

---

34 the] Q1; a Q2–F   35 RICHARD] F; *King.* Q1 (*so to end of play*)   37 sometimes] Q1; sometime Q3–F   38 tak'st] F; takest Q1   39 thy last] Q1; my last Q2–F   41 thee] Q2–F; the Q1   42 betid] Q1; betide Q2–F   43 'quite] Q1 (quite); quit F griefs] Q1; griefe Q2–F   44 tale] Q1; fall F   50.1 *and others*] CAPELL; *not in* Q1, F

33 **fawn on rage** bow to (Bolingbroke's) wrath
    humility servile tameness
34 **Which** who
35 **beasts** Richard plays on the lion theme by naming as beasts (in the moral sense) those who have betrayed him.
    aught anything
37 **sometimes** former
38 **Think I am** think of me as if I were
39 **leave** farewell
42 **long ago betid** that happened long ago (probably modifying 'tales' in the previous line, though the actual antecedent is understood: 'events')

43 **'quite their griefs** match the sadness of their tales
46 **For why** on account of which (referring to the mournful tales). See Abbott 75.
46–8 **the senseless . . . out** the insentient embers ('brands') will be in sympathy with the sad tone of your moving story and, out of pity, extinguish the fire with their weeping
49 **some** i.e. 'brands' (46)
50.1 Once again Northumberland appears as a kind of dark angel.
52 **Pomfret** i.e the castle at Pontefract in Yorkshire
53 **order ta'en** an arrangement made

RICHARD

Northumberland, thou ladder wherewithal   55
The mounting Bolingbroke ascends my throne,
The time shall not be many hours of age
More than it is, ere foul sin gathering head
Shall break into corruption. Thou shalt think
Though he divide the realm and give thee half   60
It is too little, helping him to all.
He shall think that thou, which know'st the way
To plant unrightful kings, wilt know again,
Being ne'er so little urged, another way
To pluck him headlong from the usurped throne.   65
The love of wicked men converts to fear,
That fear to hate and hate turns one or both
To worthy danger and deservèd death.

NORTHUMBERLAND

My guilt be on my head, and there an end.
Take leave and part, for you must part forthwith.   70

RICHARD

Doubly divorced! Bad men, you violate
A twofold marriage—'twixt my crown and me,
And then betwixt me and my married wife.
[*To the Queen*] Let me unkiss the oath 'twixt thee and
          me—
And yet not so, for with a kiss 'twas made.   75
Part us, Northumberland: I towards the north

---

62 know'st] Q2–F; knowest Q1   66 men] Q1; friends F   71 you] Q1; ye F   74 *To the
Queen*] ROWE; *not in* Q1, F

55–9 In *2 Henry IV* these lines are directly, if
    a little inaccurately, quoted by Boling-
    broke, when, as Henry IV, he laments
    the loss of Northumberland's loyalty
    (3.1.65–72). Shakespeare seems to have
    forgotten that Henry was not present to
    hear them when they were first spoken.
    The prophecy as a whole (57–65) rests on
    the awareness of virtually everyone in
    the audience that it will come true.
58–9 **gathering . . . corruption** The meta-
    phor is of a boil or abscess coming to a
    'head' and leaking pus.
61 **helping** having helped
63 **unrightful** illegitimate

64 **Being . . . urged** with only the slightest
    provocation
66 **love . . . fear** love between wicked men
    soon changes to suspicion. Richard is all
    too aware of the fragility of political
    alliances forged for personal gain.
68 **worthy** well-deserved
70 **Take leave** i.e. of each other. Northum-
    berland addresses both Richard and his
    Queen.
74 **unkiss** undo the marriage vow with a
    kiss; but Richard immediately recognizes
    the inappropriateness of the suggestion,
    since their vow was originally sealed with
    one (75).

Where shivering cold and sickness pines the clime,
My wife to France, from whence set forth in pomp
She came adornèd hither like sweet May,
Sent back like Hallowmas or short'st of day.   80

QUEEN
And must we be divided, must we part?

RICHARD
Ay, hand from hand, my love, and heart from heart.

QUEEN
Banish us both and send the King with me.

NORTHUMBERLAND
That were some love but little policy.

QUEEN
Then whither he goes, thither let me go.   85

RICHARD
So two together weeping make one woe.
Weep thou for me in France, I for thee here.
Better far off than, near, be ne'er the nea'er.
Go count thy way with sighs, I mine with groans.

QUEEN
So longest way shall have the longest moans.   90

RICHARD
Twice for one step I'll groan, the way being short,
And piece the way out with a heavy heart.
Come, come, in wooing sorrow let's be brief,
Since wedding it there is such length in grief.

---

78 wife] QI; Queene F   84 NORTHUMBERLAND] F; *King* QI   88 off than, near,] URE; off than neere‸ QI; off, then neere, F nea'er] CAPELL (*subs.*); neare QI–F (*subs.*)

77 **pines the clime** brings misery to the region

78 **in pomp** with ceremonious pageantry

80 **Hallowmas** All Saints' Day, 1 November

84 QI gives this line to Richard, but assigning it to Northumberland, as in F, is more appropriate and more effective. The latter intrudes into the grieving couple's melodious couplets with a harsh reminder of what drives the world of the play: 'policy'.

86 **So . . . woe** i.e. when we both weep, we together make a single woe (even if we are separated)

88 An obscure line made more obscure by the early punctuation; Ure's punctuation

(adopted here) enables the following gloss: 'it is better that we should be far from each other than, though hear in place, be no closer to meeting or to happiness'. The phrase 'never the near' was proverbial (Dent N135.2).

89 **count** measure

90–2 In l. 89, Richard has proposed that they should mark their journey with sighs and groans, and so the Queen infers that she will suffer more heartache, since her way is longer; but he offers to double his groans to stretch out the pain of his journey and so match her anguish.

94 **there . . . grief** will mean such a long period of suffering

One kiss shall stop our mouths, and dumbly part.   95
Thus give I mine and thus take I thy heart.
　　[*They kiss*]
QUEEN
Give me mine own again, 'twere no good part
To take on me to keep and kill thy heart.
　　[*They kiss again*]
So now I have mine own again, be gone
That I may strive to kill it with a groan.   100
RICHARD
We make woe wanton with this fond delay,
Once more, adieu, the rest let sorrow say.   *Exeunt*

5.2 *Enter the Duke and Duchess of York*
DUCHESS
My lord, you told me you would tell the rest,
When weeping made you break the story off
Of our two cousins coming into London.

96.1 *They kiss*] ROWE; *not in* Q1, F   98.1 *They kiss again*] ROWE (*subs.*); *not in* Q1, F
　5.2] F (*Scoena Secunda.*); *not in* Q1   0.1 *Enter . . . York*] Q1 (*Enter Duke of Yorke and the
Dutchesse*); *Enter Yorke, and his Duchesse.* F

---

95 **stop our mouths** silence us
97–8 **'twere . . . keep** it would be wrong on
my part to keep. The witty trading of
kisses is reminiscent of *Romeo and Juliet*
1.5.92–109, when the lovers first meet
and volley words and kisses—though
they are full of expectation, while here
the tone is sombre and forlorn.
99 **mine own** i.e. my heart
101 **make woe wanton** trifle with our
unhappiness
fond foolish
102 **the . . . say** let our sorrow pronounce
all the goodbyes that we cannot say in
person
5.2 The action shifts to a domestic interior
to illustrate various consequences of
Richard's fall as they affect a single
noble household. The first part (up to
Aumerle's entrance at 40.1) follows
tonally from the previous scene, continuing the motif of Richard's fall and
humiliation with York's tale of Henry's
triumphant entry into London and the
correspondingly wretched situation of
the former King who follows. (In Holin-

shed, the two processions take place on
different days but Shakespeare sharpens
the contrast by juxtaposing them.)
Though Richard's unhappy entry has
actually preceded his meeting with
Isabel presented in 5.1, the fact that we
hear of it later provides an emotional
underpinning for York's story. The
second part of the scene presents an
almost farcical treatment of the deeply
serious theme of conspiracy and possible
regicide. Conflicted in his loyalties
throughout, York feels sympathy for
Richard and some underlying discontent
with Henry, but he also believes that
fidelity to the new King is enjoined by
heaven (37–40). Perhaps compensating
for his uneasiness concerning Bolingbroke, York does not hesitate to impeach
his own son. But his wife feels no
such compunction and her heartfelt
opposition to York's decision leads to
the domestic squabble about boots and
horses that ends the scene on a comic
note.

3 **cousins** i.e. Richard and Bolingbroke

YORK

Where did I leave?

DUCHESS   At that sad stop, my lord,

Where rude misgoverned hands from windows' tops   5

Threw dust and rubbish on King Richard's head.

YORK

Then as I said the Duke, great Bolingbroke,

Mounted upon a hot and fiery steed

Which his aspiring rider seemed to know,

With slow but stately pace kept on his course   10

Whilst all tongues cried 'God save thee Bolingbroke!'

You would have thought the very windows spake,

So many greedy looks of young and old

Through casements darted their desiring eyes

Upon his visage, and that all the walls   15

With painted imagery had said at once

'Jesus preserve thee! Welcome Bolingbroke!'

Whilst he from one side to the other turning,

Bareheaded, lower than his proud steed's neck,

Bespake them thus, 'I thank you, countrymen.'   20

And thus still doing, thus he passed along.

DUCHESS

Alack poor Richard, where rode he the whilst?

YORK

As in a theatre the eyes of men

After a well-graced actor leaves the stage

11 Whilst] Q1; While Q2–F   thee] F; the Q1   17 Jesus] Q1, F (Iesu) thee] F; the Q1
18 one] F; the one Q1   22 Alack] Q1; Alas F rode] Q1; rides Q2–F

5 **rude misgoverned** barbarous and intemperate

9 **Which . . . know** that seemed to recognize his ambitious rider. 'Which', i.e. the horse, is probably the grammatical subject of 'know', though it could be the object, and 'rider' the subject.

13 **greedy** eager

14 **casements** window frames (here indicating open windows)

16 **painted imagery** The faces in the windows are compared to a painted cloth or mural, like those that sometimes graced civic pageantry.

19 The details suggest a play-acted humility, a motif continued in 23–6.

21 **still** continually

23–6 A famous passage, not least because of its metatheatrical reference. While the audience may well be led to think about the actual actors playing the two principals, it would also be prompted to think about the monarch as an actor on the political stage, a point made saliently by Queen Elizabeth herself. 'We princes', she is reported to have said in 1586 (in reference, not incidentally, to the parliamentary petition for the execution of Mary Queen of Scots), 'are set on stages in the sight and view of all the world duly observed; the eyes of many behold our actions; a spot is soon spied in our garments, a blemish quickly noted in our doings' (Holinshed, p. 1583).

Are idly bent on him that enters next,   25
Thinking his prattle to be tedious,
Even so, or with much more contempt, men's eyes
Did scowl on gentle Richard. No man cried God save him,
No joyful tongue gave him his welcome home,
But dust was thrown upon his sacred head,   30
Which with such gentle sorrow he shook off,
His face still combating with tears and smiles,
The badges of his grief and patience,
That had not God for some strong purpose steeled
The hearts of men, they must perforce have melted   35
And barbarism itself have pitied him.
But heaven hath a hand in these events
To whose high will we bound our calm contents.
To Bolingbroke are we sworn subjects now
Whose state and honour I for aye allow.   40

  Enter Aumerle

DUCHESS
Here comes my son Aumerle.
YORK   Aumerle that was,
But that is lost for being Richard's friend,
And, madam, you must call him Rutland now.
I am in Parliament pledge for his truth
And lasting fealty to the new-made King.   45
DUCHESS
Welcome my son. Who are the violets now
That strew the green lap of the new-come spring?
AUMERLE
Madam I know not, nor I greatly care not.

---

28 gentle Richard] Q1; *Richard* F   40.1 *Enter Aumerle*] F; *not in* Q1

---

25 **idly** indifferently, without much interest
26 **prattle** chatter
32 **combating with** struggling between
33 **badges** marks, signs
36 **barbarism itself** even barbarians
38 **To . . . contents** we calmly circumscribe our happiness by conforming to God's high (perhaps inscrutable?) designs
40 **state** high position
 for aye for ever

41–3 **Aumerle that . . . now** Aumerle lost his dukedom on the accession of Bolingbroke and so his father carefully observes that they must now refer to him by his earlier and less exalted title, Earl of Rutland.
44 **pledge** York had made a pledge in Parliament, guaranteeing the loyalty of his son.
46 **violets** i.e. the newly planted favourites recently sprung up under the sun of Bolingbroke. The image continues the recurrent plant metaphors.

God knows I had as lief be none as one.
YORK
Well, bear you well in this new spring of time   50
Lest you be cropped before you come to prime.
What news from Oxford, do these jousts and triumphs hold?
AUMERLE
For aught I know, my lord, they do.
YORK
You will be there, I know.
AUMERLE
If God prevent it not, I purpose so.   55
YORK
What seal is that that hangs without thy bosom?
Yea, look'st thou pale? Let me see the writing.
AUMERLE
My lord, 'tis nothing.
YORK   No matter then who see it.
I will be satisfied. Let me see the writing.
AUMERLE
I do beseech your grace to pardon me,   60
It is a matter of small consequence,
Which for some reasons I would not have seen.
YORK
Which for some reasons, sir, I mean to see.
I fear, I fear—
DUCHESS   What should you fear?

52 do . . . hold] Q1; Hold those Iusts & Triumphs F   55 prevent it] CAPELL; preuent Q1–F
58 see] Q1; sees F

49 **as lief** rather
50–1 **bear . . . prime** York elaborates his wife's metaphor and, perhaps remembering the fate of Bushy et al., reminds his son of the danger posed by the arch-gardener, Bolingbroke.
50 **bear you well** behave wisely
51 **prime** full maturity ('prime of life'), with a pun on *prime* = spring
52 **do . . . hold** are the plans for the tournament ('jousts and triumphs') still on
56–72 This faintly absurd sequence depends on Aumerle's allowing part of a secret and deeply incriminating document to stick out from under his shirt or coat, ripe for his father's suspicious eye to see

(though Shakespeare took the incident from Holinshed (p. 515), he makes it seem less believable than in the chronicle). The same motif appears in *Lear* (*History* Sc. 2.27–44, *Tragedy* 1.2.28–46), but there it is a trick by which Edmund fools Gloucester into thinking that he has discovered something Edmund *wants* to hide, while the truth is that Edmund *wants* his credulous father to 'discover' it.
56 **seal** wax impression carrying the bearer's insignia. Since it is attached by a strip to the main document, it may be liable to hang out, though Aumerle's carelessness is hard to fathom.

’Tis nothing but some bond that he is entered into   65
For gay apparel ’gainst the triumph day.

YORK

Bound to himself? What doth he with a bond
That he is bound to? Wife, thou art a fool.
Boy, let me see the writing.

AUMERLE

I do beseech you pardon me, I may not show it.   70

YORK

I will be satisfied. Let me see it, I say.

He plucks it out of his bosom and reads it

Treason, foul treason! Villain, traitor, slave!

DUCHESS

What is the matter, my lord?

YORK [*calls offstage*]

Ho! Who is within there? Saddle my horse.
God for his mercy, what treachery is here!   75

DUCHESS

Why, what is it my lord?

YORK

Give me my boots, I say, saddle my horse.
Now by mine honour, by my life, by my troth,
I will appeach the villain.

DUCHESS   What is the matter?

YORK

Peace, foolish woman.   80

DUCHESS

I will not peace. What is the matter, son?

---

66 ’gainst] Q1; against Q2–F   day] Q1; *not in* Q2–F   71.1 *He . . . reads it*] Q1; *Snatches it* F
73 What is] Q1; What’s F   74 *calls offstage*] MOWAT AND WERSTINE; *not in* Q1, F   74 Who is]
Q1; who’s F   75 God] Q1; Heauen F   76 is it] Q1; is’t F   78 by mine] Q1; by my F by my
life . . . troth] Q1; my life, my troth Q2–F   81 son] F; Aumerle Q1

---

65 **bond** promissory note (which, as York
rightly observes in 67–8, would normally
be held by the creditor not the debtor)
66 **gay** splendid
    ’gainst . . . day in preparation for the day
of the tournament (see 52)
74 **Who is within** Whether a servant
actually enters or not is uncertain; the
decision will affect the comedy, since it

would clearly be funnier if a servant
comes on, is sent off to saddle the horse
and then almost immediately called back
(77) to fetch the boots.
77 This line may be shouted offstage, or the
servant may have entered only to be sent
off again (see previous note).
79 **appeach** denounce, accuse

AUMERLE

Good mother, be content. It is no more
Than my poor life must answer.

DUCHESS   Thy life answer?

YORK

Bring me my boots.—I will unto the King.

His man enters with his boots

DUCHESS

Strike him, Aumerle! Poor boy, thou art amazed.   85
[*To servingman*] Hence villain, never more come in my
   sight.

YORK

Give me my boots, I say.

DUCHESS

Why York, what wilt thou do?
Wilt thou not hide the trespass of thine own?
Have we more sons or are we like to have?   90
Is not my teeming date drunk up with time,
And wilt thou pluck my fair son from mine age
And rob me of a happy mother's name?
Is he not like thee, is he not thine own?

YORK

Thou fond mad woman,   95
Wilt thou conceal this dark conspiracy?
A dozen of them here have ta'en the sacrament

84.1 *His man . . . boots*] Q1; *Enter Seruant with Boots.* F (*after* 83)   86 *To servingman*] POPE
(*subs.*); *not in* Q1, F

83 **answer** pay for
84.1 The slapstick comedy accelerates (see
   74 n.) as the servant enters with the
   boots and then is harassed by the
   Duchess.
85–6 The Duchess tries to recruit Aumerle to
   chase out the servant, but he remains
   motionless, 'amazed' (stunned), so she
   takes matters into her own hands.
87 The servant is no doubt comically confused, caught between mistress and
   master, but manages to creep back to
   give York his boots; he might then stay to
   help York don the boots (providing more
   opportunity for comic business) and then

exit with him at l. 111, or he might leave
earlier, dismissed by his master as the
latter's argument with the Duchess heats
up. A 2009 Vancouver production, in a
clever comic move, had the Duchess seize
the boots from the servant and hold them
behind her back while she taunted her
husband.
89 **thine own** your own child
91 **teeming date** time of childbearing
   drunk up worn out
97 **ta'en the sacrament** received the
   Eucharist (as a pledge to carry out the
   plot). See 4.1.328–9 and n.

And interchangeably set down their hands
To kill the King at Oxford.

DUCHESS   He shall be none.

We'll keep him here. Then what is that to him?   100

YORK

Away fond woman! Were he twenty times my son
I would appeach him.

DUCHESS   Hadst thou groaned for him

As I have done, thou'dst be more pitiful.
But now I know thy mind: thou dost suspect
That I have been disloyal to thy bed   105
And that he is a bastard, not thy son.
Sweet York, sweet husband, be not of that mind,
He is as like thee as a man may be,
Not like to me or any of my kin,
And yet I love him.   110

YORK

Make way, unruly woman.   *Exit*

DUCHESS

After, Aumerle! Mount thee upon his horse,
Spur post, and get before him to the King,
And beg thy pardon ere he do accuse thee.
I'll not be long behind. Though I be old   115
I doubt not but to ride as fast as York,

99–100 He shall . . . him?] *as* F; *lines ending* 'heere,' 'him?' Q1   101–2 Away . . . him] *as* Q1; *prose* F   102–3 Hadst . . . pitiful] *as* ROWE 1714; *lines ending* 'done,' 'pittifull' Q1, F   103 thou'dst] ROWE 1709; Thou wouldst Q1; Thou wouldest F   108 a man] Q1c, F; any man Q1u   109 or any] Q1c; or a Q1u; nor any F

---

98 **interchangeably** reciprocally. The oath was drawn up in as many parts as there were conspirators and each man signed each copy as a guarantee of faith (Black, p. 305).

101 **Away fond woman** York either waves her off as she seeks to interfere with him and his boots, or moves to prevent her from knocking around the poor servant, whom she may well have been accosting.

102 **groaned** i.e. in childbirth

103 **pitiful** sympathetic

112 **his horse** The Duchess apparently directs her son to intercept York and appropriate his horse before the old man can struggle into the saddle that has been prepared for him (something Aumerle

must fail to do since we hear nothing else about it). All the early texts agree on this reading, which might have resulted from a misinterpretation of Holinshed, though he states fairly clearly that Aumerle 'took his [i.e. his own] horse' and beat his father to Windsor where the King was staying (p. 515). Black sees the Duchess's directive as 'entirely in keeping with [her] character' (p. 307) and Ure thinks that Shakespeare 'increases the drama by suggesting that Aumerle steals his father's horse'. Just as likely, however, is the possibility that 'his' is simply a slip for 'thy'. Certainly the rest of the Duchess's speech suggests that York will be riding his own horse, and she hers.

And never will I rise up from the ground
Till Bolingbroke have pardoned thee. Away, be gone.

Exeunt

5.3 *Enter Bolingbroke with Percy and other lords*
BOLINGBROKE

Can no man tell me of my unthrifty son?
'Tis full three months since I did see him last.
If any plague hang over us, 'tis he.
I would to God, my lords, he might be found—
Enquire at London 'mongst the taverns there,   5
For there they say he daily doth frequent
With unrestrainèd loose companions,
Even such they say as stand in narrow lanes
And beat our watch and rob our passengers,
Which he, young wanton and effeminate boy,   10
Takes on the point of honour to support
So dissolute a crew.

---

117 And] Q2–F; An Q1

5.3] F (*Scoena Tertia.*); *not in* Q1   0.1 *Enter . . . lords*] F (*subs.*); *Enter the King with his nobles* Q1   1 BOLINGBROKE] F (*Bul.*); *King H.* Q1 (*so throughout scene*) (*sometimes omitting* H.) tell me] Q1; tell F   4 God] Q1; heauen F   9 beat . . . rob] Q1; rob . . . beate F   10 Which] Q1, F; While POPE   11–12] *as* F; *one line* Q1

---

117 **from the ground** i.e. from her knees (since she will kneel before the King to entreat pardon)

5.3 The Aumerle sub-plot continues with the arrival of the whole family one by one at Windsor to make their pleas to Bolingbroke, whose judicious handling of the conspiracy contrasts with Richard's vacillation in the face of challenge. As in 5.2, a deadly serious issue—both the plot itself and Aumerle's role in it—takes a comic turn, especially after the arrival of the Duchess, when, as Bolingbroke himself observes, 'Our scene is altered from a serious thing | And now changed to "The Beggar and the King"' (78–9). Still, the emotional intensity of the mother's appeal for the pardon of her wayward son and the dark intransigence of the unyielding father, who would rather see his son dead than admit dishonour to his family, emerge powerfully in the midst of the comedy. The scene begins with the first mention of what will become the major theme of the *Henry IV* plays—the 'unthrifty' prodigality of the young Prince who will eventually become Henry V—thus providing a context for the drama of another rebellious son in what follows.

1 **unthrifty** wasteful, extravagant

6 **frequent** keep company

9 **watch** watchmen, officers
passengers passers-by

10 **Which** as to which (Abbott 272). Frequently emended to 'while', but there are a number of instances in Shakespeare where 'which' is used in similarly loose ways.
effeminate unmanly (because of his penchant for wine and women over more manly pursuits such as jousts and courtly scheming)

11 **Takes on the** makes it a

PERCY

  My lord, some two days since I saw the Prince
  And told him of those triumphs held at Oxford.

BOLINGBROKE

  And what said the gallant?   15

PERCY

  His answer was he would unto the stews
  And from the common'st creature pluck a glove
  And wear it as a favour, and with that
  He would unhorse the lustiest challenger.

BOLINGBROKE

  As dissolute as desperate; yet through both   20
  I see some sparks of better hope which elder years
  May happily bring forth. But who comes here?

     Enter Aumerle amazed

AUMERLE

  Where is the King?

BOLINGBROKE

  What means our cousin that he stares and looks so wildly?

AUMERLE

  God save your grace, I do beseech your majesty   25
  To have some conference with your grace alone.

BOLINGBROKE

  Withdraw yourselves and leave us here alone.

              [*Exeunt Percy and the other lords*]

  What is the matter with our cousin now?

AUMERLE [*kneeling*]

  For ever may my knees grow to the earth,
  My tongue cleave to the roof within my mouth,   30
  Unless a pardon ere I rise or speak.

---

13 PERCY] F (*Per.*); H. *Percie* Q1   14 those] Q1; these F   21 years] Q1; dayes F
22.1 amazed] Q1; *not in* F   24] *as* Q1; *two lines ending* 'stares' 'wildely?' F   27.1 *Exeunt . . .
lords*] CAPELL (*after* Hanmer); *not in* Q1, F   29 kneeling] ROWE (*subs.*); *not in* Q1, F   30 the]
DYCE 1864 (*conj.* Lettsom); my Q1, F

13 **since** ago
14 **held** to be held
15 **gallant** fine young gentleman (sarcastic)
16 **stews** brothels
17 **common'st creature** lowest whore
20 **desperate** reckless
  both Referring to the two qualities mentioned earlier in the line: 'dissolute', 'desperate'.

22 **happily** possibly (with a pun on the more common meaning)
22.1 *amazed* As at 5.2.85, Aumerle is beside himself.
29 **grow . . . earth** An image used later by his mother (105).
31 **unless** unless you grant

BOLINGBROKE

Intended or committed was this fault?
If on the first, how heinous e'er it be
To win thy after-love I pardon thee.

AUMERLE

Then give me leave that I may turn the key   35
That no man enter till my tale be done.

BOLINGBROKE

Have thy desire.

[Aumerle locks the door.]
The Duke of York knocks at the door and crieth

YORK (*within*)

My liege, beware, look to thyself.
Thou hast a traitor in thy presence there.

BOLINGBROKE

Villain, I'll make thee safe.   40

AUMERLE

Stay thy revengeful hand, thou hast no cause to fear.

YORK

Open the door, secure foolhardy King.
Shall I for love speak treason to thy face.

---

35 I may] Q2–F; May Q1   36 be] Q1; me F   37.1 *Aumerle . . . door*] CAPELL (*subs.*); *not in*
Q1, F   37.2 *The Duke . . . crieth*] Q1; *Yorke withiu.* F (*in margin*)   38 *within*] F (*after* 37); *not in*
Q1   42 foolhardy] F (*subs.*); foole, hardie Q1   43 face.] This edition; face, Q1; face? Q2–F

32–4 Bolingbroke is prepared to pardon a
criminal intention but not a crime.

34 **win thy after-love** Shrewd as always,
Bolingbroke thinks about the necessity
of maintaining a strong alliance with the
York family.

37–85 The potentially farcical business with
the multiple locking and unlocking of
the door has an important underlying
element: control of access to the king's
person.

40 Johnson added a direction followed by
most editors: '*Drawing* [*his sword*]';
certainly Bolingbroke makes some kind
of threatening move, as Aumerle's 'Stay
thy revengeful hand' makes clear, but
he might brandish some other kind of
weapon.

42 **secure** over-confident

43 **Shall I . . . face** i.e. let me in so that, out
of fidelity, I can speak directly to you

about treason. Most editors treat this line
as a question (following F's punctuation),
meaning something like: 'Must I because
of my love and loyalty speak treason,
i.e. by calling you "foolhardy"' (Ure). But
this common interpretation omits
entirely the idea behind 'to thy face'.
Much more likely, the line is not meant
as a question at all (as Q1's comma
would suggest), but as a plea, and the
'treason' York wants to speak about is
not his own, but Aumerle's. Thus, as
Black observes (p. 314, citing *Taming of
the Shrew* 4.1.139, 'Shall I have some
water'), the phrase 'Shall I' probably
means something like 'let me'. The
putatively Shakespearian poem, 'Shall I
die', where the interrogative and imperative usages seem both to be in play, might
also be apposite.

267

Open the door or I will break it open.

  [*Bolingbroke opens the door to admit York, then relocks it*]

BOLINGBROKE

What is the matter, uncle? Speak,   45

Recover breath, tell us how near is danger

That we may arm us to encounter it.

YORK

Peruse this writing here and thou shalt know

The treason that my haste forbids me show.

AUMERLE

Remember as thou read'st thy promise passed,   50

I do repent me, read not my name there,

My heart is not confederate with my hand.

YORK

It was, villain, ere thy hand did set it down.

  [*To Bolingbroke*] I tore it from the traitor's bosom, King.

Fear and not love begets his penitence,   55

Forget to pity him lest pity prove

A serpent that will sting thee to the heart.

BOLINGBROKE

O heinous, strong and bold conspiracy!

O loyal father of a treacherous son!

Thou sheer immaculate and silver fountain   60

From whence this stream through muddy passages

Hath held his current and defiled himself!

Thy overflow of good converts to bad

44.1 *Bolingbroke . . . it*] WILSON (*subs.*); *Enter Yorke.* F; *not in* Q1   45–6] *as* STEEVENS; *lines ending* 'breath,' 'daunger,' Q1, F   49 treason] Q1; reason F   56 lest] OXFORD (*conj.* Craven); lest thy Q1, F   62 held] Q1, F; had F

44.1 Bolingbroke must relock the door after admitting York to prepare for the business of the Duchess's attempt to break into the conversation (73 ff.).

47 **us** ourselves (the royal plural)

49 **haste . . . show** my breathlessness (the result of 'haste') prevents me from speaking about

50 **passed** just made

52 **hand** Aumerle refers to his signature on the document.

60–2 York's lineage is compared to a crystal-clear fountain whose 'current' has been 'muddied' by the soil of Aumerle's crime. Cf. the Duchess of Gloucester's comparison of the royal family to vials of blood (1.2.12 ff.).

60 **sheer** pure (*OED a.* 4), or possibly an adverb meaning 'absolutely' (*OED adv.* 1a)

62 **his . . . himself** its . . . itself

63 **converts** has changed (through Aumerle's behaviour)

And thy abundant goodness shall excuse
This deadly blot in thy digressing son.   65
YORK

So shall my virtue be his vice's bawd
And he shall spend mine honour with his shame,
As thriftless sons their scraping fathers' gold.
Mine honour lives when his dishonour dies,
Or my shamed life in his dishonour lies.   70
Thou kill'st me in his life: giving him breath,
The traitor lives, the true man's put to death.
DUCHESS (*within*)

What ho, my liege! For God's sake let me in!
BOLINGBROKE

What shrill-voiced suppliant makes this eager cry?
DUCHESS [*within*]

A woman, and thy aunt, great King, 'tis I.   75
Speak with me, pity me, open the door,
A beggar begs that never begged before.
BOLINGBROKE

Our scene is altered from a serious thing
And now changed to 'The Beggar and the King'.

---

67 And] Q2–F; An QI   71 life:] F (*subs.*); life, QI   73 *within*] F (*Dutchesse within.*); *not in*
QI   God's] QI; heauens F   74 shrill-voiced] Q3 (*subs.*)-F; shril voice QI   75 *within*]
CAPELL; *not in* QI, F   thy] QI; thine F

64 **And** 'But' would seem more appropriate
since the King is saying that despite
Aumerle's muddying of the stream,
York's 'abundant goodness' will compensate for that 'blot'.

65 **digressing** errant, wayward

66 **bawd** someone who arranges illegitimate
sexual encounters. If, that is, Bolingbroke
uses York's virtue as a motive to pardon
Aumerle, he will be prostituting that
virtue.

68 **As . . . gold** as prodigal sons spend
their fathers' hard-earned money. The
comparison no doubt hits home with
Bolingbroke who has begun the scene
with a lament about his own 'unthrifty'
son.
scraping working hard to amass money
(often pejorative). See *OED*, scrape, *v.* 5a:
'to gather by great efforts, or penurious
or trifling diligence', cf. the modern
phrase, 'to scrape out a living'. *OED*
actually cites this line to illustrate a

different meaning, 'miserly', but that
seems incorrect given that York is clearly
on the side of the 'scraping fathers'.

69–72 'My honour depends on his dishonour dying (i.e. his being executed for
treason), otherwise I will live a life of
shame as a result of his dishonour. If you
allow him to live, you put me to death;
allowing him breath means that the
traitor will live on while I, the true man,
will die.' York, in his eagerness to get his
point across, keeps repeating himself.

74 **What . . . cry** It's hard not to hear a note
of irony in this line.

78 Bolingbroke, despite the gravity of the
situation, recognizes its comic potential.

79 **The Beggar and the King** Probably a
reference to a popular ballad telling the
story of King Cophetua and a beggar
maid with whom he fell in love (only the
title is pertinent to the present situation).
Shakespeare refers to it several times,
twice in *Love's Labour's* as well as in
Romeo and *2 Henry IV*.

My dangerous cousin, let your mother in—   80
I know she's come to pray for your foul sin.
YORK
  If thou do pardon whosoever pray,
  More sins for this forgiveness prosper may.
  This festered joint cut off, the rest rest sound,
  This let alone will all the rest confound.   85
      Enter Duchess of York
DUCHESS
  O King, believe not this hard-hearted man.
  Love loving not itself, none other can.
YORK
  Thou frantic woman, what dost thou make here,
  Shall thy old dugs once more a traitor rear?
DUCHESS
  Sweet York, be patient; hear me, gentle liege—   90
      [*She kneels*]
BOLINGBROKE
  Rise up, good aunt.
DUCHESS   Not yet, I thee beseech.
  For ever will I walk upon my knees
  And never see day that the happy sees
  Till thou give joy, until thou bid me joy
  By pardoning Rutland, my transgressing boy.   95
AUMERLE
  Unto my mother's prayers I bend my knee.
      [*He kneels*]
YORK
  Against them both my true joints bended be.

---

81 she's] F; she is Q1   84 rest rest] Q1; rest rests F   85.1 *Enter . . . York*] F (*Enter Dutchesse.*); *not in* Q1; *placed after* 81 OXFORD   90.1 *She kneels*] ROWE; *not in* Q1, F   92 walk] Q1; kneele F   96.1, 97.1 *He kneels*] ROWE; *not in* Q1, F

---

80 Aumerle once again turns the key (see 37.1), here to allow entry rather than prevent it.

82–5 Another sententious speech from York, this time warning the King that pardoning whoever might pray for mercy (Aumerle in the present case) is likely to foster 'more sins', while to cut off the corrupt limb will keep the rest of the body 'sound'.

82 **pray** prays, begs forgiveness (subjunctive)

85 **confound** destroy

87 **Love . . . can** Like her husband, the Duchess tends toward the sententious in her entreaties: 'love begins at home'.

89 **dugs** breasts (contemptuous)
   rear nurse (lit. 'raise', 'bring up')

[*He kneels*]
Ill mayst thou thrive if thou grant any grace.

DUCHESS
Pleads he in earnest? Look upon his face:
His eyes do drop no tears, his prayers are in jest,   100
His words come from his mouth, ours from our breast.
He prays but faintly and would be denied,
We pray with heart and soul and all beside.
His weary joints would gladly rise I know,
Our knees shall kneel till to the ground they grow.   105
His prayers are full of false hypocrisy,
Ours of true zeal and deep integrity.
Our prayers do out-pray his, then let them have
That mercy which true prayer ought to have.

BOLINGBROKE
Good aunt, stand up.

DUCHESS   Nay, do not say 'stand up'.   110
Say 'pardon' first and afterwards 'stand up'.
And if I were thy nurse, thy tongue to teach,
'Pardon' should be the first word of thy speech.
I never longed to hear a word till now—
Say 'pardon' King, let pity teach thee how.   115
The word is short but not so short as sweet,
No word like 'pardon' for kings' mouths so meet.

YORK
Speak it in French, King. Say '*pardonnez-moi*'.

DUCHESS
Dost thou teach pardon pardon to destroy?
Ah, my sour husband, my hard-hearted lord   120

98 Ill ... grace] Q1; *not in* F   105 shall] F; still Q1   109 prayer] Q1; prayers F
110 BOLINGBROKE] Q2 (*subs.*)-F: *yorke* Q1   111 Say] Q1; But F   118 *pardonnez-moi*] Q1
(Pardonne moy); F (*Pardon'ne moy*)

98 **grace** mercy
100 **in jest** not serious
102 **would be** (a) ought to be (Abbott 329);
   or, perhaps, (b) would like to be
105 The Duchess echoes her son's image
   from earlier in the scene (29).
   shall F's correction of Q1's 'still' makes
   better sense and contrasts more tellingly
   with 'would' in the preceding line.
112 **nurse** nanny (one of whose tasks would
   be to teach the child to speak)

117 **meet** fitting
118 *pardonnez-moi* forgive me (an apology
   for *not* complying with a request)
119 **pardon pardon** Cf. 'rest rest' (84) and
   other inversions of normal word order
   throughout this sequence; the self-
   consciousness of the language, especially
   the frequent straining for rhyme, produces an awareness of artifice that to
   some degree mitigates the potential
   threat of the scene.

That sets the word itself against the word.
[*To Bolingbroke*] Speak 'pardon' as 'tis current in our land,
The chopping French we do not understand.
Thine eye begins to speak—set thy tongue there
Or in thy piteous heart plant thou thine ear   125
That, hearing how our plaints and prayers do pierce,
Pity may move thee 'pardon' to rehearse.

BOLINGBROKE
Good aunt, stand up.

DUCHESS   I do not sue to stand.
Pardon is all the suit I have in hand.

BOLINGBROKE
I pardon him as God shall pardon me.   130

DUCHESS
O happy vantage of a kneeling knee!
Yet am I sick for fear. Speak it again—
Twice saying 'pardon' doth not pardon twain,
But makes one pardon strong.

BOLINGBROKE   I pardon him
With all my heart.

DUCHESS   A god on earth thou art.   135

---

125 thy piteous] Q1*c*, F; this piteous Q1*u*   130 God] Q1; heauen F   134–5] *as* DELIUS; *three lines ending* 'strong.' 'heart.' 'art.' Q1, F

---

121 **word . . . word** The same phrase appears
   at 5.5.13–14, where it refers to those who
   cite different parts of scripture to nourish
   contradiction.
123 **chopping** shifty, untrustworthy (because it changes the meaning of words);
   cf. chop-logic = sophistical argument
   (*OED* 1).
124 The Duchess notices a change in
   Bolingbroke's expression, which she is
   quick to capitalize on.
125–7 The image is anatomically bizarre:
   the ear becomes part of the heart which,
   once it hears the Duchess's lamentations
   ('plaints') and entreaties, will be moved
   by pity to pronounce ('rehearse') pardon.
128 **sue** beg
131 **vantage** advantage (her submissive
   posture is paradoxically a benefit)

133 **twain** divide in two (*OED v.*). As Ure
   suggests, the Duchess apparently means:
   'to say pardon twice is not to divide it but
   to double it', though it is possible that
   'twain' means simply 'two individuals'.
134–5 **I . . . heart** Most editors follow Pope
   in inverting the two part-lines, since the
   arrangement in all the early texts (a
   unanimity not to be taken lightly) produces an internal instead of an end-
   rhyme ('heart' / 'art'). However it is at
   least arguable that the internal rhyme
   captures the excitement of the moment
   better than the rather pedantic rearrangement.
135 **god on earth** Alluding, though with a
   comic touch, to the Tudor doctrine of
   divine right, much played upon by Richard earlier in the play, as well as by Carlisle and York himself.

BOLINGBROKE

But for our trusty brother-in-law and the Abbot
With all the rest of that consorted crew,
Destruction straight shall dog them at the heels.
Good uncle, help to order several powers
To Oxford or where'er these traitors are.   140
They shall not live within this world, I swear,
But I will have them if I once know where.
Uncle, farewell, and cousin, adieu.
Your mother well hath prayed, and prove you true.

DUCHESS

Come my old son, I pray God make thee new.   145

Exeunt

[**5.4**] *Enter Exton and Servants*

EXTON

Didst thou not mark the King, what words he spake?
'Have I no friend will rid me of this living fear?'
Was it not so?

SERVANT   These were his very words.

---

136 and the] Q1; the F   143 and cousin] Q1, F; and cosin too Q6; and, cousin mine
DYCE; and cousin, so OXFORD; and so, cousin FORKER (*conj.* Craven)   145 God] Q1; heauen F
5.4] STEEVENS; *no scene break* Q1, F   0.1 *Enter . . . Servants*] F; *Manet sir Pierce Exton, &c.*
Q1   3, 6 SERVANT] F; *Man* Q1   3 These] Q1; Those F

---

136 **brother-in-law** The Duke of Exeter (and
    Earl of Huntington), husband of Boling-
    broke's sister, a leader of the conspiracy;
    though mentioned in a different context
    at 2.1.281, he plays no other role in the
    play.
137 **consorted** plotting (i.e. having con-
    sorted together to form a plot)
139 **powers** military units
142 **if I once** as soon as I
143 **and cousin** This line, because it lacks
    a syllable, has been subjected to
    emendation ever since Q6 (see textual
    notes). But we would rather not fetishize
    regularity at the expense of theatrical
    speech. We prefer imagining a brief,
    meaningful pause around 'cousin' since
    Bolingbroke has just finished saying what
    he will do to Aumerle's co-conspirators
    and might silently remind his cousin of
    what could have been *his* fate.
144 **prove you** be sure you prove yourself
145 **make thee new** Referring to the
    Christian idea of men being made new

by faith (2 Corinthians 5: 17), as in the
baptismal rite ('Therefore if any man be
in Christ, let him be a new creature';
cited by Ure).
5.4 This little scene returns us to political
machinations and leads directly into that
of Richard's murder. Holinshed describes
how Henry, 'at his table', drops a broad
hint, quoted in abbreviated form by
Exton in his opening speech: 'Have I no
faithful friend which will deliver me of
him, whose life will be my death and
whose death will be the preservation of
my life?' (p. 517). The implications for
Henry's character, and for the realpolitik
of courtly life, could hardly be clearer.
There is no marked scene break in F
though editors since Steevens have
supplied one. In Q1, there is a curious
direction for Exton et al. to remain on
stage, even though they have clearly not
been present during the mini-drama concerning York's family. See Introduction,
p. 111–12.

EXTON

   'Have I no friend?' quoth he. He spake it twice
   And urged it twice together, did he not?   5

SERVANT

   He did.

EXTON

   And speaking it, he wishtly looked on me,
   As who should say 'I would thou wert the man
   That would divorce this terror from my heart'—
   Meaning the King at Pomfret. Come, let's go,   10
   I am the King's friend and will rid his foe.   *Exeunt*

[**5.5**] *Enter Richard alone*

RICHARD

   I have been studying how I may compare
   This prison where I live unto the world,
   And for because the world is populous
   And here is not a creature but myself,
   I cannot do it. Yet I'll hammer't out.   5

---

7 wishtly] Q1; wistly Q3–F   11 *Exeunt*] F; *not in* Q1
  5.5] STEEVENS; *Scaena Quarta.* F; *not in* Q1   0.1 *alone*] Q1; *not in* F   1 I may] Q1; to Q2–F
5 hammer't] F; hammer it Q1

4–5 **twice . . . twice** Holinshed mentions no such repetition, which Shakespeare has apparently added for emphasis.

7–9 Since we have not witnessed the interaction, we are left to decide whether Exton's interpretation of Henry's look is accurate or derives mainly from a desire to ingratiate himself and further his ambitions.

7 **wishtly** fixedly, meaningfully

5.5 The tragic temperature of the narrative reaches its high point in this scene, in which Richard redeems himself from some of his folly, displaying both psychological and physical courage as well as a surprising strength. His tendency to weave words in a self-conscious way has not abandoned him but is tuned, at least at times, to a more precise and honest kind of introspection. And for the first time he speaks in soliloquy, a strategy that, by allowing us to share his thoughts, builds on the sympathy that has been growing since his removal from the throne. Shakespeare may have been influenced by Daniel, who also gives Richard a soliloquy as he gazes out the window soon before his death (see Introduction, pp. 53–4). The two meditations are, however, very unlike in theme, Daniel's focusing on the difference between commoners and kings, Shakespeare's on a commonality that unites everyone: no man, Richard concludes, 'With nothing shall be pleased till he be eased | With being nothing' (40–1). The murder scene that follows is based generally on Holinshed (p. 517), but Shakespeare adds to it a number of intimate touches, such as the exchange with the groom.

5 **Yet . . . out** The mind is like a forge, where a smith hammers molten metal into significant shapes. Richard resolves to work his thoughts like such metal, despite the incompleteness of the analogy between his prison and the world that he has been 'studying' (1) to establish.

My brain I'll prove the female to my soul,
My soul the father, and these two beget
A generation of still-breeding thoughts;
And these same thoughts people this little world
In humours like the people of this world,   10
For no thought is contented. The better sort,
As thoughts of things divine, are intermixed
With scruples and do set the word itself
Against the word, as thus: 'Come little ones',
And then again,   15
'It is as hard to come as for a camel
To thread the postern of a small needle's eye.'
Thoughts tending to ambition, they do plot
Unlikely wonders—how these vain weak nails
May tear a passage through the flinty ribs   20
Of this hard world, my ragged prison walls,
And for they cannot, die in their own pride.

13–14 word . . . word] Q1; Faith . . . Faith F   14–15] *as* WELLS; *one line in* Q1, F   17 small
needle's] Q1; Needles F

6–11 **My brain . . . contented** Though he is
alone in his prison, he will 'generate' a
population of thoughts that will fill up
his 'little world' (both his mind and the
prison) and, like people, fail to be content.
The male soul and the female brain will
be the parents of this 'still-breeding' population (which is 'continuously increasing' and yet also deadlocked because the
thoughts breed stillness).
10 **humours** disposition, temperament
11 **better sort** i.e. of thoughts, compared to
the 'better sort' of people
13 **scruples** doubts
13–14 **set . . . word** A repetition of 5.3.121
(see note to that line).
14–17 **Come . . . eye** Two seemingly contradictory quotations from the new testament, which are closely associated in all
three synoptic gospels (Matthew 19: 14
and 24, Mark 10: 14 and 25, and Luke
18: 16 and 25). In the first Jesus invites
the children to come to him since 'of
such is the kingdom of God' (Luke 18: 16)
while the second proclaims the difficulty
of the rich man entering heaven (though
Richard leaves out the idea of wealth,
thereby increasing the opposition
between the passages). As far back as the
fourth century, the harshness of the

second quotation has been mitigated
either by identifying 'needle's eye' as a
small gate or by defining 'camel' as a
cable-rope. Ure suggests that Shakespeare perhaps 'compromised between'
the two interpretations 'in his choice of
words', since 'postern' = small gate, but
'thread' suggests the common meaning
of needle, while at the same time linking
to 'postern' if we take 'thread' in the sense
of 'threading one's way through' a
narrow restricted place (*OED v.* 4a,
where this line is cited). However we
interpret the biblical reference, it is
evident that Richard is questioning
whether he will be saved and comforted
as an innocent sufferer, or judged like a
powerful man.
18 **Thoughts . . . ambition** i.e. in contrast
with the 'better sort' of thoughts (11)
20 **flinty ribs** The walls of the castle, imaged
as a human body (cf. 3.3.31 and 5.1.3
and nn.).
21 **ragged** rough
22 **they** Referring in the first instance to his
fingernails, but quickly shifting to refer
to his ambitious thoughts, which are
unsuccessful in their 'plot' (18) since his
nails are unable to scratch through the
walls, and thus the thoughts 'die'.

Thoughts tending to content flatter themselves
That they are not the first of fortune's slaves,
Nor shall not be the last—like silly beggars   25
Who sitting in the stocks refuge their shame
That many have and others must sit there,
And in this thought they find a kind of ease,
Bearing their own misfortunes on the back
Of such as have before endured the like.   30
Thus play I in one person many people
And none contented. Sometimes am I king,
Then treasons make me wish myself a beggar
And so I am. Then crushing penury
Persuades me I was better when a king,   35
Then am I kinged again, and by and by
Think that I am unkinged by Bolingbroke
And straight am nothing. But whate'er I be,
Nor I nor any man that but man is
With nothing shall be pleased till he be eased   40

27 sit] Q3–F; set QI   29 misfortunes] QI; misfortune F   31 person] QI; prison Q2–F
33 treasons make] QI; Treason makes F   38 be] QI; am F

23–30 The last kind of thoughts Richard considers are those that provide a modicum of comfort by reminding him that he shares his misfortune with countless others; this reflection aligns him with society's outcasts ('beggars'), who console themselves with similar ideas.

24 **fortune's slaves** people who rise and fall with the vagaries of fortune

25 **silly** simple

26 **stocks** An instrument of punishment, in which the person to be punished was placed in a sitting position with his ankles confined between two scalloped planks of wood. (*OED*, stock, *n.*[1] 8a).

26 **refuge . . . shame** take refuge from their shame by reminding themselves

29–30 **Bearing . . . like** i.e. 'Thoughts tending to content' (23) find ease because they recognize that they are like others in having to bear their own misfortunes

31 Here, as frequently in the play and in Shakespeare's culture, kingship is imaged as a role, like that of an actor, the word 'person' carrying with it a double sense of 'character' and 'human being'. Richard is caught between the roles he imagines for himself.

34 **penury** poverty

39–41 **Nor I . . . nothing** No person will be pleased with anything until he come to terms with the fact that he is, indeed, nothing (the double negative is an intensifier, not a 'positive'); 'eased | With being nothing' may refer to an acceptance of death, as many commentators have urged, but Richard seems to be thinking about an almost existential nothingness. This is a key realization for him as it is later for Lear. In a production at Stratford's Other Place in 2000, these lines were used as a thematic thread, spoken by Richard at the beginning, the Queen before the garden scene, and Bolingbroke at the end, as well as at this point, driving home the dilemma of kingship and Richard's contradictory relation to it.

With being nothing.
   The music plays
                 Music do I hear?
Ha, ha, keep time. How sour sweet music is
When time is broke and no proportion kept.
So is it in the music of men's lives;
And here have I the daintiness of ear   45
To check time broke in a disordered string,
But for the concord of my state and time
Had not an ear to hear my true time broke.
I wasted time and now doth time waste me,
For now hath time made me his numb'ring clock: 50
My thoughts are minutes and with sighs they jar
Their watches on unto mine eyes, the outward watch,
Whereto my finger like a dial's point
Is pointing still in cleansing them from tears.
Now sir, the sound that tells what hour it is   55

---

41 *The music plays*] Q1; *Musick* F (*following* 38)   46 check] Q1; heare F

41 ***The music plays*** The source of the music is unspecified and mysterious, thus enhancing the uncanny atmosphere of the moment.

42 **keep time** Apparently the musician(s) momentarily lose the rhythm, which leads to the ensuing meditation in which Richard notes his ability to hear discord in music and contrasts it with his failure to hear it in the political world.

43 **proportion** the relation between pitches or duration of notes (*OED n.* 8a)

45 **daintiness of ear** acuity of hearing (continuing the musical analogy)

46 **check** censure

47 **concord** harmonious functioning

48 **my true time** the proper rhythm of my time as king (punning on 'time' in its usual and its musical sense)

49–58 The wordplay on musical time leads to yet another elaborate analogy, now comparing the passage of time with his own body and emotions.

49 **wasted . . . waste** squandered . . . lay waste to

50 **numb'ring clock** i.e. a clock with numbers that measures the passing hours

51–7 **My . . . bell** The passage is obscure and has generated much frustrated commentary. Richard's face, especially his eyes, is the dial of the clock ('outward watch'), his finger the hand pointing at one of the dial numbers (identified with a weeping eye), and his thoughts and sighs the mechanism that drives the clock; that is to say, they register the sad passing of time just as the clock's 'jarring' (ticking) marks the intervals of minutes and hours ('watches', 52). This produces in the eyes ('the outward watch', with a further pun on visual watching) a flow of tears, while the accompanying 'groans' toll out the hours by striking the heart, 'which is the bell'. Just how the groans can both strike the heart and be the sound produced by it remains unexplained and is a feature of the passage that has dismayed commentators (see Black, pp. 333–4).

52 **watches** (a) marks on the clock indicating minutes and hours; (b) periods of time spent watching (remaining anxiously awake)

54 **still** continuously

55 **Now sir** Richard, extending and seeking to explain his strained conceit, addresses an imaginary interlocutor, or perhaps the audience.

Are clamorous groans which strike upon my heart,
Which is the bell. So sighs and tears and groans
Show minutes, hours and times. But my time
Runs posting on in Bolingbroke's proud joy,
While I stand fooling here, his jack o' the clock.   60
This music mads me, let it sound no more,
For though it have holp madmen to their wits,
In me it seems it will make wise men mad.
Yet blessing on his heart that gives it me,
For 'tis a sign of love and love to Richard   65
Is a strange brooch in this all-hating world.
    Enter a Groom of the Stable

GROOM
  Hail, royal prince!
RICHARD   Thanks noble peer,
  The cheapest of us is ten groats too dear.
  What art thou, and how com'st thou hither,
  Where no man never comes but that sad dog   70
  That brings me food to make misfortune live?

GROOM
  I was a poor groom of thy stable, King,
  When thou wert king, who travelling towards York

---

56 which] Q1; that F   58 hours and times] F; times, and houres Q1   60 o' the] F; of the Q1   66.1 *Enter . . . Stable*] Q1; *Enter Groome.* F   69 com'st] F; comest Q1   70 never] Q1; euer Q5–F

---

58 **times** Not normally a unit of time like 'minutes' and 'hours', but perhaps meaning 'ages'; F seems to reflect this interpretation and thus places 'times' after the other two elements producing a more logical sequence.

59 **posting** hurrying

60 **jack o' the clock** A small figure on old clocks who strikes the bell at regular intervals; Richard's futile sighs mark Bolingbroke's joyful hours.

62 The ancient idea that music can be effective therapy for the mentally troubled persists to this day.
  have holp may have helped (subjunctive: see Abbott 366)

66 **strange brooch** unlooked-for jewel

67–8 **Thanks . . . dear** Alert to language as always, Richard responds wittily to the groom, reminding him that he and the

groom are 'peers' (equals), since he is no longer a prince; punning on 'royal' and 'noble', both of which are words for coins, he declares that the groom has priced him too high ('dear'), since a royal is worth ten groats (forty pre-decimal pence) more than a noble.

70 **sad** gloomy, even surly

72–80 The groom's affecting tale of his loyalty to Richard and the failure of Richard's horse to show analogous sympathy helps to establish the King's vulnerability as well as his power to evoke devotion in his subordinates. The coronation procession described by the groom should not be confused with Bolingbroke's earlier triumphal march into London, as depicted by York (5.2.7 ff.).

With much ado at length have gotten leave
To look upon my sometimes royal master's face. 75
O how it erned my heart when I beheld
In London streets that coronation day
When Bolingbroke rode on roan Barbary,
That horse that thou so often hast bestrid,
That horse that I so carefully have dressed. 80
RICHARD
Rode he on Barbary? Tell me, gentle friend,
How went he under him?
GROOM
So proudly as if he disdained the ground.
RICHARD
So proud that Bolingbroke was on his back?
That jade hath ate bread from my royal hand; 85
This hand hath made him proud with clapping him.
Would he not stumble, would he not fall down,
Since pride must have a fall, and break the neck
Of that proud man that did usurp his back?
Forgiveness, horse! Why do I rail on thee 90
Since thou, created to be awed by man,
Wast born to bear? I was not made a horse
And yet I bear a burden like an ass,
Spur-galled and tired by jauncing Bolingbroke.
Enter Keeper to Richard with meat
KEEPER [*to Groom*]
Fellow, give place, here is no longer stay. 95
RICHARD
If thou love me 'tis time thou wert away.

---

76 erned] Q1; yern'd F   79 bestrid] F; bestride Q1   83 he] Q1; he had F   85 ate] Q1, F
(eate)   94 Spur-galled] F; Spurrde, galld Q1   94.1 *Enter . . . meat*] Enter one to Richard with
meate. Q1; *Enter Keeper with a Dish.* F   95 *to Groom*] ROWE; *not in* Q1, F

76 **erned** saddened
78 **roan** Variegated in colour, often indicat-
    ing a mix of reddish brown and white.
    Barbary The horse's name, derived from
    its pedigree as an Arabian breed.
79 **bestrid** straddled
85 **jade** nag
    ate Q1 and F both read 'eate', an old form
    of 'eaten', and pronounced 'et', as 'ate'
    often is in Britain even today.

86 **clapping** patting
88 **pride . . . fall** proverbial (Tilley P581)
94 **Spur-galled** gashed by spurs
    tired wearied, but also torn to pieces (*tire*
    = tear flesh in feeding: *OED v.*^{2} 2)
    jauncing prancing, or making the horse
    prance
94.1 *meat* food
96 Richard is aware of the danger to his
    loyal followers as well as to himself.

279

GROOM

What my tongue dares not, that my heart shall say.

Exit Groom

KEEPER

My lord, will't please you to fall to?

RICHARD

Taste of it first, as thou art wont to do.

KEEPER

My lord, I dare not. Sir Pierce of Exton,   100

Who lately came from the King, commands the contrary.

RICHARD

The devil take Henry of Lancaster and thee!

Patience is stale and I am weary of it.

[*He beats the Keeper*]

KEEPER

Help, help, help!

The murderers, Exton and servants, rush in

RICHARD

How now, what means death in this rude assault?   105

Villain, thy own hand yields thy death's instrument.

[*He seizes a servant's weapon and kills him with it*]

Go thou and fill another room in hell!

[*He kills another.*] *Here Exton strikes him down*

That hand shall burn in never-quenching fire

That staggers thus my person. Exton, thy fierce hand

97.1 *Exit Groom*] Q1; *Exit.* F   99 art] Q1; wert Q5–F (wer't)   103.1 *He . . . Keeper*] ROWE (*subs.*); *not in* Q1, F   104.1 *The murderers . . . rush in*] *The murderers rush in.* Q1; *Enter Exton and Seruants.* F   106 thy own] Q1; thine owne Q5–F   106.1 *He . . . it*] HANMER (*subs.*); *not in* Q1, F   107.1 *He kills another*] POPE (*subs.*); *not in* Q1, F   *Here . . . down*] Q1, F (F *omits* Here)

---

98 **fall to** begin eating

99 The keeper is supposed to taste the food first in order to demonstrate that it isn't poisoned.

102 The line is taken verbatim from Holinshed (p. 517), where it is accompanied by Richard's attack on the 'esquire' with a 'carving knife', after which the murderers rush in.

105 An obscure line; Kittredge suggests, 'What does Death mean by assailing me so violently?', though Staunton's interpretation of 'means' as second person

('mean'st') and addressed to one of the murderers is also possible ('What, mean'st thou my death by this brutal assault?').

106–10 Richard's surprisingly powerful resistance and his success in killing two of his attackers indicate a physical boldness and a strength of character not always given full scope in performance.

109 **person** his royal self, body as well as persona (indeed the two are not really separable)

Hath with the King's blood stained the King's own land.   110
Mount, mount, my soul, thy seat is up on high
Whilst my gross flesh sinks downward here to die.

                      [*He dies*]

EXTON

As full of valour as of royal blood.
Both have I spilled. O would the deed were good—
For now the devil that told me I did well   115
Says that this deed is chronicled in hell.
This dead King to the living King I'll bear—
Take hence the rest and give them burial here.

             [*Exeunt with the bodies*]

[**5.6**] *Flourish. Enter Bolingbroke with York, other lords and*
     attendants

BOLINGBROKE

Kind uncle York, the latest news we hear
Is that the rebels have consumed with fire
Our town of Ci'cester in Gloucestershire,
But whether they be ta'en or slain we hear not.
    Enter Northumberland
Welcome my lord, what is the news?   5

NORTHUMBERLAND

First, to thy sacred state wish I all happiness.
The next news is I have to London sent

112.1 *He dies*] ROWE (*subs.*); *not in* Q1, F   118.1 *Exeunt*] ROWE; *Exit.* F; *not in* Q1 *with the bodies*] CAPELL (*subs.*); *not in* Q1, F

5.6] STEEVENS; *Scoena Quinta.* F; *not in* Q1   0.1–2 *Flourish . . . attendants*] F (*subs.*); *Enter Bullingbrooke with the duke of Yorke.* Q1   1 BOLINGBROKE] F; *King* Q1 (*so throughout scene*)

113–16 Exton's sudden remorse is described briefly by Holinshed and treated more fully in Hall. As Ure points out, murderers in *Edward II* and *Woodstock*, as well as in *2 Henry VI* (*Contention* 3.2.2–3) and *Richard III* (1.4.266–8), also experience pangs of conscience.

5.6 The final scene begins with news (condensed from Holinshed) of Henry's success in clearing the land of rebellion, and hence in solidifying his own power (1–29). Exton's entry with the body and Bolingbroke's repudiation of both Exton and his deed are Shakespeare's invention and drastically change the tone, adding

an ominous suggestion of further unrest, marked by Henry's anxiety about the fact that blood has sprinkled him to make him grow (46). His resolution to visit the Holy Land as a form of penance, though it is repeated at the beginning of *1 Henry IV*, is never realized, and, in an ironic conclusion to his whole reign, he ends up dying in a palace room called 'Jerusalem', thereby fulfilling an ambiguous prophecy that he would die in a place of that name (*2 Henry IV* 4.3.365–9). So his hope to 'wash this blood off from my guilty hand' is never realized.

3 **Ci'cester** Modern Cirencester.

The heads of Salisbury, Spencer, Blunt and Kent.
The manner of their taking may appear
At large discoursèd in this paper here.   10
BOLINGBROKE
We thank thee, gentle Percy, for thy pains
And to thy worth will add right worthy gains.
    Enter Lord Fitzwater
FITZWATER
My lord, I have from Oxford sent to London
The heads of Brocas and Sir Bennet Seely,
Two of the dangerous consorted traitors   15
That sought at Oxford thy dire overthrow.
BOLINGBROKE
Thy pains, Fitzwater, shall not be forgot,
Right noble is thy merit, well I wot.
    Enter Percy and [the Bishop of] Carlisle [as prisoner]
PERCY
The grand conspirator, Abbot of Westminster,
With clog of conscience and sour melancholy   20
Hath yielded up his body to the grave;
But here is Carlisle, living to abide
Thy kingly doom and sentence of his pride.
BOLINGBROKE
Carlisle, this is your doom:
Choose out some secret place, some reverend room   25

---

8 Salisbury, Spencer] F; Oxford, Salisbury Q1   12.1 *Lord*] Q1; *not in* F *Fitzwater*]
Q6; *Fitzwaters* Q1–F *(Fitz-waters)*   17 Fitzwater] Q6; Fitz. Q1; *Fitzwaters* F *not*] Q2–F; *nor*
Q1   18.1 *Enter . . . Carlisle*] *Enter Percy and Carlile* F; *Enter H. Percie.* Q1c; *Enter H Percie.*
Q1u *the Bishop of*] ROWE; *not in* Q1, F   *as prisoner*] WILSON *(subs.)*; *not in* Q1, F   25 reverend]
Q3–F; reuerent Q1

---

8 **Spencer** Q1 reads 'Oxford' but F corrects
the historical error (the Earl of Oxford
was not involved in the conspiracy);
Spencer had been Earl of Gloucester
under Richard but was stripped of his
earldom by Henry.

Blunt and Kent Sir Thomas Blunt,
one of the Abbot of Westminster's co-
conspirators, is a different person altogether from Sir Walter Blunt, who dies
at Shrewsbury in *1 Henry IV*. The Earl
of Kent is the former Duke of Surrey,
who intervenes in favour of Aumerle
at 4.1.65–72, but who has lost his
dukedom.

12.1 Fitzwater earlier demonstrated his
allegiance to Bolingbroke by stepping
in as Aumerle's second accuser
(4.1.34–44).
20 **clog of conscience** burden of guilt
23, 24 **doom** judgement, punishment
25–9 Henry's pardoning of Carlisle is historically accurate (he was later given a
country vicarage). Shakespeare's introduction of it here adds a dimension to his
representation of the character of Henry,
whose action is morally generous as well
as politically astute.

More than thou hast, and with it joy thy life.
So as thou liv'st in peace, die free from strife,
For though mine enemy thou hast ever been,
High sparks of honour in thee have I seen.
Enter Exton [and others] with a coffin

EXTON

Great King, within this coffin I present   30
Thy buried fear. Herein all breathless lies
The mightiest of thy greatest enemies,
Richard of Bordeaux, by me hither brought.

BOLINGBROKE

Exton, I thank thee not, for thou hast wrought
A deed of slander with thy fatal hand   35
Upon my head and all this famous land.

EXTON

From your own mouth, my lord, did I this deed.

BOLINGBROKE

They love not poison that do poison need,
Nor do I thee. Though I did wish him dead
I hate the murderer, love him murderèd.   40
The guilt of conscience take thou for thy labour
But neither my good word nor princely favour.
With Cain go wander thorough shades of night

29.1 *and others*] CAPELL (*subs.*); *not in* Q1, F   *a*] F; *the* Q1   35 slander] Q1; slaughter Q2–F
43 thorough shades] CAMBRIDGE; through shades Q1; through the shade Q2–F

26 **joy** enjoy
29.1 **coffin** The coffin is probably, given the
final line of the scene, borne in on a bier
and may be open or not. If it remains
open it offers the opportunity for an
effective stage picture: the living body of
the new King set against the dead, but
still present, body of the old: a theatrical
representation of the doctrine of the
king's two bodies (see Introduction,
p. 17).

35 **slander** i.e. a deed that will cause slander,
especially of the King who, people will
say, is the real perpetrator of the crime;
cf. 1.1.113 and note.
38–40 A brutally honest statement of the
realpolitik that motivates Bolingbroke's
public actions.
43 **Cain** The first and hence the prototypical
murderer, banished to live as a 'fugitive
and a vagabond' (Genesis 4: 12); see
1.1.104 and note.
thorough through

And never show thy head by day nor light.

                         [Exit Exton]

Lords, I protest my soul is full of woe   45
That blood should sprinkle me to make me grow.
Come mourn with me for what I do lament
And put on sullen black incontinent.
I'll make a voyage to the Holy Land
To wash this blood off from my guilty hand.   50
March sadly after. Grace my mournings here
In weeping after this untimely bier.   *Exeunt*

44.1 *Exit Exton*] WELLS; *not in* Q1, F   47 what] Q1; that F   51 mournings] Q1; mourning F

44 **light** Perhaps a candle; it has long been thought that the word could be a misprint for 'night', though the identical rhyme suggests otherwise. If it is, the meaning is just as obscure, since Exton has just been banished into the night, so it makes little sense for him to be told not to show his head there.

44.1 **Exit Exton** Presumably Exton is forced to retire at this point, perhaps with a gesture from the King; his presence would hardly be welcome in the final moments, though were he to remain in the background, it would intensify the sombre and uncertain feeling which characterizes the play's conclusion.

48 **incontinent** immediately, quickly

49–50 Perhaps ironically recalling Richard's evocation of Pilate in the deposition scene (4.1.239–42); see also headnote.

52 **after** Suggesting a procession in which the nobles will follow Henry and Richard offstage.
untimely premature (referring to Richard's death for which the bier is a kind of metonymy)

INDEX

This is a selective guide to words and phrases annotated, as well as to medieval and early modern political figures, early modern texts and authors, place names, and theatre practitioners referred to in the Introduction and/or commentary notes. Important themes and issues referred to have also been included. Asterisks identify entries that supplement the information given in the *Oxford English Dictionary*.

Index

American Literature

Authors in Context

British and Irish Literature

Children's Literature

Classics and Ancient Literature

Colonial Literature

Eastern Literature

European Literature

History

Medieval Literature

Oxford English Drama

Poetry

Philosophy

Politics

Religion

The Oxford Shakespeare

A complete list of Oxford World's Classics, including Authors in Context, Oxford English Drama, and the Oxford Shakespeare, is available in the UK from the Marketing Services Department, Oxford University Press, Great Clarendon Street, Oxford OX2 6DP, or visit the website at www.oup.com/uk/worldsclassics.

In the USA, visit www.oup.com/us/owc for a complete title list.

Oxford World's Classics are available from all good bookshops. In case of difficulty, customers in the UK should contact Oxford University Press Bookshop, 116 High Street, Oxford OX1 4BR.